D1195901

OXFORD STUDIES IN AFRICAN AFFAIRS

General Editors

JOHN D. HARGREAVES *and* GEORGE SHEPPERSON

PAN-AFRICANISM AND EDUCATION

PAN-AFRICANISM AND EDUCATION

A STUDY OF RACE
PHILANTHROPY AND EDUCATION
IN THE SOUTHERN STATES
OF AMERICA AND EAST AFRICA

BY

KENNETH JAMES KING

CLARENDON PRESS · OXFORD

1971

Oxford University Press, Ely House, London W.1

GLASGOW NEW YORK TORONTO MELBOURNE WELLINGTON
CAPE TOWN SALISBURY IBADAN NAIROBI DAR ES SALAAM LUSAKA ADDIS ABABA
BOMBAY CALCUTTA MADRAS KARACHI LAHORE DACCA
KUALA LUMPUR SINGAPORE HONG KONG TOKYO

PRINTED IN GREAT BRITAIN BY
RICHARD CLAY (THE CHAUCER PRESS) LTD,
BUNGAY, SUFFOLK

TO PRAVINA

Acknowledgements

THIS BOOK has been made possible through the co-operation of a large number of individuals and institutions in Africa, America, and Britain.

For a variety of services and kindnesses I should like to thank the librarians and staffs of the Library of Congress; the Missionary Research Library; Rhodes House Library; the National Library of Scotland; Edinburgh University Library and the Centre of African Studies; and the Macmillan and University College Libraries in Nairobi. The officers and attendants of the British Museum and the Public Record Office have been extremely helpful, as were the staff of the Commonwealth Office Library. Very great assistance in archive research has been received from the officers of the Phelps-Stokes Fund of New York, and the staff of Edinburgh House, London, and I must thank especially the archivists of the Tuskegee and Hampton Institutes for much help in locating materials. I owe a great deal also to the committees of the Church Missionary Society, the American Friends' Board of Missions, the Presbyterian Church of East Africa, and the National Council of Churches of America, for permission to use their archives.

I acknowledge most gratefully the grants received from the Scottish Education Department and the Aberdeenshire Educational Trust towards my research tour in America.

Thanks are naturally due to all those mentioned in primary source interviews, and in particular I should like to acknowledge the advice of T. Ras Makonnen, who gave generously of his time to read and comment on my work. I owe special debts of gratitude to Professor George Shepperson, who, apart from reading the manuscript, gave his invaluable assistance at various stages of my work, and to Christopher Fyfe, for his deep personal interest in my subject and for his critical reading of the whole work. Besides these there are many friends and workers in related fields whose assistance through conversation and discussion it would be hard to overrate. For all this aid, and for my wife's continual inspiration, I stand in debt.

K.J.K.

Contents

List of Plates

List of Maps

The author would like to acknowledge the use of photographic material from the following sources, which are also identified in the text:
The Museum of Modern Art, New York; Edinburgh University Library; the *East African Standard*; Tuskegee Institute archives.

Abbreviations

A.I.M.: Africa Inland Mission.
A.M.F.: Agricultural Missions Foundation.
A.S.U.: African Student Union.
B.T.W.: Booker T. Washington Papers.
C.M.S.: Church Missionary Society.
C.M.S.A.: Church Missionary Society Archives.
C.S.M.: Church of Scotland Mission.
E.A.A.: East African Association.
E.A.I.N.C.A.: East African Indian National Congress Archives.
E.A.S.: East African Standard.
E.H.: Edinburgh House.
F.A.M.: Friends' Africa Mission.
F.A.M.A.: Friends' Africa Mission Archives.
H.A.I.: Hampton Institute Archives.
H.D./R.P.A.: History Department, Research Project Archives, Nairobi.
I.M.C.: International Missionary Council.
I.M.C.A.: International Missionary Council Archives.
I.R.M.: International Review of Missions.
KEDAR: Kenya Education Department Annual Report.
K.I.A.: Kenya Institute of Administration.
K.N.A.: Kenya National Archives.
K.T.W.A.: Kavirondo Taxpayers' Welfare Association.
L.B.E.A.: Leader of British East Africa.
L.C.: Library of Congress.
M.R.L.: Missionary Research Library.
N.A.A.C.P.: National Association for the Advancement of Coloured People.
N.I.T.D.: Native Industrial Training Depot.
P.C.E.A.: Presbyterian Church of East Africa Archives.
P.R.O.: Public Record Office.
P.S.F.A.: Phelps-Stokes Fund Archives.
R.R.M./G.C.: Robert R. Moton papers: General Correspondence.
R.R.M./L.C.: Robert R. Moton papers: Local Correspondence.
S.E.F.: Southern Education Foundation.
S.M.P./E.S.A.: Secretariat Minute Papers; Entebbe Secretariat Archives.
T.U.A.: Tuskegee Institute Archives.
U.C.N.: University College, Nairobi.
U.N.I.A.: Universal Negro Improvement Association.
Y.B.A.: Young Baganda Association.

PLATE I

Mohammed Jama, first East African student at Tuskegee Institute, alights from the train at Cheechaw, near Tuskegee, Alabama. (Tuskegee Institute Archives.)

Introduction

IN THE summer and autumn of 1909, a party to shoot big game was moving slowly through the East Africa Protectorate, led by Ex-President Theodore Roosevelt and his son Kermit. Although there was not yet any education department in the territory, the American visitors interested themselves in the mission stations and in their industrial training of the Africans.[1] Less formally, they gave a stimulus to learning among their own gun-bearers and especially to one of Kermit's men, Juma Yohari, a Swahili from the coast. Possibly this man's first education came from the Roosevelts, with their illustrated tobacco and chocolate cards, which he puzzled over 'until he could identify the brilliantly colored ladies, gentlemen, little girls and wild beasts'.[2] In any case, his good humour and loyal service found considerable favour, and he therefore gained a pledge from Roosevelt before the party left: it was a letter promising an education in a school called Tuskegee Institute, should Juma's son ever manage to cross the Atlantic.

Almost six years later, on 24 October 1915, Mohammed Jama stepped from the train at Cheechaw, the little station in rural Alabama nearest to the school at Tuskegee, and thus became the first East African in this school of 1,300 Negro[3] students.[4] He almost certainly never saw the school's founder and first president alive, for Booker Washington was carried back to Tuskegee to die three weeks later; but he may well have pondered on the personality and philosophy of the man whose school could be recommended by a President of the United States as far afield as Africa.

[1] T. Roosevelt, *African Game Trails: An Account of the African Wanderings of an American Hunter-Naturalist* (New York, 1910), pp. 144–5; cf. also *Hearing and Doing*, Publication of the Africa Inland Mission, Brooklyn, ix (Jan. 1925), 1.

[2] Roosevelt, op. cit., pp. 390–1. For a picture of Juma Yohari, see illustration therein facing p. 318.

[3] Despite the widespread substitution of the word 'Black' for 'Negro' in the United States during recent years, it has been decided for the sake of uniformity to retain the word Negro in the text, as this is the term invariably used by the many writers quoted.

[4] Registry of Students, Tuskegee Institute, Ala. For an illustration of Mohammed Jama arriving at Tuskegee, see Plate 1. Mohammed Jama was not the first East African student to seek education in the Southern States; he had been preceded by a young Masai student some six years before: see pp. 245–6.

Something of Washington's ideas began to become clear as Mohammed settled down to get the sort of education for which he had travelled and worked.[1] He could barely read or write on his enrolment, so there was no doubt in his own mind that he must secure 'an education from the standpoint of books'.[2] He worked consequently with great enthusiasm and determination at these, but showed little corresponding eagerness for the strong industrial courses at Tuskegee. When, therefore, the institute failed to correct his prejudice against these, Roosevelt himself was called upon to write Mohammed an exhortation upon manual training:

> Now, will you read this to Mohammed Jama . . . What we are trying to make everybody in this country understand is that working with a man's hands, that is, industrial activity, is even more important than a literary education. Mohammed can never be a clerk in this country; he will never know enough; but he can be a very good man with his hands doing industrial work.[3]

Within a few months of this, nevertheless, Mohammed Jama had left after only one and a half years at the school, unable apparently to reconcile his notion of education with what the school or the President thought best.

This bald tale of one African's disappointed mission to the Southern States is an episode in the history of the educational pan-Africanism with which this study will be concerned. The term is used advisedly, for there is no more convenient way of describing the complex interrelationships between Africans, American Negroes, and their white sponsors in education. It must serve to cover the magnetic appeal for Africans of the Negro schools and colleges in the Southern States; equally it must comprehend the fervent desire of American Negroes to carry their own educational privileges to their African brethren. And it must, finally, extend to the role of those whites—whether missionaries, philanthropists, or individuals like Roosevelt—who believed that the education of Africans and the education of American Negroes were a single interdependent problem.

In particular, this study will assess the achievement of one agency,

[1] File on Mohammed Jama, Tuskegee Registry.

[2] 'Memo to Mr. Scott Regarding Mohammed Jama', 10 Oct. 1916, Box 312, Booker T. Washington Papers, Library of Congress, Washington, D.C. (hereafter B.T.W./L.C.)

[3] Roosevelt to E. J. Scott (Secretary of Tuskegee Institute), 13 Oct. 1916, in R. R. Moton Papers, General Correspondence (hereafter R.R.M./G.C.), 1916, Tuskegee Institute Archives (hereafter T.U.A.).

the Phelps-Stokes Fund, which might legitimately claim to have had this concern for pan-African education at the heart of its work from the very beginning. It would certainly have been difficult in 1911, the date of its foundation, to point to any body of comparable influence which had written into its charter, as one of its chief ends, 'the education of negroes, both in Africa and the United States'.[1]

At one level, what follows will therefore be a review of the priorities of a small fund in its expenditure of well over a million dollars on African and American Negro education during a period of twenty-five years. At another level, it will, through a case study of Kenya, trace the variety of ways in which the experience of the American South was introduced by the work of the Phelps-Stokes Fund into the thinking of individual missionaries and government officials. It will also assess its influence more generally upon the development of an educational policy for African colonies over a generation. And although ostensibly a study of an education suggested for Africans and American Negroes, it will in practice be something more complex, since many East Africans and American Negroes insist on regarding education as an essentially political matter.

Ultimately it may be possible to show that Mohammed Jama's voyage was not so much an isolated incident as part of a larger movement in which African initiative and determination in the search of a fuller education are seen against a background of often conflicting white and American Negro counsels.

[1] T. J. Jones, *Educational Adaptations: Report of Ten Years' Work of the Phelps–Stokes Fund, 1910–1920* (New York, *c.* 1921), p. 16. Some of the small Negro liberal arts colleges had the same aim, however; see H. M. Bond, 'Forming African Youth', in *Africa from the Point of View of American Negro Scholars* (Présence Africaine, Dijon, 1958), pp. 248–9; also, *Fisk University Catalogue* (Nashville, Tenn., 1884).

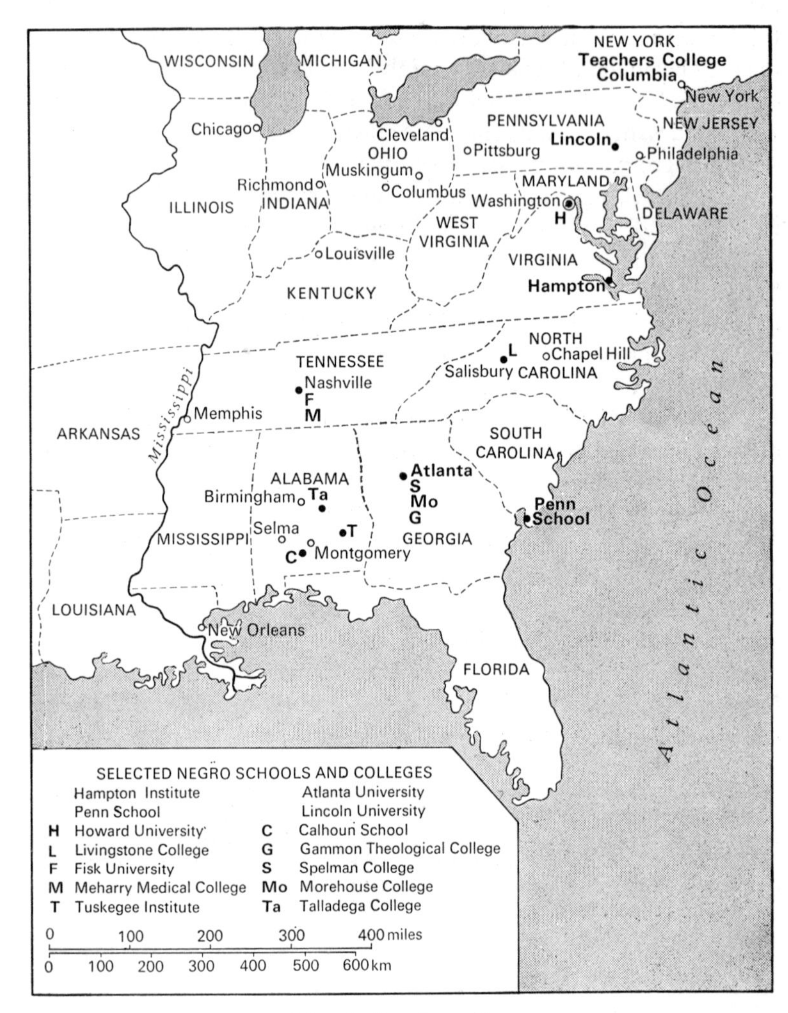

Map 1. Southern States

CHAPTER I

Africa and American Negro Education: The Beginnings

THE YEAR 1881 marked two educational beginnings which should figure in any general history of African education. In January Edward Wilmot Blyden, the West Indian scholar of African descent, delivered his inaugural address as president of Liberia College, Monrovia;[1] and in May a twenty-five-year-old Negro of slave descent, Booker T. Washington, was called from his teaching post at Hampton Institute, Virginia, to found a school for Negroes in Tuskegee, Alabama.[2] These events might seem very remote from each other, especially as the educational philosophies of the two principals were apparently at odds. Blyden had started on his term of office with a long discussion of 'The Aims and Methods of a Liberal Education for Africans',[3] while Washington had decided that the industrial education of Hampton should provide the model for his own school curriculum.[4] But the difference between them was much less than this suggests; they were both convinced that they must reject for their own people the conventional forms of western education. In so doing, they pioneered criteria for Negro education that would in the 1920s and 1930s become standard for educating Africans throughout the period of indirect rule.

The possibilities of a marriage between Hampton's industrial training and Blyden's re-defined African education had become first

[1] For Blyden's career as a Liberian educator, see H. R. Lynch, *Edward Wilmot Blyden: Pan-Negro Patriot 1832–1912* (London, 1967), Ch. 7.

[2] B. T. Washington, *Up From Slavery. An Autobiography* (first published New York, 1901; references to new (popular) ed., London, n.d.), pp. 135–6; also B. Mathews, *Booker T. Washington: Educator and Inter-racial Interpreter* (London, 1949), pp. 61–4. Dr. Louis Harlan is preparing a biography of Washington. For the young Washington, see Plate II.

[3] E. W. Blyden, 'The Aims and Methods of a Liberal Education for Africans', in *Christianity, Islam and the Negro Race* (first published London, 1887; references to reprint in African Heritage Series (Edinburgh, 1967), pp. 71–93).

[4] Washington, op. cit., pp. 149–50.

apparent two years before, in 1879. Although Hampton had been founded only a decade earlier, its energetic white president, General S. C. Armstrong,[1] had already felt that its methods might have particular relevance for African youth, and had suggested to Blyden through the American Colonization Society that three 'first-class African boys' could be educated at his institute.[2] This offer was not at first particularly welcomed by Blyden. He had been becoming increasingly convinced that Africa had a sufficiently valuable civilization of its own, in the traditions of which its youth might be educated without imitating the West. Indeed, too often such western education had not only obscured African culture, but had taught students to accept its permanent inferiority in any comparative scale of civilization.[3] He therefore wrote back to General Armstrong that he could not 'too much insist upon the idea that Africans, to be useful at home among their people, must be educated among the circumstances where they are expected to live.'[4]

Blyden's educational theories were, however, precisely those upon which Armstrong had founded Hampton in 1868, and which differentiated it from many of the other Negro schools and colleges established for the freedmen after the Civil War.[5] Education for him had primarily practical value, and was strictly governed by the conditions of Negro life in the white South. If that white community was deeply prejudiced against any competitive political or professional role for Negroes, then the educational system must be planned accordingly, and Negroes prepared for the sort of life open to them.[6] Both Blyden and Armstrong further believed that their education should find its inspiration and fulfilment in the unsophisticated life of the rural communities inland, and avoid as far as possible contami-

[1] The most valuable published source for Armstrong's methods in Negro education is the early issues of the *Southern Workman*, the monthly publication of Hampton Institute from 1871 (complete run in Ogden Memorial Library, Hampton Institute, Va.). Cf. also Suzanne Carson, 'Samuel Chapman Armstrong: Missionary to the South' (John Hopkins Univ., Md., Ph.D. thesis 1952), and F. G. Peabody, *Education for Life: The Story of Hampton Institute* (New York, 1919).

[2] *Southern Workman*, ix (Feb. 1880).

[3] Blyden, op. cit., pp. 75–6, 91–2.

[4] Blyden to Hampton Institute, 20 Nov. 1879, printed in *Southern Workman*, ix (Feb. 1880).

[5] Cf. A. Meier, *Negro Thought in America, 1880–1915: Racial Ideologies in the Age of Booker T. Washington* (Ann Arbor, Michigan, 1963), pp. 88–9.

[6] For this reason, Armstrong's maxim 'Education for Life' was to some extent ambiguous.

Booker T. Washington as a young man. (Tuskegee Institute Archives.)

nation by the cities and the seaboard.[1] Their new kind of training should therefore aim to avoid the traditional alienation of the educated man from his own people. Instead it would deliberately educate him with the return to his own community in mind. Thus, Armstrong explained to Blyden, Hampton would ideally suit the proposed African students, by putting them just a little ahead of the communities which they would return to lead:

> We believe however that the Hampton drill would avert the danger of 'walking on their heads', because of its ground work of elementary and industrial training, which tends to keep its students right end up.
>
> Men fitted for the conditions of a simple civilization will succeed in it. Those who are schooled up to the needs and duties of a higher or later plane, do not always land on their feet when forced by circumstances upon one that is lower or earlier.[2]

Here Armstrong was already predicting a solution to a problem that would be central to missions in Africa in the twentieth century: the creation of a rurally-based African leadership, made content, through education, with gradual advance:

> The Hampton School is attempting an answer to this question. It finds itself a school for civilisation . . .
>
> Give new but moderate cravings and the means of supply, and there is great gain to the student. He is content with his old home when he returns to it; he has a relative ascendancy among his people; not so great as to make for him an isolated and lonely place, but enough to stimulate him, and lead others to emulate and follow him . . .
>
> We believe that some of Dr. Blyden's boys would gain by a course at Hampton, and that they would go back to Africa right side up, and do good work for that country.[3]

When Blyden made his second visit to Hampton in 1882, there was an indication that he now recognized the eminent suitability of the Hampton training for his own Liberia College, and as preparation for work in Africa. After his speech to the institute, no less than twelve Hampton students had agreed to transfer to Liberia College and finish their training there. Some of them, he no doubt hoped, might eventually fall in with his larger plans for American Negro

[1] Cf. Blyden, 'Aims and Methods of a Liberal Education', pp. 73, 92. For the original aim of Hampton Institute, see MS. HI. 12778, American Missionary Association Papers, Fisk University Library, Nashville, Tenn.

[2] *Southern Workman*, ix (Feb. 1880). [3] Ibid.

emigration by deciding to settle in Liberia.[1] However, Blyden's proposals for studying in Monrovia were only part of a growing enthusiasm for Africa among the student body of the day.

One of Hampton's alumni, Ackrell E. White, had been a missionary to the Mende of Sierra Leone since the late 1870s, and this had brought not only regular reports on West African conditions, but also the occasional African student to Hampton. White, too, firmly associated himself with Blyden's pleas that American Negroes, and especially educated ones from the colleges, should help Africa by emigrating there:

> The Doctor [Blyden] said to me when I last saw him, that the redemption of Africa was waiting for the return of her sons from America and that she is only to be redeemed by her sons. I fully agree with the Dr. in this. Africans must redeem Africa. I believe the time will come when every black man will look to Africa as his country and his home . . . I hope every student who heard Dr. Blyden's address may feel it his duty to help Africa.[2]

It is interesting to note that one student who was exposed directly to both Blyden's and White's calls for service in Africa was W. M. Sheppard, the future champion of African rights as a pioneer missionary to the Congo.

During the beginnings of this pan-African educational activity, Armstrong's particular interpretation of industrial training had been gaining ever-widening support among Northern and Southern whites. It was a process much helped by the term 'industrial' with its complex of moral, political, and educational overtones.[3] 'Industrial' came, in fact, to be an extremely convenient shorthand term in Hampton's first decade. For the Southern whites it signified disavowal of all political ambition on the part of the Negroes, and a readiness to stay in the South as a steady labour supply. The Northern whites of missionary and philanthropic disposition were gratified by the insistence upon the 'morality' of the Hampton industrial work, and felt able to continue liberally to support a system which Armstrong stressed was primarily 'for the sake of character'.[4] The tendency to regard some form of industrial education as peculiarly appropriate

[1] Blyden's speech to Hampton students, printed in *Southern Workman*, xii (Jan. 1883), 9. Cf. Lynch, op. cit., pp. 115, 159.

[2] A. E. White, letter to *Southern Workman*, xii (Jan. 1883), 9.

[3] Cf. Meier, op. cit., pp. 85–99; also pp. 36–7, below. The term 'industrial', both in this passage and subsequently, refers to simple forms of trade training or manual training in Negro schools. This included elementary agricultural work.

[4] Mathews, op. cit., p. 47; Meier, op. cit., p. 92.

to the current stage of Negro development was given great stimulus and semi-official approval by the foundation of the million-dollar Slater Fund in 1882.[1] Not only were its own grants largely awarded to encourage industrial courses, but it attracted other moneys for the same cause. Moreover, throughout this first decade of the operations of the Slater Fund at least, there was little to suggest that industrial education was being imposed upon unwilling recipients. Most of the so-called liberal arts colleges for Negroes allowed the establishment of industrial sections, in some cases substantial plants,[2] and opposition appears to have been restricted to a very few.[3] There was certainly no national Negro spokesman to oppose the trend which Armstrong had first encouraged.

It did, however, become increasingly likely that Negro opposition to industrial education would arise after September 1895. In that month Booker Washington—by now presiding over a school that had grown fast on the same industrial lines as Hampton[4]—delivered his Atlanta Exposition address.[5] It was a masterly explanation of the political and educational compromise upon which Hampton and Tuskegee had prospered, and a statement of the concessions necessary to achieve such prosperity. The very clarity with which it laid bare the foundations of Tuskegee's success increased the chances of reaction, for Washington had almost assured whites that the schooling and general status of Negroes would for the foreseeable future benefit by abandoning both political agitation and the quest for higher education.[6] There was nothing new in the short address, except that the unspoken agreement of twenty years' standing had been publicly analysed and elevated into a political programme.

[1] See first annual report of the Slater Fund, 1883, quoted in T. J. Jones, *Negro Education. A Study of the Private and Higher Schools for Colored People in the United States* (Dept. of Interior, Bureau of Education, Bulletin 1916, No. 38, Washington, 1917), p. 257; also early reports and papers of the Slater Fund, now held by Southern Education Foundation (hereafter S.E.F.), Atlanta, Ga.

[2] For Negro approval of industrial education during this period, see Meier, op. cit., pp. 93–5.

[3] Lincoln University, Pa. was one of the few to resist; see Bond, 'Forming African Youth', p. 255.

[4] The only substantial difference between Hampton and Tuskegee was that Tuskegee had an entirely black faculty from the president downwards.

[5] The speech is reproduced in Washington, op. cit., pp. 265–73; cf. Meier, op. cit., pp. 100–2.

[6] Washington, op. cit., pp. 268, 271. Despite Washington's disavowal of political aims, the creation of Tuskegee itself was the direct result of black political power in Alabama; see S. Carmichael and C. V. Hamilton, *Black Power. The Politics of Liberation in America* (New York, 1967), p. 125.

Nor indeed did any immediate reaction to this speech come from the man who would shortly symbolize, for both American Negroes and Africans, the rejection of the Tuskegee compromise and the defence of the Negro's higher education. W. E. Burghardt DuBois in fact remained remarkably close to Washington's own position until the end of the century.[1] He had been a graduate of Fisk University, gained his doctorate at Harvard, and from 1897 had been lecturing in Atlanta University; but at this stage he saw nothing sinister in the prominence given to industrial education through the Slater Fund and other agencies.[2] In his own blueprint for education, written between 1897 and 1900, *A Rational System of Negro Education*, there was, if anything, a tendency to play down the need for a large body of college-educated Negroes, while a very strong case was made out for industrial institutes:

> There is room for a large normal or industrial institute for Negroes in every southern state, and in some states two, possibly three, could be well supported.
>
> Turning now to preparatory schools and colleges, there is undoubtedly a field among the Negroes for limited work of high grade in these lines. Two or three small well equipped colleges could easily supply the needs of the whole south and could gather a hundred or more students apiece.[3]

Within three years, however, revolt against the preponderance of industrial education had grown much more articulate, and one of the first signs of this was a powerful address, *Shall We Commercialize the Negro?*, delivered in 1901 at the Gammon Theological Seminary, South Atlanta, by R. J. Bigham, one of the white leaders of the Methodist Episcopal Church, South:

> In my opinion industrial education, even with its sideline of a little learning, will, if not safeguarded and undergirded by higher and distinctive intellectual training for the race, forge the chains of a servitude on the black man from which he will never recover . . . I have known these people face to face all my life, and have studied them carefully for many years. I believe that they were never before so threatened since they landed

[1] Meier, op. cit., p. 198. For the details of DuBois's early academic and political life, see F. L. Broderick, *W. E. B. DuBois: Negro Leader in a Time of Crisis* (Stanford, 1959), and E. M. Rudwick, *W. E. B. Dubois: A Study in Minority Group Leadership* (Phila., 1960).

[2] W. E. B. DuBois, *The Negro Artisan*, Atlanta University Publication No. 7 (Atlanta, 1902), p. 39.

[3] W. E. B. DuBois, 'A Rational System of Negro Education', MSS. 1897–1900, DuBois Papers, Park Johnson Archives, Fisk University, Nashville, Tenn.

here, and I urge that the ablest men undertake at once a very sober and vigorous campaign in the interest of the higher education of the Negro.[1]

President Tucker of Dartmouth College had already made similar points about the priority of higher education for the Negro leaders.[2]

DuBois was therefore by no means initiating a trend when his famous attack on the educational and political assumptions of industrial education was published in the spring of 1903. The novelty in this essay, 'Of Mr. Booker T. Washington and Others',[3] consisted in DuBois's fixing his indictment upon the man who, more than any other, had become the symbol of compromise through industrial education. He did not quarrel with Washington over industrial education as such, but because the Tuskegee programme of conciliating the South and promoting industrial education had been erected into 'a veritable Way of Life' for all Negroes in the United States.[4] Where Washington in his Atlanta address had begged forgiveness for Negroes in presuming to go straight from slavery to college studies,[5] DuBois retorted that historically the university had always preceded the school, and that Tuskegee itself had only been made possible by the presence of teachers trained at the liberal arts colleges.[6] But, what was more important than his challenge to Washington's disparagement of higher education, DuBois had marked out in bold strokes the political consequences that could follow from the acceptance by a depressed people, like the Negroes, of a different set of educational standards from those of the dominant group. The education of a dependent race had in fact once and for all been shown to be very much a political affair. DuBois's analysis was not going to prevent Tuskegee's insights from being applied increasingly over the next thirty years to subject peoples in India and Africa; it did begin, however, to provide for such peoples a rational platform from which allegedly educational reforms could be scrutinized for their underlying political implications. Although there were undeniably some truly progressive educational methods employed by Washington, it would

[1] R. J. Bigham, *Shall we Commercialize the Negro?* (S. Atlanta, Ga., 1901), pp. 6, 8.

[2] Ibid., p. 8.

[3] W. E. B. DuBois, 'Of Mr. Booker T. Washington and Others', in *The Souls of Black Folk. Essays and Sketches* (Chicago, 1903; references to 'Crest' paperback edn., New York, 1961), pp. 42–54.

[4] Ibid., p. 43. [5] Washington, op. cit., pp. 266, 268.

[6] DuBois, *Souls of Black Folk*, pp. 79, 83–4.

always be possible from this date to consider these as much dictated by white supremacy as by modern educational theories.

It was highly significant that this dispute over the politics of Negro education should have taken place at a time when both Washington and DuBois were beginning to interest themselves in Africa; for it involved the translation to that continent of the increasingly emotive terms, industrial and college education. The full dimensions of this American Negro conflict would not, however, become apparent in African education for some years; and initially, at least, DuBois and Washington appear to have acted in unison over Africa.

This extension of their interest to Africa was not particularly original in the context of the late 1880s and 1890s; it would have been much more strange if they had shown no concern. Africa was very much more prominent then than when Edward Blyden had first visited Hampton in 1874. Negro missions to Africa were especially important, and the call to serve in Africa was frequently made to the Negro colleges. The result was that many hundreds of Negro students volunteered for African service in the late 1880s and early 1890s, under the influence of Bishops Taylor and Turner. This enthusiasm was reflected in the creation during 1894 of the Stewart Missionary Foundation for Africa, specifically to prepare American Negroes for missionary work in Africa.[1] Indeed, in the same year as Washington's Atlanta Exposition address, this great movement for African mission was symbolized by a famous congress on Africa in the same city.[2] In addition, African students were appearing more frequently in Negro colleges, and themselves urging their American brethren to take up educational work in Africa.[3]

When, therefore, Washington was in London in 1899, it was

[1] H. M. Bond, 'The Origin and Development of the Negro Church-related College', *The Journal of Negro Education*, xxix, No. 3 (Summer, 1960), 223–4; E. S. Redkey, 'Bishop Turner's African Dream', *Journal of American History*, liv. No. 2 (1967), 271–90. Cf. also the lecture on African mission by Dr. James Stewart, of Lovedale, S. Africa, to Hampton students in Dec. 1893, printed in *Southern Workman*, xxiii (Jan. 1894), 13–15.

[2] J. W. E. Bowen (Ed.), *Africa and the American Negro. Addresses and Proceedings of the Congress on Africa held under the auspices of the Stewart Missionary Foundation for Africa, Dec. 13–15, 1895.* (Atlanta, Ga., 1896). For Blyden on this congress, see Lynch, op. cit., p. 137.

[3] For John Dube, an African student from Natal, who lectured at Tuskegee and Hampton, see *Southern Workman*, xxvi (July 1897), 142. For John Chilembwe, the Nyasaland student, in the States, see G. Shepperson and T. Price, *Independent African* (Edinburgh, 1958), p. 92. For Zulu students at Lincoln University, Pa., see Bond, 'Forming African Youth', p. 252.

natural that he should be sought out by the West Indian, African, and American Negro organizers of the 1900 Pan-African Conference, to join them in arranging its programme.[1] Nor in his early contact with pan-Africanism was Washington so ready to silence all protest against white rule as his 1895 address might have suggested. Some of the subjects to be discussed the following year at the 1900 conference were nothing if not inflammatory: 'The Cruelty of Civilised Paganism, of which our Race is the Victim'; 'Europe's Atonement for her Blood-guiltiness to Africa, is the loud cry of Current History'; 'Organised Plunder versus Human Progress has made our race its Battlefield'.[2] Yet Washington could publicly support this in England and encourage Negro attendance: 'I beg and advise as many of our people as can possibly do so, to attend this conference. In my opinion it is going to be one of the most effective and far-reaching gatherings that has ever been held in connection with the development of the race'.[3] One of those who attended and played a leading role at this conference in July 1900 was DuBois, and he, unlike Washington, was prepared without reservation to carry its spirit of outspoken protest back with him to the Southern States.[4]

Washington's somewhat uncharacteristic approval of protest policies in Africa may be largely explained by his desire to show on this European trip that many classes of people, especially Negroes, were much worse off outside the United States. It was also designed to dissuade American Negroes from emigrating to Africa. His accounts of bloodshed and cruelty in Africa, and particularly the treatment of Africans by Cecil Rhodes, all showed 'pretty conclusively that a return to Africa for the Negro is out of the question . . . the adjustment of the relations of the two races must take place here in America'.[5]

Nevertheless, he was not opposed to Tuskegee's providing short-

[1] B. T. Washington, 'The Pan-African Conference—Its Object and Its Promoters', an article written in London, 25 July 1899, and printed in *Some European Observations and Experiences* (Tuskegee Institute Press, *c.* 1900), p. 8.

[2] Ibid., p. 9.

[3] Ibid., p. 9. Cf. Imanuel Geiss, 'The Development of Pan-Africanism in the Twentieth Century', a paper read at the Centre of African Studies, Edinburgh University, 1965; also G. Shepperson, 'Pan-Africanism and "Pan-Africanism": Some Historical Notes', *Phylon*, xxiii, No. 4 (1962), 354.

[4] W. E. B. DuBois, 'To the Nations of the World', a conference address printed in *An ABC of Color: Selections from over a half century of the writings of W. E. B. DuBois* (Berlin, 1964), pp. 19–23.

[5] Washington, *Some European Observations and Experiences*, pp. 10–11.

term technical assistance for economic development in Africa; and on the first day of this century three Tuskegee graduates and one member of staff had arrived in Togo to help develop cotton culture under the aegis of a German colonial development company, a scheme which eventually employed nine Tuskegee graduates over a ten-year period.[1] The project had a significance beyond its strictly limited economic success, for it revealed to Washington and colonial officials the possibility of the more general application of Tuskegee principles in Africa, not only in isolated industrial schemes but throughout entire school systems. By 1904 Washington was noting the effect of the Togo project upon German colonial thinking: 'The Germans have been so strongly impressed with these effects of industrial training upon the natives, that they have decided to introduce into all the schools of that colony a system for the training of boys in handwork'.[2]

The initial demonstration of Tuskegee methods and principles in Africa was followed shortly afterwards by a parallel scheme in the Anglo-Egyptian Sudan, employing four more 'Captains of Industry', as Washington called these young Tuskegee pioneers.[3] They were also employed in Nigeria and possibly in the Belgian Congo, and another team came close to being used in British East Africa for cotton growing.[4] In South Africa, too, there came a gradual recognition that Tuskegee might have a peculiarly relevant lesson to teach traditionally-minded missionaries in Africa; Washington was actually consulted by the South African Commissioner for Education on the problem of organizing education in the Transvaal and the Orange Free State, and gave it as his opinion that there was 'no very great difference between the native problem there and the Negro problem in America'.[5]

Soon the idea had occurred to Robert Park, Washington's closest white adviser, that all the informal contacts between Tuskegee and Africa in the field of industrial education should be given greater publicity. He suggested in 1905 that Washington should write an

[1] L. R. Harlan, 'Booker T. Washington and the White Man's Burden', *American Historical Review*, lxxi, No. 2 (Jan. 1966), 442–6.

[2] B. T. Washington, *Working with the Hands* (London, 1904), p. 230.

[3] Harlan, 'Booker T. Washington', p. 447.

[4] Ibid. For East Africa, see J. K. Jones to Washington, 5 Sept. and 23 Sept. 1907, Box 351, B.T.W./L.C. For later attempts to use Negroes in East Africa, see III *passim*, and pp. 154–5, below.

[5] Harlan, 'Booker T. Washington', pp. 448–9.

article 'recommending that the Powers in Africa, the missionaries and educators, to come together in an international conference to devise means for the systematic extension of industrial training in Africa'.[1] The moment was particularly opportune, Park felt, for Tuskegee to give a lead in the industrializing of mission activity, since both missionaries and governments seemed ready to review their traditional educational activities. The conference did not take place for several years,[2] but in Tuskegee conviction was growing that its philosophy had a very special role to play in this form of educational pan-Africanism. Emmett J. Scott, the secretary of the institute, described and explained the magnetic appeal of Tuskegee in an article of the following year:

> This intercourse has been fostered partly by a sentimental interest that the Negroes in America feel in the land from which their ancestors came and by the desire of the native people to see what men of their own race have accomplished in this country towards mastering the white man's civilisation. But the chief reason why graduates have been induced to go to Africa and students from Africa have been led to come here is because both the white men who ruled in Africa and the natives who are ruled there have come to believe that in this school a method and a type of education has been evolved which is peculiarly suited to their needs.[3]

Appeals continued to come to Tuskegee in the next few years, seeking Washington's advice on educational problems in Africa.[4] It was probably a combination of events in 1910 and 1911, however, that finally decided him to hold the major international conference that Park had suggested. Washington had been in Europe in the late summer and autumn of 1910, and it is possible that he had made some contact while in England and Scotland with those missionary leaders and educationists who had recently been taking part in the first World Missionary Conference in Edinburgh during June 1910; this was especially likely, since the conference had recommended that African missionaries should pay particular attention to Tuskegee and

[1] Park to Washington, 25 Sept. 1905, Box 30, B.T.W./L.C. For Park, see Mathews, op. cit., pp. 259–60.

[2] For continuing educational contacts between Washington and Africa in the early years of the century, see E. W. Smith, *Aggrey of Africa* (London, 1929), p. 146; Mathews, op. cit., p. 243; and Shepperson, 'Pan-Africanism and "Pan-Africanism"', p. 354.

[3] E. J. Scott, 'Tuskegee in Africa and Africa at Tuskegee', typescript, *c.* 1906, Box 335, B.T.W./L.C.

[4] For the appeal from Liberia especially, see Mathews, op. cit., pp. 241–54.

Hampton.[1] A contributory factor may also have been an invitation in 1911 to undertake an educational tour of the West Indies.[2] But it was probably his continuing disagreement with DuBois, as much as anything else, that led him to describe Tuskegee methods before an international audience. DuBois had, after all, recently gained a position of considerable influence in the National Association for the Advancement of Coloured People (N.A.A.C.P.), which had been founded in 1910 as an organization pledged, among other things, to protest on racial issues and spread propaganda abroad. A great deal of this agitation was fostered by its official organ, the *Crisis,* which began its stormy career under DuBois's editorship in November 1910. The following year he had achieved further prominence, in a way Washington disapproved, in his role as one of the United States secretaries in the Universal Races Congress in London.[3]

Whatever influence DuBois may have indirectly had in the timing of the project, the International Conference on the Negro at Tuskegee in April 1912 certainly met a wide demand for information about Washington's methods.[4] Delegates came from eighteen foreign countries and from twelve different religious denominations; the majority representation was naturally from the West Indies and the American South, but there was a scattering of white and Negro workers from Africa.[5] As far as can be ascertained, however, only one native African attended.[6]

Washington himself saw the conference as having a double objective: first, to inform leading missionary and colonial educators about

[1] For some of the influential people Washington met in England and Scotland, see *My Larger Education* (London, 1911), pp. 257–61; also *The Times* (London) 19 Sept. 1910; see further p. 50, below.

[2] See p. 30, below.

[3] For the continuing disagreement with DuBois, see Rudwick, op. cit., pp. 131, 133–4, and especially over DuBois's prominence at the Universal Races Congress, pp. 142–8.

[4] R. E. Park, 'The International Conference on the Negro', *Southern Workman*, xli (June 1912), 348. The conference was given a semi-official status by the presence of the Hon. P. P. Claxton, U.S. Commissioner of Education, Bureau of Education, Washington.

[5] For example, James Denton, principal of Fourah Bay College, Sierra Leone; Dr. William Sheppard, Negro missionary of the Southern Presbyterian Church in the Congo; Bishop Isaiah Scott, of the Methodist Episcopal Church, Monrovia. The only evidence of East African interest was from the Lumbwa Industrial Mission, British East Africa, see O. H. Scouten to Washington, 2 May 1912, Box 61, B.T.W./L.C.

[6] Mark Casely Hayford, brother of the distinguished Gold Coast nationalist, J. E. Casely Hayford.

the methods of Tuskegee, and then 'to see to what extent the methods employed here can be applied to the problems concerning the people in countries that are peopled by the darker races'.[1] Thus he was by then quite explicitly regarding Tuskegee's education as in some way peculiarly appropriate to non-whites generally, and anticipating, by this policy of attracting white and Negro visitors to his institute, those agencies which after his death would make Tuskegee the very model of 'correct' African education.

The conference was, however, most notable for demonstrating the variety of people who considered the Tuskegee system relevant to Africa. If it had not become clear before, it was obvious by then that attitudes to Tuskegee could be extremely complex. Apart from the straight dichotomy over the rights and wrongs of industrial education, there was a whole cluster of political myths associated with Tuskegee, and this was particularly true of African attitudes towards it. E. W. Blyden, for instance, had paid very little attention to the level on which DuBois had attacked Tuskegee, but saw it rather as a 'noble monument' to black enterprise, and as the most solid evidence of 'what the African can do for himself'.[2] Several other Africans, who were not able to attend the conference, held similar views. An Ethiopian Church in Johannesburg interpreted the meeting as an endorsement of black independence in African mission work—scarcely a position that Washington would have subscribed to himself.[3] From the Gold Coast the noted nationalist writer, J. E. Casely Hayford, made no mention of Tuskegee's industrial aspects in his letter to the conference, emphasizing instead the spirit of racial solidarity for which Tuskegee stood, and hinting at a wider political end:

> There is an African nationality, and when the Aborigines of the Gold Coast and other parts of West Africa have joined forces with our brethren in America in arriving at a national aim, purpose and aspiration, then indeed will it be possible for our brethren over the sea to bring home metaphorically to their nation and people a great spoil.[4]

[1] Park, 'The International Conference on the Negro', p. 348.

[2] E. W. Blyden, 'West Africa Before Europe', *Journal of the African Society*, ii (July 1903), 372. Blyden died in fact two months before the conference, but he had written a message of encouragement which was read out to the delegates.

[3] 'The Negro in Conference at Tuskegee Institute', *African Times and Orient Review*, i, No. 1 (July 1912), 11.

[4] Ibid., pp. 10–11.

It seems that with many Africans it was not so much the white money behind Tuskegee as the black president and all-black staff that gave it much of its appeal. This certainly accounted for the publicity given to the conference in the newly founded pan-African journal, the *African Times and Orient Review*.[1] Its editor, Duse Mohammed Ali, gave wide coverage to 'The Negro in Conference at Tuskegee Institute' in the first issue of his journal, and followed that with a long article by Booker Washington in the second number.[2] Some two years later this same sense that Tuskegee stood out as an island of black pride and racial solidarity won the early admiration of Marcus Garvey, the Jamaican leader of the Universal Negro Improvement and Conservation Association.[3]

There was a similarly broad spectrum of white approval for Tuskegee at the conference. Just as in the United States the white North and white South could sink their substantial differences in common support for Tuskegee's industrial features, so now in Africa white fighters for African rights could share admiration for Tuskegee with more conservative thinkers. Thus E. D. Morel, who had played a major part in publicizing the scandals of rubber exploitation in the Congo, addressed a paper to the conference which showed how he could combine the highest approbation for the achievements of African culture with a demand for Tuskegee-type education.[4] His very esteem for African civilization made him the more anxious to grasp at anything which would prevent Africans from becoming deracialized. Nor did Morel share the anthropologist's view of an African life that must be sheltered in its simplicity from the outside world. Like Blyden, whom he quoted in his paper, he was concerned to protect a highly developed civilization:

The average individual is surprised without measure to learn of the existence of African *cities* (I do not mean European cities in Africa, but African cities, built by Africans, and inhabited exclusively by Africans) with written records hundreds of years old; of African industries which give healthy employment to tens of thousands of African men and women;

[1] Ibid., pp. 9–11; Geiss, op. cit., p. 7. Ian Duffield is preparing a biography of Duse Mohammed Ali for his Ph.D. thesis at Edinburgh University.

[2] B. T. Washington, 'Tuskegee Institute', *African Times and Orient Review*, i, No. 2 (Aug. 1912), 48–53.

[3] Garvey to Washington, 12 Apr. 1915, Box 939, B.T.W./L.C. Garvey's intention to visit 'the great institution' at Tuskegee was frustrated by Washington's death in October of that year. See, however, p. 223, below.

[4] Washington had met Morel during his 1910 European tour.

of an African civilisation superior in some of its social aspects to the western civilisation of today.[1]

As, however, missionary education had so far had the effect of creating an educated élite that had lost interest in its own culture, Morel was now prepared to support a system like Tuskegee's, which promised the development of a whole society along the lines of its own genius.

Maurice Evans, the South African, who was representing the African Society at the conference, reached the same conclusions by a somewhat different route, but equally invoked Blyden in support of his policy.[2] In his view Africans were not destined as a race to make any contribution in the areas of European mastery. There was little point in supporting an African educational system that believed it important to produce 'a few learned or artistic prodigies'.[3] Rather, they should be educated to fulfil better what they most naturally were—'a race of peasants living by and on the land'.[4] What was needed therefore was some model of an educational system that was not designed exclusively for white people, and there was none more obvious or successful than Tuskegee.

For different reasons both Morel and Evans feared the consequences of de-Africanization, and both believed that it should be the function of the school to maintain a pride in things African. In supporting Tuskegee's education as a remedy for the increasing westernizing of African societies, they failed, however, to raise questions that would remain significant over the next thirty years. Was industrial education really any more 'African' than academic western education? Could curricular changes in African schools radically alter the pattern of African aspirations, and break their determination to conform to the standards of the white world? Were there real justifications for the growing white conviction that what was good for the Negro in the Southern States was good for the Negro in Africa?

These were only a few of the questions that were not discussed, when they might very usefully have been, at the Tuskegee International Conference. Questions were, however, raised concerning

[1] E. D. Morel, 'The Future of Tropical Africa', *Southern Workman*, xli, No. 6 (June 1912), 353–4.

[2] M. S. Evans, 'Education among the Bantu of South East Africa', *Southern Workman*, xli (June 1912), 363–8. See further, M. S. Evans, *Black and White in the Southern States: A Study of the Race Problem in the United States from a South African Point of View* (London, 1915), p. 135.

[3] M. S. Evans, 'Education among the Bantu', p. 367. [4] Ibid.

how the American Negro missionaries could best serve their African brethren within the framework of white rule,[1] and much thought was also given to how the American Negro colleges and schools could best prepare their African students for valuable work among their own people.[2]

It is fitting perhaps that from a conference held at Tuskegee there should have come no very precise statement of conclusions. So many otherwise conflicting groups found it possible to support Tuskegeeism for such widely differing reasons that only the most generalized statement of conclusions was feasible. A degree of co-operation had certainly been achieved, but it would remain to be seen whether the agreement over the declarations could survive Booker Washington's death just three years later. The conference ended nevertheless on a note that seemed both optimistic and prophetic:

> The International Conference on the Negro has opened up a new field of co-operation among those interested in the Negro race; Tuskegee has become a great experimental station in racial education and a center of Negro life; the questions which were raised for discussion will affect native races in all parts of the world.[3]

[1] 'The Negro in Conference at Tuskegee Institute', p. 12.

[2] Park, 'The International Conference on the Negro', pp. 348–9.

[3] Ibid., p. 352.

CHAPTER II

Tuskegee, Philanthropy and the Missionary Societies

BY THE time of Washington's death in 1915, his hopes that Tuskegee would become the experimental centre for the education of the Negro world seemed more likely to be fulfilled than they had been at the time of the International Conference on the Negro. In the interval, the two agencies in America and Britain principally concerned with the development of education in backward areas had been reassessing their policies on educational aid: in England, Christian foreign mission policy, especially that concerned with Africa, was becoming progressively disenchanted with providing undifferentiated western education, and was casting about for a more suitable alternative, while in America there was a parallel desire on the part of the philanthropic funds operating in the Southern States to specialize their benefactions, and define more clearly the type of Negro education most deserving of aid. Both streams converged on Tuskegee, and the result was to transform into respectable educational theory what had begun as Tuskegee's compromise solution to racial discrimination. Industrial education had originally been introduced as a guarantee that the Negro would continue to provide a low-level labour supply for the white South; Tuskegeeism was now to be reinterpreted on the Negro's behalf as the first stage of the revolution against the traditional European and American concept of the school. In practice, however, this new educational justification for Tuskegee would never be entirely free from the old political implications of caste education, such as had made the Washington–DuBois dispute so bitter. Thus dissension would continue no less fiercely in the decade after Washington's death, only it would now be a feud between DuBois and those philanthropic foundations which interpreted Washington's policy. In particular, the mantle of Washington would fall on the Phelps-Stokes Fund, and on its educational director, Dr. Thomas Jesse Jones.

Jones, whose name was to be intimately linked for thirty years with the idea of industrial education for Negroes, had himself been nurtured in North Wales amidst simple rural crafts. His grandfather was a village blacksmith and his father a saddler.[1] Although the family left for America when he was only eleven, he retained from that most nationally-conscious part of Wales a fierce pride in what he considered his Celtic nature. Years later in Africa he strove to turn Africans from the 'British Grenadiers' to their own local songs by singing selections of Welsh airs.[2] In America he had his undergraduate education largely in the South, at Washington and Lee Universities, and transferred for his M.A., B.D., and Ph.D. to New York's Columbia University and Union Seminary. During his doctoral research he came much under the influence of his professor, Dr. Franklin Henry Giddings, whose emphasis on the importance of 'consciousness of kind' as a guiding principle of sociology was to remain central to Jones's own thinking. Indeed, his growing fascination with racial distinctions was early encouraged by his Ph.D. investigations of the Jewish and Italian communities living in a New York city block.[3]

He was in fact still engaged in his studies at Columbia when the invitation to come South arrived from Armstrong's successor at Hampton, Dr. H. B. Frissell, in 1902. In this novel school community of 150 white staff, 600 Negro and some 100 Red Indian students, there was a further opportunity for developing his early ideas on the distinctive contributions of the various races. It seems possible, moreover, that his race-consciousness and his convictions on the separateness of peoples grew more rigid in the South for a rather more personal reason; curiously enough this was alluded to by the famous traveller and Africanist, Sir Harry H. Johnston, who was visiting Hampton's staff in 1908:

> One of them interested me more than the others. This was Mr. Thomas Jesse Jones, a Welshman, born and bred, of wit and discernment. Though he was a nice-looking man, he belonged, as he humourously explained, to that dark type of southern Welshman who is particularly Iberian or

[1] 'In Memoriam, Thomas Jesse Jones', Phelps–Stokes Fund Archives (hereafter P.S.F.A.). See also *Reports of the Principal, Hampton Institute* (Hampton, Va., 1902–5).

[2] J. E. K. Aggrey to Mrs. T. J. Jones, 11 March 1921, printed in *Education for Life: The Phelps-Stokes Fund and Thomas Jesse Jones. A Twenty-fifth Anniversary, 1913–1937* (New York, 1937), p. 94.

[3] E. W. Smith, *Aggrey of Africa*, pp. 68–9. T. J. Jones, *Sociology of a New York City Block* (Columbia Univ. Press, 1904), summarized in Jones, *Essentials of Civilisation* (New York, 1929), p. xiv.

North African in appearance; and he complained that this slight suggestion of the pre-historic Negroid worried him at times when his journies extended into the Southern States. He was apt to feel timorous as to whether his brown eyes and dark hair might not cause him to be recommended by a tram-conductor or a railway official, to take the car or portion of the car, reserved for people of colour.[1]

It was this man who would gain for himself over the next ten years the reputation of being one of America's foremost experts on the Negro.

His first posts were as director of the Hampton research department and lecturer in sociology. In the former he began the process of collecting data of comparative racial achievement in the fields of economic and social development. This material would provide him, he felt, with his first opportunity to attack the race problem by the uncontroversial presentation of Negro and white statistics. If racial prejudice was the result of ignorance and distortion, then it might best be tackled by a cool assessment of the facts of black and white development. Through the medium of his classes on social studies and civics, he worked to impart an attitude towards racial inequalities that did not involve antagonism. His students heard his earliest attempts to lessen racial tension; they were taught to re-think the whole concept of racial injustice, and explain the apparent difficulties of the Negroes or the Red Indians in the 'social Darwinist' categories of the day. Thus there was really no such thing as racial discrimination or racial oppression, but 'natural difficulties'[2] common to every race as it evolved on its slow time scale. The element of determinism in such a philosophy made it possible to label as 'precocious' or 'not natural' individuals in lower stages who set themselves against the 'social forces controlling and limiting the development of races'.[3]

Most important, Jones was provided with a system of thought that could assess the value of such phrases as 'social equality', 'Negro domination', and 'Negro independence'. These terms did not, as he saw it, correspond to anything appropriate to the present stage of Negro development, and their use could only be construed as forms of untimely incitement to political consciousness. The precise connotation he gave to independent Negro effort is worth noticing at this

[1] H. Johnston, *The Story of My Life* (London, 1923), p. 418. For a photograph of Jones, see Plate VI.

[2] T. J. Jones, 'Social Studies in the Hampton Curriculum', *Southern Workman*, xxxiv (Dec. 1905), 689.

[3] Ibid.

point, since it was an issue that decidedly coloured his thinking both in America and later in Africa. He indicated his usual line of approach when the subject arose in his social studies classes: ' "Negro Independence" is a shibboleth used by a certain number of Negroes to persuade the race into their own power and away from the influence of the whites. The power of this phrase has been growing in the ranks of those who are more influenced by unfounded beliefs and hearsay evidence than by actual knowledge.'[1]

This unsympathetic rejection of any legitimate aspirations which might lie behind the idea of Negro independence effectively limited the meaning of his keyword, co-operation; it could now signify only the acceptance of substantial white influence in the leadership of Negro activity. In this respect perhaps Hampton did not provide a particularly fortunate introduction to the problems of interracial co-operation; membership of a predominantly white teaching staff of almost one hundred and fifty[2] was not necessarily a good preparation for dealing with Negroes' demands to lead their own institutions. Co-operation to Jones also signified an insistence that no political differences need be so radical that common ground could not be found. Any measure of agreement was preferable to admitting irreconcilability. He was to devote much of his life to showing people the possibilities of collaboration, and for this at least Hampton had provided relevant training. Its very existence was based upon just such a small area of common ground between the white North, the white South, and the Negro people, a position which, as every president of Hampton was aware, made supreme demands upon diplomacy. One had commented: 'In the delicate and difficult task of trying to be fair to our Northern white supporters, our large Negro constituency and our sincerely valued Southern white friends, we cannot hope, I suppose, to please and satisfy all three groups all of the time.'[3] This, however, was to be Jones's most characteristic activity, whether in Atlanta, or later in Nairobi and Capetown; to work for unity and compromise whenever there was the danger of racial, economic, or political views hardening into non co-operation. Soon he had mastered a technique for use in conflict situations, the first and most essential

[1] T. J. Jones, 'Social Studies in the Hampton Curriculum', *Southern Workman*, xxxvi (Jan. 1907), 44.

[2] This number constituted the largest concentration of white teachers in the Southern States in any Negro college or school.

[3] J. E. Gregg to Governor Trinkle, 11 July 1925, in R.R.M./G.C. (1925), T.U.A.

feature of which was the tactical avoidance of what could be considered the most sensitive issues. Following the principles of Booker Washington, he became convinced that, in the Southern situation at any rate, there was absolutely no advantage to be gained for Negro education by antagonizing the whites. Jones therefore operated a personal ban on the use of all terms which implied criticism of the white South; lynching, social equality, Negro rights, discrimination. Instead, some small constructive achievement would be alluded to, and then at least negotiations for co-operation might begin.

One of his first practical attempts to give expression to this philosophy was the endeavour to bring about a reconciliation between the traditionally rival schools of thought on Negro education: the industrial and the literary, and, behind these, the political creeds of Washington and DuBois.[1] Jones wished to associate the academic researches of DuBois with the practical advances in social welfare for which Hampton had made a stand. More particularly there seemed to be a possibility of combining DuBois's Atlanta University conference for the study of Negro problems with the annual Hampton conference.[2] A provisional arrangement was therefore made between Jones and DuBois that these two centres, with their very different traditions, should co-operate in the production of publications in 1907 on 'The Negro Home'.[3]

More important than the actual study was, to Jones's mind, the opportunity for channelling DuBois's energies away from unrealistic speculations by personal involvement in local community welfare. It was to be Jones's first skirmish in a campaign which lasted for over thirty years to counteract the effect of DuBois's radical investigations of racial problems. Before the differences between them finally crystallized, Jones thought it quite possible that DuBois might be won over to constructive rather than critical policies:

> Hampton and Atlanta can much more easily co-operate than Tuskegee and Atlanta. Beginning thus at the points of least divergence on a concrete proposition there is a strong possibility that the larger harmony can be brought about.

[1] For DuBois's critique of the near-monopoly held by Hampton and Tuskegee over Northern funds for Negro education in the South, see DuBois to Miss Davis, 1917, Frissell Papers, Hampton Institute Archives (hereafter H.A.I.).

[2] The Atlanta University Publications which were the product of these annual conferences were, Jones admitted, required reading for any serious student of the race problem. See also Broderick, *W. E. B. DuBois*, pp. 41–2.

[3] Jones to G. F. Peabody, 13 Aug. 1906, Jones File, H.A.I.

DuBois as one of the leaders of the race must be reckoned with. He is much in need of the training that comes from the effort to enlist ignorant men in good movements. At present he is too largely an impractical idealist.

For all these reasons, namely the larger co-operation which may be brought about among the leaders and schools of the colored race, the success of the work in Georgia, the training which DuBois may receive, it seems to me quite important that this co-operation of conferences should be undertaken.[1]

The scheme would, if it had been successful, have had the same basis as an earlier attempt by Booker Washington and his white supporters to have DuBois attached to Tuskegee as a member of staff,[2] and it failed for the same reason; that DuBois was not prepared to stifle criticism of the white South or, for that matter, of Hampton's industrial philosophy. Indeed, as if to prove this point, only two months after his conversations with Jones, he attended the Hampton summer school, and delivered a lecture on industrial education, roundly condemning Hampton as the 'center of this educational heresy'.[3]

Little had so far come of this particular initiative in co-operation, but in another field Jones had met with more success. Through the network of the Coloured Y.M.C.A., he had come across in November 1904 a young African of his own age who, he immediately recognized, was working on the same lines as himself. This man, J. E. K. Aggrey, after spending his first twenty-three years in the Gold Coast, had recently graduated from Livingstone College in North Carolina. Although a product of that classical education so contrary to the ideals of Hampton, he did not share DuBois's attitude to industrial education. The week after their meeting Jones invited him to visit and preach at Hampton,[4] and there thus began in an informal way what would later become one of Jones's major activities: the promotion of Hampton's methods to Africans.

Given the background of Jones's fear of the Negro radical, it is not improbable even at this early stage that there was an element of

[1] Ibid. For the failure of direct co-operation between Atlanta and Tuskegee in the Committee of Twelve, see Broderick, op. cit., p. 72.

[2] Broderick, op. cit., pp. 65–6.

[3] W. E. B. DuBois, 'Self Assertion and the Higher Education', an address delivered before the Summer School, Hampton Institute, 1906, p. 6, DuBois Papers, Park Johnson Archives, Fisk University, Nashville, Tenn.

[4] Smith, op. cit., p. 70; for an account of Aggrey's first visit to Hampton, see also *Southern Workman*, xxxiv (Jan. 1905), 60.

PLATE III

competition with DuBois involved in presenting Hampton's constructive approach to Aggrey.[1] But Aggrey's effect upon Jones must be regarded as incalculably more significant, for here was a Negro who combined high intelligence with the greatest interracial tact, and whose desire to aid his own common people was, apparently, his sole reason for aspiring to further education. Moreover, there was none of the insistence on rights and talk of protest that was becoming increasingly characteristic of DuBois. For practical purposes, however, the connection with Aggrey did not bear fruit until Jones extended his attention beyond the Southern States.

For the moment, Jones was working in Hampton's research department on the assumption that the correct presentation of the facts of Negro, White, and Indian differences and abilities would go a long way towards easing racial tensions. To this end his sociology courses in Hampton were designed to expose the commonest misconceptions about race; a proper appreciation of racial differences would, he thought, be a brake on unrealistic ambitions in Negroes and Indians, as much as it would stimulate white concern for the lower races. Even the objectives of the courses he taught were mapped out in strictly racial terms for the *Hampton Bulletin*:

The aim in the study of sociology is to gain an understanding of
(1) Race differences as shown in physique, health, birthrate, and death rate, illiteracy, economic conditions, and crime.
(2) Race differences, mental and moral, as shown in the efficiency of such organisations as the home, the church and the club.
(3) The relation of these differences to the progress of the Negro and Indian races, and especially their bearing upon the social situation in the Southern States.
(4) THE DANGER OF IMPULSIVE ACTION OR UNCONTROLLED EMOTION WHETHER IN RELIGIOUS OR POLITICAL MATTERS.[2]

During these early years at Hampton, Jones was slowly gathering together the elements of an educational theory appropriate to Negro people. Initially, as can be seen from the above statement, his

[1] Dr. Herbert Aptheker has mentioned to the writer that there is substantial evidence of Aggrey's interest in and personal overtures to DuBois at this early period contained in the DuBois Papers in his possession.

[2] *Report of the Principal, Hampton Institute* (Hampton, Va., 1910), pp. 31–2. For an exceedingly valuable photographic account of Hampton taken two years before Jones first went to teach there, see *The Hampton Album* (Museum of Modern Art, New York, 1966). See Plate III, for a social studies class at Hampton in 1900.

educational theory depended on an antecedent racial theory. Increasingly, however, as he began to reach a wider and more critical audience, the theoretical racial argument was dropped and there was substituted an appeal to statistics. For if figures could show that in certain agreed essentials, such as adequate housing, health, skilled work, Negroes were particularly backward, it could be suggested that their education should concern itself with such deficiencies, without raising the delicate question of whether the Negro *qua* Negro ought to have a special type of education. The premises were thus apparently shifted from racial differences to Negro needs as defined by comparative statistics. There was now a possibility that with reliable figures Jones might give respectability to Hampton's and Tuskegee's race-oriented curriculum.

It was therefore quite in accordance with this programme for Jones to take up a temporary appointment with the United States Census Bureau for the 1910 census. His assignment there was to supervise the collection of Negro data, and it was hoped that he would be successful in getting 'the facts in regard to the negroes' where the Census Bureau believed it had so far failed.[1] This was in itself significant, for it meant that Jones was already not only regarded as an authority on the Negro, but also had his confidence.

Certainly up to the end of 1910 his relations with DuBois had remained cordial; and, despite the earlier abortive attempt at cooperation, DuBois was even now prepared strongly to exhort Jones to join his newly formed N.A.A.C.P.[2] Both men had in this year left the relative obscurity of their teaching posts at Hampton and Atlanta for public positions, with full-time opportunity to develop their own increasingly divergent interests. As research director of the N.A.A.C.P., DuBois now had a platform provided by liberal white finance, and as editor of its organ, the *Crisis*, a personal vehicle of radical protest.[3] It was, however, as inconceivable for Jones to play a part in the N.A.A.C.P. as it had been earlier for DuBois to throw himself into organizing a better housing movement in rural Georgia. He explained to President Frissell of Hampton the difficulty of cooperating with DuBois on such terms:

Dr. DuBois has written urging me to join his association. I would like

[1] Frissell to Peabody, 10 Nov. 1909, Frissell letterbook, 1910, H.A.I

[2] Jones to Frissell, 1 Oct. 1910, Jones File, H.A.I.

[3] Broderick, op. cit., p. 92.

to help present the actual condition of the Negro race through that association, but I am afraid of an organisation mainly composed of people who do not know the situation and one that has for its chief purpose the presentation of the complaints of the colored people. Complaint, when it must be made, is more effectively made by those who believe and present the good and the progress.[1]

A break between the two men had become by this time almost inevitable, and relations were finally severed in November 1911, after what Jones described as 'a very unpleasant experience with DuBois'.[2] What the particular issue was that convinced Jones of the 'impossibility of working with DuBois in any continued way' can only be conjectured; but then every issue of the *Crisis* in that first year of its publication contained some editorial or comment that Jones would have considered a disastrous setback to his own interracial philosophy.

It is just possible, however, that the dispute might have developed from Jones's suggesting that the census figures could be made to show an increased need for industrial training among Negroes. Much of the material that had been collected specifically on Negro education corroborated his own views on the various types of training suitable for Negroes and, in particular, he hinted to Booker Washington that he was 'more deeply convinced than ever before of the educational value of industrial training'.[3] Understandably, Washington was delighted at support for his programme coming from such an influential source, and assured the president of Hampton that the cause of Negro education would have received 'a black eye'[4] without Jones's invaluable work. When Washington added, 'We must all stand by him,'[5] it becomes even more likely that Jones's work would have been resented by some sections of Negro opinion opposed to increased industrial training.

However this may have been, Jones had certainly been for some time moving closer to Tuskegee, and to Washington personally. Two years earlier he had shown in regard to Tuskegee his firm conviction that constructive propaganda could be a solvent of race hatred, by

[1] Jones to Frissell, 1 Oct. 1910. Two of the original published objectives of the N.A.A.C.P. in 1911 which might well have disturbed Jones were: 'to begin immediately a scientific study of Negro schools' and 'to make foreign propaganda . . .', quoted in H. A. Bullock, *A History of Negro Education in the South, from 1619 to the Present* (Harvard, 1967), p. 212.

[2] Jones to Frissell, 25 Nov. 1911, Washington File, H.A.I.

[3] Jones to Washington, 10 Feb. 1911, Box 426, B.T.W./L.C.

[4] Washington to Frissell, 14 Sept. 1911, Washington File, H.A.I.

[5] Ibid.

persuading Washington to set up a department of records and research.[1] He had personally selected and trained the director of the department, Monroe Work, in the techniques which he had himself been using at Hampton, and had thus created another agency which would authoritatively promote the Tuskegee–Hampton system as the model of Negro Education. In 1911 he suggested that he might accompany Booker T. Washington on an educational tour of the West Indies which Washington had been planning. In the process Jones was already voicing a desire to become an expert on Negro education beyond the limits of the U.S.A.[2]

It was ten years before this desire 'to make comparative studies of colored people in other parts of the world'[3] came to fulfilment. However, his move from the Census Bureau to the Federal Bureau of Education, as a specialist in the education of racial groups, gave him the opportunity in 1912 greatly to extend his knowledge of and influence over Negro education in the States. The Bureau had itself very little direct power over the educational developments in the various States, being at this time more of a centralized statistical office; the positions of greatest personal influence in the allocation of educational funds for the South lay with the officers of the philanthropic foundations. In practice, however, even these had comparatively little room for manoeuvre, since it was their implicit policy that educational moneys should be appropriated in ways that did not conflict with the wishes of the Southern white governments.[4] The consequence was that much philanthropic money was devoted to the promotion of low-level industrial training of the Tuskegee type, and more often than not Washington played the role of consultant or distributor of such aid.[5] Something of this tendency to channel philanthropic aid through Washington, as the interpreter of what was educationally feasible in the South, is shown clearly in his negotiations with the recently founded Phelps-Stokes Fund.[6] These were shortly to lead to a collaboration of the Phelps-Stokes Fund with

[1] Washington to Jones, 8 June 1908, Box 374, B.T.W./L.C.

[2] Jones to Washington, 10 Feb. 1911. [3] Ibid.

[4] For the General Education Board's financial policy in the South, see, for example, *The General Education Board: An Account of its Activities, 1902–1914* (New York, 1915), pp. 8, 9, 203, 209.

[5] Meier, op. cit., p. 114.

[6] A valuable biographical sketch of Miss Caroline Phelps Stokes, whose will created the Fund, is contained in Jones, *Educational Adaptations*, pp. 7–22. For the essential background to the Phelps-Stokes Fund, see Jones, *Negro Education*, pp. xi–xiv.

Jones and the Bureau of Education in a nation-wide survey of Negro education.

Jesse Jones and the Negro Education Report

After the incorporation of this Fund in 1910, the first official move of the secretary to the trustees, Anson Phelps Stokes, was a letter to Booker Washington inquiring what use he could suggest for five or ten thousand dollars.[1]

Washington was in no doubt that such a sum could be instrumental in accomplishing what he had long regarded as a necessity: distinguishing the worthy from the unworthy small denominational Negro schools.[2] This would require a survey of the entire field, and it would then be possible to begin the process of 'killing out' the poorer schools and encouraging those with reasonable backing.[3] No doubt an important consideration with Washington was the possibility of exposing the numerous schools which had jumped on to the industrial bandwagon. It was a measure of Tuskegee's success that, by then, the very addition of the name 'industrial' to a struggling school could make Northern appeals more successful. Washington outlined his general intention to Robert Park,[4] the man whom he hoped would direct this unpopular survey:

> As you know, there is nothing more needed in the South than to state exactly to the public what these schools are doing, especially the supposed industrial schools. A lot of them are doing fake work, others are trying to do good work but do not know how. We want to get the truth to help the schools and for the sake of the public. Of course such a report will create a great stir.[5]

When the decision had been reached to survey all the Negro schools in the South, including high schools, colleges, and universities, the scheme came to the attention of Jones. It naturally seemed the ideal opportunity to substantiate and expound his growing faith in the merits of industrial education. Consequently, after much persuasion, he was able to show Anson Phelps Stokes the advantage of such surveys being carried out under his own direction and with the

[1] Washington to Phelps Stokes, 6 May 1911, Box 440, B.T.W./L.C.

[2] Ibid.

[3] Washington to Phelps Stokes, 15 May 1911, Box 440, B.T.W./L.C.

[4] Dr. Robert Park had achieved national status as the secretary of the Congo Reform Association a few years earlier; see also p. 15, n. 1.

[5] Washington to Park, 6 Oct. 1912, Box 61, B.T.W./L.C.

cooperation of the Bureau of Education and the Phelps-Stokes Fund.[1]

Any educational report whose aim is to expose frauds and recommend models can expect a controversial reception; but there were special factors involved in reporting on Negro education in the Southern States that might have suggested a more objective assessor than Thomas Jesse Jones. In a situation where the majority of the facilities for Negro college, secondary and teacher-training courses in the South were supported by funds from the North,[2] Jones's survey would inevitably appear as a guide to absentee philanthropists on where to place their educational investments.

There was another great danger in this recommending of suitable Southern schools to Northern philanthropy: that Jones might be unable to avoid following the traditional canon of philanthropic funds: 'Unto him that hath it shall be given'. It might be difficult in this delicate task of differentiating successful from unsuccessful schools, to do sufficient justice to schools whose educational standards, management, and teachers were second-rate through perpetual lack of adequate finance. Such schools would more often than not be the little institutions of coloured denominations or struggling independent Negro schools; in all likelihood they would have no white staff. On a static assessment of their value it would be a temptation to dismiss them as bad propositions for philanthropy.

There would be difficulties, too, in reporting on effective industrial education. For, with good industrial education considerably more costly than the traditional academic curriculum, it might be difficult to determine whether a school with inadequate industrial education was in this state through poverty or preference for academic work. Most difficult of all, and indeed the test of Jones's impartiality, would be his treatment of the Negro liberal arts colleges. Founded and taught by Northerners in the flush of enthusiasm for equal Negro rights after the Civil War, they had barely survived the subsequent period of Southern demand for industrial education, and now in the philanthropic age their tenaciously-upheld classical curricula commanded very little support.[3] Almost their only asset was their alumnus and protector, W. E. B. DuBois. Now they would be individually analysed by a man firmly committed to the opposite of everything to which they

[1] Jones to Frissell, 9 Nov. 1912, Jones File, H.A.I. Also Washington to Phelps Stokes, 9 Nov. 1912, Box 464, B.T.W./L.C.

[2] Jones, *Negro Education*, p. 8.

[3] On the hand-to-mouth financing of DuBois's Atlanta University Publications, see Broderick, op. cit., pp. 56–7.

had stubbornly clung. They had not fared well in the era of informal philanthropy, when Washington had presided over the distribution of aid; it seemed doubtful if they would do any better once Jones had professionalized philanthropic benefactions under the aegis of the Bureau of Education.

In fact it is unthinkable that in 1913 any man would have been chosen for this survey whose views did not coincide with the reigning Hampton–Tuskegee philosophy of special Negro education. It was known that Jones had prejudged the issue between the industrial and literary kinds of education: his function would therefore be to judge all Negro schools by what were widely thought their own special criteria, and set his judgements as far as possible within the framework of statistics.

The results of his subsequent three years of visiting schools and compiling evidence was the most impressively produced two-volume report, *Negro Education: A Study of the Private and Higher Schools for Colored People in the United States.*[1] It claimed for itself a constructive lack of bias; all that had been aimed at throughout was 'to determine the real educational needs of the people and the extent to which the school work has been adapted to these needs'.[2] Yet, for all the pages of statistics, graphs of rural population and production, and details of income and endowment, the two volumes were in fact an extended exercise in special pleading, a restatement of Armstrong's conviction that 'the temporal salvation of the colored race for some time to come is to be won out of the ground'.[3] The assumptions upon which the whole investigation rested were summed up in an address which Jones delivered to the National Education Association in the year he began the survey. They may be quoted at length as the most fitting preface to an assessment of his *Negro Education.*

The most impressive commencement exercise that I have ever witnessed was that of a farmer boy at Tuskegee last May. He stood upon the platform of the beautiful church surrounded by the common tools and the common animals and common foods without which we could not live. There were the stove, the bed, and the table, the plow, the spade and the hoe; the saw, the hammer and the plane, the horse, the cow and the pig. Surrounded by these evidences of a democratic education, he stood erect, a splendid

[1] The report was in two volumes, Bulletin No. 38 and No. 39 (hereafter Bulletin No. 38 and Bulletin No. 39).

[2] Bulletin No. 39, p. 2; see also Bulletin No. 38, p. xii.

[3] Quoted in Bulletin No. 38, p. 104. Cf. also Washington, *Up From Slavery*, p. 116.

specimen of young manhood entirely unconscious of his uniform, the simple blue overalls of a farmer. He explained in dignified clear English a scientific chart showing exactly how to obtain the greatest possible returns from an acre of soil and still leave that soil ready for other crops. It was all most interesting and impressive, but to me the climax of his splendid efforts came when quite unconsciously he lifted from the platform a box containing what he described to be the farmer's best ally. His simple words were eloquent with meaning as he showed that out of that box of barnyard manure came prosperity and comforts, and pleasures and education and religion to the man who is democratic enough to recognise its value.[1]

Quite apart from the confusion of democracy with rural simplicity —the traditional American Jeffersonian approach—this passage anticipated one of the priorities of the report: the place of rural education in Negro life. A determined effort was made in the chapter on rural education to demonstrate that it was not prejudice but unchallengeable statistical facts that made rural education so essential to the Negro. If the 1910 census showed that eighty per cent of Southern Negroes lived in country districts, then it followed that agricultural education must be the mainstay of the curriculum.[2]

This type of static educational prescription, which reappeared a decade later in Africa,[3] took little account either of the urbanization process or of the victimization of Negroes in rural life. Rather, the movement to the towns was noticed only to be dismissed as a 'delusion',[4] while reports of white violence and higher lynching rates in rural areas had been, Jones suggested, exaggerated out of proportion.[5]

To counteract the general indifference of the Negro towards rural studies, it was only necessary to correct his conviction that literary studies were made for prosperity, and to use the entire school system to prove that the 'most substantial gains made by the race are in the rural communities'.[6] Again, the 1910 census provided what Jones thought decisive evidence of the rural Negro's advantage: more Negroes owned farms and were tenant farmers in 1910 than in 1900. Why this should have been selected as a more substantial gain than the voting rights and freedom from lynching in any Northern city, Jones did not explain. With sublime faith in the power of the school to change the pattern of social and economic forces which were

[1] T. J. Jones, 'The High School and Democracy', an address before the National Education Association at Salt Lake City, 1913; copy in H.A.I.

[2] Bulletin No. 38, p. 99. [3] See p. 206

[4] Bulletin No. 38, p. 99. [5] Ibid. [6] Ibid.

driving rural Negroes to the North, he pleaded principally for a curricular reform: 'The emphatic conclusion of this study is therefore that the first step in rural education should be the enthusiastic advocacy of the theory and practice of gardening, for every colored pupil.'[1] Not surprisingly, in the volume of individual school assessments and recommendations, over fifty per cent of the schools visited received as one of their recommendations 'that the theory and practice of gardening should be included as part of the regular course'.[2] Not even DuBois's old teaching college at Atlanta was exempt. It came perilously close to provocation to accuse certain 'educational leaders of the colored people'[3] of being indifferent to agricultural progress, and then to suggest that Atlanta University make better use of its garden, hennery, and dairy herd.[4] DuBois rose to the challenge. When he came to assess this part of Jones's report, he dismissed, in a highly critical article, most of the arguments for rural studies as 'propaganda' or untruth,[5] and on Jones's anti-urbanization he commented: 'The advance of the cities has been greatest for all people, white and colored, and for any colored man to take his family to the country districts of South Georgia in order to grow and develop and secure an education and uplift would be idiotic.'[6]

It must be reiterated that Jones, in pressing for the primacy of rural needs, was entirely representative of policy among the great philanthropic foundations in the South. Without exception their efforts were centred on rural betterment; the General Education Board had, in the general public apathy over rural schools, appointed white State supervisors through the State departments of education. Their aim was, beyond the general stimulus of the local community, to work for curricular reform, 'especially along industrial and domestic lines'.[7] DuBois construed their priorities rather differently; 'it is this board that is spending more money today in helping Negroes learn how to can vegetables than in helping them to go through college.'[8] Similarly, at the lower county level, the Jeanes Fund supported a devoted corps of travelling women teachers to encourage interest in simple rural industries,[9] and the Rosenwald Fund

[1] Ibid., p. 97. [2] Bulletin No. 39, *passim.*
[3] Bulletin No. 38, p. 99. [4] Bulletin No. 39, p. 215.
[5] W. E. B. DuBois, 'Negro Education', *Crisis*, xv, No. 4 (Feb. 1918), p. 177.
[6] Ibid. [7] *The General Education Board, 1902–1914*, p. 195.
[8] DuBois, 'Negro Education', p. 177.
[9] L. G. E. Jones, *The Jeanes Teacher in the United States: 1908–1933* (Chapel Hill, 1937), *passim.*

concentrated on rural school buildings.[1] Through the Phelps-Stokes Fund, Jones was merely combining in a single educational theory their various rural preferences.[2]

Nor was there anything particularly novel in Jones's advocacy of industrial training as a Negro priority. What novelty there was consisted in 'proving' the need for industrial training from the census figures, thus providing a more reputable basis for such courses than the traditional 'industry is good for the Negro' approach. At this point, however, Jones's procedure broke down; figures were adduced from the census to show the distribution of Negroes in the South by trades; but no attempt was made to differentiate skilled from unskilled workers, nor were any comparative figures for white workers given. It was simply claimed as obviously important from the tables that the coloured people should 'grasp every opportunity for industrial training'.[3] The whole argument was vitiated by Jones's decision to avoid anything controversial—in this case the role of the white labour unions in preventing Negro access to skilled trade training. Indeed, DuBois very early saw this as the crucial point about what he considered the 'decadent' trades taught at the majority of Negro industrial schools,[4] and his description had ample confirmation some thirty years later from Gunnar Myrdal: '*In spite of all the talk about it, no effective industrial training was ever given the Negroes in the Southern public schools*, except training for cooking and menial service.'[5]

The economic value of industrial work was, however, only a small part of the benefits credited to the Hampton–Tuskegee conception of industry. Most important in any industrial proposals for Negro education were the famous character-forming qualities of trade training; not that the morality of industry was not urged for white children also at this period, but it was thought particularly suitable for the allegedly more unruly and emotional nature of Negro peoples. It first gained general currency in Armstrong's attempts to transform the old slave natures of his freedmen,[6] and also found its way into educational prescriptions for the Negroes of Africa.

[1] Bulletin No. 38, pp. 166–7.

[2] Jones became educational director of the Phelps-Stokes Fund in 1913.

[3] Bulletin No. 38, pp. 84–5. [4] DuBois, 'Negro Education', p. 175.

[5] G. Myrdal, *An American Dilemma: The Negro Problem and Modern Democracy* (New York, 1944), p. 899. See also, E. Franklin Frazier, *The Negro in the United States* (revised edn. New York, 1957), pp. 461–2.

[6] Jones reproduced several of Armstrong's axioms on the uplifting value of labour in Bulletin No. 38, pp. 81–2; the pithiest of these was 'Morality and

PLATE IV

Military uniform for Hampton students, 1900. (*Hampton Album*, Museum of Modern Art, New York.)

There was a yet broader interpretation of the value of industrial training than this. Both Armstrong and Jones believed that the Hampton–Tuskegee type of industrial school could eliminate the distinction between academic and vocational studies. In Jones's words, 'the underlying principle of these schools is the adaptation of educational activities, whether industrial or literary, to the needs of the pupil and the community.'[1] What this educational slogan concealed was for the aspiring Negro a basically reactionary principle: the educational diet was to be limited and defined by the most pressing needs of the backward rural communities. 'Needs' had already been defined for predominantly Negro communities by Jones as sanitation, health training, improved housing, and increased industrial and agricultural skills. On his utilitarian criteria, what was necessary in these spheres was 'real' and 'democratic', and what did not contribute directly to remedying communal backwardness was 'artificial' and 'selfish'. Latin and foreign languages, therefore, were by definition not needed in the schools that served the small rural communities.[2] Although the point was clothed in the quasi-sociological language of 'adaptation' and 'community-consciousness', it was the lineal descendant of Booker Washington's ridiculing the Negro boy reading a French grammar in a broken down shack.[3] 'Adaptation of education to the needs of the community' was thus a principle radically to differentiate Negro education from white, and it would have ensured in its application that the school population did not advance beyond the pace of the community.

It was mentioned earlier that Jones's experience of teaching only in a white-dominated Negro institution might not have been the best background for understanding the aspirations of the small, independent Negro schools. He had shown little sympathy with 'Negro independence' generally, and now suddenly the fate of a large number of independent schools lay in his hands. Jones could have no quarrel with independent schools as such, for Tuskegee and Hampton came into this category. These, however, were large, nationally-

---

Industry generally go together.' It was a direct consequence of his belief that emotion and sloth had to be trained out that military uniforms were worn in Hampton and Tuskegee; see Plate IV.

[1] Bulletin No. 38, p. 81.

[2] For a curious description of the ideal Latin teacher (as Jones thought), see Appendix I.

[3] DuBois, *Souls of Black Folk*, p. 43, Washington, *Up From Slavery*, p. 154.

known corporations strictly supervised by their boards of trustees, and, as in the case of Atlanta and Fisk also, white representation on the boards was considerable. What Jones did question was the value of the little schools at the lowest level of education, where supervision was nominal if it existed at all. He could only recommend that, if they could not be run down, they should be transferred as soon as possible to private or public educational boards, and that 'the founding of new independent schools should be vigorously discouraged'.[1] Such advice might be considered appropriate in a situation where local or state authorities desired actively to reorganize the educational system, but no such situation obtained in the Southern States. Indeed, the very existence of the independent schools was a pointer to the apathy and hostility of the white authorities.

When the individual reports on these independent schools, contained in the second volume of *Negro Education*, are considered, Jones's policy for the gradual 'killing out' of poorer schools becomes more obvious.[2] It usually consisted of a short factual survey, with an appropriate recommendation for the benefit of potential donors:

Holmes Industrial Institute
Principal: B. R. Holmes.
A small, disorderly school doing five grades of elementary work. It was founded five years ago by the principal and has a nominal board of trustees. It is supported by private subscriptions.
Attendance: Reported enrollment, 250. There were 40 pupils present on the day of visit.
Teachers: Total 4; all colored: male 3, female 1.
Financial: There were no financial records except memoranda. The school was supported by donations amounting to $1,200 a year.
Plant: Estimated value, $2,000. Consists of one very poor frame building unceiled. The windows were broken and the place very dirty. The children were sitting on boards and boxes. A dilapidated printing press covered with dust constituted the industrial equipment.
Recommendations: In view of the condition and management of this school it cannot be recommended as worthy of aid.
Date of visit: January, 1915.[3]

Of the sixty small independent schools included in the report, twenty-seven were said to be not needed or not to be worthy of any aid; on

[1] Bulletin No. 38, pp. 126–7.

[2] There was a section on the independent schools in each State at the end of every chapter; it was prefaced by some general warning that such schools were 'doubtful ventures for outside philanthropy'; e.g. Bulletin No. 39, p. 254.

[3] Ibid., p. 256.

five, no favourable recommendation could be made; eight did not merit anything beyond local donations, and must not look further afield; nine should be taken over by the county as soon as possible; with some others, benefactors were advised to channel their aid through the white county officials; and three schools only should continue unchanged.[1]

What was objectionable in this method of improving Negro education was the publicizing of the findings on a national scale. These were not confidential reports for the use of local school supervisors, but were published in an edition of 12,500 and circulated with the greatest care 'to those who would make the largest use of them'.[2] With independent schools, at least, the main purpose was the protection of the Northern benefactors, for the reports had not been concerned to analyse the social and political forces that had given rise to such defective institutions. A final guide to Negro education had been compiled,[3] and however a school might subsequently attempt to make improvements and extend its usefulness, it stood little chance of outside support once it had gained Jones's disapproval.[4] Such signal distrust of local Negro initiative in education was not a good augury for the time when Jones would transfer his attentions to African education, and be faced with the multiplying pockets of independence in the African bush schools.[5]

His most delicate task, after disposing of the independent schools, was to examine the Negro colleges of the traditional type. There was certainly a case for pointing out that many Negro 'colleges' and 'universities' did not deserve their classification, even on the most liberal definition of college status.[6] Applying, therefore, certain national standard requirements for college work, Jones was able to show that only three institutions, Fisk and Howard Universities, and Meharry Medical College, merited their names.[7] A second group of fifteen institutions which claimed 'Secondary and College courses' demonstrably contained ninety per cent secondary students, while a further group of fifteen advertising 'college subjects' had clearly in Jones's view neither the staff nor the equipment necessary.[8] So far this was firm, if unpopular, ground.

[1] Ibid., *passim*. [2] Jones, *Educational Adaptations*, p. 31. [3] Ibid., p. 27.

[4] C. G. Woodson and C. H. Wesley, *The Negro in Our History* (6th edn., Washington, 1931), p. 505.

[5] See pp. 119–20.

[6] For instance, the fake Latta University; see Bulletin No. 39, p. 459.

[7] Bulletin No. 38, pp. 54–67. [8] Ibid., p. 60.

The report soon abandoned its comparative objectivity, and introduced Jones's idea of what was appropriate in Negro colleges. There was a strong general condemnation of Negro student aspirations, and in particular of 'their almost fatalistic belief not only in the powers of the college, but in the Latin and Greek features of the course'.[1] Yet there was no mention of the Latin requirements of the leading northern colleges for which some of the Negro students were preparing, nor was any consideration given to DuBois's point that 'for Negro . . . schools voluntarily and alone to cut themselves off from the educational system of the land as established by the white universities, is suicide'.[2] True to the theme that Jones had developed earlier, the argument against the traditional college courses was carried on more in terms of morality (the selfishness of Negro students in seeking personal advancement at the expense of their own communities) than of the socio-economic pressures that made for conformity with the white educational system. Clarity was not furthered, certainly, by making an artificial and outworn distinction between college studies and real life: 'The majority of them [Negro colleges] seem to have more interest in the traditional forms of education than in adaptation to the needs of their pupils and their community. Ingenuously some of their leaders have been urging secondary schools to prepare their pupils for college rather than for life.'[3]

Much of this would have little significance if Jones had simply been writing another of the many Dewey-influenced reinterpretations of American schooling, but enough has been said already to show the impossibility of any such purely pedagogical survey of Negro education. Too many forces in the American South wanted confirmation of their prejudices against Negro colleges for Jones not to have realized the political consequences of his strictures. It is highly likely that he must have realized equally well his power to reduce Northern philanthropy even further by the slightest reluctance to approve Negro college work. For this reason, crucial importance attached not so much to his discussions of principles but to the volume of descriptions and recommendations for specific colleges.

Here, in this exceedingly delicate discrimination between the worthy and the unworthy, Jones made a variety of financial recommendations. These ranged from the encouragement of liberal support to the strongest disapproval of any donations at all. Thus Calhoun

[1] Ibid., p. 56. [2] W. E. B. DuBois, *Crisis*, xx, No. 3 (July 1920), 120.
[3] Bulletin No. 38, p. 56.

School and Penn School, which Jones believed had best adapted their activities to the simple needs of the community, inspired the report 'the financial aid necessary' and the recommendation that 'ample funds' be provided to continue their work;[1] while, at the other extreme, it was noted that the majority of the independent schools were 'not worthy of aid'.[2]

No university or college received any such outright general call for donations as had Calhoun and Penn Schools. Some financial aid was urged for Atlanta, but specifically for strengthening its manual department, and for Fisk for its training institute and social service studies; Howard, in a series of recommendations which included the need for the theory and practice of gardening, should receive support specifically for medical work.[3] The remainder of the fifteen Negro institutions doing secondary and college work were not mentioned as candidates for aid. It was not that patrons were positively discouraged from contributing to their work, but the general tone of Jones's recommendations was scarcely such as to inspire confidence. Although Lincoln University was actually in a Northern state, the criticisms it attracted from Jones were representative:

> Recommendations: 1. That in view of the isolation of the institution from contact with the colored population of the country, the teachers become better acquainted with the actual conditions and needs of the people by frequent visits to colored schools in the South. 2. That in the effort to raise the standards of admission to college special care be exercised that there shall be no neglect of secondary subjects. 3. That the time given to foreign languages be not allowed to limit the time for courses in economics, sociology, teacher-training, hygiene and sanitation. 4. That rural economics, including the theory and practice of gardening, be made a part of the regular course for college and theological students. 5. That the dormitory and dining room be so supervised as to develop sound ideas of home life.[4]

What effect the report had in influencing colleges to adopt the values pioneered at Tuskegee and Hampton is much less easily gauged. Certainly during the three years of visits and preparations, Jones was put in a position of quite extraordinary influence over Negro school and college presidents, who realized the long-term importance of a favourable comment in print. DuBois went so far as to allege that Jones had actually ordered some presidents to resign if

[1] Bulletin No. 39, pp. 60, 485. [2] Ibid., p. 256.
[3] Ibid., pp. 154, 215, 538. [4] Ibid., p. 691.

they wished their schools to receive approval.[1] What substance if any there was in this allegation is less important than the fact that DuBois was prepared to make it quite openly in a leading *Crisis* article. What little evidence does exist shows a readiness in some quarters to fall in with Jones's curricular preferences. It can hardly have been coincidence that brought the following letter from the president of Morehouse College, one of the Atlanta group, just six months before the publication of Jones's report:

> You may be interested to know that the following announcement was made at our commencement exercises on Wednesday of this week:
> 'The College has put at the disposal of seven college men in the agricultural class, a horse, a wagon, plow, garden tools, hand-spray and insecticide, garden seeds and plants to be used in aiding the people of the community with their gardens'.[2]

This letter of John Hope, president of Morehouse College, well expressed the tendency of the whole report, namely, the extension of Tuskegee–Hampton education by the threat of philanthropic displeasure. The Tuskegeeism recommended in its pages had nothing of the independent spirit that E. W. Blyden and Duse Mohammed Ali had so admired:[3] it had now become, through Jones's work, synonymous with the spirit of deference, the very mode and form of an education scientifically proved to suit the Negro people. This form of Tuskegeeism would, as DuBois saw, create a breed of philanthropists' Negroes, and stifle the freedom for which the Negro college had stood:

> There follows easily the habit of having no patience with the man who does not agree with the decisions of such boards. The Negro who comes with his hat in his hand and flatters and cajoles the philanthropist—that Negro gets money. If these foundations raise, as they do in this report, the cry of fraud they have themselves to thank. They more than any other agency have encouraged that kind of person. On the other hand, the Negro who shows the slightest independence of thought or character is apt to be read out of all possible influence not only by the white South but by the philanthropic North.[4]

[1] W. E. B. DuBois, 'Thomas Jesse Jones', *Crisis*, xxii, No. 6 (Oct. 1921), 254. What DuBois resented most was the quasi-dictorial position of one man over the fortunes of many institutions for Negroes. An exchange of correspondence between Jones and Washington reveals something of what DuBois and Woodson suspected but could not prove: see Washington to Jones, 26 Dec. 1914, and Jones to Washington, 9 July 1914, Box 506, B.T.W./L.C.

[2] Hope to Jones, 1 June 1916, John Hope Papers, Morehouse College, Atlanta, Ga.

[3] See pp. 17–18.

[4] DuBois, 'Negro Education', p. 178.

In the volume of praise which greeted the publication of Jones's report there were few, apart from some Negro college presidents, to heed what DuBois thought its 'sinister danger'.[1] Jones had successfully evolved a programme for educating the Negro that met with the approbation of Northern philanthropists and white Southerners. Indeed, newspapers in the South went so far as to hail the report as testimony that the Federal Bureau would limit educational activity to elementary, agricultural, and industrial subjects.[2] In this they could hardly be blamed, for what concessions had been made in the report to the higher education of Negroes had been all but swamped by Jones's enthusiasm for industrial and agricultural education, and his general adaptation of standards to Negro needs. He had not perhaps managed to please all three Southern communities all of the time, but he had certainly given Washington's formula a national currency. It was now, in this new, more professionalized guise, ready to be carried by Jones to Negroes further afield.

British Missions, Africa, and the Industrial Interest.

The publication of the Negro Education report marked the institutionalization of the Tuskegee philosophy for the education of Negroes within America. During the period in which Jones had been gradually elevated to the position of the expert on Negro education, there had, however, been a parallel movement in Britain, which had similarly been reaching a consensus of opinion on the relevance of Tuskegee for their purposes. These were the British missionary societies and colonial educationists, and particularly those concerned with the African field. Although the parallel cannot be pressed too closely, they had experienced disillusionment with the value of a western literary education for backward people, similar to that of the post-reconstruction period in the American South. To understand something of the enthusiasm with which the working model of Tuskegee was embraced in the first decade of the twentieth century, however, it is important to note that the opinion that it was necessary to differentiate the style of African education from that of the West had been gradually forming since the previous century.

For the first forty years of the last century there was little enough policy-making on African education, beyond the assumption that

[1] Ibid. For a surprisingly sympathetic view of DuBois's attitude towards Jones, see Peabody (millionaire philanthropist) to J. H. Dillard (president of the Jeanes Fund), 26 Oct. 1921, (Box 15), Peabody Papers, L.C.

[2] *Tuskegee Student*, xxix, No. 20 (1917), 1.

what was good for the Charity Schools of England and Scotland was good for the African. Consequently such missions as the Church Missionary Society (C.M.S.) and the Wesleyans had no qualms about transferring to their 'Recaptive' pupils in Freetown, Sierra Leone, or their Cape Coast scholars, the benefits of the 'National' or 'British' monitorial systems prevailing at home.[1] By the 1840s, however, this form of basic literary education was under fire from a number of quarters. There were those, determined to grapple with the still-flourishing African slave trade, who wished, under the banner of legitimate trade, to invade interior Africa, and, through a combination of white capital and African enterprise, to supplant the old trade by the new.[2] The corollary of this 'Bible and Plough' remedy was, of course, that Africans should be trained to develop those industries most appropriate to their areas. Despite the failure of the great Niger expedition of 1841, which had aimed at blazoning forth this new formula for African redemption, the idea did not die. It was taken up by Henry Venn, secretary of the C.M.S. from 1842 to 1872, and with him perhaps more than with any other individual, proposals for trade training were founded on convictions about African capacity and initiative. A policy of industrial scholarships to England could quickly form a strong middle class of African entrepreneurs, and their new national consciousness could then dispense with Europe's leading-strings. His aim was to enable Africans through such training

to act as Principals in the commercial transactions, to take them out of the hands of European traders who try to grind them down to the lowest mark. We hope that by God's blessing on our plans, a large body of such Native independent Growers of cotton and traders may spring up who may form an intelligent and influential class of Society and become the founders of a kingdom which shall render incalculable benefits to Africa and hold a position amongst the states of Europe.[3]

If Venn's proposals aimed at the independence of the African in both church and state, however, there was a much larger group which believed that African education should be conditioned by the need

[1] C. P. Groves, *The Planting of Christianity in Africa*, i (London, 1948), 278–9; also P. D. Curtin, *The Image of Africa* (London, 1965), p. 264. Cf. P. J. Foster, *Education and Social Change in Ghana* (Chicago, 1965), pp. 52–3.

[2] T. Fowell Buxton, *The African Slave Trade* (London, 1839) and *The Remedy: Being a Sequel to the African Slave Trade* (London, 1840), see (*passim*). Also K. O. Dike, *Trade and Politics in the Niger Delta* (Oxford, 1956).

[3] J. F. Ade Ajayi, *Christian Missions in Nigeria, 1841–1891* (London, 1965), p. 85.

simply to produce the raw materials for the European economies. It was this attitude that had led to the refusal of the request by some Calabari Chiefs in 1828 for sugar and cotton processing machinery;[1] Africans could have technical education but not technology. When the first authoritative statement on colonial education was made by the Education Committee of the Privy Council in 1847, it affirmed the primacy of industrial education for Africans, but not Venn's sort; it was to be an education designed to make the African an improved peasant through practical training, and teach generally 'the domestic and social duties of the coloured races'.[2]

There was already explicit in these recommendations a rejection of the assimilationist philosophy of African education, and the beginnings of a mood that would become even more pronounced as Europe listened increasingly to the new pseudo-scientific racism of Robert Knox and Count de Gobineau during the 1850s. As the century wore on, the products of the assimilation era, especially the Creoles of the West Coast settlements, became more and more frequently the objects of ridicule. Members of the race-oriented Anthropological Society of London, such as R. F. Burton and Winwood Reade, were not slow to contrast the Islamic dignity of the unspoilt interior African with the pretensions of the Creoles, and draw the obvious conclusions about the value of Christian missionary education.[3] Africans, too, joined the antimission chorus, foremost among them Edward Blyden and James Johnson, the Sierra Leonean. Although neither of them had anything very specific to recommend on technical education (indeed Blyden himself doubted if technical ability was properly part of the African racial endowment), they were both vehement on the need for African education to go off the white standard. 'The Negro or African', Johnson affirmed, 'should be raised upon his own idiosyncrasies.'[4] To the many Europeans in the 1890s, therefore, casting around for a solution to what was variously described as the problem of the educated African, the over-supply of clerks, the mission boy, or the black Englishman, the most appropriate way of Africanizing education was to make it industrial.

Mary Kingsley, who shared Blyden's distaste for the Europeanizing

[1] Ibid., p. 54, also Curtin, op. cit., pp. 426–7. [2] Foster, op. cit., p. 55.

[3] C. Fyfe, *A History of Sierra Leone* (Oxford, 1962), pp. 335, 338.

[4] Quoted by Blyden in 'Christian Missions in West Africa' from his *Christianity, Islam and the Negro Race*, p. 64. For Johnson, see E. A. Ayandele, 'An Assessment of James Johnson and his place in Nigerian History', Pt. II, *Journal of the Historical Society of Nigeria*, iii, No. 1 (Dec. 1964), 73–101.

education of the Coast Africans, affirmed in the mid-1890s that there was 'no immediate use for clerks in Africa'; all Africa would need for the next two hundred years at least was a supply of 'workers, planters, plantation hands, miners and seamen'.[1] She was therefore pleased to note that almost every mission on the coast had either just constructed a technical school or was in the process of doing so.

The missions themselves had begun to follow such a course for a number of reasons; in part they were influenced by the sheer hostility towards traditional mission products at a time when Africans were being slowly edged out of the higher posts in the Colonial Civil Service.[2] Partly also some form of technical education was a natural outgrowth of the expanding mission station; it provided an inexpensive way of staffing mission estates and mission houses, which were increasing in sophistication as lady workers volunteered in larger numbers.[3] But apart from this trend towards the self-supporting mission (a common feature of many Catholic missions), there were signs of official encouragement from home. The importance of industrial training had been underlined at the international level in one of the resolutions of the Brussels Conference Relative to the African Slave Trade in July 1890.[4] In the same month a group of influential C.M.S. leaders at the Keswick Convention addressed their central committee on the need to recognize the industrial factor in mission work. The C.M.S. response to this was significant for the way in which it linked Africa and industry; it was recommended that 'missionaries assigned to Africa, or to uncivilized places, should have some industrial training', and although no other part of the mission field needed technical training at all, it was urged 'that simple industrial training should be given in all schools in West Africa, and that Freretown in East Africa, should have an industrial training establishment maintained at full efficiency'.[5]

[1] Mary Kingsley, *Travels in West Africa* (London, 1897), p. 671.

[2] Cf. D. Kimble, *A Political History of Ghana, 1850–1928* (Oxford, 1963), pp. 93–105.

[3] Oliver, *The Missionary Factor in East Africa* (2nd edn., London, 1967), p. 213. Cf. Bishop Tucker, 'Report to the Commission', Item 796, 1910 World Missionary Conference Papers, Missionary Research Library (hereafter M.R.L.) New York, p. 22.

[4] Article II/1, *General Act of the Brussels Conference Relative to the African Slave Trade*, 2 July 1890.

[5] R. Maconachie, 'On the Education of Native Races (C.M.S.)', in *Special Reports on Educational Subjects*, Vol. xiv, XXVI, Cmd. 2379 (H.M.S.O. London, 1905), p. 226.

There had, of course, been missions, such as the Basel, and some of the South African institutions, which had had a thoroughly industrial character for a good part of the century,[1] but it was particularly during the last decade that industrial departments began to become fashionable. 1893 saw the start of the Hope-Waddell Institute in Calabar, designed by Dr. Laws of Livingstonia; this was followed by Bishop Ingham's technical institute in Freetown in 1895, one in Brass in 1897, and another in Onitsha in 1898; the same year a technical department was opened in the government school at Accra, and in 1899 a separate government technical school was opened in Lagos.[2] Meanwhile, in East Africa, following on the work of Krapf on the coast and Alexander Mackay in Uganda, the East African Scottish Mission began its industrial experiments in Kibwezi in 1891,[3] and there was a further development of technical education in Mengo, Uganda. There, in the first years of the twentieth century, philanthropic companies were started by Sir T. F. Buxton to process the products and employ the trainees of the C.M.S. in East Africa.[4]

When, therefore, Booker Washington made his first widely publicized visit to Britain in the summer of 1899, and had his autobiography published two years later, he was certainly not recommending a method of Negro education that was unheard of or untried in some British missionary circles.[5] His value to those who were attracted to the industrial ideal was that his work provided an example of twenty years' success in technical expansion, but, much more important, Tuskegee (unlike Lovedale, Freretown or Freetown) was the first outstanding example of the black man's turning to industrial education of his own accord.

Interestingly enough it appears to have been Southern Rhodesia which first actively canvassed in this century the idea that Tuskegee might hold the key to colonial and mission education in Africa. The

[1] W. J. Rottmann, 'The Educational Work of the Basel Mission on the Gold Coast', in *Special Reports*, Vol. xiii, Cmd. 2378 (London, 1905), pp. 297–307, also J. Stewart, *Dawn in the Dark Continent* (Edinburgh, 1906), Ch. vii.

[2] E. A. Ayandele, *The Missionary Impact on Modern Nigeria, 1842–1914* (London, 1966), pp. 296–8; E. Ashby, *Universities: British, Indian, African* (London, 1966), p. 156.

[3] Maconachie, op. cit., pp. 228–9, 245; B. G. McIntosh, 'The Scottish Mission in Kenya, 1891–1923' (Univ. of Edinburgh Ph.D. thesis, 1969), pp. 53, 58, 111–12.

[4] T. F. Buxton, 'Missions and Industries in East Africa', *Journal of the African Society*, viii (Apr. 1909), pp. 279–87; also Oliver, op. cit., pp. 214–15.

[5] Washington, *Up From Slavery*, p. 339.

example from which Rhodesia might best learn, urged its first inspector of schools, was not the literary education of Cape Colony provided for the natives by 'misguided enthusiasts who believed that black men and white were equal', but rather that of the Southern States. There at least Negroes, after a period of pursuing the illusory ideal of book learning, had realized their mistakes; and the dangers of such deceptive courses had been largely avoided by the more recent trends at Hampton.[1]

In Britain itself approval for differentiating the education of Negro people from that of white, along Tuskegee lines, seems to have come first from the Board of Education's brilliant comparativist and director of special inquiries, Michael Sadler. His 'Education of the Coloured Race', published in 1902, may also have been inspired in part by direct contact with Washington (they had been in correspondence the previous year when Sadler had visited Hampton),[2] but in any case it began his long involvement in spreading the values of Tuskegee and Hampton beyond the limits of the United States. To a large extent one aspect of the history of colonial and mission education policy in Africa over the next thirty years was to be a series of variations on and developments of Sadler's early theme:

> The work which is going forward in the industrial and agricultural training schools for the coloured race in the United States, is one of great significance. Lessons can be learned from it which are of value for those engaged in education in parts of the British Empire; for example, in West Africa and the West Indies, where there are large black populations.[3]

Most of the aspects of Tuskegee's organization that would subsequently appeal to many hundreds of missionaries from Africa had already been noted: an educational formula to fight urbanization; a school life that could compensate for a backward home; and 'the kind of *practical* instruction which the coloured people would specially need'.[4]

The one element that Sadler did not particularly stress was Tuskegee's and Hampton's political and economic value to a white-

[1] H. E. D. Hammond, 'The System of Education in Southern Rhodesia (1890–1901): Its Origin and Development', *Special Reports on Educational Subjects*, Vol. xiii, XXVI, Cmd. 2378 (1905), pp. 164–6.

[2] Sadler to Washington, 23 Sept. 1901, box 209, B.T.W./L.C.

[3] M. E. Sadler, 'The Education of the Coloured Race' (Nov. 1901), in *Specia Reports*, Vol. xi, XXIX (London, 1902), p. 559.

[4] Ibid., p. 544.

dominated society, and their implicit rejection of competition in the higher skills and professions. This omission was remedied by Sir Harry Johnston. The lavishly illustrated results of his visit to the U.S.A. in 1908, *The Negro in the New World*, was a striking advertisement for the usefulness of Hampton and Tuskegee, and struck a further blow at the struggling Negro colleges.[1] No less than forty-six pages were needed adequately to describe the advantages of the Hampton–Tuskegee method, while Lincoln University, Berea College, and Wilberforce University were dismissed in half a page of ridicule for their 'useless classics', 'old fashioned, incorrect history' and their 'Old Testament and seventeenth-century theology'.[2] Johnston expanded a little on the point that Sadler had missed:

> These colleges and universities are well enough . . . but they merely train clergymen, lawyers, politicians, petty officials, school masters . . . third-rate writers, a few geniuses . . . but they don't solve the tremendous need of the United States for field-hands—INTELLIGENT field-hands; they don't turn out cooks—and cooks, as Booker Washington points out . . . are more necessary than preachers. They don't sent out into Twentieth-Century-America, machinists, inexpensive electricians, plumbers, builders, bricklayers, carpenters, cabinetmakers, gardeners, stockmen, sawyers, hydraulic engineers, painters, tailors, dressmakers, bootmakers, metal-workers and laundry hands.[3]

In Africa, Tuskegee was thus coming to stand for a number of different approaches to education and political development, but two main schools of thought, at least among the whites, had made themselves clear: Tuskegeeism for the white man's country, designed to prevent the political growth of Africans while increasing their value to the economy; and Tuskegeeism for black Africa, soon to be associated with indirect-rule doctrines of keeping the African true to his own best nature. The former had been seen already in Rhodesia, and was restated for South Africa in Dudley Kidd's *Kafir Socialism*.[4] The other view found early support from the British Resident in Ibadan, Nigeria: the Yoruba people, he explained, might yet be saved from the perils of denationalization by having a Tuskegee set down in their midst; its teachers would be sent to the mother institute for three years' training, and would return to implement a completely

[1] H. Johnston, *The Negro in the New World* (London, 1911).
[2] Ibid., p. 386.
[3] Ibid., p. 403. In exchange for this welcome publicity, Washington reviewed Johnston's book in the *Journal of the African Society*, x (1910–11), 178.
[4] D. Kidd, *Kafir Socialism* (London, 1908), p. 265.

Africanized curriculum; the medium of instruction would be Yoruba and all textbooks would be translated into that language.[1]

This aspect of Tuskegee had a powerful effect too upon the Governor of the Gold Coast, Sir John P. Rodger, who toured the industrial schools of the Southern States, and on his return appointed a committee in 1908 'to revise educational rules, establish a training institution for teachers, to establish a technical school, and to introduce hand and eye, industrial and agricultural training into the schools'.[2]

For the first ten years of the century, publicity for Tuskegee was still the result of scattered individual enthusiasms, but in 1910, at the first World Missionary Conference in Edinburgh, came the beginnings of institutionalized recognition. Commission III, at that historic gathering, was given the brief to determine the form of education that might accompany 'the evangelisation of the world in this generation'.[3] Continent by continent past errors were assessed and new recommendations made. Expert evidence was culled from all over the world, and included not only the witness of Professor Michael Sadler, who was a member of the commission, but also a submission from Thomas Jesse Jones. Whatever the specific source, the methods of Hampton and Tuskegee received the strongest possible approbation, and especially, although not exclusively, for Africa. For, in the eyes of the commission, while industrial education was generally recommended for the mission field, its application to Africa was 'especially urgent'.[4] In Africa the commission was thus mainly concerned to correct the absence of industrial and agricultural instruction; and, in no less than three conspicuous places, missions were reminded that 'the value of industrial and agricultural training for the negro race is abundantly proved by the experience of the Normal and Agricultural Institute at Hampton, Virginia, and the Normal and Industrial School at Tuskegee, Alabama'.[5]

Even though the two schools had been given an important place in the official statement of policy, the commission had been aware of the

[1] C. H. Elgee, 'Memorandum on the System of Negro Education in the United States of America, with a study of its practical application to our West African Possessions, November 1905', Box 992, B.T.W./L.C.

[2] T. J. Jones, *Education in Africa* (New York, 1922), pp. 141–2.

[3] This was the great call of the 1910 conference.

[4] *Education in Relation to the Christianisation of National Life: Report of Commission III* (World Missionary Conference, Edinburgh, 1910), p. 302.

[5] Ibid., pp. 213, 277, 302.

fact that it would require personal study tours of the Southern States before specific changes could begin to take place in Africa itself. The real watershed in the 'Hampton for Africa' policy might therefore be more properly marked not by the 1910 conference but by the visits to Hampton in 1912 of two men who, as much as any others, were profoundly to influence the course of African education for the next generation: A. G. Fraser and his brother-in-law, J. H. Oldham.

Although for the next twelve years Fraser was more particularly involved in promoting rural education and teacher training in Ceylon he was subsequently joined by Jones's protégé, J. E. K. Aggrey, in establishing a university in the Gold Coast on African lines.[1] In 1912, however, his admiration for General Armstrong's methods was unreserved; 'A visit to Hampton', he proclaimed in the newly founded *International Review of Missions*, 'is to the missionary worth more in education than a dozen conferences. It is a missionary institution under ideal conditions.'[2] Such enthusiasm convinced Oldham, who was editor of this journal, and secretary to the continuation committee set up by the World Missionary Conference, that he should investigate. Late in 1912, the briefest of visits assured him that Hampton might hold the answer to missionary education. He explained his new-found ambitions to Dr. Frissell, Hampton's president:

> The two days which I spent at Hampton were one of the richest experiences of my life and I shall never be able to forget all your great kindness. I learned more than I think I have ever before in the same amount of time. My great desire is to serve in any way that I can to make the work of Hampton bear fruit in other countries to the largest extent possible.[3]

Oldham's quite unusual gift for sowing ideas that he had taken up among influential people was at this stage largely responsible for increased publicity for Hampton and Tuskegee in the short time before war broke out in Europe. For, as he had reflected on the American visit, he had convinced himself that one of his chief tasks must be 'to make the experience of Hampton fruitful in the work of Protestant missions in Asia and Africa'.[4] On his own initiative, therefore, he

[1] Cf. W. E. F. Ward, *Fraser of Trinity and Achimota* (London, 1965).

[2] A. G. Fraser, 'Impressions of Hampton Institute', *International Review of Missions* (hereafter *I.R.M.*), i (1912), 713.

[3] Oldham to Frissell, 15 Oct. 1912, Oldham File, H.A.I.

[4] Oldham to Frissell, 2 Nov. 1912, Oldham File, H.A.I.

sent the education secretary of the continuation committee to Hampton,[1] and successfully urged his American counterpart, Dr. John Mott, to pay a similar visit.[2] Plans were then set on foot for a number of key people in the mission field to go on educational exchanges, and through *I.R.M.*, Dr. Frissell was able to stress the value of his industrial education.[3] Even Booker T. Washington (or at any rate his 'ghost writer', Robert Park) was prevailed upon to link the position of Tuskegee with the situation of the mission school in Africa, in a contribution to the same journal entitled 'David Livingstone and the Negro'.[4]

There remained one further figure who was to visit the South at this time, and absorb Hampton ideas on educational research—C. T. Loram, of South Africa. Currently engaged on work identical to that of Jesse Jones, he was attempting to collect statistics to support a new theory of African education. From Booker Washington and Professor Work he sought figures which might convince his fellow whites that 'with proper training and education the negro can be made a valuable asset to any country'.[5] He needed ammunition, he told Washington, to refute the notions of criminality, laziness, and intermarriage held by South Africans about the Negro.

Until this point, Jones, Oldham, and Loram, the men who were to constitute a triumvirate on education in Africa after the war, had scarcely known of each other's existence. But on the publication of Loram's *Education of the South African Native*,[6] and Jones's *Negro Education* in the same year, Oldham began to draw the separate strands together in a seminal review of their findings. 'Christian Missions and the Education of the Negro' was the start of a formidable era of educational co-operation.[7] The moment was opportune for Oldham; he had characteristically foreseen that the large-scale entry of governments into traditional missionary preserves after the war

[1] Oldham to Frissell, 24 Apr. 1914, Oldham File, H.A.I.

[2] Ibid. John R. Mott had been chairman of the Edinburgh World Missionary Conference, 1910, and of the continuation committee; he was also general secretary of the World's Student Christian Federation, and of the National Council of Y.M.C.A.'s of America.

[3] H. B. Frissell, 'The Value of Industrial Education', *I.R.M.*, iv (1915), 420–31.

[4] B. T. Washington, 'David Livingstone and the Negro', *I.R.M.*, ii (1913), 224–35.

[5] Loram to Washington, 27 Dec. 1914, Box 523, B.T.W./L.C.

[6] C. T. Loram, *The Education of the South African Native* (London, 1917).

[7] J. H. Oldham, 'Christian Missions and the Education of the Negro', *I.R.M.*, vii (1918), 242–7. Jones thought so highly of Oldham's commentary that he reproduced the whole of it in his *Educational Adaptations*, pp. 24–7.

was inevitable. Much mission education would, he felt, almost certainly be assumed by government unless radical improvement could be made. In the two volumes of these men he found both the necessary sharp critique of missionary efforts and an appropriate remedy. Not only was the unsuitability of the traditional literary school demonstrated authoritatively for the Negro of Africa and America, but both volumes proclaimed a new doctrine of educational adaptation.[1] In a summary of their conclusions, Oldham accepted their teaching on differentiation, with all its ambiguous use of the 'real' and the 'actual':

> It is insisted that education must be closely related to the actual life of those who have to be taught. It must take account of their instincts, experiences, interests as distinct from those of people living in quite different conditions. Its aim must be to equip them for the life which they have to live. Hence the main emphasis must not be on a purely literary curriculum, such as still prevails in many schools, but on training in such necessities of actual life as health, hygiene, the making and keeping of a home, the earning of a livelihood and civic knowledge and spirit.[2]

Oldham was not content merely to act as a propagandist for Jones's and Loram's ideas; he had been working for some time on a scheme to utilize Hampton's lessons in India. Its characteristic emphasis on the needs of the community seemed eminently suitable for what then looked like the beginnings of a mass movement of low-caste Indians towards Christianity. In January 1917, a 'Hampton for India' project was mooted, with the idea of establishing 'an institution for the creation of truer educational ideals and methods'.[3] While it would not attempt to reproduce Hampton's structure in India, it would seek to capture all its peculiar success in enlisting its graduates for community service, and in correcting the dominant literary pattern of education by its industrial programme. The scheme soon broadened into an India-wide concern for the improvement of village education. A survey was necessary, and A. G. Fraser, the obvious choice, was provisionally commissioned to lead a deputation to study the situation. His conclusions, it was hoped, would show the way to a sound village education, whose 'object would be not ordinarily to

[1] Loram was calling for special Bantu education as early as 1914; Loram to Frissell, 20 Oct. 1914, Loram File, H.A.I.

[2] Oldham, 'Christian Missions and the Education of the Negro', p. 245.

[3] Memorandum on an Educational Institution for meeting the needs of the Mass Movements in India, January 18, 1917' (conference of British Missionary Societies), H.A.I.

attract the young Christian villagers away from their villages by education, but to make them good villagers'.[1]

For the moment the plan had to remain in reserve, awaiting the end of the war. At the end of 1918, however, circumstances suddenly changed, and the influence of Hampton on the Village Education Commission promised to be very much more immediate: Jones was invited to direct it.[2] The change of leadership had arisen very naturally out of Jones's first meeting with Oldham when he was returning from a special mission to France, but it took on a somewhat different colour in the light of Jones's most recent activity.

During the war Jones had considerably enhanced his reputation as an expert on the Negro, and not only in the narrowly educational sphere. As special collaborator in the Department of the Interior, he had recently been working on the more political aspects of Tuskegee-ism, and had been attempting, with the full support of the War Department, to get at the facts of the Negro soldiers' morale in France. His experience there in December 1918, with Dr. Moton, Negro president of Tuskegee, had convinced him that he must make it his major concern to contain and divert the growing racial dissatisfaction of the Negro troops, and work for their peaceful return to civilian life in the States.[3] Jones's intimate knowledge of Negro leaders was relied on by the War Department, and this enabled him with Moton's help to select twelve 'absolutely reliable' Y.M.C.A. Negroes to help to pacify the Negro labour battalions in the French ports.[4] His further plans for using Mrs. Booker Washington as an agent for lowering the temper of the troops were almost set in motion, but were eventually abandoned in case Negro radicals might point to the project as evidence that 'the War Department and Tuskegee are in league to persuade the Negro to be submissive'.[5]

Concurrently in the States Jones organized the establishment of an

[1] Resolution of conference on Indian education, reported in Ward, op. cit., p. 122.

[2] Oldham to Jones, 17 Jan. 1919, File 314, Edinburgh House (hereafter E.H.), London, now transferred to International Missionary Council Archives (hereafter I.M.C.A.), Geneva.

[3] Jones to Moton, 13 Feb. 1919, R.R.M./G.C. (1919), T.U.A. Robert Russa Moton, President of Tuskegee Institute in succession to Booker Washington, had graduated from Hampton Institute in 1890 and had taught there until Washington's death in 1915.

[4] Miss I. Tourtellot to Moton, 14 Feb. 1919; Jones to Moton, 29 Mar. 1919, R.R.M./G.C. (1919), T.U.A.

[5] Jones to Moton, 27 Mar. 1919, R.R.M./G.C. (1919), T.U.A.

Inter-racial Committee for After War Cooperation.[1] Like his *Negro Education* report, this had the very delicate aim of finding an area of common ground for negotiation somewhere between white prejudice and black aspirations. As executive secretary of this committee, Jones outlined his views characteristically:

> The preaching of world democracy and the disturbance attending the world war has given rise to what Dr. Dillard has aptly called 'Great Expectations'. These 'Great Expectations' are held in two groups. (1) The white people have 'Great Expectations' that the negro soldiers are returning 'bumptious' and impossible. (2) The negro leaders have 'Great Expectations' that democracy in all its implications is coming immediately . . .
> The Committee is of the opinion that it is important to select the possible improvements rather than the program of complete change which the negroes themselves would advocate.[2]

This organization, especially in its early months, reflected Jones's preoccupations with the dangers of Negro radicalism; but it also brought into the open the political assumptions that had underlain much of his educational work, and in general hinted at the value of Tuskegeeism in dealing with a new problem—the post-war demands of colonized peoples for self-determination.

Something of this new enlargement of Jones's educational reputation seems to have been apparent to Oldham as he negotiated for Jones to lead the commission to India. For, while acknowledging Hampton as the inspiration for the Indian commission, he warned Jones emphatically against giving educated Indians the impression that the 'Indian people as a whole were a backward or a depressed class'; they would strongly resent being given a prescription appropriate to the Negroes' political status in the American South. For this reason the very name 'Hampton' had been scrupulously avoided in discussing the project with Indians.[3]

Before Jones's diplomacy could be tested in India, however, the commission's leadership reverted to Fraser.[4] For, despite Jones's enthusiasm for the scheme, the conditions of the Phelps-Stokes

[1] Jones, *Educational Adaptations*, pp. 90–3. See further p. 188.

[2] Minute of first meeting of the Committee on After War Co-operation (17 Mar. 1919), R.R.M./G.C. (1919), T.U.A. The committee changed its name soon after to the Inter-racial Commission.

[3] Oldham to Jones, 17 Jan. 1919, File 314, now I.M.C.A., Geneva.

[4] See further *Village Education in India. A Commission of Inquiry* (London, 1920).

Fund's act of incorporation limited its interests to 'the education of negroes, both in Africa and the United States'. In addition to this legal disqualification, Jones had in these same months of January and February 1919 been thinking seriously of transferring his attention to Africa.

This new interest might be partly explained by the express terms of the Phelps-Stokes Fund's charter; it is not improbable, however, that an element of competition with DuBois's African programme prompted Jones to move now in this direction. DuBois had, after all, been in France at the same time as Jones and Moton, and, it was well known, was making preparations for his first Pan-African Congress in February 1919. Jones may well have begun to realize the logical extension of his feud with DuBois into the African arena, for certainly it was at this point that he started to press the urgency of an African survey upon the officers of the Phelps-Stokes Fund.[1] Within a month, a perfect opportunity had presented itself; a request was made through the North American Missionary Conference by the Baptist Foreign Missionary Society that a survey of West African education should be undertaken by the Phelps-Stokes Fund and that Dr. Jones should be requested to carry it out.[2] Their agreement marked the beginning of the first Phelps-Stokes Educational Commission.

Representatives of the various interests that were to co-operate on the Commission had been slowly drawing together over the previous decade and a half. From South Africa, Jan Smuts appointed C. T. Loram to travel seven thousand miles with the commission;[3] Oldham ensured the co-operation of the European governments and missionary societies;[4] and the influence of Tuskegee was apparent in the assumption by the Foreign Mission Conference of North America that the main task of the commission would be to 'study and report upon the industrial education adapted to the needs of the African'.[5]

There was one very important respect in which the Phelps-Stokes African commission differed from the earlier *Negro Education* report; it would not lay itself open again to the charge which DuBois had then

[1] Moton to Phelps Stokes, 19 Jan. 1919, Box 71, Peabody Papers, L.C.

[2] Minutes of the Committee of Reference and Counsel of the Foreign Mission Conference of North America, 28 Feb. 1919, p. 11, Archives of the Division of World Mission and Evangelism, Inter-Church Centre, New York.

[3] Jones, *Education in Africa*, p. xxii. [4] Ibid.

[5] Minutes of the Committee of Reference and Counsel, 4 Dec. 1919, Minute No. 88.

made, 'that the Phelps-Stokes Fund find it so much easier to work *for* the Negro than *with* him'.[1] J. E. K. Aggrey was called from the relative obscurity of Livingstone College to be a member of the Commission. It was a courageous and almost unprecedented move for such an international commission. An African Negro himself would help to report on the 'Great Expectations' of West Africans and their aspirations for full western education. He must be prepared in West Africa to advocate industrial education and patience where his hearers would expect talk of universities and self-determination, and in South Africa he must suffer discrimination with a smile. It would not, Jones saw, be easy, for it was essentially a task in which only the Tuskegee spirit, and the good offices of its president, could bring success:

I desire also to inform you that I have asked Mr. Aggrey to come to the Tuskegee Conference. I am eager that he shall have another contact with Tuskegee and with you before he leaves for Africa . . . Mr. Aggrey's position on the committee will not be an easy one. Prejudice and misunderstandings are as difficult in Africa as they are in any part of the United States. Very confidentially, I would say that it may be impossible for us to take Mr. Aggrey to South Africa . . . In view of the difficulties that may arise, I am eager that you help Mr. Aggrey to take a broad view with regard to even the narrowness of white people.[2]

[1] DuBois, 'Negro Education', p. 177.
[2] Jones to Moton, 17 Jan. 1920, R.R.M./G.C. (1919), T.U.A.

CHAPTER III

East Africa, Pan-Africanism and the American Negro before the Phelps-Stokes Commission

DURING THIS period, when Hampton and Tuskegee were gaining considerable popularity with missions and governments for their relevance to Africa, certain groups of Africans in Kenya and Uganda had been forming their own view of American Negroes. Indeed, a whole range of contacts with Negroes in America had been experienced by a small minority of East Africans in the years before the Phelps-Stokes Commission's second African tour of 1924, and its commendation of Tuskegee and Hampton. There were three most significant aspects of this East African interest in the American Negro: the pan-Africanism of the earliest nationalist movements in Kenya and Uganda; American Negro missionary activity in East Africa; and the part played by African students in American Negro colleges. Combined experience in these three areas had made some East Africans aware of the wide extent of potential aid from American Negroes before Aggrey and Jones pleaded for the specific adoption of Tuskegee's educational and political philosophy.

The first opportunity for extended contact between East Africans and American Negroes was provided by the First World War, and in particular by the role of the Coloured Y.M.C.A. of America in relation to the Native Carrier Corps in the East African campaign. It arose very largely from the initiative of a young American Negro of Shaw University, Max Yergan, who in 1916 answered a call to work as Y.M.C.A. secretary among Indian troops in Bangalore, and was shortly afterwards transferred at his own request to work with the African troops in British East Africa.[1] His success in this field was so outstanding in alleviating the often appalling conditions of the Carrier Corps[2] that the Y.M.C.A. headquarters in New York were cabled, with the full authority of the military command, to send six

[1] C. H. Tobias, 'Max Yergan', *Crisis*, xl (July 1933), p. 155.

[2] Cf. J. W. Arthur's wartime letters from Tanganyika, Arthur Papers, Edinburgh University Library. Also D. C. Savage and J. F. Munro, 'Carrier Corps Recruitment in the British East Africa Protectorate', *Journal of African History*, vii, No. 2 (1966), 313–42.

additional Negro secretaries.[1] There was a ready response, and within a few months Yergan was joined by other graduates of American Negro colleges: Lloyd from Howard, Ballou from Knoxville, Ritchie from Fisk, Pritchett from Lincoln, Sherard from Atlanta, and the Rev. W. P. Stanley from Baltimore.[2]

Seven Y.M.C.A. aides in East Africa might seem a very small part of the total American Negro involvement in the First World War; but if it is seen in the context of the long-frustrated desire of educated Negroes to work on equal terms with whites for the improvement of the peoples of East Africa, it has great significance. It was certainly seen by DuBois as a major rift in the long-standing prejudice against American Negroes in African missions, and he was quick to give publicity through the *Crisis* to the full range of these secretaries' exploits and their success. An article by Jesse E. Moorland, the senior secretary of the International Committee of Coloured Men's Y.M.C.A.s, rehearsed in almost Pauline terms the histories of shipwreck, loss of possessions, fever, and drowning that featured in their African service;[3] but he also saw the wider implications of this episode: 'This means more than a Y.M.C.A. movement; it means a movement which will open the doors of this great continent in a way they have never been opened to such of our young manhood and womanhood who will be willing to give others the chance they themselves have had.'[4]

The white secretaries, too, who worked alongside Max Yergan's contingent, could not help remarking on the great post-war possibilities for Negro mission that were suggested by this first American Negro educational enterprise in East Africa. The great advantage that the college-educated Negroes seemed to have in dealing with the wide assortment of South African, West African, West Indian, and local troops did not go unnoticed,[5] especially as it was assumed,

[1] C. R. Webster (War Work Secretary), 'Annual Report for the year ending September 30th, 1917', in 'Reports of Foreign Secretaries 1917', Vol. ii, 940, Y.M.C.A. Historical Library, New York.

[2] J. E. Moorland, article on Max Yergan and the Y.M.C.A. in East Africa, *Crisis*, xv, No. 2 (Dec. 1917), 68.

[3] Ibid., pp. 65–8. Ritchie and Pritchett lost all their possessions when their ship was mined off Capetown. Later Ballou was drowned off Dar es Salaam, and Pritchett died in trying to rescue him. Yergan was invalided home after a two-year period.

[4] Ibid., p. 68.

[5] A. Perry Park (army secretary, Y.M.C.A., Lahore), 'Annual Report for the year ending September 30th, 1917', in 'Reports of Foreign Secretaries 1917', Vol. ii, 994, Y.M.C.A. Historical Library.

perhaps more readily by Y.M.C.A. secretaries than by traditional missionaries, that 'this great pioneer mission work ought to appeal very strongly to the colored community of America, for it is essentially their own'.[1] Nor was the Y.M.C.A. unaware of the difficulties in promoting such a programme of co-operation between trained Negro leaders from the Southern States and African youth; but they were most anxious to prevent the growing tendency in African governments to categorize all American Negroes with African aspirations as virulent pan-African revolutionaries. On the basis of their East African experience they felt they could make a justifiable distinction:

> There are those whose interest goes along the line of a great Pan-African political movement in antagonism to the White. There are those on the other hand who have a deep sense of missionary obligation and who feel that through education, through play, through religious leadership, through industrial and agricultural effort, through the promotion of co-operative credit, adapted to meet African conditions, in co-operation between leaders of all races will the largest result come.[2]

This latter was certainly the category to which these first American Negro secretaries belonged, and it is interesting to note how their co-operative attitude in racial matters anticipated the amazing interracial sensitivity of J. E. K. Aggrey in Kenya six years later.[3] It differentiated them from some of the other colonial troops, whose tendency to voice complaints at discriminatory wartime treatment had frequently to be assuaged by 'their consecrated commonsense and unselfish service'.[4] They were held in high regard by the white officers 'for their sterling manhood and their humble yet confident bearing',[5] and it is not surprising in these circumstances to learn that 'one of the secretaries addressed the white troops on "Booker T. Washington" and his earnestness and striking appeal for the men of his race sank into the hearts of the white men who heard him and had its effect there'.[6]

There was, however, a prodigious amount of work to be done

[1] Ibid., p. 999; see also K. Saunders, 'A Forward Move in Africa', *Southern Workman*, lxix (Feb. 1920), 84.

[2] E. C. Carter to O. Bull, 26 July 1921, Yergan File, Y.M.C.A. Historical Library.

[3] See pp. 113–4.

[4] A. Perry Park, 'Annual Report for the year ending September 30th, 1917', p. 994.

[5] Ibid., p. 995.

[6] Ibid.

among the Africans, many of whom had been uprooted for the first time from the relative isolation of mission stations in the Reserves, and were forming their impressions of wartime 'civilization' in the large military camps throughout East Africa. Yergan found hundreds of mission Christians bewildered by this life without any army chaplains to turn to, and proceeded, first at the religious level, to organize undenominational activities and study that united African Christians of different sects.[1] Further initiatives were taken in recreational work. But by far the most important, for many Africans, was the chance which the secretaries provided of beginning or continuing their education. Yergan realized the peculiar challenge of this work and its far-reaching consequences, and gave much attention to the extension of literacy through the medium of night schools in at least six centres;[2] a technical school was taken over from the railway department in Nairobi, and two of the secretaries had charge of the training of seventy Africans for both clerical and manual skills.[3] Indeed, many hundreds of men and boys in the camps learnt their first stumbling sentences at the hands of these seven Negroes; and if it was later to become a cause of rancour that American Negroes were no longer allowed into East Africa to teach, the reason lay partly in the conspicuous success of their first Negro educational mission, and in the team's knowledge that they had the enthusiastic support and good will of the local Africans. Yergan made the point forcibly:

> If anyone has doubt as to the desire and ability of the African to take profitable advantage of such opportunities, he has but to know what goes on in these schools. Men and boys who will spend from two to three hours over a slate or the alphabet after having worked for eight or ten hours under an African sun, must have the desire, and to be able to master the alphabet, write one's name and read a little within the surprisingly short space of four weeks are strong evidences of Native ability . . . Arab, Swahili, Kikuyu and many other tribes crowd into these school huts where our secretaries with Native assistants are trying to help meet this need in their lives.[4]

[1] Max Yergan, 'The Y.M.C.A. with Native Troops and Military Laborers in East Africa', Moorland Collection, Howard University Library, Washington D.C., pp. 2–3.
[2] Ibid., p. 8.
[3] C. R. Webster, 'Annual Report for the year ending September 30th, 1918', in 'Reports of Foreign Secretaries 1918', Vol. ii, 735.
[4] Yergan, 'The Y.M.C.A. with Native Troops and Military Laborers in East Africa', p. 8.

It is still an open question exactly what links were formed with the senior, mission-trained native Kenyans and Ugandans who made up a significant portion of the Carrier Corps. Whether or not evidence appears later of contact between any of these Negro graduates and some of the activists who were soon to achieve prominence through African political movements, it is certain that the presence of these seven men was a very potent advertisement for American Negro education in the Southern States. Yergan himself frequently drew attention to the educational opportunities in the Negro colleges of America, and he was probably in a small way responsible for encouraging East Africans to think of American Negroes as their brothers, and to expect increased help from them. He gave an interesting example of this after one of his lectures in East Africa:

> When I was through, I went outside and sat on the trunk of a tree. Presently one of our boys came out and said, 'You say back in America you have schools and colleges and churches'. 'Yes'. 'And you say you have this thing called ambition and hope, and then you say you are literally our brothers and sisters, that the same blood which flows through you flows through us here. If that is the case, why have so many of you remained in America so long? Why are you alone here?'[1]

In the minds of the white secretaries of the Y.M.C.A. and the national councils in India, Britain, and America, there was never any question that this East African channel of service would remain open after the war. It had far outgrown the exigencies of the war's demands in its one and a half years, and when Max Yergan was encouraged in March 1920 to accept the national secretaryship of East Africa, serving under the English National Council, but deriving his support from the coloured men's department of the International Committee in America, a permanent link between American Negroes and the East African field seemed about to be established.[2]

After Yergan's acceptance, formal approval was being obtained through the Colonial Office for his beginning work in autumn 1920, when the barrier came down. A short note from the Governor of Kenya's personal secretary informed the English National Council that Sir Edward Northey did 'not consider it advisable to introduce into East Africa negroes of a different calibre from those to be found

[1] M. Yergan, speech delivered at Atlantic City, Sept. 1921, copy in the Y.M.C.A. Historical Library.

[2] Minutes of the Foreign Committee of the Y.M.C.A., 18 Dec. 1919, Y.M.C.A. Historical Library.

in East Africa itself'.[1] Very serious implications were raised by the terms of Northey's refusal. It apparently placed an embargo on any Negro of greater education or higher sophistication than Kenyan Africans, and left no place for Negro co-operation in the work of improvement in East Africa.

Although it becomes apparent from a further confidential letter to the Y.M.C.A. that Northey was also opposed to the scheme on the grounds that all the Europeans 'arriving by every mail in this country' must receive the Y.M.C.A.'s full attention before the Africans received any,[2] it is possible that an experience during his wartime service in Nyasaland provided a further reason for the ban on Yergan. There he may well have been party to the discussion of the John Chilembwe rising, and have paid some attention to its roots in American Negro radicalism and educational service in Nyasaland.[3] At any rate, native welfare in Kenya was to be the prerogative of the European missionaries with their African assistants and not an occasion to use 'an imported Negro'.[4] However unjust the decision was in the case of Yergan, it did not, in the highly explosive state of Colonial Office–Kenya relations at that time, seem to the Y.M.C.A. or to Oldham to be an auspicious moment to press for a reversal of policy.[5]

Yergan was shortly, after some considerable difficulty, to gain entry to another African country; but even though this particular attempt to establish a link between the educated youth of the Southern States and of East Africa proved impossible, interest in alliances with American Negroes did not end there. It was taken up by two of the young nationalist political associations in Kenya and Uganda.

Pan-African politicians in East Africa

The exact origins of the Young Baganda Association (Y.B.A.) are still a little unclear. Certainly both government sources and reliable testimony from the association itself would place its formal inauguration in 1919;[6] but it is possible that, as with other early East

[1] G. R. Sandford to O. H. McCowen, 26 May 1920, Box 67, World Service—Foreign Work (hereafter Box 67), Y.M.C.A. Historical Library. For Ex-President Theodore Roosevelt's strong commendation of American Negroes in East Africa ten years earlier, see Roosevelt, *African Game Trails*, p. 10.

[2] Northey to McCowen, 24 Sept. 1920, Box 67, Y.M.C.A. Historical Library.

[3] See G. Shepperson and T. Price, *Independent African, passim.*

[4] Northey to McCowen, 24 Sept. 1920.

[5] Carter to E. C. Jenkins, 29 Nov. 1920, Box 67, Y.M.C.A. Historical Library.

[6] *Buganda Annual Report, 1919–20* (Entebbe 1920), Secretariat Minute

African political associations, there was a period of informal co-operation between the founding members some time before they formed an official organization. For this reason, therefore, it is dangerous to condemn as mere speculation J. H. Driberg's belief that the informal inception of the Y.B.A. could be dated from as early as 1915, 'in which year it is certain that John Chilembwe, the leader of the abortive Nyasaland rising, sent his revolutionary emissaries to invite the co-operation of the Baganda'.[1] It is not known whether Driberg had any evidence for this fascinating suggestion, or for his further alarmist report that the Y.B.A. was in fact a cover for an armed revolutionary committee led by chiefs;[2] on the other hand, what most marked the activities of this educated pressure group was respect for constitutional procedures.[3] Composed very largely of sons of chiefs, it did nevertheless make determined efforts for a short time to overcome the sectarianism which had characterized so much of Uganda's social and political history. It embraced, therefore, Protestants, Catholics, and Moslems, and saw itself as 'the youthfulness of the nation,' indeed 'the only Association in Uganda Territories mainly devoted to the interests of its country in general'.[4] Despite this image, however, the Y.B.A. remained small and exclusive—often not much above thirty members—and there is little evidence that it intended radically to broaden its basis of recruitment.[5]

Papers (hereafter S.M.P.) No. 1138, Entebbe Secretariat Archives (hereafter E.S.A.); also J. R. Kamulegeya to the secretary, Negro Farmers' Conference, Tuskegee Institute, 13 Sept. 1921, R.R.M./G.C. (1921), T.U.A.

[1] Driberg (Assistant District Commissioner) to the Chief Secretary to the Government, Entebbe, 23 Apr. 1920, 'Notes on the Young Baganda Society', C.O. 537/947, Public Record Office (hereafter P.R.O.).

[2] Ibid. The Government of Uganda were, however, very sceptical; Coryndon to Milner, 19 Jan. 1921, C.O. 537/948, P.R.O.

[3] See the statement of their objectives and their general aims in the *Direct Apeal* [*sic*] *of The Young Baganda Association to General Public in Uganda, Kenya, Tang'anyika, and Zanzibar Territories and also to Over-seas Lovers of Africans* (Mengo, 1922), copy in East African Indian National Congress Archives (hereafter E.A.I.N.C.A.). For a detailed treatment of the development of the Y.B.A. within the context of post-war Buganda politics, see K. J. King, 'The Young Baganda Association: Some Notes on the Internationalisation of Early African Politics in Buganda', *Journal of African and Asian Studies* III, i (1969), 1–25.

[4] The Y.B.A. to the Colonial Secretary, 12 Mar. 1921, S.M.P. 6538, E.S.A. Cf. also the *Direct Apeal*, p. 1.

[5] E. B. Kalibala, 'The Social Structure of the Baganda Tribe of East Africa' (Harvard Univ. Ph.D. thesis 1946), p. 522. Also, Sturrock, Provincial Commissioner Buganda to Chief Secretary, 27 Aug. 1921, in Coryndon to Milner, 20 Sept. 1921, C.O. 537/949, P.R.O.

In Kenya, on the other hand, political organizations among the young Africans developed some two years later. Their appeal was very much wider, since their leaders voiced grievances more serious than anything with which the Young Baganda were concerned. Against a general background of land alienation, increase in settlers' political power, the Native Registration Ordinance, and the doubling of hut and poll taxes, the actual move towards African political organizations was sparked off by a concerted effort among Europeans in the private sector to reduce native wages by one-third.[1] In central Kenya, protest against this was centred on a Kikuyu, Harry Thuku, a born organizer and a man whose political philosophy increasingly cut across tribal, racial, national, and religious boundaries.[2]

Initially, on 7 June 1921, he had become the proposed secretary of a group which called itself provisionally the 'Young Kikuyu Association', possibly on the analogy of the Y.B.A.[3] But as Thuku was aiming at a national youth movement, such a designation was obviously not inclusive enough for the very mixed communities of African urban workers and it was never ratified. By 11 June, Thuku and his associates had abandoned it in favour of 'The (proposed) African Association'.[4] They used the new organization principally to protest against the injustice whereby European soldier-settlers had not only got land free of charge, but wanted now to give their African 'fellow ex-soldiers' a reduction in wages.[5] Only two weeks

[1] The general background to the emergence of African politics in Kenya is well covered in H. D. Hooper, 'The Development of Political Self-consciousness in the Kikuyu Native', Oldham Papers, E. H. Also valuable is Norman Leys's letter to the Colonial Secretary, 7 Feb. 1918, Oldham Papers, E.H. See also G. Bennett, *Kenya. A Political History* (London, 1963); J. Nottingham and C. G. Rosberg, *The Myth of 'Mau Mau': Nationalism in Kenya* (Nairobi, 1966). Cf. also J. Kangethe, 'The background to Politics in Kenya' a translation from *Uria Kenyatta Atwarirwo Ruraya ni K.C.A. Kuma 1928 Nginya 1930* (Nairobi, *c.* 1947), University College Nairobi, History Dept. Research Project Archives (hereafter U.C.N./H.D./R.P.A.) D/3/4.

[2] For Thuku see G. Bennett, 'The Development of Political Organisations in Kenya', *Political Studies*, v, No. 2 (June 1957), 118–30; Nottingham and Rosberg, op. cit., pp. 36–55; K. Kyle, 'Gandhi, Harry Thuku and early Kenya Nationalism', *Transition*, vi, No. 27 (1966), 16–22. For a more detailed account of his contribution to the development of modern politics, see K. J. King, 'The Nationalism of Harry Thuku: A Study in the Beginnings of African Politics in Kenya', *Trans-Africa* I, 1 (1970).

[3] Thuku, letter to the *East African Standard* (hereafter *E.A.S.*), 10 June 1921, H. D. Hooper, *Africa in the Making* (London, 1922), pp. 36–7.

[4] The (Proposed) African Association to the Acting Colonial Secretary, 11 June 1921, E.A.I.N.C.A.

[5] Ibid. The European farmers were, incidentally, successful in their campaign.

later, however, on 1 July, the title was finally settled, and it was almost unanimously agreed that they should be called the East African Association (E.A.A.).[1] The new name was not only trans-tribal, but, like the East African Indian National Congress, cut across national boundaries within East Africa.[2]

Thuku was soon engaged in a double campaign, against the colonial government, and against those government-appointed Chiefs who presumed to represent the people. In the process he began to put substance into the title of the association by canvassing support among the Kamba in the autumn of 1921. Apparently response was cool.[3] In another part of the country, however—Nyanza—his movement struck a sympathetic chord among those Kavirondo who were themselves beginning to build up a similar organization. By 23 December 1921 they were in touch with Thuku, and had assured him that they were 'struggling' with him for the country, and had even contributed financially to his central funds.[4] Indeed, the mass meeting of 23 December which launched the Young Kavirondo Association in western Kenya promised to send Thuku further financial support, thus marking, incidentally, one of the earliest examples of Kikuyu–Kavirondo nationalist co-operation. There is some slight evidence also that some Masai groups, and particularly the Keekonyokie, were also aware of the need for political organization, and appear to have founded a Masai Association in response to the same sorts of forces.[5] Exactly what connection this association had with the E.A.A.

[1] Hooper, 'The Development of Political Self-consciousness'. There has been a continuing tendency among East African historians to link Thuku's name primarily with the Young Kikuyu Association (Y.K.A.). There is, however, no evidence that the Y.K.A. existed in anything but a provisional form, and that for only four or five days. The title had possibly also been a deliberate rejection of the idea that the rural, conservative Kikuyu Association, led by the senior Chiefs, could represent all Kikuyus.

[2] For some further discussion of the implications of this new title, see J. M. Lonsdale, 'Some Origins of Nationalism in East Africa', *Journal of African History*, ix (1968), 126, n. 28.

[3] Nottingham and Rosberg, op. cit., p. 47.

[4] Thuku to M. Njeroge (secretary of the Kikuyu Association), 23 Dec. 1921, n Bowring to Churchill, 25 Jan. 1922, C.O. 533/275, P.R.O. Cf. also Nottingham and Rosberg, op. cit., pp. 55–60, and K. M. Okaro-Kojwang, 'Origins and Establishment of the Kavirondo Taxpayers' Welfare Association', in B. G. McIntosh (Ed.), *Ngano: Nairobi Historical Studies* 1 (1969), 120–1. There is no evidence that Thuku himself engaged in political campaigning in Kavirondo country, as has been claimed, for instance, by the *Oxford History of East Africa*, Vol. ii, 357.

[5] See further K. J. King, 'A Biography of Molonket ole Sempele', in King and Salim, *Kenya Historical Biographies* (Nairobi, forthcoming 1970). For another

is not yet clear, but it seems certain that Molonketole Sempele, with his vivid experience of racial prejudice in the Southern States, played an important part in radicalizing the younger Masai.[1]

At all events, Thuku was increasingly ready to preach the need for black solidarity as the year wore on: 'Now if anyone wants friendship with us we also want to be friendly with him, but with him who does not want to be friends with us, we do not want friendship, even if he is a European, may he perish at a distance. But it is no use for us black people to quarrel amongst ourselves.'[2]* Unlike the Y.B.A., Thuku's association had a mass appeal, his meetings on occasion being attended by up to 25,000 people. Although the Young Baganda had cultivated non-denominationalism, Thuku embraced Christians, non-Christians, and Moslems in a much more deliberate way, and made the success of his non-sectarian policies a central theme in his publications:

> I was very delighted to be travelling to the meeting at Ngenda, because I was accompanied by the school teacher, Samuel Okoth, a Christian from Maseno, and two Moslems, their names were Abdullah Tairara and Ali Kironjo; the going was delightful all through, and we travelled as brothers (kama Ndugu moja) and I saw no difference between the Kavirondo and the Kikuyu, or between the Christian believer and the believer in Islam; and I was very pleased too in that we fulfilled the command of the Lord God, that you should love your neighbour as yourself.[3]

Thuku's other allies in East Africa were the Indians, at this time fighting bitterly for equal rights and representation, and ready to seek support from any body similarly oppressed by white supremacist aims. The E.A.A. announcement of an Afro-Indian *entente* on 10 July 1921 encouraged widespread allegations among all sections

---

hint of Masai interest in Thuku, see Lonsdale, 'Some Origins of Nationalism', p. 126.

[1] The Revd. J. T. Mpaayei, interview, Oct. 1968.

[2] Thuku to Njeroge, 23 Dec. 1921.

[3] Thuku, *Tangazo*, 17 Feb. 1922, (*East African Chronicle Press*), Nairobi. With the exception of *Sekanyolya*, produced monthly by Nairobi Baganda from Dec. 1920, this edition of *Tangazo* is the earliest example of the indigenous Kenyan African press. The first issue was in Dec. 1921, and four or five others were produced in Feb. and Mar. 1922. For Thuku's publications in general, see King, 'The Nationalism of Harry Thuku'. I am indebted to Mr. Opadia Kadima for the translation from the Swahili. The original is in Coryndon Papers 17/2, MSS. Afr.s. 633, Rhodes House, Oxford.

* No alteration has been made in the English used by Africans, either here or elsewhere in this study.

of the white community that Thuku and his association were being ruthlessly manipulated by the Indians.[1] Certainly the Indians, and particularly M. A. Desai, the editor of the radical *East African Chronicle*, advised Thuku on political procedure, and co-operated to the full in the printing of Thuku's official correspondence and his broadsheets. But much of the settler and missionary talk of the monthly salary of thirty pounds paid to Thuku by the Indians, and the high-powered cars lent him for his tours of the Reserves was the merest speculation.[2] Thuku himself gave the lie to much of this by pointing out that 'the Natives do not need to be told by the Indians that they are not masters in their houses'.[3] He was not opposed to Indians' having equal rights in Kenya, but he did not live up to the European image of himself as a tool of the Indians when he pointed out the need for reciprocity: 'I can strongly say that if Home Authorities will grant equal rights to Indians I have no objection, but we Natives must have such rights also in our countries including India.'[4]

It was Thuku's controversial position on the Indian question that originally forged a link with the Y.B.A. Some five months earlier the Y.B.A. had itself created a furore in Buganda by claiming that Afro-Indian relations were 'very cordial', and that 'the Indian Community is helpful to natives in more than one direction'.[5] Consequently the secretary of the Y.B.A. Joswa Kamulegeya, began a correspondence with Thuku, and the process led both men to realize that their associations had common goals, and that the division between Kenya and Uganda was artificial. In fact, it led Thuku to make one of the earliest declarations on 'closer union' in East Africa between these two infant African political organizations:

It has been very interested to me and my Association also to receive your letter with remark that my aim is yours, it is quite true because I recognise no difference between the natives of Kenya and Uganda, so far

[1] Cf. Hooper to Oldham, 4 Mar. 1922, East Africa–Kenya File (File Q–A), E.H., also Arthur to W. Paton, 23 Aug. 1924, A/37, Presbyterian Church of East Africa Archives (hereafter, P.C.E.A.), Nairobi.

[2] For some new material on the question of aid from Indian sources to Thuku's association, see King, 'The Nationalism of Harry Thuku', also Hooper to Oldham, 4 Mar. 1922, and Nottingham and Rosberg, op. cit., pp. 40, 46.

[3] Thuku to Desai, 2 May 1922, reprinted in *E.A.S.*, 22 Aug. 1922.

[4] Thuku to Kamulegeya, 9 Sept. 1921, enclosed in Northey to Churchill, 4 May 1922, C.O. 533/277, P.R.O. For evidence of the close friendship between Desai and Thuku, see the correspondence between the two men published in the *E.A.S.* (wkly edn.), 26 Aug. 1922.

[5] 'Address presented by Baganda to Indians', *E.A.S.*, 26 Jan. 1921.

as our future status and education concerned. What is good for the Native of Uganda is equally as good for the Native of Kenya.[1]

Thuku's growing co-operation with the Young Baganda, however, opened up for him a new international area of alliance with New World Negroes, for by the summer of 1921 Kamulegeya had been in correspondence with one sector of American Negro opinion for two years, and had received much of the American Negro literature and propaganda coming to Uganda. This contact had arisen through his developing a correspondence with the president of Tuskegee Institute, Robert Moton, after the war, and his successful attempt to gain a place there for his younger brother, Danieri Kato. The choice of Tuskegee was interesting. For over a decade Ugandans had shown a keen interest in continuing their education to a level beyond that of their own most advanced school, Budo, and it had become not uncommon for aspiring students to proceed from there to Trinity College, Kandy, Ceylon, under the principalship of A. G. Fraser.[2] The war had, however, given men like Kamulegeya (himself a Kandy graduate) a knowledge of Negro affairs beyond East Africa, and they had learnt of the existence of the large, predominantly Negro colleges of the United States from the West Indian and West African troops, or possibly directly from the seven Y.M.C.A. secretaries.[3]

Whatever the combination of influences that suggested the American South to Kamulegeya (and the impact of Booker Washington's own publications must not be discounted),[4] Danieri Kato became in June 1920 the first Ugandan entrant to Tuskegee.[5] In this way a regular channel of information between the Y.B.A. and New World Negro politics was opened up. It also worked in the opposite direction, and Kato must be assumed to be responsible for the first mention of the Y.B.A. in a North American graduate thesis; in 1922 Kato's lecturer in African history, S. M. Nkomo from Rhodesia,

[1] Thuku to Kamulegeya, 9 Sept. 1921.

[2] For Fraser in Uganda, Kandy, and later in Achimota, see Ward, *Fraser of Trinity and Achimota*, also Mrs. A. G. Fraser, interview, Sept. 1967.

[3] Other young educated Baganda who were making inquiries at this time to Negro colleges were Sirwano Kulubya (not a member of the Y.B.A., but soon to distinguish himself as Treasurer to the Kabaka's Government, and as Ugandan delegate to the Joint Parliamentary Committee on Closer Union in East Africa), and E. B. Kalibala, a Budo-educated teacher in the C.M.S. Mengo High School.

[4] Kalibala, for instance, believed it was his reading of *Up from Slavery* that first determined him to make for Tuskegee. (Interview, Jan. 1969.)

[5] Registry of Students, Tuskegee Institute, Ala.

stated in his pan-Bantu thesis at Chicago University, that, along with the South African Native Congress, 'the Baganda Young Peoples' Association' had worked 'to resist European penetration at the expense of native rights'.[1]

As will be seen later,[2] Tuskegee was at this period very far from being the safe model of Negro education which it was often represented as. Rather, it had a strong African orientation, and gave much attention to the question of American Negro involvement in Africa. Thus, a personal interest had been taken in Max Yergan, and money raised for him, by the student body.[3] In this environment Kato had access to a wide range of American Negro thought; and that he took a keen interest in the same problems as his brother in Uganda is evident from his delivering a lecture to the African Student Union (A.S.U.) of America on 'What are the prospects for the American Negro in Africa?'[4]

Kamulegeya had not, however, been content to await his brother's arrival in Tuskegee before seeking first-hand information on American Negro activities. Already by March 1920 he had received directly from Moton copies of American Negro papers and periodicals, especially the *Crisis* and the New York *Age*.[5] These he had read with great interest, and had circulated among 'several bodies in our community, who, some of them, have decided to subscribe to those two papers'.[6] It is worth noticing here that, despite the tendency in informed missionary and philanthropic circles to stress the difference between the safe, Tuskegee-type Negroes and the more radical followers of DuBois, it was in all likelihood the president of Tuskegee himself who was the first man to send DuBois's periodical, the *Crisis*, to the young African nationalists of Uganda.

Equally important in turning the minds of the younger Baganda to the American South was Marcus Garvey's publication, the *Negro World*. Although it is not known on whose initiative it first entered Uganda, there is little doubt, on the evidence of E. B. Kalibala, who

[1] S. M. Nkomo, 'The Customs of the Bandowo Folk considered with a view of adding certain new arguments to the generally accepted view of the Unity of the Bantu race' (Univ. of Chicago, M.A. thesis 1922), p. 4.

[2] See pp. 222–5.

[3] Yergan had lectured to the students in Mar. 1921, and they had agreed on a target of $250 to be raised in his interest during April, R.R.M./L.C. (1920), T.U.A.

[4] Fifth annual conference of the A.S.U., printed in the *Tuskegee Student*, xxxiv (Mar. 1924), 5.

[5] Kamulegeya to Moton, 4 Mar. 1920, R.R.M./G.C. (1919), T.U.A.

[6] Ibid.

had been trying to get to the Southern States since 1919, that its arrival was a new, 'sensational development'. By reason of its 'beautiful' portrayal of outstanding Negroes, and because it was published in English, the young Baganda 'were overcome with the *Negro World*'.[1]

The consequence of the circulation of both the *Crisis* and the *Negro World* in East Africa was, of course, greatly to increase interest in American Negro education, because of the prominence given in their advertising to the Negro colleges.[2] Indeed, so rapid was the growth of this interest that by May 1922 it had reached the attention of Uganda's Governor Coryndon. He regarded 'with especial anxiety a desire, which has become more marked of late, on the part of several chiefs of different tribes, to send their sons to America, and notably to the great institution of Tuskegee for education.'[3]

In addition to Danieri Kato, there would be in the Governor's mind, Hosea Nyabongo (the nephew of the Omukama of Toro at that time), who had successfully entered Tuskegee in early 1922.[4] Such young men, so Coryndon feared, would be considered handsome prey by Marcus Garvey's Universal Negro Improvement Association (U.N.I.A.);[5] he had little doubt that 'leaders of Negro political aspirations in the Southern States will eagerly seize an opportunity for influencing and helping to educate sons of chiefs of this Protectorate'.[6] An attempt was made, therefore, to obtain the Colonial Office's consent to his refusing all passports for Ugandans wishing to go to the Southern States. Churchill, the Colonial Secretary, agreed.[7] The ban, which lasted for a number of years, seems to

[1] Kalibala, op. cit., p. 533, and interview, Jan. 1969.

[2] The Y.B.A., for instance, seems to have had good information on opportunities overseas for higher education; see Y.B.A. to the Colonial Secretary, 12 Mar. 1921, S.M.P. 6538, E.S.A.

[3] Coryndon to the Colonial Secretary, 30 May 1922, C.O. 536/119, P.R.O. It is possible that Coryndon, with his very considerable background of administration in southern Africa, may have come to certain conclusions on the American Negro element in S. African 'Ethiopianism', and desired to prevent its occurrence in Uganda.

[4] Danieri Kato and J. R. Kamulegeya were the sons of Joswa Kate Mugema, a Muganda county chief, who had been deposed in 1919 for his leadership of the anti-medicine Malakite movement. For Kate, see F. B. Welbourn, *East African Rebels* (London, 1961), 31–53. For other evidence of Baganda in Negro colleges at this time, see Reuter's correspondent in the *Daily Telegraph*, 22 Nov. 1921.

[5] Coryndon to Northey, 28 June 1922, enclosed in Northey to Churchill, 14 July 1922, C.O. 533/279, P.R.O.

[6] Coryndon to the Colonial Secretary, 30 May 1922.

[7] Archer to Devonshire, 14 Aug. 1923, C.O. 533/126, P.R.O.

have been immediately effective in the case of Absolamu Sabirye, who had been persistently trying to reach Tuskegee.[1] Even Kalibala was able finally to reach the Southern States in 1925 only via a spell in an English theological college.[2] It certainly had the effect of cutting down the number of younger Baganda who had been approaching administrative officers for information and prospectuses on the Southern Negro colleges.[3] In its own way, however, this African enthusiasm for education in the American South was one of the reasons that led the Uganda Government to establish a form of higher education locally, in the new Makerere College. This point was well made by a government official at the very time that Coryndon was blocking the way to the Southern States:

> I think we may be able to prevent young men going abroad for education, at any rate to Alabama, for the next two or three years, but each year will become more difficult, and there will come a time when we shall no longer be able to do so. We must if possible anticipate this time by providing an advanced course of study locally.[4]

Coryndon's intention in erecting the barrier had been 'to discourage as far as possible the connection which is gradually becoming established between East Africa and the Southern States',[5] but action came too late. Links had by then been formed for over a year between both the E.A.A. and the Y.B.A. and the three main streams of New World Negro movements, associated with the names of Moton, Garvey, and DuBois. The deliberate policy of involving the American Negro leadership in their political struggles was embarked on together by Thuku and Kamulegeya, but because of the long-standing

[1] H. T. C. Weatherhead, 'Memorandum re Educational Facilities in Uganda Protectorate for Boys who at present go to England, America or Ceylon', in 'Annexure to the Minutes of the P.C.'s Conference 1922', S.M.P. 6538, E.S.A. I am grateful to Mr. Tom Watson for allowing me to consult his file of material copied from the E.S.A.

[2] E. S. Kalibala, interview, Jan. 1969, also E. B. Jarvis, Colonial Secretary, to Canon Grace, 27 Apr. 1923, No. 3374, Minute 59, E.S.A.

[3] C. S. Nason (Asst. D.C.) to Moton, 2 Mar. 1922, R.R.M./G.C. (1922), T.U.A.

[4] E. L. Scott, 'Memo on Higher Education', 30 June 1922, E.S.A. In this connection it is interesting to note that considerable pressure had been put on D. K. Kyebambe, the Mukama of Toro, by the Governor, Lord Lugard, and others, to prevent him sending his two sons to English universities; Kyebambe to Coryndon, 3 June 1921, S.M.P. 6538, E.S.A. It should be noted that Makerere opened in 1922 with fourteen students taking low-level technical courses.

[5] Coryndon to Northey, 28 June 1922.

informal contact between Kamulegeya and Tuskegee the first move came from his association. Now, in his official capacity as secretary of the Y.B.A., he approached the N.A.A.C.P. in New York. This was a natural first step, since the *Crisis* had been in circulation in Uganda for over a year, and it was all the more likely on account of the publicity that DuBois was giving to pan-Africanism in these last few months before the second Pan-African Congress.[1] A reply was sent from the N.A.A.C.P., promising help in any way possible, and although the exact terms of the N.A.A.C.P. letter are not yet known, it is more than likely that DuBois would have confirmed the importance of the alliance between the U.S.A. and East Africa.[2]

Apart from the imminence of the Pan-African Congress, there is an intriguing factor which may have influenced Kamulegeya in his cultivation of Negro support. It appears in his next letter, addressed this time to Tuskegee, to the members of the Negro Farmers' Conference. Kamulegeya reveals that he may have had added encouragement to seek such alliances: 'This Association was advised more than twice by Political men and lovers of Africans that we ought to affiliate with our brothers who are over-seas such as yourself here in United States of America and others in Africa and elsewhere.'[3] While the phrase 'Political men and lovers of Africans' could conceivably refer to DuBois, it is much more probably an allusion to non-Negro encouragement. It could well be to some of Thuku's and Kamulegeya's friends in the Indian National Congress of East Africa, and it is just possible that additional encouragement may have come from a pan-Islamic body termed 'the Khalifate party' by one of the acutest observers among the missionaries. Its representative in Nairobi was one of Thuku's main supporters, and its alleged aim was to make 'a bid for a big anti-white combination throughout Africa'.[4] Whatever the immediate stimuli, however, this move to incorporate the American Negroes in their struggles was the culmination of a slowly-growing Negro consciousness that extended beyond the frontiers of tribe, nation, and continent.

[1] For the bulletins issued by DuBois in these pre-conference months, see an example in DuBois to Moton, 25 Feb. 1921, R.R.M./G.C. (1921), T.U.A. On the second Pan-African Congress, see W. E. B. DuBois, 'A Second Journey to Pan-Africa', *New Republic*, 7 Dec. 1921, pp. 39–42.

[2] The reference to the approach to the N.A.A.C.P. occurs in Kamulegeya to the Negro Farmers' Conference, Tuskegee, 13 Sept. 1921, R.R.M./G.C. (1921), T.U.A.

[3] Ibid.

[4] Hooper to Oldham, 4 Mar. 1922, File Q–A, E.H

It was only now, in the frustration and disenchantment of post-war conditions in East Africa, that what had been a gradual, informal process of establishing contacts became a political necessity. Kamulegeya stressed to Tuskegee the unity and strength in such an alliance with its potential for reciprocal aid: '. . . not only to the friendship but also to seek co-operation and support from time to time. You know, dear brothers, that unless we Negroes get proper education and understand modern civilised ways, we will never be advanced and enjoy all the priveleges of the citizens of today; we should therefore love one another.'[1]

A characteristic of Kamulegeya's letter, which brought it into marked contrast with Thuku's international appeals, was its conspicuous lack of rancour against whites. It was rather a quiet appreciation that, although in Uganda the best land was in the hands of the Africans, it was more likely that they would learn to make the best use of their assets through other Negroes than through Indian traders or the white government. The burden of the letter thus came to be a request for a commission of the Negro farmers to visit Uganda and advise them on how best to develop their land.[2] That the full development of their agricultural resources should have been the first request of the Young Baganda in 1921 was all the more interesting in view of the common missionary attitude to urban, educated Africans; three of Uganda's leading C.M.S. missionaries felt that in 1925 they were breaking new ground when they suggested bringing agricultural graduates of Tuskegee and Hampton to help correct the Baganda's distaste for agriculture.[3]

Of course the absence of political grievances in Kamulegeya's letter may not mean any more than that he had a more sophisticated awareness of Tuskegee's characteristic interests than Thuku, and would therefore understand that President Moton would be more likely to be sympathetic to the economic forms of pan-African co-operation, without too many political overtones. He had, after all, corresponded earlier with Moton over economic matters, and in the process he had given notice of what may be one of the earliest East African examples of an attempt to form trade links between Africans and American Negroes, such as had become common in West

[1] Kamulegeya to the Negro Farmers' Conference, 13 Sept. 1921.

[2] Ibid.

[3] Memorandum of H. Mathers, H. M. Grace, and H. F. Wright, presented to the Phelps-Stokes Fund after their tour in the Southern States, 23 Oct. 1925, File B–3, P.S.F.A. See further p. 195.

Africa by this time.[1] What result if any came from these early gropings in the field of economic interchange, or from the request to the Negro farmers, can only for the moment be conjectured; but again it must be stressed that, as with so much else in the realm of East African–American Negro relations in the 1920s and 1930s, it is the attempt that is important, however frustrated it may have been.

Harry Thuku's letter to Tuskegee preceded Kamulegeya's by five days; its tone was, however, radically different, and coming as it did just two months after the founding of the E.A.A., it constitutes one of the fullest statements of Thuku's views at that time. Stylistically it was the product of his Indian friends at the *Chronicle* office, but the sentiments were manifestly his own. These contents were hardly, however, attuned to Tuskegee's ear, consisting as they did of a lengthy, generalized critique of the twenty years of British justice and rule that Kenya had experienced. Although, therefore, it is not surprising that such a narrative of naked exploitation apparently gained no response from Moton, it is important to examine Thuku's image of Tuskegee, especially as his was a not uncommon attitude among African nationalists.

It appears that Thuku was as much impressed by Tuskegee's apparent independence and self-sufficiency as by anything else. This factor contrasted very pointedly with his own dependent position, where he relied so heavily upon the co-operation of his Indian associates for printing, publications, and the wording of his official papers. He would almost certainly have read some of the Tuskegee publications channelled through Kamulegeya,[2] all printed at the Tuskegee Institute Press, and would have remarked on Tuskegee's ability to buy land from whites, build its own plant, hire its own black staff, and be apparently beholden to no man for anything. In Kenya, on the other hand, there had been almost no attempt by Africans to provide for themselves independently the benefits which most of the immigrants enjoyed; and, while not ungrateful for white and Indian philanthropy, Thuku jibbed at the compromises in educational and political progress that such dependence entailed:

We must frankly confess that we are not without warm friends and

[1] Kamulegeya to Moton, 4 Mar. 1920, R.R.M./G.C. (1919), T.U.A. For further evidence of East African economic pan-Africanism, see the Rev. Prince U. Kaba Rega [*sic*] to Moton, 23 Mar. 1918, R.R.M./G.C. (1919), T.U.A.

[2] Thuku to the secretary of Tuskegee Institute, 8 Sept. 1921, mentions that he had read 'books and newspapers' dealing with Negro conditions in the States, R.R.M./G.C. (1921), T.U.A. (See further Appendix II.)

sincere sympathisers among European Missionaries and benevolent Indians (East Indians) to whom we owe so much of our improved life of few of us. These friends have been helping us as much as they can, and in their own way; but with all this, we are convinced that this is totally inadequate and insufficient to dispel our present illiteracy and ignorance we have steeped in and to safeguard our position as human beings or to avert the impending danger which seems so imminent to our view.[1]

Thuku was, in his admiration of Tuskegee, unaware of the very considerable compromises by which Washington and later Moton had gained enviable financial security in exchange for far-reaching social, political, and educational concessions to the white North and South. In his ignorance, Tuskegee undoubtedly appeared as an island of black defiance to the traditions of the white South, or, as Thuku put it, 'our asylum where the hunted down-trodden and oppressed Negro may hasten to seek for help or advice in all times of danger.'[2] Thuku was not the first to attach to Tuskegee this important mythical element of independence,[3] and the frequency with which such a view would keep recurring was to prove only one of the difficulties Jones would encounter in preaching his own image of Tuskegee throughout Africa.[4]

Beyond the apparent independence and self-sufficiency of Tuskegee, however, there lay the attraction of its educational system, which assured a large supply of leaders, teachers, and skilled men. This educational machinery seemed to be completely lacking to Thuku as he surveyed the twenty years of 'petty efforts' by the Kenya Government in education, whose purpose was 'ostensebly to impart technical and elementary education to the natives but at an expense totally disproportionate to the revenue extracted from them'.[5] There was the almost complete lack of skilled professional people among the Africans to break the vicious circle of poor education for themselves, and the only remedy seemed to Thuku the acquisition of exactly those 'imported' Negroes that Northey had the previous year prescribed:

We suffer beyond imagination from the want of such men and leaders of our own race to guide us in every walk of life, and the result is that our progress in the sphere of Trade Industry Agriculture and the last but not the least important politics is seriously hampered . . .

[1] Ibid. [2] Ibid. [3] See pp. 17–8.
[4] See Ch. VIII, *passim*.
[5] Thuku to the secretary of Tuskegee, 8 Sept. 1921.

The necessity therefore of having our own man—a skinsman brother, and a leader, who has devoted his life and renounced everything for the elevation and uplifting of a primitive race like ours, which is even now scarcely free from the shackles of the slavery days will be too obvious for further elaboration. It gives me the greatest pleasure to learn that despite the stubborn adverse evil influences the Negro race in America has been successful in producing many large hearted men like Booker T. Washington and establishing Institutes like the Tuskegee. We regard such men as our saviours . . . Such being the feeling I am therefore anxious to be informed if a Booker T. Washington or a Du Bois can be spared for founding a 'Tuskegee' in the African wilds and for the holy Mission of up-lifting and emancipating the hopeless, hapless struggling 3,000,000 nude Native souls from deep ignorance, object porvity, and grinding oppression of the white settlers of this Colony of Kenya.[1]

The apparently anomalous suggestion that DuBois should found a 'Tuskegee' is not such a contradiction as it first seems; it must be remembered that Thuku would consider its foundation to be a defiant act of racial pride, and not an educational compromise with the white settlers. Even if he was aware of the divisions within the American Negro leadership, it is doubtful if he would regard them as more important than the need for black racial solidarity.[2]

In fact Thuku might just as easily have suggested Garvey as the founder of his independent black school. He had, after all, communicated with him on the same day as he had with Moton. Although the original letter has not survived, it is likely that it would have been in the same vein as the one to Tuskegee. It is known certainly that he had asked Garvey 'for an advice and help',[3] and received both shortly afterwards, in the form of U.N.I.A. pamphlets.[4] Also, it was not long after that date that the *Negro World* began to enter Kenya in small numbers.[5] Whether or not it arrived as a direct result of Thuku's request is not absolutely clear, but it would be difficult to exaggerate the sort of effect it began to have from 1921 onwards. As C. L. R. James has noted, it had a circulation far beyond the ordinary:

[1] Ibid.

[2] For Thuku's remark, 'It is no use for us black people to quarrel amongst ourselves,' see Thuku to Njeroge, 23 Dec. 1921.

[3] Thuku to Kamulegeya, 9 Sept. 1921.

[4] I am indebted to Dr. J. Mangat for mentioning this material in the E.A.I.N.C.A.

[5] Acting Commissioner of Police to the Colonial Secretary, 26 Apr. 1922, in Northey to Churchill, 4 May 1922, C.O. 533/277, P.R.O.

Jomo Kenyatta has related to this writer how in 1921 Kenya nationalists, unable to read, would gather round a reader of Garvey's newspaper, the *Negro World*, and listen to an article two or three times. Then they would run various ways through the forest, carefully to repeat the whole, which they had memorised, to Africans hungry for some doctrine which lifted them from the servile consciousness in which Africans lived.[1]

It is a further interesting speculation, therefore, whether it was the exposure to this new type of Negro journalism, very different in tone from that of the *Crisis* and the New York *Age*, that gave Thuku the stimulus to begin issuing his own radical broadsheet, *Tangazo*. Its circulation understandably soon caused considerable unrest.[2]

How frequent communication between the two organizations was cannot yet be known with any certainty, but in addition to the process of direct correspondence, further publicity was given to Garvey's programme by Daudi Basudde. He was, like Thuku, an ex-telephone operator, who had been removed in 1920 from his post in Maseno School, Nyanza, for inciting the pupils to strike over the change in Kenya's status from protectorate to colony.[3] During the next year he had gone to England for just eleven days during September, with the aid of the Indian Associations in Kisumu and Nairobi,[4] and had come back full of the significance of Garveyism for Africa. Strong circumstantial evidence makes it very likely that he would have made contact on his return with both Thuku and Kamulegeya, especially as he was to use the pages of *Sekanyolya* to give publicity to his impressions. It could not have but given a stimulus to both men to hear of the effect Garvey's might was having upon the Europeans:

He [Marcus Garvey] is who is the head of the wonderful group which exists today, which has a membership of close on five millions. It has under consideration the questions of Africa for the Blacks and is called the 'Universal Negro Improvement Association'. It is convinced that the four hundred million Blacks in the world will undoubtedly acquire a Kingdom in their land of Africa. This man Garvey, the work which he has done

[1] C. L. R. James, *The Black Jacobins: Toussaint l'Ouverture and the San Domingo Revolution* (2nd edn. New York, 1963), p. 397. I owe this reference to Professor Ali Mazrui.

[2] On the effect of *Tangazo* in the Reserves, H. D. Hooper commented that 'Many of them contained attacks on missions or missionaries. They alienated considerable native feeling.' 'The Development of Political Self-consciousness'.

[3] J. M. Lonsdale, 'Archdeacon Owen and the Kavirondo Taxpayers Welfare Association', in 'Proceedings of the East African Institute of Social Research held at Kivukoni College, Dar es Salaam, January 1963', p. 4.

[4] Nahame (?) Kasim to Desai, 11 Aug. 1921, E.A.I.N.C.A.

cause all people to be afraid and the fame of him will spread to all lands. When I left he was about to visit in England and in Paris in France.[1]

That something beyond a formal relationship existed between Garvey's U.N.I.A. and Thuku's E.A.A., however, is suggested by the very tone of Garvey's reaction to Thuku's arrest and the subsequent shooting of twenty-five Africans protesting against his detention. It must therefore have come as something of a shock to the Colonial Office, which considered Garvey to be not 'much concerned with the primitive natives of Kenya',[2] to receive the following telegram four days after the protest meeting:

> Four hundred million Negroes through the Universal Negro Improvement Association hereby register their protest against the brutal manner in which your government has treated the Natives of Kenya East Africa. You have shot down a defenseless people in their own land for exercising their rights as men; such a policy will only tend to aggravate the many historic injustices heaped upon a race that will one day be placed in a position to truly defend itself not with mere sticks, clubs and stones but with the modern implements of science. Again we ask you and your Government to be just to our race for surely we shall not forget you. The evolutionary scale that weighs nations and races, balances alike for all people. We feel sure that some day the balance will register a change.[3]

The American Negro as Missionary to East Africa

An issue common to both Kamulegeya's and Thuku's relationship with New World Negroes was their demand for personal guidance in educational and agricultural development at the hands of their Negro brethren. In both cases no American Negro came. While it is possible that nothing militated against their particular requests other than the lack of a favourable reaction on the part of Tuskegee, the fact inevitably raises the more general question of access for American Negro missionaries and educators to colonial Africa in the twentieth century.

It was a topic of the greatest delicacy and explosiveness, and

[1] Translation by W. E. Owen in *Sekanyolya* of part of reported interview with Daudi Basudde, Jan. 1922, File 'Indians in Kenya', E.H. It seems likely that Basudde may have confused the imminent Pan-African Congress of DuBois with Garvey. The latter's world tour was not projected until 1923.

[2] Minutes on Garvey to Lloyd George, 20 Mar. 1922, C.O. 533/290, P.R.O.

[3] Garvey to Lloyd George, 20 Mar. 1922, C.O. 533/290, P.R.O. Cf. also, Amy Jacques Garvey (compiler), *Philosophy and Opinions of Marcus Garvey* (first published New York, 1923; 2nd edn. London, 1967), Pt. 1, 43.

although it was widely discussed during the first four decades of the twentieth century, little detailed evidence of attitudes to Negro mission has survived. This is understandable; as neither colonial governments nor white missionary societies wished to practise overt discrimination against Negro missionaries *qua* Negroes, there tended to be an absence of definite rulings for or against Negro missionaries in general, and a preference for judging cases according to their individual merits.[1] This naturally led to a high level of suspicion if Negroes felt themselves to have been rejected unfairly. Precisely because evidence of discrimination was almost unobtainable, and what little there was would not readily be vouchsafed to those most eager to find it, the area was deeply scarred with rumours and protracted ill feelings against those most suspected of frustrating the Negro's legitimate mission.

For instance, in Kenya and Uganda there appear to have been no Negro missionaries between the two world wars,[2] but even the most determined investigator might have found it difficult to prove that this was necessarily the result of discriminatory policies; for, on the one hand, many of the white East African missionaries would openly encourage Negro students to awake to their missionary responsibilities in Africa;[3] and, on the other, it was hard to determine whether any candidates had come forward, and, if they had, whether they had been adequately qualified. It was moreover well known that many American Negro students had not the slightest interest in the missionaries' continued appeals to fulfil their obligations in Africa (hence the phrase 'I ain't lost nothing in Africa', frequently heard among Negro students in the 1920s).[4] Yet, despite the inevitable sketchiness of the primary sources, the subject must bear further investigation, if for no other reason than because two most distin-

[1] For the attempt of some Negroes to settle in the East Africa Protectorate in 1911, see M. P. K. Sorrenson, *Origins of European Settlement in Kenya* (O.U.P. Nairobi, 1968), pp. 262–3.

[2] Except the American Negro wife of Ernest Kalibala, whose independent school near Kampala was sponsored by the Negro Baptists at the very end of the thirties; see pp. 243–5

[3] Especially relevant was J. W. Arthur's speech at Tuskegee; see p. 195, and J. W. C. Dougall's speech at Hampton; see p. 154.

[4] Major Walter Brown (commandant, then dean of men at Hampton Institute from the early 1920s), interview, May 1967. For some of the sparse background on this subject, see E. Ross, *Out of Africa* (Friendship Press, New York, 1936), pp. 154–66. Also, H. Isaacs, *The New World of Negro Americans* (New York, 1963), p. 124; and C. Clendenen and P. Duignan, *Americans in Black Africa up to 1865*, Hoover Institution Series, No. 5, (Stanford, 1964), 64.

guished Negro scholars continued over a period of twenty years to believe that opportunities for Negro mission had been deliberately reduced by white agencies, and that Thomas Jesse Jones bore partial responsibility.

Max Yergan's attempted entry to East Africa as international Y.M.C.A. secretary was a case in point. It had involved a large number of different individuals and organizations: the English National Council of the Y.M.C.A. and its American equivalent, the secretary of the British Conference of Missionary Societies, the Colonial Office, the Kenya Government. Only Yergan and the Coloured Y.M.C.A. of America who were to support him knew nothing of the Governor's prohibition. The next year, however, Yergan's entry to South Africa was to become a *cause célèbre*, and engender the bitterest suspicions among the Negro communities in the States, uniting in the process the resentment of DuBois, Carter Woodson, and Tuskegee.

After the rebuff in Kenya, the English National Council had entered into negotiations with the Y.M.C.A. of South Africa to accept Yergan. Progress had been made easy by Yergan's substantial record of service in East Africa, and arrangements were nearing completion for his initiating Y.M.C.A. work among native South Africans, when an unforeseen difficulty occurred. Oswin Bull, the general secretary of the Y.M.C.A. in Capetown, had suddenly become dubious about the project. This was partly, as Bull saw it, because the climate in South Africa as a whole had been becoming more hostile to American Negroes through the 'egregious antics of Martin Garvie [*sic*]',[1] but that there was a more specific reason was revealed confidentially to John Mott, general secretary of the International Committee of Y.M.C.A.s:

> My own personal hesitancy is perhaps increased by conversation in the past few days with Dr. Jesse Jones of the Phelps-Stokes Commission and also Dr. Loram . . . I find him (Loram) exceedingly doubtful about lending support to the matter of inviting Yergan. He does not know the man of course and it is possible that he is influenced in part by Dr. Jesse Jones, who is apparently a little bit doubtful about the attitude of Moreland and your other Coloured Y.M.C.A. leaders and (perhaps for want of knowing him better) classes Yergan with them.[2]

Jones at this point early in 1921 had just entered South Africa on

[1] Bull. to Mott, 18 Feb. 1921, Box 67, Y.M.C.A. Historical Library.
[2] Ibid.

the first Phelps-Stokes Commission and had been travelling with Dr. Loram of the Native Affairs Commission, who had substantial influence in government circles and was widely regarded as the foremost authority on native education. When the subject of Yergan's entry had been broached, Loram had consulted Jones's intimate knowledge of American Negro leadership, and had been convinced that it would be wise first to 'make sure of Mr. Yergan's belief in and practice of co-operation'.[1] In fact Jones had communicated to both Loram and Bull his own classification of Negroes, and in his own desire to ensure that the South African Y.M.C.A. started on satisfactory lines, had explained that the Coloured Y.M.C.A. in America was composed of both the 'Pan-African Negro with a violent antipathy to co-operation with white people', and 'the co-operative type, that realises that progress has got to be made in co-operation, not in antagonism'.[2]

He pleaded for time to find out which Yergan was, and set in motion machinery to do this; Moton of Tuskegee was cabled for his opinion,[3] and when Aggrey had rejoined the commission after his journey in Angola, he too was sounded.[4] Meanwhile J. H. Oldham had taken advantage of being in New York to prosecute his own inquiries into Yergan's record with the Phelps-Stokes Fund.[5] The result was, naturally enough, that the most complete endorsement of Yergan was eventually received, which placed him 'in the front rank of sane and wise leaders' in America.[6] In the interval, however, Jones had certainly been prepared to counsel delay; he had suggested to Dr. Bridgeman, a leading missionary of the American Board in Johannesburg, that the issue might be the safer for his own personal investigation of Yergan after the Phelps-Stokes tour, and in such a controversial matter his words were significant:

> Dr. Jones' final word was—'Can't you let the matter lie over until my return to America when I can go into the question with those interested there?' I now think it advisable to conform to this suggestion, if possible. While Dr. Jones did not say so, I assume that he would not wish his opinion to come to the ear of our negro brethren.[7]

[1] Jones to Miss Tourtellot, 19 June 1921, R.R.M./G.C. (1921), T.U.A.
[2] Carter to Bull, 26 July 1921, Box 67, Y.M.C.A. Historical Library.
[3] Jones to Miss Tourtellot, 19 June 1921.
[4] Carter to Bull, 26 July 1921.
[5] Miss Tourtellot to Moton, 23 May 1921, R.R.M./G.C. (1921), T.U.A.
[6] Jones to Miss Tourtellot, 19 June 1921.
[7] C. Patton to Jenkins, 7 May 1921, Box 67, Y.M.C.A. Historical Library.

This was, however, precisely what happened, and somehow the Coloured Y.M.C.A. became acquainted with the contents of Oswin Bull's original letter revealing Jones's role in the matter. To the Coloured Y.M.C.A. and Yergan in particular this must have appeared exactly the sort of subtle pressure that they may well have suspected had operated in Yergan's finally not going to East Africa. There they had no evidence; but with this letter before them, their frustration exploded.

Yergan felt bound to explain the delay in his mission to those most closely concerned with providing his financial support, and in doing so he raised the broader issue of Jones's categorization of Negroes into safe and unsafe. The implication of Jones's action was that any Negro applicant for the mission field must be assumed to be dangerous until proved innocent:

> It is easy to see how the added opposition of Thomas Jesse Jones caused the Government to take the position it did. I might add here that this man Jones is attempting to do in Africa precisely what it is claimed he did in America, namely, to assign all colored people to one of the two so-called 'schools' and then to say that those of one of these 'schools' cannot undertake to minister to the needs of the race. But his action goes further, for it will tend to prevent any colored man serving in a missionary capacity in Africa.[1]

The repercussions of what seemed the blatant prejudging of this pioneer missionary spread out through the Negro world. Tuskegee, with its current strong interest in the American Negro obligation to Africa,[2] had been one of the earliest to protest, and certainly the African representatives of the Tuskegee Y.M.C.A. (which included Daniel Kato) helped to draft the indignant note to John Mott, even before the leakage.

> The delay of Mr. Max Yergan's sail for service as missionary secretary among our brothers in Africa, is causing great concern among the NINE HUNDRED young men who constitute the student membership of the Tuskegee Association . . . Most especially do we covet our 'birthright of privilege' to make our distinct contribution toward the salvation of Africa; and we want to be acquainted with the barriers which are delaying your plans for the African work.[3]

[1] Yergan to J. J. Rhoads, 22 Apr. 1921, R.R.M./G.C. (1921), T.U.A.
[2] See further Ch. viii.
[3] Tuskegee Students' Y.M.C.A. to Mott, 31 Mar. 1921, R.R.M./G.C. (1921), T.U.A. Yergan had been lecturing in Tuskegee shortly before this letter of protest.

It came also to the attention of Dr. Carter G. Woodson, the founder and director of the Association for the Study of Negro Life and History, and seemed to him to be an extension to Africa of the white control which he believed interfered with so much of Negro welfare work in the States. Again, much importance must be attached to the seriousness of the charges brought against Jones, as they indicate how widespread suspicions of white manipulation must have been before this particular piece of evidence came their way. The incident is the only explanation of why the scholarly objectivity of his *History of the Negro Church* is interrupted that same year by a single page of unscholarly invective on the subject of white selection methods: 'His business now', he concludes his sketch there of Jones, 'seems to be that of furnishing the world with "handpicked" Negro leaders to damn even the Natives of Africa'.[1]

It no longer mattered exactly how much weight Jones's intervention had had on the decision of the South African Government; it was sufficient that he had urged the greatest caution. And if, Dubois and Woodson argued, he was culpable in the African arena, was it not *a priori* likely that he had been even more active than they had suspected in Negro welfare organizations, and had used similar methods? DuBois thus used the occasion to demonstrate how this was only the culmination of years of activity by Jones, during which Negro college presidents, Y.M.C.A., Y.W.C.A., and other welfare workers had been selected and rejected on the advice of one white man.[2] Though many of the charges would be impossible to prove, both DuBois and Woodson felt sure that the handpicking of Yergan was simply an extension of the monopoly Jones had held over Y.M.C.A. appointments after the First World War.[3]

By this time the fictitious aspects of the case were as firmly believed in as those admitting of some proof, and, more than this, the whole reputation of the Phelps-Stokes Report on West and South Africa was at stake in this test case of its chairman's attitude to the Negro. Not surprisingly both Jones and Loram went to considerable trouble to have the decision of the South African Government reversed, and to reassure their white and Negro constituencies that the misunder-

[1] C. G. Woodson, *The History of the Negro Church* (Washington, 1921), p. 309.

[2] DuBois, 'Thomas Jesse Jones', pp. 254–6.

[3] Ibid. See also p. 54.

standing had been cleared up.[1] Their combined pressure achieved this on 13 July 1921, and Yergan sailed at last for Capetown in November.[2] In view of the fact that he was seriously considering attending DuBois's second Pan-African Congress two days before the ban was withdrawn,[3] it is interesting to speculate what the result might have been for Yergan if the embargo had remained.[4] Despite its satisfactory settlement, the incident would leave many raw nerves, and long after Yergan's work in South Africa was actually receiving financial aid from the Phelps-Stokes Fund itself,[5] it remained an emotional reference-point in Negro memory.[6]

The controversy had blown up not because Jones had wished to practise exclusion of Negro missionaries in general, but through his passionate conviction that Negro missionaries could be found who might have the same beneficial effect upon white governments' stereotyped ideas of Negroes as Aggrey had been having during the Commission's journeys. It was his intention to facilitate the placing of Negroes of Aggrey's type in Africa, but the process demanded a sharper division of Negroes into two readily distinguishable categories than was either feasible or realistic.

Jones certainly bore some responsibility for transferring to the African context his concept of the American Negro in a dualistic universe, where the forces of co-operation battled with those of protest. In America the Negro organizations, from the Y.M.C.A. and the Negro churches to the Negro colleges, were at stake, and Jones considered that the chief threat came from DuBois and the N.A.A.C.P., as he explained confidentially to John Mott:

Their (N.A.A.C.P.) policy is avowedly that of protest. It is therefore natural that they should endeavor to capture the colored leadership and

[1] That the incident had left adverse impressions on white Y.M.C.A. members as well is shown by Carter's comments, after the ban had been lifted, to Jenkins, 30 July 1921 (Box 67, Y.M.C.A. Historical Library): 'Jones has done a great work in Africa on this trip—But it strikes me he is about 20 years behind the times in some things. I don't think he really trusts and believes in the coloured people to the extent a man in his position should'.

[2] Yergan to Moton, 26 Nov. 1921, R.R.M./G.C. (1920), T.U.A.

[3] Yergan to Jenkins, 11 July, 1921, Box 68, Y.M.C.A. Historical Library.

[4] For Yergan's eventual break with the co-operative approach to South Africa, 15 years later, see Yergan to F. V. Slack, 6 Mar. 1936, File E-3, P.S.F.A., also p. 250.

[5] Jones to Yergan, 11 Apr. 1927, File E-3, P.S.F.A.

[6] C. G. Woodson, 'Thomas Jesse Jones', *Journal of Negro History*, xxxv (Jan. 1950), 107–9.

the colored organisations for their program. While we cannot condemn them for their efforts, it seems to me it is the duty of those of us who are interested in the constructive and co-operative programs of such institutions as the schools and the churches to avoid entangling alliances with organisations whose primary functions are protest.[1]

Jones conceived of the struggle for Africa no differently, except that there Marcus Garvey could be as powerful an opponent as DuBois's pan-Africanism. Nor is there any evidence that his interest in communicating this, for him, crucial division between the Negro wings diminished as the result of the Yergan affair. As both Jones and DuBois were in England in August 1921,[2] each winning support for his own view of Africa's greatest needs, Jones might well have felt an added incentive to put the case for Tuskegeeism in Africa to those many missionaries and other influential officials he met. Indeed, to at least two leading authorities on Kenya, Handley Hooper of the C.M.S.,[3] and Norman Leys,[4] a most astringent critic of white Kenya, Jones seems to have presented in the summer of 1921 a strong case for Tuskegee's relevance to racial problems in Africa.

The next year these conversations with Jones returned to Hooper's mind when he saw evidence in Harry Thuku's papers 'of correspondence with Marcus Garvey and his lieutenants',[5] and the notion that the Phelps-Stokes Fund might, in alliance with Tuskegee, counter this threat was now pressing: 'You may remember that I urged you to get the Tuskegee folk to embark upon some form of literary propaganda which might be used out here to familiarise the natives with the ideals of that particular school, before they were prejudiced by the reports of other negro associations.'[6] White missionaries, Hooper realized, would not be very effective agents of Tuskegeeism on their own; he proceeded to imply that there might be a need to employ Tuskegee-type Negroes themselves if an organization was to be established in Kenya adequate to counteract the efforts of radical American Negroes.[7] Thus Garvey's and DuBois's propaganda caused Negro missionaries to be both more in demand and more minutely scrutinized for flaws than ever before.

Clearly the Negro missionary question would soon have to be

[1] Jones to Mott, 20 Feb. 1920, R.R.M./G.C. (1920), T.U.A.

[2] Jones had just returned from the Phelps-Stokes West Africa Commission, and DuBois was preparing for the second Pan-African Congress.

[3] H. D. Hooper's *Leading Strings* (C.M.S. London) was written this year.

[4] For Norman Leys, see further p. 129.

[5] Hooper to Oldham, 10 Aug. 1922, File Q–A, E.H. [6] Ibid. [7] Ibid.

debated within the Conference of British Missionary Societies and its American counterpart, the Foreign Missions Conference of North America. It was no accident that close attention began to be paid to the subject in the year of the Yergan incident; in September 1921 steps were taken by the Committee of Reference and Counsel of the Foreign Missions Conference to set up a committee to study the problems connected with the appointment of Negro missionaries to Africa.[1] Dr. Oldham, who was present *ex officio*, made the interesting comment that the Phelps-Stokes journey of Jones and Aggrey could conceivably have the effect of facilitating the entry of American Negroes of 'a certain type'.[2] On the larger issues of missionary policy on the question he favoured postponing radical decisions for two years, until the meeting of the International Missionary Council (I.M.C.). The committee appointed did, however, submit its report which, besides asking for a fuller investigation, concluded that 'the problem is by no means an easy or a simple one'.[3]

Pressures were beginning to build up which would make it difficult indefinitely to shelve the matter, and not only among American Negroes; Africans too were lending their weight to the same cause. Aggrey had been touring the Southern Negro colleges in the autumn of 1921, and turning the students' minds to African mission. He urged them to consider Yergan's departure as 'an entry wedge'[4] to the continent, and reminded them that the time had come 'when black people themselves ought to do something'. Further, the A.S.U. of America was taking up the issue of its American Negro brethren at the World Student Federation Conference at Peking, and pointing out firmly how the present 'closed door' policy was a contradiction of that Christianity which the Europeans had brought them.[5]

In the end a move was forced on the missionary societies by Governor Coryndon, now of Kenya, who, on receiving a routine Colonial Office circular on missionaries, made the proviso that no Negro missionaries should be admitted to Kenya.[6] In itself this move was no more than a corollary of the Governor's earlier embargo on

[1] Minutes of meeting, 22 Sept. 1921, of the Committee of Reference and Counsel of the Foreign Missions Conference of North America, Division of World Mission and Evangelism, Interchurch Centre, New York.

[2] Ibid. [3] Committee of Reference and Counsel, minute of 8 Dec. 1921.

[4] J. E. K. Aggrey, speech to Hampton students, Oct. 1921, preserved in Monroe Work's file on 'The Negro', 1921, T.U.A.

[5] C. H. Tobias, 'Young Men's Christian Associations in American Negro Colleges', *The Student World*, xvi, No. 2 (Apr. 1923), 60–1.

[6] Coryndon to Devonshire, 19 Feb. 1923, C.O. 533/293, P.R.O.

his African students' going to Negro colleges, but it was, he admitted, further influenced by the American Negro aspect of the Chilembwe rising, and the potential for subversion which the Thuku incident had revealed among the Kenyans.[1]

The Colonial Office naturally had to seek authorization from the British Conference of Missionary Societies for Coryndon's new policy, and they were relieved to find its secretary, J. H. Oldham, 'quite sympathetic', as they had anticipated.[2] Oldham wished to do in the religious sphere what Jones had attempted in the political sphere—to make a distinction between 'negroes trained at Tuskegee or under Booker Washington influences, and those trained in schools in which the Christianity taught was purely of the Psalm singing, prayer-meeting variety'.[3] The former might be valuable for West Africa, the latter, Oldham felt, should be banned from Africa entirely, and, for the moment, even the Tuskegee type should be excluded from Kenya. As to the best means of achieving the Governor's wishes for Kenya, it was felt wisest to avoid a governmental decree but to leave the matter to the missionary societies to manage in their own way. Oldham would ensure that his American counterpart, Fennell P. Turner, 'damped down any movement in the direction of sending Negro missionaries to East Africa',[4] at any rate until the matter had been more fully discussed by the I.M.C. later in the year. In explaining the policy to Turner, Oldham continued to keep the door open for the eventual use of the Tuskegee type:

> I said I was certain that the missionary societies both in Great Britain and America were fully alive to the difficulties involved and that there would be no disposition to press proposals which the Government would find embarrassing. The problem is, How to secure the safeguards which the Government requires in the way which will least give rise to objection and criticism and will not bar negroes trained at Tuskegee when Colonial Governments are willing to avail themselves of the help of this kind of negro, as I believe they are in West Africa.[5]

This policy lasted until July 1923, when advantage was taken of Turner's presence for the I.M.C. Conference[6] to call a meeting of

[1] Ibid. [2] Ibid., minute on Despatch. [3] Ibid. [4] Ibid.

[5] Oldham to Turner, 27 Mar. 1923, C.O. 533/305, P.R.O.

[6] There was cautious approval given to Negro missionaries' working in Africa during the session of the I.M.C. conference; see Minutes of 16 July 1923, in *Minutes of International Missionary Council* (London, n.d.). Such approval must be reconsidered in the light of the meeting at the Colonial Office three days later; see p. 89, n. 2 below.

Oldham, Turner, Bottomley of the Colonial Office, and Governor Coryndon to work out a policy for the longer term. Obviously Negro missionaries could not simply be treated as prohibited immigrants, as in the case of Marcus Garvey's application to come to Kenya in May 1923.[1] Matters must be arranged more diplomatically. Yet it is revealing in this situation, and in the light of American Negro suspicions of this period, what concessions the secretary of the Foreign Missions Conference of North America was prepared to make to Coryndon's stand. Turner volunteered to inform all the recognized missionary societies that Negro missionaries for Kenya would not be welcome, and for the unrecognized societies, he would readily allow his committee to take the line that they 'could not be regarded as equal to the responsibility of looking after negro missionaries'.[2] It could therefore be arranged for any such applications to be turned down by the Passport Central Office in New York in collaboration with himself. Presented with such a readiness to co-operate, Governor Coryndon realized that his object could be achieved without the colonial government's making a specific ruling. With the proviso, presumably due to Oldham, that the 'best type of negro missionaries (e.g. the 'Tuskegee' type)'[3] could be considered for Kenya, he felt that any public and formal discouragement of Negroes such as Turner had offered was both unnecessary and potentially dangerous to Kenya's good name. Coryndon, having thus avoided any discriminatory legislation, 'was well content to leave the matter to Mr. Turner's good offices in individual cases . . . without any reference to the Colonial Government's wishes.'[4] It was a serious concession that had been made by the North American Secretary, for he had assumed total responsibility for interpreting the Governor's wishes. Even though the so-called Tuskegee type was a specific exception to general policy, the result of adopting this distinction of Jones and Oldham would inevitably be to make the Tuskegee missionary more unobtainable than ever. Nor would the visit of Aggrey to Kenya the next year help to lessen the mythical nature of the

[1] Note on Despatch destroyed by statute, Gov. 32018, 29 May 1923, P.R.O. For the Uganda Government's rejection of a highly qualified West Indian doctor (Wallace) in the same month, see A. R. Cook to acting Public Medical Officer, May 13 1923; minute from Scott (Asst. Secretary of Native Affairs), 29 May 1923; and Jarvis to Cook, 6 June 1923, S.M.P. 4689, E.S.A.

[2] Minutes of meeting, 19 July 1923, C.O. 533/305, c.o. 16050, P.R.O.

[3] W. C. Bottomley to Oldham (copy to Turner), 21 July 1923, Archives of the Committee of Reference and Counsel, Interchurch Centre, New York.

[4] Ibid.

Tuskegee missionary and make him more attainable.[1] Aggrey's quite remarkable intelligence and co-operativeness would increase the demand for such a Negro and simultaneously create more unattainable standards.

Exactly how Turner used his extremely influential and delicate position in judging Negro missionary applications, not only for Kenya, but for all African countries, is not known. Certainly, however, during the early 1920s, the agencies, such as the Stewart Missionary Foundation, most intimately connected with sending Negro missionaries to Africa, noted with some incredulity the gap between the professions of European missionaries on the subject and the manifest difficulty in practice of entering Africa. Dr. Martin commented on the anomalies of the situation from the Foundation's point of view in the very month when lines of policy were being worked out in London:

> Dr. James Henderson [of Lovedale] on tour in America is reported as saying in a series of addresses he has delivered in this country that there is an open door for the American Negro workers, who are well trained as teachers, and social workers and similar callings, on the continent of Africa. We rejoice in this good word of promise to the ambitious student in America who is committed to the uplift and redemption of Africa. We have not found it quite so easy for our people to gain access to Africa . . . for an American Negro however well prepared to find access to the schools of Africa as a teacher, or to enter the continent as a preacher, Y.M.C.A. worker or in any form of social uplift work has been understood as a difficult undertaking. May a new and better day of privilege soon come.[2]

Even if it was scarcely an 'open door' policy that the missionary societies had been developing with the Government, Jones and Oldham were now under some obligation to show the value of their sharp distinctions between Negroes. Nor would occasions be lacking. For in both Uganda and Kenya progressive missionaries would be sufficiently impressed by Aggrey's co-operative brilliance to demand American Negroes of his type for their own work. Oldham proceeded to explain to Jones one of these schemes suggested by a C.M.S. missionary to Uganda; the combination of caution with the disinclination to initiate the scheme in Kenya may well imply the continuing force of Coryndon's policy:

[1] See pp. 191–2.

[2] D. D. Martin, 'The open door for American Negroes in Africa', *Foundation*, xiii (July/Aug. 1923), 7.

I think you are agreed that we must do something to bring about the co-operation of the American coloured people in the uplift of the African race; and are also agreed that the experiment can succeed only if it is made under the most favourable conditions ... I am inclined to think however that the experiment could be made much more hopefully in the beginning under missionary than under Government auspices and that Uganda is a more favourable field than Kenya . . . The relation of the coloured community in America to Africa is a matter of such magnitude, importance and difficulty that it deserves the best thought that we can give to it.[1]

As it is the question of the general policy to be adopted towards the Negro missionary by the European and American Boards that is under consideration at the moment, the obstacles peculiar to some of these schemes may be deferred until after the Phelps-Stokes Commission in East Africa has been examined. Clearly, however, much more thought had now to be given in Oldham's view to marking out some legitimate place for the American Negro in Africa. It was fortunate that a convenient occasion was approaching, in the 1926 Le Zoute conference on the Christian mission in Africa. Both Jones and Oldham were on the business committee of this conference and, it may be assumed, were pre-eminently responsible for the appointment of a strong committee of thirty-four leading figures from missionary, government and philanthropist fields who might give the subject their fullest attention. The Phelps-Stokes Fund was strongly represented on the committee: Dr. Anson Phelps Stokes was chairman, and other members of the Phelps-Stokes Commissions serving were A. W. Wilkie, Dr. Thomas Jesse Jones, Dr. C. T. Loram, and Dr. J. H. Dillard. Also important were J. H. Oldham and Sir Frederick Lugard, and, by a nice juxtaposition, the Colonial Secretary of Kenya, E. B. Denham, and Max Yergan.

While the entire two pages of findings and recommendations are a highly significant commentary on the subject, certain features are particularly relevant in view of what has been seen of the informal agreements between governments and mission secretaries.[2] First, it was claimed that the present difficulties derived either from the obstacles placed in the Negroes' way by African governments, or from the unsatisfactory results of some American Negroes' work in

[1] Oldham to Jones, 4 June 1925, File 314, E.H., now I.M.C.A., Geneva.

[2] E. W. Smith, *The Christian Mission in Africa: a study based on the proceedings of the International Conference at Le Zoute, Belgium. September 14th to 21st, 1926* (London, 1926), pp. 122–4.

Africa.[1] There was no suggestion that white mission boards might in any way bear partial responsibility. So far from even hinting at this, there was included, as one of the chief recommendations, a proposal that Negroes should be increasingly required to go out to Africa 'under the auspices of responsible societies of recognised and well-established standing'.[2] In addition to thus proposing that Negroes should generally work through responsible societies, any Negro missionary society applying to initiate work in Africa should similarly be encouraged to work through a society of longer standing, and should direct its special attention to the unevangelized districts. The committee recognized that these recommendations were an incomplete and unsatisfactory series of steps along a complex route. They had made concessions to governmental fears of independent Negro missionaries operating in Africa, and in doing so had possibly made it more rather than less hard to serve as a Negro missionary, for there would now be additional complicated decisions about salary and status involved in serving within the framework of a well established white society.

If the Le Zoute conference had not produced a charter for the American Negro's mission in Africa, and had reached its conclusions without self-criticism, there was clearly nothing tactfully guarded in the study that DuBois felt compelled to make on the subject some two years later.[3] Of the 'responsible societies of recognised and well-established standing'[4] that the Le Zoute conference had referred to as preferable vehicles for American Negro service, DuBois revealed, as the result of a questionnaire, that of the 793 missionaries sent to Africa by such societies as 'the United Presbyterian; the United Mission Society; the United Brethren; the Africa Inland Mission; the Friends; the Brethren in Christ; the Southern Baptists; the Women's General Missionary Society of the U.P.C.; the Lutherans; the Sudan Interior Mission; there is not a single American Negro'.[5] These figures were only slightly less startling for the boards which did have some tradition of engaging Negroes; but considering that it was very largely these boards which had drawn up the recommendations of the Le Zoute committee for a deliberate drive to encourage Negro missionaries, little progress appears to have been made in the three years.[6]

[1] Ibid., pp. 122–3. [2] Ibid., p. 124.
[3] W. E. B. DuBois, 'Missionaries', *The Crisis*, xxxvi, No. 5 (May 1929), 168.
[4] Smith, *Christian Mission in Africa*, p. 124.
[5] DuBois, 'Missionaries', p. 168. [6] Ibid.

DuBois might be relied on to spell out quite openly the failings of white American Christianity, but that he was not fabricating a grievance that was not more widely felt is shown by evidence from a much more conservative quarter. Tuskegee's long experience of adjusting its ideals to Southern white racism had given its graduates the reputation of being extraordinarily co-operative; and it will be remembered that both Oldham and Jones had tried to convince missionary Boards of the need to distinguish Tuskegee men from other sorts of Negro. Yet, for all this, it does not appear that men with the 'Tuskegee spirit' found it any easier to enter Africa than Garvey's lieutenants. For instance in 1924, when a well-wisher suggested supporting some student at Tuskegee who might be thinking of the African mission field, the president, Robert Moton, was forced to point out that although he had quite a number of students ready to go to Africa, there was absolutely no sense in supporting them through college for missionary careers when at the end of it no organization would be willing to enlist them.[1]

Nor was it any easier for Tuskegee men even after Le Zoute; for when Moton was criticized by a white Alabaman in 1930 for not attending sufficiently to African missions, his readiness to explain the normally unmentioned aspects of Negro mission is the greater testimony to real grievance:

> Over against these facts is the equally significant one that the Presbyterian Church of North America has steadfastly *refused* to send any American Negroes, whatever their qualifications, to work in Africa though dozens of them have offered themselves for this service. It is also true that the European Governments have refused to admit American Negroes to serve as missionaries in their respective territories . . . I think I am safe in saying that no other workers in Africa face such great obstacles either on the field itself or in attempting to enter the field as American Negroes, in spite of which they are found there today doing their best in as noble a spirit of self-sacrifice as any workers who have ever gone there.[2]

It was mentioned earlier that when Thuku and Kamulegeya appealed to Tuskegee for American Negro educators and advisers, no answer came, or if it did it has not survived. There may have been extremes of expression in Thuku's letter which could account for its not being attended to, and Kamulegeya's request may have seemed a little unrealistic. There is a sense, however, in which Moton answered

[1] Moton to A. D. Reynolds, 10 Apr. 1924, R.R.M./Misc. (1918–34), T.U.A.

[2] Moton to Miss L. Robertson, 7 May 1930, R.R.M./G.C. (1930), T.U.A.

these letters with the words quoted above, and some of the workings of white missionary accommodationism that have been seen in this chapter also form part of the answer.

Those early ventures in pan-Africanism failed to achieve their most concrete object, the introduction of American Negroes as the collaborators of the young politically-minded Africans. But no failure or proscription could prevent the slowly-growing consciousness of Negro unity that white prejudice had nurtured. The wiser of the missionaries in East Africa saw that these pan-African aspirations of the young Africans were modelled on the internationalism of the European and Indian communities in their midst. Handley Hooper believed such growth in articulate, unified form along the colour line was inevitable, and that only one measure could prevent it from taking a dangerous turn:

> Much as we may desire to isolate the several fields and problems of the negro world, the presence of the European with his world-wide interests and the Indian with his nationalistic newspapers will defeat our purpose.
>
> West Africa, South Africa, East Africa and the negro element in America will not always remain separate entities in a black world. The interests of the negro are no longer tribal in extent, and his instincts will prompt him to seek a wider federation for his self-expression. The boundaries of this new confederacy will almost inevitably be suggested by colour. The subtle bonds of racial hope will defy the difference of local problems, and artificial political restriction. The only way to counter-act the complications which will arise is to foresee them, and to provide without delay a wise and liberal education which will minimise causes of complaint and will frustrate the mischievous machinations of self-appointed agitators.[1]

There was only three years' delay between Hooper's writing this in 1921 and the coming to Kenya of the Phelps-Stokes Educational Commission. It would have many problems to face, and conflicting aims to reconcile; but there was one which might well deserve its especial attention—the aspirations of the group whose educational ambitions and political consciousness had been heightened in part by contact with the same Negro South from which the Phelps-Stokes Commission drew its inspiration.

[1] Hooper, *Leading Strings*, pp. 8–9.

CHAPTER IV

The Phelps-Stokes Commission in Kenya

THE SECOND Phelps-Stokes Commission arose out of the success of the first, whose origins were traced in Chapter II. In fact, during the three years (1920–3) that separated the sailings of the two missions to Africa, an educational policy considered appropriate to Africans had begun to evolve, which commanded the support of leading missionaries, colonial educationists, and even the Colonial Office itself. This had been quite largely due to the very wide appeal in post-war Africa of Jones's formula for adapted Negro education.

It was not that there was anything particularly novel in Jones's approach to Africa. Individually the points he emphasized had been known to one African educationist or another for the best part of a hundred years. The importance of industry and agriculture had been noted as early as the 1847 Select Committee of the Privy Council, and had been fully exemplified in the work of the Basel Mission, and at Lovedale, Blantyre, and Livingstonia.[1] The notion that education should be adapted to the African— 'adaptation' was the keyword of the West Africa commission—had been Blyden's theme for some forty years, and had been shared by Henry Venn and James Johnson. The Africanization of the curriculum had been the stock in trade of the indirect rulers of northern Nigeria, and had found its way into the Bo School for Chiefs' sons in Sierra Leone.[2] The priority of rural village education, with its counterpart of a healthy, contented peasantry, spanned the century from the export of English village life to the Sierra Leone settlers in the 1810s to Alek Fraser's Village Education Commission of 1920.[3] What was new was the

[1] See further Foster, *Education and Social Change in Ghana*, pp. 54–6; and Curtin, *The Image of Africa*, p. 427. On the industrial philosophy of Lovedale, Livingstonia, and Blantyre, see Stewart, *Dawn in the Dark Continent* Chs. vii, viii. See also pp. 44–7 above.

[2] For the Bo School prospectus, 29 Sept. 1905, see C. Fyfe, *Sierra Leone Inheritance* (London, 1964), pp. 303–7. For northern Nigeria, see Sonia F. Graham, *Government and Mission Education in Northern Nigeria, 1900–1919, with special reference to the work of Hanns Vischer* (Ibadan, 1966).

[3] Fyfe, *A History of Sierra Leone*, pp. 128, 131, *Village Education in India. A Commission of Inquiry* (London, 1920); cf. also Ward, *Fraser of Trinity and Achimota*, ch. vii.

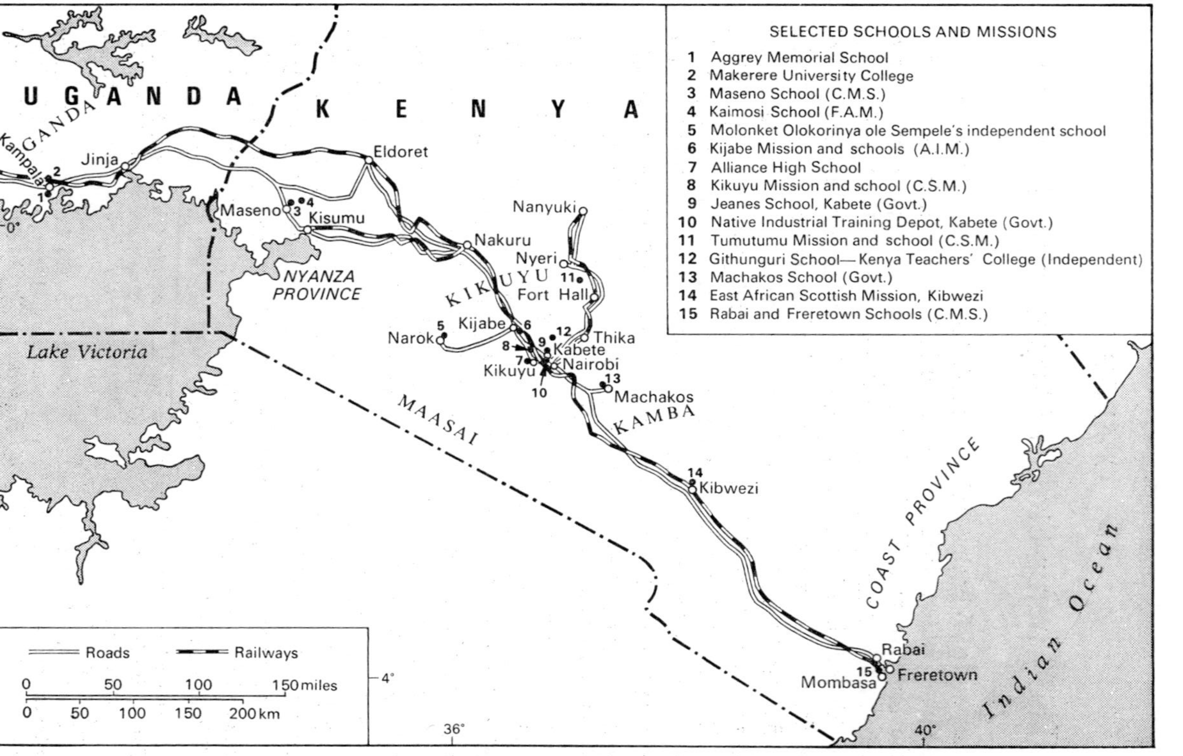

Map 2. Kenya and Eastern Uganda

attempt to demonstrate the importance of these principles through case studies and analyses of individual schools in western Africa from Monrovia to Capetown.

There were two self-evident general principles to be applied to African as to Negro education in the States: adaptation and community consciousness, and these two values could be best embodied in schools through emphasis on what Jones called the 'Simples' of health, home life training, industry (including agriculture), and recreation.[1] The work of the Phelps-Stokes Commission had been therefore to assess several hundred schools by these criteria, ranking them by the extent of their adaptation to the 'realities' of African conditions; western academic curricula were thus less real than agricultural schools, and nothing was more unrealistic than Greek or Latin in an African school.[2]

These principles—almost slogans—of African education were particularly compelling to both mission and government. They suggested a fresh start from the grass roots in the village schools, and the principle of community consciousness accorded well with the traditional anti-élitism of so much educational policy in Africa. Moreover, adaptation and the concern for the African-ness of education answered adequately the many people who were disturbed by the detribalization and the destruction of African life and culture. Adaptation and indirect rule could easily coexist.

The impact of the first commission was also attributable to Jones's flair for publicity, and his production of the really authoritative-looking *Education in Africa*, which presented his recommendations with a masterly battery of data and photographs. There had been nothing quite like this in the field of African education, and, even if there were close correspondences with Jones's *Negro Education* report, few probably noticed that whole passages had been lifted intact from his earlier work.[3]

The case for African education's departing from white, western standards was presented more cogently than before, and there was a corresponding response from influential educators in many parts of West and South Africa who had themselves been moving towards such a conclusion. It placed a seal of international approval on the plans of individual men, endorsing their own initiatives in adapting

[1] Jones, *Education in Africa*, pp. 16–37.
[2] Ibid., pp. 26, 67, 76, 109–11.
[3] Ibid., pp. 60–1, 66–7, 70–4, for example.

western education to the African environment. It was precisely because the commission confirmed the soundness of his own experiments that Governor Guggisberg of the Gold Coast could greet *Education in Africa* as 'the book of the century.'[1] South African educators too, although differing very radically from Guggisberg over Africans' ultimate educational and political status, felt their moves towards differentiating African from European education had been blessed by the commission. It was not to be the last time that adaptation was interpreted as education 'along their own lines'.[2]

Undoubtedly another factor that contributed to the success of the commission was its quasi-political role in promoting interracialism in several areas of racial tension. The tour had revealed James Aggrey's quite extraordinary gifts for creating racial harmony; he spoke several hundred times to black, white, and mixed audiences, and, sharing the platform with his white colleagues, embodied the Tuskegee spirit of reconciliation and co-operation in the face of militant black nationalism and anti-European feeling. The political significance of his presence was noted by the African lecturer at the South African Native College, D. D. T. Jabavu, in a very penetrating account of Aggrey's tour of South Africa:

> His African origin was a real advantage to him for it gave him the ear of the whites who otherwise, on account of their dread of Ethiopian doctrines, are always suspicious of American Negroes; whilst it secured him the attention of the indigenous Africans who, ever since the reports of Marcus Garvey's Black Star Fleet, have had their eyes turned to overseas Negroes for succour from the prevailing economic depression as well as for liberation from the injustice of the white man in whom they are tending to lose faith. He convinced the former in a single address more effectually than any amount of argument has done in a generation, that in the British colonies and America there are Negro intellectuals who have assimilated European culture in its refined form with rational mentality; while he disillusioned the latter of the African Republic mirage, giving them instead an edifying message of self-help based on Booker Washington's principles and on Christian ethics.[3]

This political aspect was of considerable importance when it came to considering a parallel commission for East Africa. The Thuku

[1] *Gold Coast, Legislative Council Debates, 1923–4*, p. 56.

[2] Smith, *Aggrey of Africa*, pp. 164–84. A. V. Murray, *The School in the Bush* (2nd edn., London, 1938), p. 306, and Appendix II, 'Education under Indirect Rule'.

[3] Biographical material on Aggrey collected in C. H. Fahs Papers, Missionary Research Library (hereafter M.R.L.), Union Theological College, New York.

troubles and the Indian crisis were very much in the minds of those pressing for an East African Phelps-Stokes Commission, and to Jones and Oldham in particular it seemed that there were few places where initiatives in co-operation were more needed than Kenya.

With Oldham the chance of another educational commission fitted into a somewhat broader strategy. For several years now he had felt that Jones had a prescription for co-operation between mission and government which, if heeded by the missions, could secure the place of the specifically Christian school as governments increasingly took control of education in Africa.[1] In addition to its other insights, the report of the West and South Africa Commission had skilfully presented an agenda for co-operation in which the role of the mission school was described as that of 'a leavening centre' or an 'experiment station',[2] and it was this notion of the mission school as the imaginative ally of the Government in African education for which Oldham now sought official approval.

Thus, very shortly after the publication of *Education in Africa* in 1922, he felt the missionary position strong enough to suggest to the Colonial Office his case for co-operation between mission and government in African education. The result was Oldham's memorandum, *Educational Policy in Africa*, a closely argued defence of the mission's place in any future government plans.[3] He was able to use the Phelps-Stokes Commission (which had been mission-sponsored) as his strongest card, to show the missionaries' determination to put their house in order. Also he began in this document the process of introducing into the mainstream of British colonial educational policy some of the characteristic Phelps-Stokes emphases. The tone of his recommendations not only followed closely Jones's *Education in Africa*, with its pleas for a differentiated African education, but pointed beyond this to the source of that adaptation in the work of the Hampton and Tuskegee Institutes:

> The aims of native educational policy are first the improvement of the life of the masses of the people. This will include the giving to them a better knowledge of the nature and cultivation of the soil, of agricultural processes and of the raising of stock, the spreading among them of a better

[1] See pp. 52–3.

[2] Jones, *Education in Africa*, p. 91. For Booker Washington's earlier use of the term 'experimental station', see p. 20.

[3] *Educational Policy in Africa: a memorandum submitted on behalf of the Education Committee of the Conference of Missionary Societies in Great Britain and Ireland* (London, 1923).

understanding of the laws of health and sanitation, the development of simple industries related to village life, the giving of a simple elementary education adapted to village conditions, the training of them in habits of industry, perseverance, honesty and thrift, and, through all these activities as well as by direct teaching, supplying them with the motives that will build up strong and stable character.[1]

The memorandum led directly to the calling of a major conference of African Governors and church leaders, with Oldham and Jesse Jones, in June 1923 by W. A. Ormsby-Gore, Under-Secretary of State for the Colonies. This decided unanimously that a Colonial Office Advisory Committee on African education should be established. There was thus centred in London a body, some of whose leading members were deeply aware of the need to avoid in Africa the mistakes of educational policy in other regions such as India, China, and the Southern States of America. Sir Michael Sadler had made specialized studies of American Negro and Indian university education;[2] Oldham, too, drew heavily on the American South, and Lord Lugard and Sir James Currie (first principal of Gordon College, Khartoum) represented some of the best thought on African education from West and East Africa respectively.[3] Indeed, it is some indication of the debt of that committee to the experience of Negro education in the United States that Jesse Jones should have been the first man seriously to be considered for the secretaryship.[4] When that proved impossible, negotiations were started to secure the South African educationist, C. T. Loram, who had played such an important role as a part-time member of the Phelps-Stokes Commission in southern Africa; and it was only when these too had failed that Hanns Vischer was appointed, his own experience having been gained chiefly from indirect-rule education in northern Nigeria.[5] Finally, Ormsby-Gore, announcing the formation of this permanent committee in the House, acknowledged that it had been largely an outgrowth of 'a most extraordinarily interesting report issued by

[1] Ibid., p. 2.

[2] 'Education of the Coloured Race', and *Calcutta University Commission, 1917–1919. Report*, 13 vols. (Calcutta, 1919–20).

[3] For Lord Lugard on education, see Lugard, *The Dual Mandate in British Tropical Africa* (London, 1965), chs. xxi, xxii, and Ayandele, *Missionary Impact on Modern Nigeria*, pp. 303–4, also Lugard, 'Education in Tropical Africa', *Edinburgh Review*, 242, July 1925, 1–19.

[4] Oldham to Ormsby-Gore, 8 June 1923; Ormsby-Gore to Oldham, 9 June 1923, File 'Africa: General: Education' (hereafter Q-E), E.H.

[5] Loram File, Q-E, E.H., also Ashby, *Universities*, p. 158.

Dr. Jesse Jones', and mentioned that an East African Educational Commission was in the planning stage.[1]

These decisions were very opportune for Oldham, apart from the protection they offered to mission interests; Governor Coryndon of Kenya had just agreed to Jones's and Aggrey's reporting on education in East Africa,[2] in the very month that a White Paper on Indians in Kenya had set forth the doctrine that, in any conflict among Kenya's mixed population, 'the interests of the African natives must be paramount'.[3] There would now be provided, Oldham saw, after three years' continuously hostile criticism of white Kenya's labour ordinances and Indian policy, an opportunity for its settlers and government to vindicate their reputation and show responsible trusteeship in education. Although Oldham had played a leading part in the organization of the years of protest,[4] he had recently begun to believe that external pressure would be insufficient to solve Kenya's deep difficulties; lasting progress, he explained to Governor Coryndon, must involve local initiatives in good will:

> It has, however, become increasingly clear to me that, while the Imperial Govt. has responsibilities which it must do its best to discharge, no *real* solution of the problems of Kenya can be reached in London, but only in Kenya itself. The things I should like to see done for the native population, if they are to be done at all, must, I am fully convinced, be done with the assent and co-operation of the European community.[5]

Following the traditions of philanthropy in the Southern States, it was the task of the commission to show the various sections of the European community that the interests of African and European were not necessarily opposed, and to win the active co-operation of the best element of the settler class in the cause of African education. For such an end the membership of the commission could scarcely have been improved upon.

In Dr. Dillard, president of the Jeanes and Slater Funds, and

[1] T. J. Jones, *Education in East Africa: A Study of East, Central and South Africa* (New York, 1925), pp. xix–xx.

[2] Bottomley to Oldham, 21 May 1923, C.O. 533/305, P.R.O.

[3] *Indians in Kenya*. Cmd. 1922 (23 July 1923), p. 10. Cf. also Files 'East Africa-Indians', E.H. See further J. Mangat, *History of Asians in East Africa* (Oxford, 1969), especially ch. iv.

[4] Oldham had played a most significant part in the protest against the 1919 Labour Ordinance in Kenya; see File on Labour, E.H. Cf. also Bennett, *Kenya*, p. 44, and N. Leys, *Kenya* (London, 1924), p. 201.

[5] Oldham to Coryndon, 16 Jan. 1924, File 'East Africa: Tanganyika: Education' (hereafter Q-R), E.H.

member of the General Education Board,[1] there was the very powerful example of the Southern gentleman wholly converted to belief in the value of education for the Negro. His assignment in Kenya was primarily to hold informal conversations with influential settlers, in the hope that they might be persuaded a little way towards realizing the value to themselves of African education. Oldham meanwhile reassured the Governor of Dillard's interracial tact:

> It would, as you are aware, be impossible for him to retain the regard and confidence of the white South, if he had any touch of the faddist or sentimentalist. At the same time he has given much of his strength to helping the negro community and furthering their education on wise lines. He is a man who, I am certain, will commend himself to the European community in Kenya.[2]

Almost as important as Dillard, and the strongest proof of his message that education need not ruin the Negro, would be J. E. K. Aggrey. If, Oldham briefed Coryndon, Aggrey's experience in South and West Africa was anything to go by, then Kenya could only benefit from his twin convictions—that education must 'begin at the bottom and not at the top,' and that no controversy or protest must endanger the chance of racial co-operation.[3] It was not that Aggrey necessarily counselled submission to white racism as a strategy in itself; rather, he had worked out a philosophy of black pride in the cultural sphere, while in the more controversial areas he assumed that white justice and altruism would respond to African patience and humility. He summarized the attitude which he would take with him to East Africa a few days before he left America to join the commission:

> Wherever I go, I shall give this message, which I have found in the colleges and universities of this continent. A new spirit is coming throughout the South and the North. Let us be patient. You can never beat prejudice by a frontal attack, because there is mere emotion at the root of it. When there is emotion at the root of anything you cannot beat it by a frontal attack. Always flank it. You can catch more flies with molasses and sugar than you can with vinegar.[4]

[1] Dillard's previous work in the Southern States is sympathetically recounted by B. Brawley, *Dr. Dillard of the Jeanes Fund* (New York, 1930).

[2] Oldham to Coryndon, 16 Jan. 1924. [3] Ibid.

[4] J. E. K. Aggrey, 'Africa', in M. Stauffer (Ed.), *Christian Students and World Problems. Report of the Ninth International Convention of the Student Volunteer Movement for Foreign Missions, Indianapolis, Indiana, December 28th, 1923 to January 1st, 1924* (New York, 1924), p. 173.

Two other members who helped to make this commission more weighty than the West and South Africa one were Major Hanns Vischer, the newly-appointed permanent secretary of the Advisory Committee on Native Education in Tropical Africa,[1] and Dr. Shantz, a leading agriculturalist in the U.S. Department of Agriculture. Missionary representation was provided by Dr. Garfield Williams of the C.M.S., and J. W. C. Dougall of the Free Church of Scotland. The commission was led by Jones, who had already been assured that Coryndon 'heartily welcomed' the tour.[2]

The commission was thus very far from having a purely educational brief; it was certainly conceived of by its chief architects, Oldham and Jones, as providing a test case of Kenya's trusteeship intentions. Education was being given a mandate status and was being opened to international inspection. It seemed possible, moreover, especially with a Parliamentary Commission to East Africa also imminent,[3] that certain large concessions to native development might be obtained, and a new advance in African education secured.[4]

In Kenya itself, apart from the general issue of a mandate for African education and development in a white settlement country (which the 1923 White Paper had sought to solve), two specific educational problems had become apparent, and had both reached crisis proportions in the month before the commission sailed. The industrial education policy of the Department of Education and its director had fallen into disrepute, and the missions felt hanging over them the threat that their influence might at any moment be reduced by a battery of government secular schools with a corresponding model teacher-training college. The latter was precisely the sort of conflict which Oldham had anticipated would arise after the war. To understand, however, the task of the commission in finding a formula for co-operation here, and in hammering out an acceptable policy for African education, it is necessary to trace something of the stubborn history of these two issues.

The process is revealing; in effect Jesse Jones in 1924 was going to sit in judgement on the educational achievements of a department whose director had for thirteen years quite deliberately worked to transfer the insights of Tuskegee and Hampton to Africa. J. R. Orr

[1] For Vischer's experience, see Graham, op. cit.
[2] Oldham to Sir H. Read, 19 Sept. 1923, File Q-E, E.H.
[3] *Report of the East Africa Commission.* Cmd. 2387 (Apr. 1925).
[4] Oldham to Vischer, 1 Feb. 1924, File Q-E, E.H.

had initiated this Tuskegee policy when the Education Department had been established in 1911, but even prior to that African education had been taking on a thoroughly industrial character. Nor was this a question of the Government's forcing an industrial policy upon unwilling missionary societies; some of the educationally more developed missions had already articulated an industrial philosophy for African schools. The C.M.S., even apart from its nineteenth century initiatives in industry on the Kenya coast, had begun actively to promote to the Government in 1908 the idea of an industrial school,[1] and parallel with this, both the Friend's Africa Mission (F.A.M.) in Nyanza, and the Church of Scotland Mission (C.S.M.) at Kikuyu and Tumutumu had for reasons of self-sufficiency and greater evangelizing impact built industry and agriculture into their mission systems during the first decade of the twentieth century.[2] Government action over the next twenty years was merely going to determine where the emphasis should be placed in industrial training.

That few questioned the premises that African education should be primarily of an industrial nature can be seen from the first report dealing with the training of Africans in Kenya. Indeed, the terms of reference given to Professor J. Nelson Fraser of Bombay in undertaking his investigation in 1909 were 'not to put forward plans for the literary education of negroes, but to consider the possibilities of developing industries amongst them'.[3] With the strongest encouragement from missionaries, Fraser was led to recommend to the Government an industrial apprenticeship scheme through indentures.[4] He reasoned that missions and government might thus begin a fruitful co-operation to replace relatively expensive Indian artisans by African; or as H. E. Scott, head of the C.S.M. put it, placing his finger very early on one of the many political aspects of industrial education:

[1] Sir J. Sadler to Secretary of State, 15 Sept. 1908, C.O. 533/47, P.R.O.

[2] Friends' Africa Industrial Mission, Minute Book 1902–1907, microfilm no. 7, i, University College, Nairobi. For the agricultural policies of the C.S.M., see H. E. Scott to Dr. Robertson, 15 Mar. 1911, P.C.E.A., A/9. The C.S.M.'s industrial policy was itself a continuation of that of its predecessor in Kenya, the East African Scottish Mission, see B. G. McIntosh, 'The Scottish Mission in Kenya, 1891–1923' (Univ. of Edinburgh Ph.D. thesis 1969), pp. 53, 58. See also map of Kenya.

[3] *Leader of British East Africa* (hereafter *L.B.E.A.*), 30 Oct. 1909.

[4] *L.B.E.A.*, 26 June 1909; also *Report of United Missionary Conference, 7–11th June, 1909* (Nairobi, 1909), also Scott to W. M. McLachlan, 9 Mar. 1909, P.C.E.A., A/3.

PLATE V

Johnstone Kenyatta 'Working with the hands' in Kikuyu Mission. (From J. W. Arthur's photograph albums, Edinburgh University Library.)

The Europeans are now beginning to see that one way of getting rid of the Indian is to train the native to take his place! I am telling everybody that that is the only solution of the problem . . . And so the Government Board may take up the policy of subsidising liberally the industrial missions for the ultimate object, not of helping mission work, but of getting rid of the Indian.[1]

In proposing an industrial formula, however, Fraser felt that he was also making an assault on those undesirable qualities—self-conceit and insolence—that were assumed to follow from giving Africans a liberal education. Interestingly enough, he turned to the Southern States of America for an antidote to the swelled head in Africa. 'It appears to me', he argued, 'there is a book by a negro which would serve to counteract this error—Booker Washington's Autobiography —which should be familiar to every one who has to deal with negro education.'[2]

With J. R. Orr appointed Director of Education, an era of government-mission co-operation in the training of African artisans began. Government grants-in-aid went, through a system of payment by results, to some eight mission schools capable of trade training, and by the First World War almost one hundred indentured apprentices had been produced.[3] Orr was not, however, content merely to administer such grants; he wanted the adoption of a policy that took into account the African's political status in a white settlement country—an education adapted to the African's psychology and to his economic needs. Well-versed in current educational literature on under-developed areas, he turned, like Fraser, to Washington for confirmation of his principles:

[1] Scott to McLachlan, 22 Feb. 1911, A/9, P.C.E.A.; also Scott to Sir P. Girouard, 9 Nov. 1910, A/9, P.C.E.A.

[2] *L.B.E.A.*, 13 Nov. 1909. Also J. Nelson Fraser, *Report on Education in the East Africa Protectorate* (Nairobi, 1909), *passim*.

[3] J. R. Orr, 'The System of Education in the East Africa Protectorate' (Dec. 1912), *Imperial Education Conference Papers, III, Educational Systems of the Chief Colonies not possessing Responsible Government* (H.M.S.O., London, 1915), pp. 34–5. Also *Evidence of the Education Commission of the East Africa Protectorate 1919* (Nairobi, n.d.), p. 180.

The indenture system, however, was from the start most unattractive to some Africans, among whom was Johnstone Kamau (now President Kenyatta). For an account of Kenyatta's refusal to apprentice himself at the C.S.M. Kikuyu, see Arthur to McLachlan, 15 Feb. 1929. File Q-A, E.H. For Johnstone Kamau working at carpentry in the Kikuyu mission prior to his refusal to indenture himself, see Plate V.

We have now our opportunity and I trust that all Educational bodies . . . will unite in adopting an uniform political doctrine. The one man alone who has given serious consideration to the problem and has done more educational work on behalf of the negro than any educational society, is himself a mulatto (I refer to Booker Washington) and he is holding his people back and attempting to divert their attention from politics to useful industry because he realises the hopelessness of competition between black and white.[1]

But when Orr claimed that the policy of his department was 'based upon the excellent work of that great negro, the late Mr. Booker Washington—a book entitled *Working with the Hands*', he intended more than that Africans should eschew politics and consider themselves uneducated until their technical achievements matched the whites.[2] He had accepted Washington's wider conviction that every people had to proceed through the stages of agriculture and industry to a state of self-sufficiency. Only then could cultural or liberal education be justified; 'With an ignorant or a poverty stricken race,' he quoted from Washington, 'the problem of bread-winning must precede that of culture.'[3] He had also taken over the notion from Washington, C. T. Loram, and Dudley Kidd that manual training was peculiarly important for its effects on African psychological development, whether it led to an artisan career or not.[4] It was these twin values of industrial training to the individual and to the native community in the Reserves that Orr sought to popularize among missionary leaders in Kenya by circulating copies of his ' "Bible" of Native education', *Working with the Hands*.[5]

However, this very devotion to Washington led Orr to desire the creation of schools that would wield as much influence over native education as Tuskegee and Hampton had in the Southern States. He felt the attraction of their non-denominationalism, in contrast

[1] Orr to Bishop Allegeyer (copy to Arthur), 25 Mar. 1912, unfiled Education Bundle, P.C.E.A.

[2] *Kenya Education Department Annual Report for 1924* (hereafter *KEDAR 1924*) (Nairobi, n.d.), p. 18; Orr to Arthur, 24 Dec. 1913, Education Bundle, P.C.E.A.

[3] Orr to Canon Leakey, 18 Aug. 1919, Education Bundle, P.C.E.A.

[4] *KEDAR 1924*, pp. 19–20. On the analogy of 'mental defectives' and 'feeble-minded' children in Europe, Orr and Kidd prescribed handwork for Africans; cf. Kidd, *Kafir Socialism*, p. 184. For Orr's knowledge of other African educationists, see Orr to E. B. Denham, 22 Nov. 1923, 'African Education in Kenya' enclosed in Coryndon to Devonshire, 10 Jan. 1924, C.O. 533/308, P.R.O.

[5] Orr to Leakey, 18 Aug. 1919.

with the internecine feuds over spheres of influence that so disfigured missionary work in Kenya. It is not surprising that at times Orr wished devoutly to create national institutions untrammelled by conscience clauses and compulsory dogmatic teaching. This had led him, indeed, to establish the first government model industrial school among the Kamba at Machakos in 1912, a scheme which he described to the Imperial Education Conference of 1915 as 'frankly and without apology based on Tuskegee'.[1] With its headmaster a former staff sergeant of the Royal Engineers, it copied from the American South too that 'semi-military discipline' thought appropriate to the evolving Negro.[2]

Machakos had appeared as an ominous move to a small number of Kenya missionaries before the First World War, perhaps principally to J. W. Arthur, head of the C.S.M. after Scott's death; but any possibility of Orr's establishing government model schools all over Kenya was ruled out by the war. Nevertheless, as Oldham had foreseen, the war years had greatly strengthened the government's determination to control the direction of education, and it was with this aim in view that an Education Commission for the East Africa Protectorate was appointed in 1918.

The commission paid considerable attention to the question of the best agency to undertake African education, and to the curriculum, and on balance the missions could be satisfied with its recommendations; great emphasis was laid upon the government's working through missionary schools. Borrowing a leaf from the book of the South African Native Affairs Commission (1903–5) they accepted that secular education could be no substitute for religious instruction, especially when Africans were abandoning their traditional value systems. They were thus able strongly to condemn Orr's proposals for a secular government teacher-training college, with its twelve government feeder schools.[3] On the question of the curriculum for African schools also, they inclined more towards missionary than settler preferences. Payment by results was summarily abolished, and although it was agreed that 'technical education should be the principal aim and object of native schools', it was nowehere suggested that this could be divorced from literary education. There were

[1] Orr, 'The System of Education in the East Africa Protectorate', p. 24.

[2] *Evidence of the Education Commission of the East Africa Protectorate 1919*, p. 186.

[3] *Report of the Education Commission of the East Africa Protectorate 1919* (Nairobi, n.d.), pp. 7–8, paras. 39, 47, 48.

other objectives for African education, they cautioned, besides creating skilled labour.[1]

On what was becoming the really crucial issue, however, the commission said nothing. Was technical and industrial education going to be primarily for the development of the native Reserves, or for the settler economy? Many of those who gave evidence to the 1919 commission had little doubt that industrial education should produce semi-skilled illiterate artisans to work for white farmers, builders, and planters.[2] As pressure grew from the post-war influx of settlers, a further Technical Education Committee was set up, which might spell out what the earlier report had left unsaid. Its recommendations were made at the height of the crisis over the political and economic future of the Indians in Kenya, and something of its crash programme for African artisans (a thousand to be trained over a five-year period) must be traced to the desire to supplant the Indians. With efficiency and the priority of the interests of the settler economy as the keynotes of their report, it was not surprising that their interest in the general education of their artisan trainees was negligible:

> It is not disputed that a workman is more efficient in proportion to his knowledge of theory, drawing and so forth. The Committee on the other hand inspected the excellent brick house built by illiterate masons and carpenters under the non-technical supervision of Cpt. F. O. B. Wilson. The Committee are of the opinion that the Colony will be efficiently served if artisans capable of erecting such a building are forthcoming within the next few years.[3]

Such determination by the Legislative Council and the settlers to have a supply of Africans outside the Reserves produced by the Education Department and missions created a reaction. Orr began to clarify his position in a number of policy statements; it was precisely not his objective to extract an artisan élite from the Reserves to serve the European economy. This was why he had borrowed the experience of the Southern States, for 'the system of Hampton and Tuskegee appears to supply by the provision of industrial training an education which affects most widely the interests and activities of the

[1] Ibid., p. 7, paras. 40, 44.

[2] Cf. Evidence of Limuru Farmers' Association in *Evidence of the Education Commission 1919*, pp. 137–43.

[3] 'Report of the Native Technical Education Committee' (3 Apr. 1923), pp. 9–10, File Q-A, E.H.

Community as a whole.'[1] Industrial education he interpreted as flooding the Reserves with new skills, developing Africa's traditional village industries, until, like Tuskegee, economically self-sufficient communities were achieved. Moreover, it appears that towards the end of 1923 he received the report of the first Phelps-Stokes Commission, and found there, naturally, ample confirmation for his Reserve-oriented village industries. His *Lessons Derived from 12 Years Administration of African Education* were consequently written with a new confidence that what he had been working for since 1911 had international approval. He wrote:

> The teachers of this Department, consider that Reading and Writing unaccompanied by work useful to the Community divorces the pupil from his tribe, gives him contempt for his own people and attracts him to the towns. They consider that whatever man does in an African village can form the object of a lesson in the elementary school . . . we are beginning to believe that elementary education should be closely related to the improvement of village activities . . . In the Kindergarten a commencement is being made with the study of flowers—their differences and their colours. Simple agriculture and the growing of a variety of European and Native foodstuffs form the next stage. It is felt that this might be followed in the different standards by the care and breeding of fowls: lessons on the qualities of cattle, sheep and goats; ghee and butter making; ploughing with home made ploughs; tree planting and the knowledge of timbers; cart making to convey produce to market; and with older boys the construction of better houses for occupation by villagers.[2]

Although this enthusiasm for improved village life did anticipate by some ten years the consensus of African educationists on rural and agricultural priorities,[3] conflict between Orr's policy and the labour shortage in the European sector became inevitable in 1923 when the education estimates for 1924 were being debated. Irritated by the incompetence of the Education Department in providing skilled labour, a group in the Legislative Council, headed by the settler leader, Lord Delamere, attempted completely to withdraw grants-in-aid from so-called technical missions, but, failing this, they succeeded in tying down all but £1,000 of the £13,000 education grant to their own specifically technical objectives. In

[1] J. R. Orr, 'Technical Education in Mission Schools', 25 June 1923, Education Bundle, P.C.E.A.

[2] J. R. Orr, 'Lessons Derived from 12 Years Administration of African Education' (21 Dec. 1923), p. 8. File on 'Kenya: Nyasaland: Zanzibar: Reports' (hereafter Q-F), E.H.

[3] See pp. 203–5.

addition, they decimated Orr's proposals for general educational aid to the Reserves, and by what seemed verbal gymnastics, they were even able to allot the reduced literary education grant to technical education. Orr had, after all, so often spoken out against exclusively literary education that the Legislative Council felt justified in preventing missions from receiving any money from government that was not earmarked for indentured apprentices. As a final touch, it was decided to revert to the system of payment by results.[1]

Judging these actions to be a vote of no confidence in his own direction and priorities, Orr appealed to the Colonial Office to have his department investigated by the Phelps-Stokes Commission when they came to Kenya in two months' time. They would certainly be able to confirm whether he was justified in accusing the Government of completely neglecting the Reserves, for he felt that the one aim of present educational policy was to ensure '*that Government shall provide education only for those African Males who are willing to serve the European Community as Artisans*'.[2] The strain of trying to fulfil his obligations to settlers, missionaries, and government, and to no less than four racial groups, would soon make Orr a sick man;[3] but that he was not at this point exaggerating the situation with which Jones would have to deal is shown by the comment of the Representative Council of the Alliance of Protestant Missionary Societies in Kenya:

> The Council is disturbed by the fact that in the Estimates for African education in 1924, the increase in the grant is for technical education only . . .
>
> The Representative Council believes that there is a conflict between the ideals of Missionary Societies and those of the Leg. Co. Education should be on the broadest possible base, whereas the grants made by Leg. Co. are on as narrow one as is possible to imagine.[4]

Here, therefore, was one problem which looked too stubborn

[1] Coryndon to Devonshire, 10 Jan. 1924, C.O. 533/308, P.R.O.; Orr to Denham, 22 Nov. 1923, in above despatch. Cf. also Orr to Coryndon, 23 Oct. 1923, Coryndon Papers, Box 5, MSS. Afr.s.633, Rhodes House, Oxford.

[2] Orr to Denham, 22 Nov. 1923.

[3] Hooper to Oldham, 20 June 1925, Hooper File (hereafter Q-K), E.H. For aspects of education according to the races, see Snehlata R. Shah, 'A History of Asian Education in Kenya, 1886–1963', (University College Nairobi, M.A. thesis, 1968).

[4] Minutes of the Representative Council of the Alliance of Protestant Missionary Societies, 19th–22nd November 1923, File Q-A, E.H. See also Hooper to Orr, 23 Nov. 1923, File Q-A, E.H.

to be resolved by any simple formula, since the most basic principles of the missions and the Director of Education seemed to be directly at cross purposes with the Legislative Council's and settlers' demands. It was at least an issue which united the department and the missions; the difficulty was that the other critical issue of government school versus mission school set the missions in opposition to both the director and the administration.

As with the industrial education question, the first stirrings of this antagonism lay back in the period after 1910, but the issue only really became critical in the weeks before the Phelps-Stokes Commission arrived. Although Orr's suggestions for government schools had received a serious setback in the 1919 Education Commission Report, the case was reopened with the unanimous proposals of the Senior and District Commissioners' meeting of 4–8 December 1923, that 'Model Government Schools should be instituted in each District'.[1] Orr immediately confirmed the recommendation, adding the gloss that 'no African should be compelled to receive doses of Catholicism or Calvinism in his endeavour to learn, and free access should be given to undenominational or even secular schools'.[2] It is not at this stage entirely clear exactly how far Orr and the commissioners were expressing an administrative preference. They do, however, seem in part to have been reflecting the beginnings of African opposition to mission education, such as would become widespread in the later twenties.[3] On the other hand, the secretary of the Protestant Alliance, J. W. Arthur (whose two C.S.M. centres had both experienced serious strikes from their apprentices during the Thuku troubles)[4] was almost certainly underestimating the element of African initiative behind the commissioners' proposals. There must have been more to it than Arthur's explanation that the commissioners were getting the Chiefs together and 'asking them if they want Govt. schools and putting it in such a way as to suggest that they may do what they like as to polygamy, drink, etc. if their children are sent to Govt. schools'.[5]

[1] 'Resolutions of Senior and District Commissioners, December 4th to 8th, 1923', enclosed in Coryndon to Devonshire, 10 Jan. 1920.

[2] Orr, *Lessons Derived from 12 Years Administration*, p. 9.

[3] Cf. T. Ranger, 'African Attempts to Control Education in East and Central Africa, 1900–1939', *Past and Present*, No. 32 (Dec. 1965), 57–85; also J. Anderson, *The Struggle for the School* (London, 1970).

[4] A. R. Barlow to Orr, 10 May 1922; H. R. A. Philp to Orr, 14 June 1922, Education Bundle, P.C.E.A.

[5] Arthur to Jones, 14 Dec. 1923, File Q-A, E.H. For a further valuable analysis of Arthur, see McIntosh, 'The Scottish Mission in Kenya', pp. 389–91.

Indeed, there was soon to be a paradox involved in any discussion of the advantages of government schools for Kenya. The Colonial Office would be inclined to discourage the notion, since it would give the settlers too strong a say in their management; while the Africans would increasingly look to government schools as affording them freedom from mission control. For the moment, it was an indication of Arthur's fear that he felt it necessary fully to brief the Phelps-Stokes Commission on the dangers of government model schools as soon as they reached Mombasa. He was able to pass on at the same time the report that Orr was planning a further invasion of mission privilege by starting a model government training school within six miles of Arthur's Scots Mission school at Kikuyu.[1]

Orr was not activated by spite in proposing this, but he had long held the conviction that teacher training was the over-riding weakness of the present system. Indeed, he had had the strongest confirmation of his views in the recent official report of E. R. J. Hussey on African education in Kenya.[2] It was, after all, the most logical priority for someone who had given so much attention to the role of Tuskegee in providing teachers for Southern schools; and it was only natural that he should now bring the proposal forward in the hope of Phelps-Stokes support. Part of Arthur's animus against him, however, was explained by the fact that Orr's model teacher-training school would not be the only scheme seeking the Phelps-Stokes Commission's blessing. For Dr. Arthur hoped that his own plan for a higher joint missionary college would gain their official approval.[3]

The Phelps-Stokes Commission were to spend three weeks in Kenya.[4] In that short time they had so to gain the sympathy of the best of the settlers that trusteeship of African education would be taken seriously. But, more difficult, an area of co-operation had to be found and proclaimed between parties who could at present only see that their ways and principles were totally opposed.

The first approach was to the settler community. As soon as Jones had given his first press conference, the settlers at least were given a

[1] Ibid.

[2] E. R. J. Hussey, *Memorandum on Certain Aspects of Arab and African Education* (Govt. Press, Nairobi, 21 May 1924), p. 3; see also Orr to Hooper, 17 Aug. 1920, File Q-A, E.H.

[3] Arthur to Oldham, 31 Dec. 1924, memorandum on the origins of the Protestant Alliance Missionary College, File Q-A, E.H.

[4] i.e. 18 Feb.–9 Mar. and 24–28 Mar. 1924. For the commission in Kenya, see Plate VI.

The Phelps–Stokes Commission in Kenya. (From the *E.A.S.* weekly edition, 8 March 1924.) Dillard, second from left in front group; Vischer, third from left in front group; Jones, fourth from left in rear grouping; Shantz, eighth from left in rear grouping; Aggrey, ninth from left in rear grouping.

very firm assurance that this particular commission was not going to call into question the fact of white settlement. This was not, however, to be done in Jones's characteristic way, by simply avoiding the whole issue—quite the opposite. White settlement was enthusiastically and publicly embraced by the three most influential members of the team; Dillard, Aggrey, and Jones, each in his own way, gave the settlers the message that they had 'reason for self-congratulation' on their civilizing mission.[1]

So far from Dillard's using his long experience of Southern education to drive a harder bargain for an educational mandate, he seemed to the white press 'a kindly soul, unlikely to hurt the feelings of anyone by harsh criticism. He tells us', continued the *E.A.S.*, 'that he is sure that we will solve our problems all right; we impress him that way.'[2] Jones himself was prepared to be a good deal more explicit, and, from Kenya's example, openly to advocate the extension of white colonization in other parts of Africa which the Commission had recently visited. In a speech widely taken to refer to the colonization of Abyssinia, he suggested that settlement was almost a necessary precondition of African redemption:

> 'If I had my way,' he said, 'I would take a cross cut of the population of Kenya—I would not want the angelic members of the population—I would take the average man, a thousand of the ordinary citizens, even the despised settler, and put them in certain parts of Africa. I know that they might work out the salvation of those parts. I am talking now in all sincerity. I am increasingly of the conviction that Africa will only work out its salvation as it comes in contact with the other parts of the world.'[3]

If any further demonstration of sympathy with the position of whites in Kenya was needed after this, Aggrey's speeches to white audiences provided it. His justification of colonization followed basically the same pattern as Jones. The general doctrine that no backward people or nation could advance independently of outside help was used to encourage white supervision, while allaying fears that Africans wished self-determination. Admittedly there was usually, for the careful listener, the quiet promotion of African rights, and the gentlest of threats that the African might not continue patiently to appeal to the white man's conscience for ever. Many of

[1] 'First Impressions', *E.A.S.* (weekly edn.) 8 Mar. 1924.
[2] 'You will solve Your Problems All Right', *E.A.S.*, 8 Mar. 1924.
Ibid. Cf. also Orr to Jones, 14 Ap. 1926, File N-1, P.S.F.A.

Aggrey's speeches had just such a double edge,[1] but there can be little doubt that his major speeches in Kenya were taken as sophisticated African confirmation for increased white settlement. The following extract showed their tendency:

> 'America is great because Northern Europe and Southern Europe came to help to make it what it is. Therefore', he said, 'let the best of the nations, especially those who have done something themselves come over here and help us that we too make make a contribution to the world (applause). We are ordinary human beings with ordinary passions and aspirations longing to be where everyone is. I am pleading with my people to be patient with the white man, and when you want things done, be patient too.'[2]

Aggrey's role had originally been more narrowly defined as the improvement of race relations, and, strictly speaking, discussion of white settlement was beyond his brief. But even within this limited sphere he scored considerable successes in interpreting the two races to each other.[3] Part of this success came from his reinterpretation for Kenya of the well-worn interracial axiom of the Southern States in the phrase, 'the leadership of the best Africans by the best white men'.[4] This was in fact a much more explicit definition of what co-operation meant than Aggrey was wont to make in Africa,[5] but then the whole trend of the commission's attitude to the whites in Kenya had been unusually conciliatory. Indeed, it seems possible that the American members of the commission exaggerated the need to identify with the white colonists, and eulogize their civilizing influence. After all, even the *E.A.S.* had felt a little overcome by 'all this flattery and appreciation', and thought that more valuable criticism could have been expected had the commission not come to Kenya direct from uncivilized Abyssinia.[6]

The larger implications of these concessions to white settlement will be examined later,[7] but Jones may well have thought such a stance a necessary preliminary to resolving the other acute educational and political conflicts in the territory.

The first of these was the impasse that had been reached between Christian missions and the Director of Education and the settlers

[1] See pp. 243–4. [2] See Jones, 'You will solve your problems'.
[3] See further pp. 191–2.
[4] Orr to Jones, 14 Apr. 1926, File N-1, P.S.F.A.
[5] Smith, *Aggrey of Africa*, p. 125, wrote, 'What does cooperation imply? I cannot find in available records that Aggrey fully defined the term.'
[6] Jones, 'You will solve your problems'. [7] See Ch. V.

over the industrial nature of African education, and whether it should be directed towards the European labour market or the African Reserves. It seemed an issue on which there could be no compromise. In practice, however, the Commission won friends on both sides by working in the crucial area where settler and mission views overlapped. Both sides had a common antipathy to merely literary education. That industrial training must provide the basis of African education was not in dispute. What was needed was to present the case for a new type of industrial education in the Reserves that would satisfy the missionary conscience without interfering with the settlers' labour supply. The argument, Jones saw, was less about industrial education than about an equitable distribution of grants-in-aid between Reserve education and the education of artisans for the towns and European areas.

Jones himself had no objection to African artisan training for the towns, and on this the settlers were reassured as soon as he had given one of his press briefings, and Aggrey had spoken to white audiences. It was not basically a distortion of either Jones's or Aggrey's views when the settlers seized on Jones's 'Gospel of the Plough' or Aggrey's 'Teach the Native to work with his hand'.[1] These slogans kept appearing in Phelps-Stokes speeches because they reflected a basic conviction that contact with the European economy, especially in industrial activities, was a valuable education for the African. Jones made it quite clear, when he came to write his report later in the year, that the Phelps-Stokes attitude to industrial training and the labour market was a refinement, but not a radical alteration of the settler position.[2] In General Armstrong's language, he outlined the value to Africans of wage labour within the European sector of the economy: 'Literally thousands upon thousands of the Native Youth have "learned by doing" many of the important processes of industry, commerce and agriculture.'[3] There was therefore not the slightest inclination on Jones's part to criticize the policy of African

[1] 'Religion in a Spade', *East Africa*, i, No. 2 (1924), 42; also Aggrey was reported in the *E.A.S.*, (weekly edn.), 8 Mar. 1924: 'He made a special plea for education through the hand so that they might produce something—"even the most infinitesimal part of a fraction".' Cf. also, E. Huxley, *White Man's Country*, ii (1914–1931), (London, 1935), p. 182.

[2] Nor was Jones's attitude to such topics as native production of coffee and cotton radically different from the settler position, see *Education in East Africa*, p. 107.

[3] Ibid., p. 86.

artisan training, over which Orr had nearly resigned. Indeed, his report on Kenya could only comment that the determination to train natives for industrial pursuits constituted a valuable educational opportunity for Kenya's Africans.[1]

Although this naturally more than delighted the settler lobby, it would still be necessary to provide evidence for the missionaries that the training of artisans for the European economy did not run counter to the demands of developing the Reserves. Some of the leading missionaries were already becoming apprehensive, and J. W. Arthur in particular viewed the settlers' jubilation with dismay, since they were 'claiming in their speeches that the Phelps-Stokes Commission is recommending exactly what they themselves think'.[2] Yet Arthur's indignation at this point is a little unexpected, for a year earlier, during the height of the Indian crisis, he had met Jones and had been pleased to gain the impression that he was 'anti-Indian and very much pro-settler', and even then it had been obvious, at a meeting between Delamere, Arthur, and Jones, that Delamere felt the Phelps-Stokes views of education accorded exactly with his own.[3]

Jones had, however, brought a scheme over from the Southern States which he felt would precisely meet the requirements of the Reserves, namely, the Jeanes Industrial Teacher system. The function of these Jeanes teachers in the States had been to travel round groups of backward Negro schools as friendly visitors, attempting to make simple industrial and agricultural improvements on the narrowly literary curriculum.[4] Here in Kenya, Jones explained, after training in a central institution, they could travel in the Reserves, stimulating the growth of local African crafts, and encouraging a less literary approach to education. As the missionaries desired, these teachers would be exclusively concerned not with the development of a few skilled artisans, but with the general improvement of the masses in the Reserves.

It seems clear that Jones, with the strongest backing from Dillard of the Jeanes Fund,[5] had decided they should present the Jeanes Scheme to the Government as the most important single chance to

[1] Ibid., pp. 116–17.

[2] J. W. Arthur, 'The Phelps-Stokes Commission' (9 Apr. 1924), File Q-A, E.H.

[3] McIntosh, 'The Scottish Mission in Kenya', pp. 383, 400–1; Arthur to Barlow, 2 July 1923, P.C.E.A./Tumutumu.

[4] Jones, *The Jeanes Teacher in the United States.*

[5] For a more detailed account of the factors involved, see p. 151.

demonstrate trusteeship for native education. The Government were ready to grant this request because it looked as if it would resolve not only the industrial education problem, but also contribute to a solution of the government-mission school controversy.[1]

This other major area of government-missionary hostility, Jones realized, had largely blown up because there were no formal lines of communication between the missionaries and the Education Department. In consequence, departmental policy from month to month had been more the subject of rumour than anything else. Probably Jones's greatest achievement, therefore, was to build up in the space of three weeks machinery for co-operation in the form of a Central Advisory Committee on African Education.[2] This body would now represent all the important educational missions in the country, as well as settlers and government; and it was due solely to Jones's persuasiveness that the previously non-co-operating missions were drawn into this central council. Both the F.A.M. and the Africa Inland Mission (A.I.M.) now had representatives on the Advisory Committee, and the Friends had for the first time been convinced that they might benefit from accepting government grants.[3]

While this constitutional basis for future co-operation had been in the negotiating stage, it had been of vital importance that the Phelps-Stokes Commission should countenance no scheme that might upset the balance. Both Orr's higher teacher-training school and Arthur's higher missionary college were therefore passed over as being too controversial, and the Jeanes scheme introduced instead. This meant, in effect, that the two alternative suggestions for higher education cancelled each other out for diplomatic reasons, and a low-level village teacher scheme was put forward on which government and missions might co-operate. For the Jeanes Central Training School would be government-run, but its trainees would be seconded from the various missions, and return to them after their course.[4]

It must be remembered that in this tactical deadlock over higher education it was not only some missionaries and the Education

[1] Ibid.

[2] A very valuable account of the tactics and diplomacy involved in this agreement is contained in J. W. C. Dougall's Journal of his tour (18 Feb. 1924 to 20 June 1924); copy in E.H. Cf. also, Arthur, 'The Phelps-Stokes Commission' (9 Apr. 1924), File Q-A, E.H.

[3] See Dougall's Journal and Arthur, 'The Phelps-Stokes Commission'; also Jones, *Education in East Africa*, pp. 119, 128, 130, 131.

[4] See Dougall's Journal and Arthur, 'The Phelps-Stokes Commission'.

Department that had been hoping for a move in the direction of further education; the education of an African leadership had been one of the main planks in the programme of Thuku and those he had influenced.[1] It would now be seen to what extent the Phelps-Stokes Commission could make contact with and satisfy African opinion on such a brief visit.

This was of course specifically Aggrey's assignment, and indeed it had been hoped that he might compile a chapter on the native viewpoint as he went round East Africa.[2] But Aggrey's time had been more occupied in preparing Africans for the new type of education than in seeking out and passing on their own preferences. Along with this went his attempt to communicate the insights in interracial philosophy that he had learnt in the Southern States. How much importance Jones attached to this function can be seen from Aggrey's speaking no less than seventy-five times in Uganda and Kenya within five weeks.[3] On the face of it, his messages of patience and loyalty appeared to the white population valuable contributions to law, order, and correct education in the country. For example, there was still, even two years after Thuku's arrest, a strong underground movement.[4] Aggrey was therefore enlisted by the C.S.M. to give their loyal Chiefs some backing for their anti-Thuku stand, and an hour was spent talking to them and advising them 'to beware of all anti-government agitation'.[5]

Despite this episode, it seems likely that Aggrey's speeches had an effect upon his African audiences directly opposite to what Jones and Aggrey himself intended. He called for Africans to be content to be truly African, and yet he was widely hailed and admired for being the 'black Muzungu' (European).[6] What was more important than his words of patience was the fact of his amazing fluency in the English language. He appeared in fact as the most vivid single advertisement for the advantages of higher literary education that

[1] See pp. 75–6; also Ranger, 'African Attempts to Control Education', p. 66.

[2] In Hanns Vischer's 'Report for the Chairman of the Advisory Committee on Native Education in Tropical Africa' (15 Dec. 1924), there is an empty docket for Aggrey's Memorandum on the Native Point of View.

[3] Aggrey to W. E. Owen, 15 Apr. 1924, Owen Papers, Acc. 83, C.M.S.A., London.

[4] Hooper to Oldham, 1 Aug. 1923, File Q-A, E.H., See further King, 'The Nationalism of Harry Thuku'.

[5] Arthur, 'The Phelps-Stokes Commission' (9 Apr. 1924), File Q-A, E.H.

[6] Hooper to Oldham, 2 Mar. 1924, Q-K, E.H.

many Africans in Kenya and Uganda would see throughout the 1920s and 1930s. It did not matter at all that Aggrey spoke out for practical training on almost every occasion; he probably, paradoxically, did more harm to the cause of industrial education in his whirlwind three weeks than the Jeanes School could undo in many months. Although, therefore, the commission had made no concessions to higher education, and in closed session had expressed grave concern at Africans' going abroad, there is strong evidence that Aggrey's American education directly stimulated Africans to think of education overseas.[1]

There was another point at which the Phelps-Stokes philosophy made contact with local African initiative. This was its certainty that the crucial undertaking for education departments and missions was the strict supervision of the thousands of tiny 'bush' or village schools. Very little significance would be attached to Jones's enthusiasm for supervising the schools at this level if he had not already shown in the States a more than educational interest in the little Negro independent schools.[2] His *Negro Education* had offered very little understanding of the aspirations that lay behind the independent schools, and now in Kenya and other parts of Africa it seemed that it was the danger of their relative independence that drew Jones's attention to the bush schools, as much as their educational inefficiency:

> Sympathetic supervision and friendly visitation of schools in Africa will improve all, double the value of a large proportion, and save many from utter failure. Without friendly direction, the village school system in parts of Africa will soon be so completely discredited as to threaten the arrest of mission activities in those areas. In view of the amount of harmful propaganda rife among Native people, Governments cannot be indifferent to the existence of a large number of small schools taught by Natives with very little education. The one hope for the continuance of such schools is the provision of sufficient supervision to guide and direct their work and influence.[3]

This potentially dangerous sector of the system where, as Jones saw

[1] Dougall, 'Journal of the Phelps-Stokes Commission', 25 Mar. 1924. For an example of Aggrey's stimulating Africans for higher education abroad, see p. 233. For Azikiwe's catching his ambitions for study in America from Aggrey, see K. A. B. Jones-Quartey, *A Life of Azikiwe* (London, 1965), pp. 25, 53.

[2] See pp. 37–9.

[3] Jones, *Education in East Africa*, p. 50; also Ranger, 'African Attempts to Control Education', p. 72.

it, the teachers were very often merely 'blind leaders of the blind' was a further reason to insist on introducing the Jeanes Teacher system.[1] It would provide a corps of Africans trained in the new ideals of adapted education, who could continuously tour the Reserves and keep a friendly watch over the areas that the white missionaries could not adequately cover.[2]

At the end of their three weeks of visits and negotiations, the commission had unquestionably created a rare degree of harmony among all concerned with African education. Missionaries who had previously thought any genuine co-operation with government impossible had quite changed their minds.[3] Vischer reported that the good element among the settlers was 'dead keen on Native education'.[4] Governor Coryndon expressed his indebtedness to the Phelps-Stokes Commission for their sympathetic understanding of every section of Kenyan opinion.[5] Even the Director of Education had been praised for his statesmanlike policies.[6] This sudden unanimity was not simply the result of Jones's persuasiveness, although that was remarkable. It would have been impossible had there not been a substantial area of agreement to be exploited. Jones's strategy had been simply to cut his way through the personal animosities and mission-government rivalries, to demonstrate how all three parties could subscribe to differentiated education for Africans. As with his earlier work in the Southern States, very little that was new had been needed to reach agreement, beyond the provision of a more sophisticated theoretical basis for the industrial education which everybody already believed in. The new outlook was never clearly defined, and it was this very ambiguity that was the cause of success. Oldham described the impression it had on many missionaries:

> I am reminded of the perplexity which existed to some extent a year or two ago when Dr. Jesse Jones came back from Africa and expounded his programme of education. 'What precisely do you want us to do?' people kept asking him. If he had been ready to supply a cut-and-dry curriculum, if he had insisted that this or that subject should be cut out or this or that activity introduced, what he was saying would have seemed so much simpler. But he consistently refused to do this. 'I do not want you

[1] Jones, *Education in East Africa*, p. 59.
[2] See Ch. VI for the working out of this experiment.
[3] Hooper to Jones, n.d. File Q-R, E.H.
[4] Vischer to Oldham, 1 May 1924, File Q-E, E.H.
[5] Coryndon to the Colonial Secretary, 20 June 1924, C.O. 533/311, P.R.O.
[6] Jones, *Education in East Africa*, pp. 118, 139.

to do anything in particular,' he kept saying. 'I want you to do from a new point of view what you are doing at present.'[1]

The ambiguity was popular with the settlers because Jones had consistently refused also to tie technical education down to improving the African Reserves.[2] For the missions, there was the challenge of experimenting with the new, adapted education and of receiving government grants for the purpose.[3] Moreover, in its readiness to inaugurate the first Jeanes Teacher Training scheme in Africa, the Kenya Government had made precisely the sort of concession to trusteeship of the African that the missionary leaders and the Advisory Committee in Britain had desired.

It might appear, nevertheless, that the Phelps-Stokes Commission could have driven a harder bargain with Kenya than the establishment of this school to train better village teachers. It must be stressed however that there was no question of their having failed to get a higher college or teacher training school. The Jeanes School was the highest concession that the American members of the Phelps-Stokes Commission wanted. It was, after all, the embodiment of the most enlightened principles of Negro education in the States; there was in it the rural emphasis and the simplicity thought so appropriate to developing peoples, together with the same spirit of community-mindedness as fired Hampton and Tuskegee. Jones himself believed that the Jeanes system was the most suitable vehicle for transplanting his whole philosophy of adapted education to Africa.[4] And as his views on African education had received in 1924 the official approval of the American and British missionary societies,[5] the Kenya Government's image changed, as far as education was concerned, from reactionary to progressive within the year.[6]

[1] J. H. Oldham, 'The relation of Christian Mission to the New Forces that are reshaping African life', in Smith (Ed.), *Christian Mission in Africa*, p. 170.

[2] Dougall to Oldham, 19 Jan. 1925, File 'Kenya: Education: Jeanes School' (hereafter Q-G), E.H.

[3] As a direct consequence of the Phelps-Stokes visit, the Government made its first grant for home training and child welfare: £500, and £2,915 was set aside for the Jeanes school. Estimates for 1925, 15 Oct. 1924, C.O. 533/314/53606, P.R.O. See also Denham to Jones, 4 June 1924, File Q-F, E.H.

[4] Jones to Oldham, 20 May 1927, File Q-G, E.H. Also Jones, *Education in Africa*, p. 54.

[5] *Christian Education in Africa: Conference at High Leigh, Hoddesdon, September 8–13, 1924*, (Edinburgh House Press, n.d.), p. 3.

[6] Note the considerable publicity given to the Jeanes School in the Annual Reports of the Education Department, especially *KEDAR*, 1928, 1930, 1931, 1932.

Before examining in a little more detail the place of the commission within the general development of Kenyan education in the 1920s and 1930s, it is worth asking whether radical changes could be expected to result from the new-found co-operation. Leaving aside the single initiative in Jeanes work in the Reserves, Jones's watchword, 'adaptation', was too broad a term to suggest any particular course except one that was different from the prevailing white system. It could therefore be equally used by a variety of people who wished education to be adapted, some for racial reasons, others for political and social, and others on purely pedagogical grounds. Indeed, this was the continuing embarrassment to any industrial programme, whether it was General Armstrong's, Albert Schweizer's, or Jesse Jones's; they attracted support from racist as easily as from progressive educators.[1] It is not therefore surprising to find that after the Phelps-Stokes Commission left, things went on very much as before. The need of the Europeans for artisans, and the gradual improvement of the Reserves could be simultaneously encouraged under Jones's slogan of 'adaptation of education to the needs of the community'.

Despite all the publicity for the Jeanes School, the production of artisans remained the priority. Mission Central schools continued compulsorily to indenture their technical students for the last three years in school. Government grants-in-aid were still weighted heavily in favour of schools giving efficient technical education, and indeed there was added inducement in the new grant agreements to build up European staffs on the technical side.[2] The trend was continued in the establishment of the Native Industrial Training Depot (N.I.T.D.), to take the indentured mission students on for a further two years of trade training. Although both the N.I.T.D. scheme and the Jeanes School were mooted for the first time at the inaugural meeting of the Central Advisory Committee for Education in May 1924, the rate of their development was significant.[3] By June the Government

[1] Compare the use made of Schweizer and Armstrong in J. H. Oldham and B. D. Gibson, *The Remaking of Man in Africa* (London, 1931), pp. 45–6, with that of H. O. Weller (supervisor of technical education in Kenya), 'The Education of the Kenyan African' (1933) in Coryndon Papers, 18/1, MSS. Afr. S. 633, Rhodes House, Oxford.

[2] *Report of the Committee on Grants in Aid for Education in Kenya* (E.A.S., Nairobi, 1925), paras. 18, 21, 28; also, C. W. Stubbs and E. E. Biss, *Report of Technical Departments of Mission Schools Receiving Grants-in-Aid* (16 Oct. 1925) (Govt. Press, Nairobi, 1925), p. 6.

[3] Minutes of Central Advisory Committee for Native Education (Kenya) for 13 May and 26 June 1924, File Q-A, E.H.

was suggesting setting aside £25,000 from the loan fund for permanent buildings at the N.I.T.D., and students in training rose swiftly from 55 in 1925, to 220 in 1926, to over 500 in 1928.[1] The Jeanes School by contrast lay becalmed without adequate staff, capital expenditure or budget from 1924 until 1927, and was set in motion then only by strong external pressures.[2] The next five years saw no relaxing of the industrial priority, and it was only when the market became glutted with N.I.T.D. graduates in 1933/4 that the Government finally abandoned the indenture of technical students at mission primary schools.[3] It is doubtful, however, whether the Phelps-Stokes Commission, even if it had wanted to, could have reversed or checked the determination of the settlers to have the labour they required. As it was, the development of the N.I.T.D. was not inconsistent with the analysis and recommendations contained in the Kenya section of the Phelps-Stokes East Africa Report.[4]

There was a more serious defect in the commission's Kenya report than this failure to comment on the industrialization of the school system; the agreement that had been secured did not take into consideration the possible reaction of the Africans themselves. Jones's concessions to the value of industrial training and his introduction of the Jeanes system were neither of them calculated to gratify African aspirations. Indeed, the unanimity he had achieved among the sections of white opinion had been precisely at the expense of the two schemes for higher education. The postponement was particularly significant in view of Arthur's college scheme at least having gone far beyond the mere planning stage. Already considerable endowments had been promised, land obtained, and the medical buildings erected.[5]

That it was not entirely abandoned was probably more due to

[1] Denham to the Colonial Secretary, 7 June 1924, C.O. 533/311/31193, and 8 July, 1924, C.O. 533/312/37308, P.R.O. Also Kenya Legislative Council Debates for 10 Mar. 1927; cf. *KEDAR 1928* (Govt. Printer, Nairobi, 1929), p. 61.

[2] See p. 159.

[3] *KEDAR 1930* (Govt. Printer, Nairobi, 1931), pp. 28–9. Also *KEDAR 1932* (Govt. Printer, Nairobi, 1933), pp. 14–17, and *KEDAR 1934* (Govt. Printer, Nairobi, 1935), pp. 21, 24. Oldham significantly greeted this as the abandonment of what he had long thought 'a thoroughly mistaken policy'. (Oldham to H. S. Scott, 12 Sept. 1933, File Q-A, E.H.).

[4] Jones, *Education in East Africa*, pp. 117, 119. There was no comment on the indenture system, nor any suggestion that the technical bias was anything but commendable.

[5] Arthur to Oldham, 31 Dec. 1924, memorandum on the Protestant Alliance Missionary College, File Q-A, E.H.

African pressure than anything else, although Arthur himself became even keener on the project when he had noticed the effect of higher education on James Aggrey.[1] However, only a month after the publication of the Phelps-Stokes Report, the Director of Education had to inform the Advisory Committee of 'a desire expressed by certain Africans to send their sons to schools in Ceylon, India, America and England'. Arrangements had been made to send two boys to the new Achimota College in the Gold Coast, and there was even an interest in going to Tuskegee.[2] This alarming enthusiasm for further education overseas could only, the committee agreed, be contained by providing locally for some sort of higher education. Arthur's proposals were meanwhile reintroduced, and sent to Edinburgh House, the headquarters of the Conference of British Missionary Societies, for their comment. A small conference was held there between Oldham, Jones, the Church of Scotland, and the C.M.S. representatives, and it was decided, on Oldham's suggestion, with the strongest backing from Jones, to change the plan from a college to a good junior high school.[3] Alliance High School, the result of this agreement, began in a small way in 1926,[4] but as far as satisfying African demand for secondary education went, it came too late and on too small a scale.

There had been African hostility to much mission education for some time, both on curricular and other grounds, and it had certainly not been lessened after Thuku had popularized the idea that the missionary was in the settler's pay.[5] When therefore Local Native Councils were established in 1925, Africans immediately began taxing themselves for an education that would be outside missionary control. Government schools, they felt, would give them greater control over their own education; and by 1929 they had presented the new Director of Education, H. S. Scott, with the problem of more than £50,000 raised by voluntary taxes specifically for non-mission

[1] J. W. Arthur, 'The Phelps-Stokes Commission', File Q-A, E.H.

[2] Proceedings of Meeting of Central Advisory Committee for African Education, 9 June 1925, E.H. Note on meeting between the Director of Education (Kenya) and the Executive Committee of the Kenya Missionary Council, 21 May 1925, in File 'Christian Council Correspondence', E.H.

[3] During the preliminaries to this conference, Jones's *Education in East Africa* was consulted by Edinburgh House, and taken to be not 'very definite' on the matter of the college; File Q-A, E.H.

[4] For further details of Alliance High School, see pp. 193–4.

[5] See p. 78, n. 2. Also report of Thuku's speech in Chief Native Commissioner G. V. Maxwell to Northey, 9 Mar. 1922, C.O. 533/276, P.R.O.

education.[1] The much-vaunted co-operation that Jones had secured was soon quite lost in months of bitter recrimination, as missions and government in turn claimed to be the best interpreter of the Africans' real demands.[2]

The crux of the problem was the same in 1929 as when Jones had been in Kenya: the achieving of a meaningful co-operation. The only difference now was that Scott's definition of co-operation contained an element that had been conspicuously lacking in the consensus that Jones had achieved:

> . . . above all that there is the attitude of the native: definitely hostile to any type of school which is not free from missionaries. When I speak of cooperation, I do not mean cooperation between the missionaries, the LNC and the Government. I can get the Government to cooperate with the missionaries, and I can get the Government to cooperate with the LNCs, but my difficulty is to get the missionaries to see the native point of view.[3]

It was this sense that the African viewpoint must be ascertained and accorded serious attention that most separated Jones's and Scott's approaches to African education. Admittedly, Local Native Councils were only in the planning stage when the commission had been in Kenya; there had, nevertheless, been indications even then that some such open expression of African resentment might be forthcoming. The commission had deliberately brought Aggrey with them to investigate the state of African feelings, and he had warned them of 'subterranean meetings and a deep rumbling that may prophesy an earthquake'.[4] Moreover, he had made it clear that African co-operation in approving the education suggested by the Phelps-Stokes Commission could not be taken for granted, since 'Africans are liable to have definite and strong views on the matter'.[5] But Jones did not let this affect his educational preferences; rather it had confirmed his conviction that the methods of the Southern States were particularly relevant to Kenya.

[1] Scott to Oldham, 10 Mar. 1929, File Q-A, E.H. The growth of the Kenya Independent Schools was partly a reaction to Government's unwillingness to use Local Native Council money for secondary education; see Ranger, 'African Attempts to Control Education', and Sally Abbott, 'The Education Policy of the Kenya Government, 1904–1935', Univ. of London Ph.D. thesis, 1969.

[2] H. S. Scott, File (hereafter File Q-A), E.H.

[3] Scott to Oldham, 17 June 1929, File Q-A, E.H.

[4] Aggrey to Owen, 15 Apr. 1924, Owen Papers, Acc. 83, C.M.S.A., London.

[5] Barlow to Miss B. D. Gibson, 24 Feb. 1926, File Q-A, E.H.

The conclusions of Jones's investigation of Negro schools in the Southern States were identical to those of the Phelps-Stokes Commission's Kenya tour: education was to be changed from the dominant white pattern; very few safeguards were to be given for higher education; and it was to be clearly understood that no education at all was preferable to certain forms of independent Negro or African school. True, there were a few passages in Jones's East Africa report which affirmed the importance of higher education, but these were overshadowed by the very strong emphasis upon adaptation to the needs of the simple village communities, and by the stress on industrial skill. As with white Southern reaction to Jones's earlier report, so in Kenya importance must be attached to what Europeans thought the commission was recommending, and, in this respect, the *E.A.S.* was representative:

> We have heard nothing more sound enunciated in Kenya on the subject of education than Dr. Jesse Jones' basic principles, i.e. that education must bear a direct relationship to (1) hygiene, (2) home life, (3) industry (or more widely the correct use of the opportunities of environment), and (4) recreation . . .
>
> The African requires to be taught his duty to himself. In his present stage to give him book learning is a waste of energy and funds.[1]

It had been intended that the supremacy of native African interests should be manifest in the Kenya report; but, if anything, it encouraged complacency and the idea that the Kenya regime required not more criticism but greater support.[2] The effect of the report was in fact to make it just a little more difficult to associate the African with the benefits of culture and deep learning, and just a little easier to laugh with Lord Delamere, Kenya's settler-king, as he praised the Phelps-Stokes Commission with the following story:

> Let me tell you a little story of the Phelps-Stokes visit. I was laid up and so they came to my house to meet a number of people and talk over their views on education. It was just at the time when people at home were talking a lot about our treatment of the Natives, and when Dr. Jesse Jones introduced a member of the delegation he said, 'Now, Lord Delamere, you will be very interested to meet Dr. Dillard whose ancestors were the largest slave owners in Alabama'. (laughter) He did not quite mean that. What he had meant to say was that when the U.S.A. had to

[1] *E.A.S.* (weekly edn.), 1 Mar. 1924. For higher education in the East Africa report, see Jones, *Education in East Africa*, pp. 43–5, 68–9, 267.

[2] Dougall to Oldham, 6 Apr. 1924, File Q-R, E.H.; see also Jones, *Education in East Africa*, p. 136.

deal with Negro education and development they had to call in the people of the South, who knew and had been brought up with the Negroes.

We still have our vagaries. A friend of mine who is here tonight visited a school in one of our Reserves. They were holding an examination, so he asked to see the paper. The first question was, 'Who was Socrates, and what was his life's work?' (loud laughter) I am sure that whatever differences we may have about the right way, that is probably the wrong way.[1]

[1] Lord Delamere, Speech at East African Dinner, printed in *East Africa* (London), ii, No. 91 (17 June 1926), 818.

CHAPTER V

The Phelps-Stokes Commissions and the Politics of Negro Education

THE PHELPS-STOKES Commissions to Africa and their published findings were very far from being isolated attempts at recommending the educational values of Tuskegee to Africa. They had grown out of the bitter conflicts to work out an education relevant to Negro political status in America, and were only one episode in the extension of those disputes to Africa. At times it was not so much that they were recommending Tuskegee as that they were promoting it deliberately to counterbalance the Africa programmes of two other American Negro creeds—DuBois's pan-Africanism and Garveyism. This fact made it increasingly difficult to regard 'adaptation' as a purely educational formula, since Garvey and DuBois (the latter with more valuable white support than he had had over Jones's *Negro Education*) showed the concept to be closely allied to African docility and continuing dependence on white leadership.

All three approaches to Africa were launched within the space of little more than a year, at the end of the First World War. Dr. Moton of Tuskegee had been directed into African affairs in December 1918 with his appointment to represent Africa at the Peace Conference,[1] and had by January decided that an educational survey of Africa might be the best contribution he could make:

> I am hoping the Phelps-Stokes Fund as soon as possible will study the African situation as Dr. Jones proposes, with a view as far as possible to helping those of the Peace Conference who will settle forever, I hope, the situation as regards Africa on a basis of human brotherhood, that is the development of the natives as the only safe method of colonization from a selfish as well as from a humanitarian viewpoint.[2]

Dubois inaugurated the first of his pan-African congresses the next month in Paris, a project which had only become a reality after

[1] Moton's role on the Presidential Peace Commission was to be on hand at the Peace Conference for consultation on African colonies. He did not in fact attend, but had some informal discussions with English and American authorities.

[2] Moton to Phelps Stokes, 19 Jan. 1919, Box 71, Peabody Papers, L.C.

Blaise Diagne, the Senegalese deputy, and Moton had intervened diplomatically with the French and American authorities.[1] There, to a relatively small Negro élite from the West Indies, Africa, and America, DuBois proposed a more radical readjustment of the African colonies than Moton was contemplating. Then on 1 August 1920, at a great international Negro convention in Harlem, Marcus Garvey blazoned forth his own declaration of the rights of the Negro peoples of the world.[2] Three weeks later the first Phelps-Stokes Commission sailed for Africa, with Aggrey groomed 'to introduce many features of Tuskegee and Hampton' wherever they went.[3]

The British missionary leaders most concerned with sending the Commission had believed from the beginning that there were serious political issues potentially involved, and were prepared to make these quite clear to Jones in the months before he left. A. G. Fraser, for instance (at this point leading his Village Education Commission to India via a tour of Negro education in the United States), found it possible to combine the greatest admiration for Tuskegee and its president with the conviction that the Phelps-Stokes Commission should be used to investigate the evils of exploitation in South and East Africa.[4] J. H. Oldham thought it conceivable that some useful alliance could be forged between Jones's ideals and those of Norman Leys, a retired medical officer. The latter's outspokenness over the Coast administration and Masai land policy in the East Africa Protectorate had earned him his dismissal,[5] but in 1919 he was, with Oldham's close co-operation, continuing his attack on settler power in East Africa by exposing the recent Labour Ordinance of the East Africa Protectorate.[6] In an attempt to initiate some form of collaboration between the two men, *Negro Education* was

[1] Moton to DuBois, 5 July 1919, R.R.M./G.C. (1919), T.U.A.; also Moton, *Finding a Way Out* (London, 1920), p. 253. For Moton and the Second Pan-African Congress, see p. 222.

[2] See Declaration in R. Buell, *The Native Problem in Africa* (New York, 1928), Vol. ii, Appendix XLIX, pp. 965–71. For an account of Garvey, see E. D. Cronon, *Black Moses* (Madison, 1955). Much recent material is contained in J. A. Langley, 'West African Aspects of the Pan-African Movements: 1900–1945' (Univ. of Edinburgh Ph.D. thesis, 1968).

[3] Aggrey to Moton, 16 Apr. 1923, R.R.M./G.C. (1923), T.U.A.; Jones to Moton, 17 Jan. 1920, R.R.M./G.C. (1919), T.U.A.

[4] Fraser to Peabody, 12 July 1919, R.R.M./G.C. (1919), T.U.A.

[5] Denham to the Colonial Secretary, 27 Mar. 1925, C.O. 533/327, P.R.O. For Leys on the Masai, see Leys, *Kenya*, pp. 86–125.

[6] For co-operation between Oldham and Leys on the labour situation in East Africa, see File on Leys (hereafter File Q-B), E.H.

recommended to Leys as 'exceedingly valuable',[1] while Jones was sent a detailed analysis of the causes and solutions of African unrest which summarized Leys's sixteen years' experience in British East Africa, Nyasaland, and Portuguese East Africa.[2]

Leys's document could have been exceedingly relevant to Jones's purposes, since he was chiefly concerned like Jones to propose a colonial policy that would make for African stability through education; moreover, he too had had first-hand experience of the results of American Negro education which had helped to confirm his African proposals. But here the similarity ended. For the Negro education Leys had in mind was that of John Chilembwe, leader of the abortive 1915 Nyasaland rising.[3] Leys deliberately stressed in this memorandum of 1918 the fact that Chilembwe's 'knowledge of English was perfect, he had read widely and had sent his sons to America for education'.[4] The point was introduced, however, not as an obvious reason for curtailing such literary education, but as a plea for even wider education, and for giving responsibility and respect to those who secured it:

> The touchstone of educational policy, and through education of all policy in Africa, is the relation of governments with the class of educated natives . . . The importance of these men lies, not in their being a necessity, as clerks and so forth, to the machinery of Government, but in their being taken as models by an increasing number of their countrymen . . .
>
> Nevertheless, to guide the thought and ambition of these men, and to gain their sympathy and cooperation, should be part of Government's deliberate policy. A place must be given them in the state comparable with their influence on society. Otherwise they inevitably pass into opposition.[5]

Although both men attached supreme importance to the role of the school,[6] it is difficult to understand how Oldham could have contemplated any form of alliance between them, for basically Leys

[1] Oldham to Leys, 3 Sept. 1919, File Q-B, E.H.

[2] Leys to the Colonial Secretary, 7 Feb. 1918, copy in File Q-B, E.H.

[3] Ibid., pp. 30–4; for the full significance of this rising, which Leys believed to be 'the first attack of a new malady', see Shepperson and Price, *Independent African*.

[4] Leys to the Colonial Secretary, 7 Feb. 1918, p. 31. For the exact nature of Chilembwe's English see Shepperson and Price, op. cit., pp. 537–8.

[5] Leys to the Colonial Secretary, 7 Feb. 1918, pp. 45–6.

[6] For Leys's views on missions and education, see Fulani bin Fulani (pseudonym for Leys), 'A Problem in East African Missions', *I.R.M.*, viii (1919), 155–72; 'Native Races and their Rulers', *I.R.M.* viii (1919), 263–6; 'Christianity and Labour Conditions in Africa', *I.R.M.* ix (1920), 544–51.

would make Africa safe by more independence and Jones by less. For industrial education, too, Leys had already stated the consequences of his own political philosophy: industrial training should aim neither at providing artisans for the European commercial community, nor at reviving village anachronisms, but primarily it should develop 'real, large-scale industries, having insatiable demand from wide markets, like cotton or oil seed growing'.[1] Scarcely surprising in the light of all this, was that sector of American Negro opinion which Leys was beginning to heed: after the 1919 Pan-African Congress in Paris, he had begun to be impressed by a 'M. Burghardt du Bois, a man of character, ability and power to lead in quite exceptional degree', and had shown some considerable sympathy for 'his new liberation campaign, to be preached to Africans'.[2]

There is, however, little evidence from the West Africa Report that Jones thought Leys's document anything more than an indirect confirmation of his own outlook. His own report was studded with references to the education of American Negroes, but they were all to that type which had received the greatest publicity in his earlier *Negro Education.* Attention was continually focused on Washington and Moton, Tuskegee and Hampton, and the little Penn School on St. Helena Island was declared to be the best model for African education.[3] The casual reader would scarcely have gained any idea that Negroes had ever aspired any higher, apart from one short passage in Anson Phelps Stokes's introduction to the volume:

> The time has passed when the old thesis can be successfully maintained that a curriculum well suited to the needs of a group on a given scale of civilization in one country is necessarily the best for other groups on a different level of advancement in another country or section.
>
> This was the natural mistake generally made by New England in dealing with the Negro in the southern states of America immediately after emancipation. For the many as distinct from the few, the results were small in comparison with those that came later based on General Armstrong's vital work at Hampton, where education was adapted directly to a people's needs. Here there was real education.[4]

[1] Leys to the Colonial Secretary, 7 Feb. 1918, p. 45.

[2] Leys to B. Turner, 3 May 1921, File Q-B, E.H.

[3] Jones, *Education in Africa*; see index for references to Hampton Institute, Jeanes Fund, Rosenwald Schools, Washington, Moton, Tuskegee, Armstrong; for Penn School, see pp. 34–5.

[4] Ibid., p. xxiii.

Furthermore, the two colleges for higher education that there were in Africa received a comment somewhat similar to that made on Lincoln and other universities in the *Negro Education* report.[1]

There were further parallels with Jones's earlier work. The general effect of the first Phelps-Stokes Report upon independent Negro initiatives was not so readily ascertainable as in America. The Yergan affair, however, had already shown Jones over-anxious to scrutinize the safety of individual Negroes for African work.[2] Nor was that an isolated episode, but part of a definite policy to play down those types of independent American Negro and African enterprise in Africa that commended themselves to DuBois and Garvey, even to the extent of not mentioning when mission stations were headed by American Negroes. An extreme example of Jones's caution in this matter was shown in his description of the work of the American Congregational Mission in Angola. In the published report, there was no mention that the oldest station of this mission was under the direction of Mr. Hastings, a native Jamaican, and another station under Mr. Hector McDowell, an American Negro graduate of Talladega College.[3] That this reticence was no accident was shown in Jones's more private account of the commission's tour:

> The home board [of the Congregational Church] plan to have Negro churches send more workers supported by themselves. It is to be hoped that the board will exercise great care in pursuing this policy. The relationship of missionaries on the field to the government and to the natives is exceedingly delicate. Our observations in Africa indicate that only the most thoughtful, cooperative type of American or English Negro can be helpful with the mission fields.[4]

More than this, there was even a parallel to the way that, in the States, Jones's word had become almost necessary to ensure philanthropic support. Mrs. Adelaide Casely Hayford, the wife of the famous Gold Coast barrister, had been in the States raising funds for a new girls' school for Sierra Leone, run in fact on model Phelps-Stokes lines.[5] Yet Jones had been instrumental in at least one donor's

[1] Ibid., pp. 109, 205, for Fourah Bay College and the South African Native College. For Lincoln University, Pennsylvania, see p. 41.

[2] See pp. 81–2.

[3] T. J. Jones, 'Journal of the West Africa Phelps-Stokes Commission', (copy in E.H.), entry for 4 Feb. 1921; p. 186; see also Jones, *Education in Africa*, pp. 239–43.

[4] Jones, 'Journal', p. 186.

[5] Adelaide Casely Hayford, 'A Girls' School in West Africa', *Southern Work-*

withdrawing her contribution, by pointing out 'the relative usefulness of money placed in a school that had no assurance of going on, or the number of schools like Tuskegee and others in this country which are assured of continuance'.[1] This incident, with several others like it, were no doubt of little enough significance in themselves. They do, however, illustrate a point which has been touched on before—Jones's fear not only of the radical Negro, but also of the uncommitted or marginal man.[2] They also put into somewhat more accurate perspective the claims for Tuskegee methods that the commission was expounding.

Once the commission had returned to England in August 1921, the confrontation between Tuskegee and pan-African propaganda for Africa was accentuated by both Jones and DuBois again being in England at the same time, and seeking to put their own points of view before various groups of people.[3] One of the people with whom they both conferred at some length during the same week was Dr. Norman Leys,[4] who was thus ideally placed to judge the issues that had divided the two men for more than ten years. He had read widely both Washington's writings and some of DuBois's work, but had not felt it necessary to judge between the two schools.[5] The outcome was not now difficult to predict. Leys began to see a good deal of DuBois, subscribed to the *Crisis*, and attended the second Pan-African Congress at the end of August.[6] For Jones it was a very

---

man, lv (Oct. 1926), 449–56. For Jones's attitude to African independent schools see further p. 239. See also Mrs. Casely Hayford's reminiscences, serialized in the *West African Review*, from vol. xxiv, No. 313 (Oct. 1953) to vol. xxv, No. 323 (Aug. 1954).

[1] Peabody to Mrs. Casely Hayford, 7 Jan. 1924, Box 20, Peabody Papers, L.C. Tuskegee itself contributed money through its Y.M.C.A. to her school; R.R.M./L.C. (1920), T.U.A.

[2] See p. 85, n. 1. For Jones's 'fear of radical negroes', see Peabody to Dillard, 7 Dec. 1921, Box 15, Peabody Papers, L.C. Cf. also DuBois, 'Thomas Jesse Jones', p. 256.

[3] Jones and DuBois had coincided once before in England, see p. 56.

[4] Leys to Oldham, 22 Aug. 1921, File Q-A, E.H.

[5] Leys to Moton, 11 Jan. 1922, R.R.M. Misc. Papers, (1922), T.U.A.

[6] DuBois met Leys at a meeting of the Advisory Committee on International Questions of the Labour Party, 26 Aug. 1921, along with Sidney Webb, John Harris, and Leonard Woolf. For Leys's views of the importance of the *Crisis*, see Leys to Miss G. Gollock, 18 Dec. 1921, 'Race' Folder, E.H., now I.M.C.A., Geneva. The Pan-African Congress (London session) took place on 28 and 29 Aug. 1921. For this second Pan-African Congress, see DuBois, 'A Second Journey to Pan-Africa', pp. 39–42.

important reverse; Leys had become convinced that the Phelps-Stokes Africa policy, as expressed by its chief architect, presupposed for Negroes a permanent status significantly different from that of whites. He confided this view at a very crucial time to Oldham, who was working on a book about Christianity and the race problem:[1]

> There is no sense whatever in trying to treat the least of human creatures as a Jesus if in his soul there are innate deficiencies. Let me give you an illustration of how intensely practical a question the alternative raises. I pressed Jesse Jones to tell me whether he thought American negroes as a whole different in nature and capacity from the Europeans they live among and whether he expected from them a different kind of future. He admitted that he did. I told him that explained everything, to me, of his differences with Du Bois and others . . . Jones in effect says it isn't wise, it isn't sensible to teach a negro child what European children are taught because as men they have a different status.[2]

It is interesting that Leys considered the issue sufficiently important for him to write direct to Moton at Tuskegee, and ask him to confirm or deny the impression he had just gained of Jones and DuBois.[3]

What Moton replied is not known, but it is clear on other evidence that Moton was not prepared to be pressed by his white supporters into a personal vendetta with DuBois. Despite this, he was increasingly being elevated by white missionary leaders into a position of Negro spokesman on Africa, which had the effect, albeit involuntarily, of throwing him into apparent competition with DuBois.

Oldham, on his second visit to Tuskegee, had co-opted Moton to be one of the representatives for Africa on the I.M.C., and Moton had therefore an influence at the highest level on missionary policy in Africa at the 1921 session.[4] Jones and Aggrey were also prominent at the same conference, and this monopoly of Phelps-Stokes and Tuskegee opinion over education in Africa understandably gave DuBois the feeling that policy-making was quite out of his hands. He commented bitterly: 'A secret conference on missionary and educational work among Negroes in Africa and elsewhere has been held at Lake Mohonk. The Negro race was represented by Thomas

[1] J. H. Oldham, *Christianity and the Race Problem* (London, 1924).

[2] Leys to Oldham, 14 Nov. 1921, Folder on Race, E.H., now I.M.C.A., Geneva.

[3] Leys to Moton, 11 Jan. 1922.

[4] Oldham to Moton, 5 Mar. 1921, R.R.M./G.C. (1921), T.U.A.; see also F. Lenwood, 'The International Missionary Council', *I.R.M.* xi (1922), 41.

Jesse Jones and R. R. Moton.'[1] Whatever DuBois's reaction, Jones's and Aggrey's personal pre-eminence in missionary conventions on Africa was assured, for they had now a quite unrivalled knowledge of mission work throughout the western, central and southern areas of Africa. It was therefore very natural that they should dominate the Foreign Mission Convention of North America when they discussed education in its 1922 session.[2] It is some indication of the success that both they and J. H. Oldham had had in pointing to Tuskegee as the source of missionary inspiration for Africa that Dr. Robert Moton should be called across to the great Scottish Churches Missionary Conference in Glasgow later that year.[3] There he linked the 'conspicuous' progress of the Negro population of America to the education of Tuskegee and Hampton, and both of these to the development of Africa. In this light, he explained, even the slave trade now appeared as the working of Providence.[4]

Marcus Garvey, however, would not be spoken for on Africa in this manner any more than DuBois. Himself an ardent admirer of Tuskegee,[5] he nevertheless felt that Moton should guard himself against manipulation; for whether Moton realized it or not, he was being used to recommend to Africans continued dependence on the white man:

> Now that the Negro has started to think for himself the white Christian leaders and philanthropists realise that it will be very hard for them to convince us to accept their 'friendly protection'. Hence they feel that the best that can be done would be to get a representative Negro to say for them what they would very much like to have said. Our friend Dr. Moton is the fittest man for such a job, because he and his institution as well as Hampton Institute . . . are the two Negro institutions that have received millions of dollars from white philanthropists to teach Negroes in the way that they should go . . .

[1] DuBois, *Crisis*, xxiii, No. 2 (Dec. 1921), 81.

[2] T. J. Jones, 'The Educational Needs of the People of Equatorial Africa', *The Foreign Mission Conference of North America: Twenty-Ninth Annual Session, 1922* (New York, 1922), pp. 168–76. See also address by Aggrey therein, pp. 176–80.

[3] D. Fraser, 'The Scottish Churches' Missionary Campaign', *I.R.M.* xi (1922), 286–94.

[4] R. R. Moton, 'Problems and Development of the Negro Race', (address at Scottish Churches' Missionary Conference, Glasgow, 17 Oct. 1922), printed in the *Tuskegee Student*, xxxii, No. 17 (1 Nov. 1922); see also 'Missionary Methods', *Tuskegee Student*, xxxii, No. 18, (15 Nov. 1922).

[5] Garvey to Moton, 1 June 1917, R.R.M./G.C. (1917), T.U.A. See further p. 18, n. 3.

We hope that no member of our race will pay any attention to what Dr. Moton says in the matter of Africa's needs, because it is strange that he had nothing to say about Africa until he was called by these white missionaries and philanthropists to speak.[1]

It was a charge that was echoed by several leading American Negroes at this time, however bitterly opposed to each other they might be on other matters.[2] What seems strange in retrospect, however, is not that the charge was made, but that it never more openly attached to Aggrey's role in the Phelps-Stokes Commissions. This may perhaps be partly explained by Aggrey's capacity for understanding of and friendship with those very Negroes most critical of Jones and the Fund, in particular Max Yergan, Carter G. Woodson, and such Coloured Y.M.C.A. leaders as Jesse E. Moorland.[3] Indeed, with the exception of his attacks on Garvey, Aggrey seems to have been determined to avoid that internecine strife that had so weakened the Negro leadership during the early twentieth century. It was a conviction he only spoke of to all-black audiences, using the following parable:

The cardinal sin of whites is arrogance—the trouble with us Africans is jealousy. If we have a leader, even a first-class one, we want to pull him down.

I once went to a lumber camp in Canada, and I saw an enormous fir being felled with ropes right up to the top—scores of men pulling. Finally down it came. 'Have you ever seen such a wonderful sight?', the foreman asked. 'It's not wonderful so much as amazing. You have missed the whole point. Look who was pulling on the ropes—Canadian Negroes! Have you ever seen one hundred Negroes pulling together?'[4]

At any rate, even if Aggrey was himself too occupied in gaining everybody's co-operation for Africa to notice the peculiar vulnerability of his role, there can be little doubt that Jones did increasingly

[1] *The Negro World*, xiii, No. 10 (21 Oct. 1922), 1. Garvey underestimated Moton's personal interest in Africa, expressed most obviously in the encouragement of African staff and students at Tuskegee, see Ch. VIII.

[2] Cf. p. 84.

[3] Aggrey to Peabody, 17 Nov. 1923, Box 18, Peabody Papers/L.C.; Aggrey to Woodson, 13 July 1927, Box 6, acc. 3579, add. 1, Woodson Papers, L.C.

[4] I am indebted for this anecdote to Mr. A. G. Fraser (son of Principal Fraser, leader of the Village Education Commission, and later of Achimota College). For a more detailed discussion of Aggrey, see K. J. King, 'James E. K. Aggrey: Collaborator, Nationalist, Pan-African', *Canadian Journal of African Studies*, iii, No. 3 (1970).

see Aggrey and others as fulfilling precisely the function Garvey had mentioned.[1]

As Jones had been under severe attack from all sectors of radical Negro opinion both during and after the West African Phelps-Stokes Commission,[2] it is not perhaps surprising that the second (East African) Education Commission and its report had an even greater propaganda content than the first. Indeed, many of its actions and much of the subsequent report can only be fully understood as part of a continuing crusade by Jones against DuBois, Garvey, and Woodson.

Much more time both in Africa and in the writing of the report was consequently spent on explaining away the recent demands for racial equality and the various forms of independence claimed by Africans. Nor was Jones concerned only to counteract radical American Negro propaganda; he was possibly also reacting to his encounter with Leys on the question of race equalities. For it was strongly denied that any rating of equalities or inequalities was valuable; instead, it was 'sound and helpful' to appreciate the reality of racial differences.[3]

On the issue of greater independence for Africans, there was a further reference to programmes for Africa politically different from his own:

> The conflicting ideals of those who would serve are in some instances as divisive and unfortunate as selfishness and prejudice. The more recent of these ideals are represented by such words as 'Self-Determination', 'Self-government', 'Self-expression'... Liberty, independence and self-determination, with their comparatively unknown or untried experiments, are far more attractive to idealistic temperaments than trusteeship, protectorate and colony, whose failures have often been allowed to over-shadow their successes. The thought of freedom seems to have far more charm than that of direction and discipline and order.[4]

As has been seen in Kenya itself, Aggrey had been of great value in preaching against Garveyism, an activity which he had later continued in southern Africa.[5] It was generally the commission's policy to leave the winning of Africans themselves to Aggrey, but on more than

[1] On Jones's scheme to finance a Negro journalist, Lester Walton, to conduct constructive propaganda among Negroes and whites, see Jones to W. W. Alexander, 22 Dec. 1922, R.R.M./G.C. (1923), T.U.A.

[2] DuBois, 'Thomas Jesse Jones', pp. 253–6.

[3] Jones, *Education in East Africa*, p. 77.

[4] Ibid.

[5] Smith, *Aggrey of Africa*, pp. 122, 124, 176; see also p. 118 and p. 223.

one occasion Jones seems to have taken the initiative himself with a local ruler, and used Tuskegee's good offices to anticipate propaganda from other Negro sources. He sought Moton's co-operation in one of these plans: 'Today I conferred with His Highness, the Sultan of Zanzibar. He is an able and delightful man. I wish you could send him *Finding a Way Out* with a brief letter of appreciation for his kindness to us. You would thus begin to bind him to you and so help avoid a relationship to the radical forces of our country.'[1]

In discussing the reports from this propagandist angle, it has been implied throughout that they could be taken as expressing Jones's views rather than those of any other members of the commission. Both reports were indeed almost entirely of his authorship, but it is significant that his monopoly over the contents had not been ceded willingly in the East Africa report. While they were still on tour, Garfield Williams and others had been so alarmed at Jones's dictating the mind of the commission that a form of joint authorship had been agreed on.[2] This had, however, been reversed on the return to London, and the Report was written by Jones alone, under a serious threat of non-cooperation from the two English authorities, Vischer and Williams.[3] Their differences with Jones can only be conjectured, but some light is thrown on possible areas of disagreement from one of Jones's co-workers at Edinburgh House.

Miss Georgina Gollock, co-editor with Oldham of the *I.R.M.*, had noted in the draft of the report the almost complete absence of any criticism of white settlers and government, and thought this was a potential danger to the report's intended objectivity. She had made therefore an attempt to have the balance redressed by Anson Phelps Stokes:

> I believe that his [Jones's] attitude may be the means of inaugurating a new kind of fellowship, a new and fuller understanding just where it is needed most; but the reality and the extent of this sympathy has a side of danger, and it is for this I think a very careful reading should be given to the Report as it nears completion. Individual sentences or paragraphs in

[1] Jones to Moton, 14 Apr. 1922, R.R.M./G.C. (1925), T.U.A. Jones was also anxious that Moton should use his influence with President Coolidge to arrange for the Prince Regent of Ethiopia, Ras Tafari (Haile Selassie) to come to the States; Jones to Moton, 6 Feb. 1924, R.R.M./G.C. (1925), T.U.A. The book mentioned was R. R. Moton's, *Finding a Way Out: an autobiography* (London, 1920).

[2] Vischer to Oldham, 8 Apr. 1924, File Q-E, E.H.

[3] Miss Gollock to Oldham, undated memo of 1924/5, File Q-R, E.H.

a certain chapter may be in true proportion. When they recur in chapter after chapter, they may make a total impression of something that is more than the truth . . . I am anxious lest there should be anything in the Report which should seem in the least degree to condone actions which are not quite worthy, or to fail to hold an even balance where the interests of the Africans are at stake.[1]

Miss Gollock was anxious that Anson Phelps Stokes should insert somewhere an explanation for this absence of criticism of the white settlers and government. He could, she suggested, stress that the commission had deliberately steered clear of political issues as beyond their brief. What Miss Gollock failed to see in the report, however, was that, far from playing down white injustice and avoiding controversy, it rather invited controversy by enthusiastically supporting a large increase in white settlement. The report gave the strongest possible backing to the idea of a great white belt extending from East to South Africa, in which South Africans would play the dominant part, and where 'possession' would be 'nine points of the law'.[2] It is not improbable, therefore, that it was with something in these assumptions that Vischer, Williams, and Shantz quarrelled.[3]

It might equally well have been the question of cultural education for Africans or the place of African leadership in East Africa that caused disagreement, for on both these matters Miss Gollock also felt that there was a danger of the report's appearing reactionary and attracting adverse criticism.[4] Indeed, it seems not impossible that the criticism she anticipated was from DuBois.[5] Her suggestions on the report, however, appear to have had no more effect on Jones than Leys had had earlier, and if she foresaw DuBois's hostility, it was probably no more than Jones did himself.

Fresh fuel was to be added to the flames of this antagonism to DuBois and his supporters soon after the commission had returned to England for the second time. It consisted of the publication in

[1] Miss Gollock to Phelps Stokes, 15 Jan. 1925, File L-1, P.S.F.A.

[2] Jones, *Education in East Africa*, pp. 82–3.

[3] H. L. Shantz to Oldham 2 June 1925, Box 314, E.H., now I.M.C.A., Geneva. For Jones's own confidential analysis of his tactics in the report, see Jones to Owen, 18 Dec. 1924, Acc. 83, Owen Papers, C.M.S.A., London; and Jones to Arthur, 18 Dec. 1924, Education Bundle, P.C.E.A.

[4] Miss Gollock to Phelps Stokes, 15 Jan. 1925, File L-1, P.S.F.A.

[5] DuBois was quick to note the praise for Jones's Report coming from *East Africa*, a magazine exclusively interested in white settlement and business throughout Eastern Africa. *Crisis*, xxx (May 1925), 40. *East Africa*, i, No. 32 (Apr. 1925), 676–8; No. 33 (May 7 1925), 694–5.

October 1924 of Norman Leys's book, *Kenya*, one of the most ruthlessly outspoken exposés of white exploitation to appear in the inter-war years. The timing was crucial; it antedated Jones's East Africa report by several months, and took good care to condemn in advance what Leys believed to be its educational heresies and its accommodation to white settlement. In three pages of passionate analysis of Jones's ideology, it demonstrated the central political importance of African education, and concluded:

> The reader may consider that too much attention has been paid to these false educational ideals. He may be assured that in Africa the obscurantist is an even greater danger than the exploiter. What the African in Kenya needs is knowledge, enlightenment, the acquisition of the appetite which makes men seek the truth. He needs these exactly as the whole human race needs them.[1]

The publicity which attended *Kenya*[2] and its attempt to discredit Jones's policies was only the beginning of a series of reverses that threatened completely to undermine Jones's position as expert on the Negro in America and Africa. DuBois had himself travelled to West Africa in the winter of 1923, and on his return had had published in a nationally respected journal his famous 'Worlds of Color'.[3] It was a sort of miniature second instalment of Leys's work, investigating the 'dark colonial shadow' that walked behind every great European power, and reserving for Britain's African governments the heaviest strictures of all; on any rating of colonial racism, DuBois argued, Britain had no competitor.[4] This was, of course, in direct contradiction to everything that the Phelps-Stokes report would claim the month afterwards, and it made both Jones and Oldham feel that something must be done to set the record straight on British colonial policy.[5]

The contemporary situation in the Negro colleges was equally crucial for Jones, and was an inevitable counterpart to the conflicts over African education and white rule. Since June 1924 DuBois had been waging a campaign to free Fisk University, his own Alma

[1] Leys, *Kenya*, p. 392.

[2] It had run through two editions before Jones's *Education in East Africa* was published.

[3] W. E. B. DuBois, 'Worlds of Color', *Foreign Affairs* (Washington), iii, No. 3 (Apr. 1925), 423–44.

[4] Ibid., p. 423.

[5] Oldham to Jones, 5 May 1925, Jones File (hereafter Q-J), E.H.

Mater, from what he considered to be the oppressive white leadership of President McKenzie. Indeed, at the Alumni commemoration address at Fisk in 1924, DuBois had suggested to McKenzie's face that he should resign and that his place should be taken by a Negro.[1] Even here there was an element of the old vendetta; Jones was the secretary of the Fisk board of trustees, and believed that McKenzie was one of the only men who had really tried to adapt Negro college education to his own ideals.[2] He assured the board that a blow would be struck for 'Fisk, Negro education and for race relationships in America and Africa' if McKenzie could weather the storm.[3] But DuBois was more than ready, for once, to come down into the arena and distribute his own printed statements among the student body, to encourage them in their protest. Student rioting broke out at least twice at DuBois's incitement, and on the most serious breakdown of order, in February 1925, the president's account left no doubt about where some of the inspiration came from:

> This Wednesday night two of these leaders told Miss Boynton that it would be of no use for the President or any other representative of the faculty to come, and that they were going to keep up this sort of thing until the President's hair was white. The disorderly students overturned chapel seats, broke windows and fired shots terrifying the neighborhood for blocks around all the while keeping up a steady shouting of 'DuBois' and 'Before I'd be a slave'.[4]

In the event, President McKenzie was forced into resignation two months later, and Jones, in complete confusion, had to admit the apparent defeat of the Hampton principle of white leadership in Negro colleges.[5] While the *Crisis* was blazing its victory to other colleges,[6] however, Jones suggested a new policy to his board: a completely coloured faculty from the president down, with W. T. B.

[1] W. E. B. DuBois, 'Diuturni Silenti', *Fisk Herald*, xxxiii, No. 1 (1924), see also L. A. Roy to Jones, 19 June 1924, File A-22, P.S.F.A.

[2] Jones to P. Cravath, 20 Aug. 1924, R.R.M./G.C. (1925), T.U.A.

[3] Ibid.

[4] F. A. McKenzie, 14 Feb. 1925, 'Letter written to an Alumnus who asked for information', File III, b.6, Acc. No. 329, McKenzie Papers, Tennessee State Archives, Nashville. Also Broderick, *W. E. B. DuBois*, pp. 163–4.

[5] Jones to McKenzie, 6 May 1925, File III, b. 6, Acc. No. 329, McKenzie Papers, Tennessee State Archives: 'I am all mixed up. I have been saying things that do not belong in Sunday School . . . Well, what next? After us, the Deluge.'

[6] DuBois thought the time appropriate for a general attack on restrictive philanthropy; see especially his 'Gifts and Education', *Crisis*, xxix, No. 4, (Feb. 1925). See further, p. 246, n. 3, and Broderick, op. cit., pp. 163–4.

Williams, a member of the staff at Tuskegee, and field agent of the Jeanes and Slater Boards, as the new President. The rationale of this proposal was exactly what Garvey had three years earlier analysed as the new philanthropic and missionary method of controlling Negroes in the post-war era. A safe Negro could more plausibly suggest unpopular methods than a white man.[1]

Jones indeed realized that the same principle might be applied equally well in the international sphere, and, if the right candidate could be found, would effectively nullify some of the recent radical statements about Africa. Here there could be no doubt whom Jones would select:

> I have been giving serious consideration to some plans for Aggrey . . . They are as follows. 1. That influences unfriendly to British Colonial policy, such as the articles in *Foreign Affairs* and the *New York Times Current History* by Dubois; Leys' book; the propaganda of Indians and others in this country, make it very desirable that the carefully presented statement of an educated African like Aggrey should be produced.[2]

Jones proceeded to outline how Aggrey's still uncompleted Ph.D., along with other articles, could be used for this larger end, and proposed that the Colonial Office could grant him study leave from Achimota College, where Aggrey was by this time assistant vice-principal.[3] As Achimota had not yet even opened, however, it was impossible at this stage that Aggrey should be spared; his role in recommending to his fellow-Africans a new kind of college that started from the bottom with a kindergarten and not a degree was much too vital.[4] Nevertheless, it was a pointer towards this more deliberate use of Aggrey in redressing slurs on British African policies that he was given the opportunity to justify the new African education on the B.B.C. in November 1925.[5]

These provisional plans for Aggrey were becoming in Jones's mind only a part of a wider scheme whereby the peculiar appropriateness of Tuskegee-Hampton education could make itself felt throughout Africa. He now projected that white men with the right experience of

[1] Jones to McKenzie, 6 May 1923; Fisk did not in the event have a black president then, since many Negro leaders, including Moton, thought it highly inadvisable; Moton to Jones, 14 May 1925, R.R.M./G.C. (1925), T.U.A.

[2] Jones to Oldham, 14 July 1925, File Q-J, E.H.

[3] Smith, *Aggrey of Africa*, p. 230.

[4] Ibid., pp. 225–45.

[5] J. E. K. Aggrey, 'The Prince of Wales College' broadcast talk, reproduced in *Southern Workman*, lv (Jan. 1926), 39–42.

Southern education should go out to each African country, paired with American Negroes who had been trained in the Hampton and Tuskegee ideals.[1] By the end of 1925 the first white educator had been selected for this programme, and had been sent to Liberia as supervisor of missionary education;[2] but, as has been seen already, the real difficulty was finding suitable American Negro partners—a task that had become doubly difficult after Woodson's and DuBois's critique of 'hand-picked' Negroes.[3]

Associated with this new conception of the value of the American Negro propagandist in Africa was the notion, now suddenly popular among mission leaders in Britain and Africa, that Dr. Moton himself should make an African tour. It had originated with Donald Fraser, who had called Moton to the Scottish Conference earlier, and was taken up by Loram.[4] Oldham too thought that 'a visit to Africa by Moton, rightly prepared for, might have a most valuable and far reaching influence'. He had evidence from Uganda that Moton could most usefully reinforce the impetus towards co-operation given by Aggrey's earlier visit, and thought it possible that he would also be welcome in Kenya.[5]

Both these projects were made even more relevant by the fact that a major conference at Le Zoute on Christian mission and education in Africa was being prepared for 1926. Organized primarily by Oldham, its educational objective was to ratify the new outlook of both the Phelps-Stokes Commissions and the Colonial Office Advisory Committee,[6] and link once and for all the development of African education with the philanthropic traditions of the Southern States.[7] Oldham, in recognition of this connection, had made it quite clear to Jones that everything would 'depend on getting over the right representatives of the coloured people in America, and of

[1] Jones to E. C. Sage, 18 Dec. 1925, File C-3, P.S.F.A.

[2] W. E. B. DuBois, 'The New African Program', *Crisis*, xxxi, No. 3 (Jan. 1926), 113–14.

[3] See p. 79 ff.

[4] Jones to Moton, 2 Aug. 1923, R.R.M./G.C. (1923), T.U.A., and Oldham to Jones, 3 Dec. 1925, File Q-J, E.H.

[5] Moton did not eventually go to Kenya or Uganda on his African tour.

[6] Smith, *Christian Mission in Africa*, *passim*. The first Command Paper of the Advisory Committee for Native Education in Africa (*Educational Policy in British Tropical Africa*, Cmd. 2374 Mar. 1925) had been timed to coincide with the publication of Jones's *Education in East Africa*.

[7] Sage (asst. secretary of the General Education Board) to Jones, 10 Dec. 1925, File C-3, P.S.F.A.

those among the whites who have been leaders in the work for the Negroes'.[1] Jones, for his part, had by now quite recovered from the upsets of the previous year, and, with a World Conference in the offing, it was a temptation to feel that Africa really might soon be won for his four 'Simples' of education.[2] The policy was there; all that was required was for Loram, Oldham, and himself to work as a triumvirate for its acceptance. He explained this, their continent-wide potential, to Loram:

> The three of us have real possibilities for the future of Africa . . . It is thus important that we shall work out the bases of cooperation . . .
>
> That Oldham shall win Mission Societies and European Governments to our education programs; that you shall help formulate the administrative problems of both schools and Governments, and of course win Governments and others to these programs; that I shall help formulate the adaptations of education and exert any influence I may have in winning the support of America.[3]

If this master plan to be ratified at the September World Conference took no account of African or American Negro reaction, that very soon occurred. Two months before the conference, DuBois delivered his most stinging indictment yet of the two Phelps-Stokes African education reports.[4] He took up the same points that he had made earlier in his critique of Jones's *Negro Education:* Jones's animus against African higher education, his fear of all forms of Negro independence, and his accommodation to the commercial requirements of the white minorities in Africa. To DuBois both Africa reports were simply further proof of the essentially political nature of Negro education: 'This is the program of Thomas Jesse Jones and the Phelps-Stokes Fund in Africa. They are defending situations like that in Kenya, warning against agitation, seeking to substitute white leadership, white teachers and white missionaries for

[1] Oldham to Jones, 5 Nov. 1925, File Q-J, E.H.

[2] See the full statement of his educational philosophy in *The Four Essentials of Education* (New York, 1926); and A. V. Murray's critique of this in *The School in the Bush*, pp. 300–4.

[3] Jones to Loram, 7 June 1926, File Q-J, E.H.

[4] W. E. B. DuBois, 'Education in Africa: A Review of the Recommendations of the African Education Committee', *Crisis*, xxxii, No. 2 (June 1926), 86–9. DuBois had shown further evidence of his continuing association with Norman Leys by devoting some considerable space in the *Crisis* to a review of Leys's *Kenya*, viz. 'Kenya—A Study of East African conditions as revealed by Norman Leys', *Crisis*, xxxi (Feb. 1926), 188–91.

colored missionaries, and decrying and discrediting the educated black man the world over.'[1]

This tirade, which concluded that 'the Phelps-Stokes Fund was making Africa safe for white folks',[2] did not fail to be heard. Indeed, the reverberations were soon felt in the Gold Coast, and Aggrey was thrown into the role, which Jones had cast for him, of counteracting DuBois's propaganda and justifying the Phelps-Stokes Fund.[3] Furthermore, Aggrey's task was not made any easier by propaganda from the *Negro World* at this time. Just a month before the Le Zoute conference, it brought out a full-page editorial, demonstrating that Africans 'need the same sort of education that Europeans need.'[4]

None of this could, of course, prevent the conference from reaching a very satisfactory consensus; its effect would come later, in making it just a little more difficult to convince Africans that they needed a specially adapted type of education. The conference itself, however, was a success on its own terms, for its membership did indeed symbolize just such a union of the Southern States and Africa as Jones and Oldham had worked for. Every major fund that worked in the American South was represented at the highest level: Dr. Dillard of the Jeanes and Slater Funds, E. C. Sage and Jackson Davis of the General Education Board, Leonard Outhwaite of the Spelman Rockefeller Board, Canon Anson Phelps Stokes and Jesse Jones of the Phelps-Stokes Fund.[5] More than this, the educational methods of the South of which Jones most approved were represented by Miss Thorn, Principal of Calhoun Coloured School, and Miss House of the Penn School[6] The extent to which the conference was an endorsement of Jones's overall vision for education was no more expressively summed up than by E. W. Smith: 'Scarcely a speech at Le Zoute was complete without the words "adaptation", "cooperation". They were reiterated so frequently that at last speakers felt inclined to apologise for pronouncing them.'[7]

As far as the attitudes of Leys and DuBois were concerned, such conspicuous missionary and philanthropic unanimity over the form of African education could only give further grounds for indignation

[1] DuBois, 'Education in Africa', p. 88. [2] Ibid., p. 89.
[3] Smith, *Aggrey of Africa*, pp. 255–7.
[4] 'The Sort of Education Africans Need', *Negro World*, xxi, No. 1 (14 Aug. 1926).
[5] Smith, *The Christian Mission in Africa*, pp. 187–8.
[6] Ibid.; for the Penn School, see further, p. 41, and pp. 184–5.
[7] Smith, *Christian Mission in Africa*, p. 92.

and dispute. Another clash over the politics of African education was inevitable. The only difference this time was that the protagonists were not DuBois and Jones, but Leys and Oldham, by now in open hostility. The complete break between these two men, who had co-operated to such effect in their resistance to Kenya's labour ordinances, had been coming for some time, but was very largely due to just those issues of race and education that the Phelps-Stokes Commission had raised but not resolved. In Leys's view, Oldham's book, *Christianity and the Race Problem*, had failed to take account of the racial undercurrents in Jones's educational theories, and had, instead of dismissing the notion of race itself as illusory, returned with 'conspicuous fairness' a verdict of not proven.[1]

It was on these grounds that Leys now castigated him for his part in spreading Phelps-Stokesism; for Oldham had not only been instrumental in getting the missionary societies to ratify Jones's adapted education, but he had also been largely responsible for it's becoming the official doctrine of the Colonial Office Advisory Committee on African Education.[2] In the bitter correspondence which they carried on in the national press over Jones's reports and African education,[3] the key term was 'adaptation', with all its widely different interpretations. For Oldham this was an educational term, for Leys a thinly disguised formula for political inferiority. The truth was that it could assuredly be both, and, as has been noticed in Kenya, it was very largely its ambiguity that temporarily secured the co-operation of all the various white groups in the cause of African education.

Although co-operation between Jones and Oldham was going to become progressively strained in the later twenties and early thirties, as Oldham's doubts about white settlers' good intentions in Eastern Africa revived,[4] there were substantial grounds during the years

[1] Leys to Oldham, 14 Nov. 1921, Folder on Race, E.H., now I.M.C.A., Geneva; also Leys to Oldham, 2 July 1924, File Q-B, E.H.

[2] N. M. Leys, *The Scots Observer*, 27 Nov. 1926, p. 13.

[3] N. M. Leys, letter to *Manchester Guardian*, 26 Oct. 1926; J. H. Oldham, letter to *Manchester Guardian*, 29 Oct. 1926; N. M. Leys, 'Christianity and Race: A New Policy for Missions', *The Scots Observer*, i, 13 Nov. 1926, p. 4. N. M. Leys, 'Missions and Governments: Objects of Christian Education', *The Scots Observer*, i, 27 Nov. 1926, p. 13; J. H. Oldham, 'African Education: Missions and Governments', *The Scots Observer*, i, 11 Dec. 1926, p. 13; N. M. Leys, letter to *The Scots Observer*, i, 18 Dec. 1926, p. 11.

[4] Cf. Oldham's membership of the Hilton Young Commission (Cmd. 3378, 1929), and commentary by Bennett, *Kenya*, pp. 67–9. See also J. H. Oldham, *White and Black in Africa: A Critical Examination of the Rhodes Lectures of General Smuts* (London, 1930); and Jones to Oldham, 17 Jan. 1930, File L-1, P.S.F.A.

1923–7 for Jones to believe Oldham committed to the same approach as himself on the best way to resolve Kenya's political crises. Oldham does seem to have adopted Jones's conviction that constant criticism from London could only impede any settlement of Kenya's race-torn politics, and that the better element among the whites on the spot should be trusted to work out for themselves problems of native welfare. In addition, he came near to letting himself be appointed the Governor of Kenya's research director, a position that would have allowed him to bring to bear on racial tensions the sort of objective analysis that Jones was in the habit of advocating.[1] Moreover, Oldham had recently written articles in *The Times*, asking for more public recognition of Kenya's progress, which Jones thought surpassed even his own 'appreciation of the terrible Nordics in that part of the world!'[2] For his own part, Jones continued in America to take every available opportunity of protecting white Kenya's image against corrosion.[3] As for West Africa, he had just successfully persuaded A. G. Fraser to release Aggrey for the important propaganda work against the detractors of British colonial policy.[4] It had begun to look as if the propaganda conflict was entering a new phase.

Aggrey's research work on the subject of Jones's choice was to be undertaken between May and November 1927. 'It is now going to be about British rule in West Africa,' he wrote to Jones. 'Those who hate Great Britain and are Anglophobists will have their eyes opened.'[5] It must remain a very open question, however, whether Aggrey's work would really have served the purpose Jones intended, even if it had been completed.[6] As it was, J. E. K. Aggrey died quite unexpectedly in New York only two months after starting on his project, with his thesis still in note form.[7]

[1] Oldham to Sir Edward Grigg (Governor), 28 July 1926, General Correspondence 1927, Grigg Papers, (John Grigg, London; microfilm at Queens University, Kingston, Ontario, Canada); Oldham to Ormsby-Gore, 'Research into Native Welfare in East Africa', Grigg Papers; Oldham to R. T. Davidson (Archbishop of Canterbury), 2 Mar. 1927, ibid.

See also G. Bennett, 'Paramountcy to Partnership: J. H. Oldham and Africa', *Africa*, xxx, No. 4, (Oct. 1960), 358.

[2] J. H. Oldham, leading articles on Kenya, *The Times*, 9 June 1926, and 10 June 1926. Jones to Gibson, 28 June 1926, File Q-J, E.H.

[3] Jones to Orr, 1 Feb. 1926, File Q-G, E.H.

[4] Smith, *Aggrey of Africa*, p. 271. [5] Ibid.

[6] Aggrey was soliciting C. G. Woodson's aid for his thesis just two weeks before he died; Aggrey to Woodson, 13 July 1927, Box 6, acc. 3579, add. i, Woodson Papers, L.C.

[7] Smith, *Aggrey of Africa*, pp. 276–7.

Aggrey's death was a much greater blow to Jones than anything else could have been. It was not simply a question of losing after twenty-five years the only African he had ever really known well. His single most perfect exemplar of Negro behaviour had been removed. For Aggrey had embodied the very spirit of the adaptation and co-operation that Jones had preached in Africa. Yet it must be seriously doubted whether the uniqueness of Aggrey had not in the long run had an unfortunate effect on Jones's view of African and American Negro progress. For Aggrey had been a continual reminder to Jones that protest was not essential to leadership, and that a Negro could reach the highest point of development without rejecting his white counsellors. Aggrey had further taken the greatest pride in the differences between races, and frequently talked of the Negro's distinctive contribution. He had even pleaded fervently for an African curriculum differentiated from that of the whites, and had worked to make that a reality at Achimota. Most important of all for its influence on Jones, Aggrey had believed the race problem soluble by the initiative of enlightened individuals, and not by political alliances. As an individual he felt complete racial equality with all his white friends, but he did not realize that the Africanization he emphasized so strongly could only enhance his already high personal status, while it might still be dangerous for Africans in general. He then proclaimed differentiation for his people's education before it was politically safe and in the process underestimated the value for others of the twenty years of undifferentiated higher education that had largely given him his own equality.

After Aggrey's death the propaganda conflict over African education continued unabated, with Jones proceeding on an opposite set of assumptions from DuBois and Leys. It was, however, becoming increasingly clear that the debate was less about education than the political futures that were open to Africans. Because of his conviction that white rule in Africa was as unchangeable as white supremacy in the Southern States, Jones believed that the most that was open to Africans was, like Aggrey, to imbibe on an individual level the Tuskegee spirit; they could then make a successful adaptation to the white *status quo*. DuBois and Leys, on the contrary, sought out those Africans who had formed or belonged to African political associations, and encouraged them to aspire to independence. It was entirely consonant, therefore, with their vision of Africans for Leys to adopt and co-operate with the secretary of the Kikuyu Central Association,

Jomo Kenyatta,[1] and for DuBois to be enlisted by the A.S.U. as 'the most logical candidate' to help them 'to do the things that will benefit Africa in its march toward race consciousness and self determination'.[2] For Jones it was no less appropriate that he should have continued to work to create such leaders as Aggrey. At this time, very few Africans could, of course, go and hear Aggrey's message in the Southern States, however; for the vast majority who did not, it was Jones's largest ambition that the Tuskegee spirit of the Southern States should come to them—as it did now to Kenya, in the form of the Jeanes School.

[1] For evidence of co-operation between Leys and Kenyatta, see Hooper to Miss Soles, 26 Sept. 1929, Letterbooks of the Africa Secretary, C.M.S.A., London. Cf. also correspondence in Winifred Holtby Papers, File 8, Hull Public Library.

[2] T. Dosuma-Johnson to DuBois, 27 Jan. 1933, DuBois papers, Park Johnson Archives, Fisk University, Nashville, Tenn.

CHAPTER VI

The Jeanes School: An Experiment in Phelps-Stokesism

. . . there is the strongest probability that none of these things are represented in the school you visit. Children are not playing games or doing any of the things they would do out of school. The music you hear will not be a Native song but the parody of a familiar European hymn . . . None of the acute problems of village housing, sanitation, water or food preparation are present either in theory or practice. Here there is no building, making or repairing with the hands, no cultivation of the garden. Instead, the brown bodies are huddled over a chart or a book. The chorus of unintelligible sounds is the sing-song of the syllables as they follow one another in meaningless succession. You will hear reading, but it will not describe, explain or appreciate any of the hundred and one real things and actions of the village at this moment. In fact, you will wonder if the schools belong to the village world at all.[1]

This impression of the bush schools of Kenya, described here by J. W. C. Dougall, had been formed by all members of the commission, and it was their unanimous presentation of the case for change at this level that had influenced the Kenya Government to proceed with the plans for the first Jeanes school in Africa. For the next fourteen years European staff at the Jeanes School and teams of African teachers trained under them attempted to remedy the village school's failings and re-order its priorities. It was hoped that this would be the first chapter of the new education in Africa, and would inaugurate a change in status and function of the village school. It would no longer be an alien institution, encouraging its pupils to leave the Reserves, but might become a lever for raising the whole standard of village life; so far from the village school's being the entry point for westernization, it could now perhaps become the demonstration model of an Africanized curriculum and embody some of the traditional values of African tribal life. In all this it would be the first substantial exemplification of Phelps-Stokes educational theory, providing in form adapted to East Africa the best experience of the American South. An assessment of the commission's effect in Kenya

[1] J. W. C. Dougall, 'Religious Education', *I.R.M.* xv, No. 4 (1926), 498.

may therefore be most legitimately based on the development of this training school, which Denham, the Colonial Secretary of Kenya, trusted would be 'a lasting memorial of the visit of the Phelps-Stokes Commission'.[1]

A closer examination of why the first Jeanes school should be founded in Kenya, when the commission had already toured West African countries and made similar recommendations,[2] raises some issues that go beyond the purely educational. At one level the presence of Dr. Dillard, president of the Jeanes Fund, on this East African Commission might be sufficient explanation for action's not having been taken on the earlier commission. Indeed, there is strong evidence that his part in urging the Jeanes system was influential in government and missionary circles; he had stressed that the most outstanding problem in the school system was that of the little bush schools, and that change there would affect the great majority of the school population.[3] But, as was seen in Chapter Four, Dillard's persuasion, even when added to Garfield Williams's and Jones's convictions that the improvement of village schools should be the first responsibility of the colonial authorities, would not alone have been sufficient to explain the immediate adoption of the Jeanes system by the Kenya Government.[4] Admittedly it was important also that the village school level was, in the Kenya context, the only uncontroversial area of education, so that the Jeanes agreement might almost seem a compromise measure in the disputes between missions and government.[5] Apart from all these factors, however, the overriding reason that progress was unusually rapid at the government level was the belief that the Jeanes scheme would be established and supported by the aid of American finance.

It seems certain that both Jones and Dillard held out to E. B. Denham the possibility of American philanthropic aid, should a viable scheme be proposed. Within a month of the commission's leaving Kenya, Denham had worked out in considerable detail a memorandum on the training of teachers for village schools,[6] and had

[1] Denham to Jones, 4 June 1924, File Q-F, E.H.

[2] Jones, *Education in Africa*, p. 54.

[3] Notes on a conversation between Dillard and Oldham, 7 May 1924, File Q-G, E.H.

[4] G. Williams, 'General Description of Educational Work in the Kenya Colony', 14 Apr. 1925, File G3/A5/0/1925, C.M.S.A., London.

[5] See p. 117.

[6] E. B. Denham, 'The Training of Teachers for Village Schools' (27 Apr. 1924), File Q-F, E.H.

presented it to the Colonial Office Advisory Committee. The staffing of the school and the training of the African teachers would, he explained, gain immeasurably from the secondment of an American educationist with the experience of Jeanes work, and aid would be forthcoming:

> I am certain that such a scheme is assured of the support of the Phelps-Stokes Commission, and I believe that if it is put before the Commission and approved by them, the proposal would receive financial backing which, as the Advisory Board is well aware, is so very essential and necessary at the present time when the finances of the Colony do not permit of Government undertaking any scheme involving a large financial outlay.[1]

The involvement of American funds in some such way in Kenya, while it appealed to the Education Department budget, was also part of a much wider political strategy of J. H. Oldham, to bring international pressure to bear on the stubborn problems of white settlement. He had conceived of the Phelps-Stokes Commission's visit itself as beginning the process,[2] and now wished that American money could continue this indirect form of control. This really amounted to creating a kind of educational mandate status for Kenya, and would, if it proved successful, provide for East Africa a parallel to the liberalizing influence of Northern philanthropy in the American South:

> It seems to me a matter of great importance that there should be some American financial contribution to the work in Kenya. In view of the peculiar difficulties of the situation there, I cannot help thinking that the co-operation of America might have a valuable psychological influence. It would be a reminder that the education of the natives is really a world concern, and would help in this way to prevent too provincial a view being taken of questions that may arise.[3]

By October 1924 some modification in Denham's plans for the form of American aid had taken place; Jones and Oldham had agreed that an American might not be the most suitable person to start an experiment in a British colony, and had successfully persuaded Dougall to accept a year's training in American Jeanes work as a preparation for directing the project.[4] The process of internationalizing the Jeanes work began with the Spelman Rockefeller Board's

[1] Ibid., p. 15; cf. also Oldham to Bottomley, 24 Oct. 1924, C.O. 533/327, P.R.O.
[2] Oldham to Coryndon, 16 Jan. 1924, File Q-R, E.H.
[3] Oldham to Dougall, 2 Apr. 1925, File Q-G, E.H.
[4] Oldham to Bottomley, 24 Oct. 1924.

appropriating money for Dougall,[1] and already the possibility of grants of several thousands of dollars a year for a five-year period was being canvassed by Dillard, to begin the improvement of 'education among the backward natives'.[2] American money for the school finally materialized in April 1925—37,500 dollars over five years—and it came quite unexpectedly from the Carnegie Corporation.[3] As there had in fact been some confusion over the awarding of the grant, there was no suggestion that it should be used for anything more specific than 'cooperation with the British Government in educational developments in Kenya Colony'.[4] Oldham immediately feared that in the absence of any conditions, it might fail completely in the larger object he intended, and simply be used by the Kenya Legislative Council as an educational economy.

The issue did not in any case arise in an acute form for some time; in the meantime, there was the much more pressing problem of staffing the institution that was to pioneer the educational revolution in Kenya. As the Jeanes School was to embody the new approach, with Jones's 'Simples' of health, agriculture, home, and recreation, the staff must be convinced that there were valuable features in African notions of health and agriculture which could be developed, and African patterns of home life and recreation on which the village school syllabus could build. Like the staff of Achimota which was being recruited under Fraser and Aggrey,[5] they must combine research into traditional African methods with their western knowledge, and consequently develop an education congruent with the African past. The principal difference between the two parallel experiments in East and West Africa was that the Jeanes School was conditioned by the fact of white settlement, and would be exclusively concerned with the Reserves.

It was perhaps partly recognition of some similarity between the political situations in the Southern States and the African Reserves that led Dougall to consider American Negroes as the first likely candidates for his staff. In view of the barriers against Negroes in

[1] Dougall to Oldham, 1 Mar. 1925, File Q-G, E.H.

[2] Oldham to Bottomley 24 Oct. 1924.

[3] Oldham to A. L. Warnhuis, 26 Mar. 1925, File on International Institute of African Languages and Cultures, E.H.

[4] F. P. Keppel (president of Carnegie Corporation) to Jones, 7 Apr. 1925, File 314, E.H., now I.M.C.A., Geneva.

[5] Cf. Smith, *Aggrey of Africa*, pp. 236–7 and Foster, *Education and Social Change in Ghana*, pp. 166–70.

Africa,[1] it is significant that, for this type of work in a semi-government institution, Oldham did not anticipate any difficulty in the plan's going through as soon as Dougall was established.[2] The idea appealed to Dr. Dillard, too, who agreed that 'undoubtedly the best possible thing for the plan of reaching the village schools would be to get a good colored man from the South who has been in the work';[3] there were several candidates who, he felt, would be ideal, and he believed financial backing could be secured. Similar support for the idea of Negro workers from America was coming from some of the leading missionaries in East Africa; in the aftermath of Aggrey's extraordinarily successful tour, they were convinced that educated Africans or Negroes would have an advantage over the European missionary in many situations.[4] As Dougall proceeded, therefore, to tour the Southern States in the early months of 1925, the plan for a Negro colleague took shape; the man would have to be approved by President Moton of Tuskegee, and would take charge of about twenty village schools in Kenya as itinerant teacher and supervisor. He would need, naturally, to be accepted by the Kenya authorities, but Dr. Dillard was ready to explain the urgency of the case to Denham as soon as a suitable candidate was found.[5]

It was not, however, an opportune moment for such a quest. Many of the Negro colleges had been in a state of considerable unrest over the nature of white patronage and white leadership since the Fisk riots of February 1925,[6] and it is noteworthy that it was the atmosphere among the students of Hampton Institute, of all places, that caused Dougall the most serious hesitation. Despite a public invitation to the Hampton students to volunteer for service in Africa, therefore, he wrote privately to Oldham: 'After my visit to Hampton, I am less confident about the wisdom of sending over an American Negro to help with the initial stages of the Jeanes work. One can hardly escape the feeling that the younger generation of educated negroes is restive, aggressive and less appreciative of the work of the whites even in such a school as Hampton.'[7] Further, whatever reser-

[1] See Ch. III, *passim*.

[2] Oldham to Dillard, 23 Feb. 1925, Oldham Papers in the possession of Dr. Kathleen Bliss.

[3] Dillard to Oldham, 6 Mar. 1925, ibid.

[4] Oldham to Jones, 4 June 1925, File 314, I.M.C.A., Geneva; Grace to Oldham, 8 Apr. 1925, File on Uganda, E.H.

[5] Dougall to Oldham, 8 Feb. 1925, File Q-G, E.H. [6] See pp. 140–1.

[7] Dougall to Oldham, 1 Mar. 1925, File Q-G, E.H. J. W. C. Dougall, 'Africa Today', *Southern Workman*, liv (Apr. 1925), 169.

vations Dougall might have had about Negro staff would scarcely have been overcome by Jones, whose traditional caution over Negro missionaries' collaborating with whites in Africa had been intensified by the series of set-backs his interracial philosophy had suffered during the year.[1] There may well have been additional factors, but at any rate the notion of using Negroes for inaugurating the Jeanes scheme in Kenya did not recur after June 1925.

The school did not open formally until October, but there was an unusually full discussion of principles and of the Jeanes philosophy both prior to its opening and in the two years following. It is therefore worth considering some of the ideals and ambitions propounded by the individuals most concerned with shaping the school.

What was to be attempted, after all, was nothing less than the conversion of the educational system from the traditional western model of élitist, academic education to one apparently more attuned to the economic and social forms of African life. The relative infancy of formal African education seemed to provide an opportunity to benefit from the experiences of two separate spheres—India and the Southern States. The Colonial Secretary of Kenya and his inspector of education had had considerable experience of education in Ceylon and India respectively,[2] and to them, no less than to the missionaries and most other educationists, Indian education provided the supreme example of what must be unlearnt for Africa. Denham set out the moral in his draft plan for the Jeanes School:

> We have therefore before us the lesson to be drawn from the history of education in India, where higher education and professors were superimposed instead of progress through village schools and village teachers upwards. What we wish to avoid in this Colony is a repetition of such disastrous experiments and the lesson we can learn is, in my opinion, that simplicity is the keynote of education.[3]

Of course India had long provided, in missionary and government circles, an example of what not to do, but it was only comparatively recently, with the growing knowledge of the achievements of the

[1] See p. 140.

[2] Denham had been Director of Education in Ceylon, 1916–20, and E. E. Biss, the inspector of education, had had long experience in the Indian educational service.

[3] Denham, 'The Training of Teachers', p. 3. For a missionary's disapproval of the Indian model, see Arthur to W. H. Beech, 10 Dec. 1912, A/10, P.C.E.A.

Southern States, that any positive alternative could be proposed. Both Hampton and Tuskegee, Oldham believed, provided a formula for combating the usual results of native education, 'the swelled head' and the openness to agitation, and if their principles could be firmly established in the new education of Africa, and the Jeanes School in particular, there was a chance that Africa could bypass the stage of Indian discontent.[1]

As for the products of the training, it was hoped that there would be secured a nucleus of new-style African leaders, who would be eager to return to the country, equipped through their 'contact with realities'[2] to resist the temptations of urban life. Exposure to some European ways in their training at the Jeanes School would give them a fresh vision of the possibilities of renewal in their villages, without separating them by too great an educational gap from these local communities. In Dougall's phrase, the teacher would be only 'a little in advance of his people'.[3] It is all the more interesting, in view of this limitation set on their education, that Dougall could still express the hope that they might 'find a few who will become leaders, like Aggrey, among the native people'.[4] Nor was the first vice-principal, T. G. Benson, less ambitious for the teachers in training, who, he felt, at his most idealistic, might have become the 'germ of a new nation'.[5]

It should not be suggested that the task of selecting suitable candidates was necessarily thought to be a light one. Indeed, few saw more clearly than Dougall the improbability that the qualities he desired would reside in more than a handful of people. The teacher must be young enough to be capable of radically changing his whole attitude to teaching, and intelligent enough to adapt his new knowledge to the differing conditions of the villages and their little schools; and yet he must have attained a maturity that would give him the ear of the local Chief and elders or of the District Officer. Most exacting of all, to maintain his loyalty to the small local communities, 'he must have passed the stage when English, certificates, and clothes are the

[1] Oldham to Major Dutton, 8 Oct. 1929, File Q-G, E.H. Cf. further, p. 215.

[2] Oldham to Dutton, 8 Oct. 1929.

[3] J. W. C. Dougall (Ed.), *The Village Teachers Guide: A Book of Guidance for African Teachers* (London, 1931), p. 103.

[4] J. W. C. Dougall, *Jeanes School Kabete: A Guide to Intercession for Staff and Friends* (Nairobi, 1928); copy in H.A.I.

[5] T. G. Benson, interview, 1966.

predominating factors in the choice of a career'.[1] In a word, what was required for a position in the Jeanes School was Dr. Loram's 'good African',[2] a figure so highly prized in the twenties and thirties, and so rarely found by those who defined him:

> As far as British policy at least is concerned, the objective of education in Africa is to produce the good African—the Native who is proud to be an African, appreciative of the finer elements in his culture, willing and anxious to accept European culture in so far as it is complementary and supplementary to his own, quite unwilling to be an imitative or unoriginal white man.[3]

The curriculum of the Jeanes School would, of course, be very largely determined by this definition of the African teacher, and the most delicate task of the European staff would then be the communication of 'an attitude of discrimination towards African and European cultures'.[4] They would have, in addition, to expend considerable energy, and make use of anthropological knowledge, in order to fulfil their aim 'to adapt conventional subjects to African life and psychology'.[5] The African Jeanes teacher, for his part, would in his two-year course have so to discern the relevance of African lore and customs that he could pass on to the teachers in the out-schools suggestions to prevent the heedless, wholesale adoption of western ways. He would also have to learn how all school subjects could be adapted and directed towards the improvement of the various villages. Arithmetic would no longer concern itself with hypothetical problems, but be used in the computation of village statistics; drama might become a vehicle of propaganda for health and agricultural improvement, and even reading and writing could be given local relevance by the collection and repetition of tribal songs and stories. It was recognized in all this that an unusual degree of resourcefulness

[1] J. W. C. Dougall, 'The Training of Visiting Teachers for African Village Schools', 1927, p. 3, File Q-G, E.H.; this is the draft of an article of the same title which appeared in *Southern Workman*, lvii (Oct. 1928), 403–14.

[2] C. T. Loram, 'Fundamental Principles of African Education', in *Village Education in Africa: Report of the Interterritorial "Jeanes" Conference held in Salisbury, Southern Rhodesia, on 27th May to 6th June, 1935* (Lovedale Press, 1936), p. 9.

[3] Ibid., pp. 9–10. The use of the term 'good African' by Loram qualifies what is said on p. 232.

[4] J. W. C. Dougall, 'School Education and Native Life', *Africa*, iii, No. 1 (1930), 54.

[5] *Jeanes School Kabete and the Work of the Village Guide* (published by the authority of the Government of Kenya Colony and Protectorate, 1931), p. 11.

and imagination would be required. For, as Dr. Dillard had noted in his Kenya tour, 'the textbooks at present in use are absolutely absurd, having no sort of relation to native life'.[1] The Jeanes teacher was being commissioned to undertake a most difficult thing, to remove the few, admittedly shaky, western supports from beneath the bush school teacher, and substitute, very largely on his own initiative, a new African syllabus and methodology. It was a tall order, and everything had to be learned from European staff through the medium of Swahili only.

Such was the general background of ideas and aspirations against which Dougall began his first job as a junior officer of the Government. All about him the highest claims were being made for the scheme that would now be put to the test. The Colonial Secretary had announced that the Jeanes School's influence was 'essential to the promotion of the education of the African on the right lines throughout the country'.[2] For Jones it was the culmination of six years' continuous involvement with African education, and the entry wedge, if successful, for a larger scheme that would cover all Africa.[3] Oldham was not naturally given to overstatement, but there is a sense in which the launching of the Jeanes School was the fulfilment of the wish he had entertained for Africa when he had first seen Hampton in 1912. The intervening years had spanned his vital connection with the successes of the Phelps-Stokes Commissions in Africa, and his initiative in the formation of the Colonial Office Advisory Committee. The Jeanes School would now be the first-fruits:

> I am of the opinion that if the proposed plans can be carried out successfully, Kenya will probably take the lead among all the British colonies in Africa in coming to grips with the real problems of the village school. The Governor said to me that he thought that the plans for the Jeanes School were in advance of anything he observed in Uganda . . . If we can provide Dougall with the proper staff I do not think that there will be anything so effective in this particular line in the whole of East Africa, or for that matter, in West Africa.[4]

When it came to the practical embodiment of these high aims, with the co-operation of the Kenya Government and settlers, the

[1] Notes on a conversation between Dillard and Oldham, 7 May 1924.
[2] Denham to Jones, 4 June 1924, File Q-F, E.H.
[3] Jones to Oldham, 20 May 1927, File Q-J, E.H.
[4] Oldham to Jones, 14 May 1926, File L-1, P.S.F.A.; also Oldham to Ormsby-Gore, 9 Dec. 1926, C.O. 533/363/xf 7877, P.R.O.

question of staffing was only one of many crucial difficulties. Nor was it the first. There was the question of whether the project would get off the ground at all in the early months, for, as Oldham had foreseen, the Kenya Education Department saw the Carnegie grant as an opportunity for educational economy rather than an inducement to innovation. Although the money had been allocated to the Jeanes School, the Director of Education was only just prevented from using it to save on building costs,[1] and Dougall then discovered that his budget for 1926 was to be £100, 'the other £1,500 having been marked by the words "to be recovered from Carnegie Grant"'.[2] Indeed the financial pre-conditions for success were probably not fully realized by the Kenya authorities until Oldham had personally intervened in his visit to Kenya in March 1926. His close connection with Governor Coryndon's successor, Edward Grigg, enabled him to explain the capital requirements of the school, and also the hard fact that it would need five or six full-time, highly-qualified European staff to train only twenty-five Jeanes teachers and their wives. But his counsel prevailed, and £8,000 was found for buildings, with the Carnegie money earmarked for salaries.[3]

It was a remarkable illustration of the effect of Oldham's pressure that the Government was prepared to sanction the institution to be run on the scale that Dougall thought necessary. The effect was to make the African Jeanes teacher the most expensive single product of Kenya's educational system. Even with the Carnegie subsidy, the tuition costs of the Jeanes teachers per head annually were, at 2,237 shillings, more than twice as much as the most expensively educated European child in government schools. More important from the viewpoint of the unofficial members of the Legislative Council, it was more than four times as much as it cost to train an artisan in the N.I.T.D.[4] For this reason it is not entirely surprising that when Lord Delamere visited the school in 1928, he should have suggested to Dougall that his Jeanes teachers might as well be sent to Eton.[5]

However, with the financial problems for the moment settled, the Jeanes School now required a team of educationists with extraordinary qualifications; they must be prepared to do both research and teaching in a semi-missionary, aggressively non-theoretical institution

[1] Dougall to Oldham, 9 Dec. 1925, File Q-G, E.H. [2] Ibid.
[3] Dougall to Oldham, 18 July 1926, File Q-G, E.H.
[4] *KEDAR 1928*, Statistical Table No. VI.
[5] J. W. C. Dougall, interview, May 1966.

and communicate their knowledge through Swahili. In 1926 an intensive search was instituted by Loram in South Africa, Jones in the United States, and Oldham and the Colonial Office appointments board in Britain, to find appropriate candidates, but they made only slow progress.[1] The case of the agriculturalist was particularly difficult and illustrated the problem posed by the qualities Dougall required:

> He must not be the type they have in the Agricultural Dept. whose attitude might be thus expressed: 'Of course the native is the worst agriculturalist in the world', nor should he be like the man they have just got out to C.S.M., Kikuyu . . . who is as keen as can be on helping the native but teaches the science in absolute detachment from native method and idea . . . We want something of Shantz's attitude which begins with curiosity as to the native thought of agriculture and native practice of the art, is prepared to develop some respect for it, and in any case will teach in relation to native practice and develop gradually from it.[2]

But by 1929 even he had been found, and there was assembled a body of six Europeans prepared to develop knowledge on an African basis.

It proved no less difficult to recruit the right type of African teacher to undergo Jeanes training. Some responsibility for this might be traced to the missions, who were understandably loath to take their best teachers out of service for a two-year course, especially as it meant a transfer of the Jeanes man from a teaching post to the role of an itinerant supervisor. The crux of the recruitment problem, however, was what Dougall had anticipated: attracting the young, intelligent, and influential. The selection of the first batch of students in 1925 highlighted the paradoxical combination of qualities they were to have; some were rejected for not being well enough educated, one for being too well educated, and the Governor let it be known that any applicants who knew any English would be ruled out.[3] The result was, with these as with many subsequent intakes, that many of them were over thirty, and their elementary education required

[1] Oldham to Dougall, 25 Mar. 1927, File Q-G, E.H. See also R. Furse, *Aucuparius: Recollections of a Recruiting Officer* (London, 1962), pp. 124–5.

[2] Dougall to Oldham, 23 May 1927, File Q-G, E.H. For an extended exercise in this attitude, see H. L. Shantz, 'Agriculture in East Africa', in *Education in East Africa*, pp. 353–401. The agriculturalist referred to in the C.S.M. was E. A. Cromack, a white teacher from Hampton Institute; see further p. 194.

[3] Biss to Dougall, 23 July 1925, from the personal papers of Mr. T. G. Benson kindly made available to the writer.

considerable amendment before they could even begin to understand the new emphasis of the Jeanes work.[1]

The staff soon found that changing the direction of African education was not as simple as Denham's *tabula rasa* conception had suggested. Within two years of the school's inauguration, Dougall had to admit that 'the African himself is in some respects the biggest obstacle to the giving of the best kind of education in Africa'.[2] The brighter students would demand to know why, if this education was as good as Dougall said it was, the white people did not practise it themselves.[3] Despite the very low level of attainment in English among many entrants,[4] there was still strong resentment at the 'no English' policy of the school, and in fact many of the Africans were determined to find elsewhere what was denied them by the official policy.[5]

Even after the school was comparatively well established, recruitment continued to be a problem, with students being sought out by the staff rather than applying in the normal way.[6] There might have been more interest in entry to the school if there had not been erected, a year after the beginning of the Jeanes work, the Alliance School, Kenya's first junior secondary school, which, for all its early professions of adapted education,[7] became a traditional academic school with a highly competitive entry. The two schools were situated within a few miles of each other, the one providing a path to further education and the possibility of entrance to the new Makerere College in Uganda, and the other demanding an attitude in its students that despised further paper qualifications. Alliance High School could lead to some of the best-paid jobs in the African Civil Service, while the Jeanes School pointed the way back to the Reserves and a life of quite extraordinary difficulty, where patience was more important than ambition. In these circumstances it is curious that Dougall should have thought it possible to attract entrants of the same calibre:

[1] T. G. Benson, interview, Sept. 1966.
[2] Dougall, 'The Training of Visiting Teachers', p. 5.
[3] J. W. C. Dougall, interview, May 1966.
[4] Dougall notes in a cyclostyled letter of 11 Nov. 1925 (Benson Papers) that there might be one compensation in the students' being able to speak hardly any English—that it would be more difficult to induce them to leave their vocations.
[5] Professor R. A. C. Oliver, interview 6 Oct. 1966.
[6] J. W. C. Dougall, Circular Letter No. 6, 8 Aug. 1927, File Q-G, E.H., and Dougall to Oldham, 26 Dec. 1928, File Q-G, E.H.
[7] See pp. 193–4.

At present there may seem to be a competition between the High School at Kikuyu and the Jeanes School. It is true that we do not need to aim at the High School standard. At the same time, if we are to get the pupils who are most able mentally to profit by this course, we should want some to come here who otherwise might go to the Alliance school.[1]

Once the African teachers and their wives had taken up residence in the Jeanes village beside the school, the question arose whether they would be intelligent enough to grasp the principle on which the school was founded—that progress for backward village communities need not be by wholesale westernization, but by the marriage of minimal western techniques with what was already of value in traditional African methods. After all, Dougall believed in retrospect that the Government as a whole had not understood the Jeanes idea. He had intended to have the philosophy of Jeanes embodied in the school buildings and teachers huts, by having improved native-style houses built by the Government: 'We had the greatest difficulty in building a hut that was not either a brick hut, which the African had never seen before, or else leaving them where they were. These [see Plate VII] were the first huts and they were not what I wanted at all. They were just brick huts, with cement floors and corrugated roofs. The idea that I had did not get over at all.'[2] Similarly Dougall felt that few of the teachers had grasped the idea that the old was better or could be bettered; they tended either to leave it as it was or do as the European did.[3]

An important part of the two-year residential programme was practice in experimental farming within the limitations of a half-acre plot; again, it was only experimental in the Jeanes sense of examining traditional African methods of agriculture for their value before encouraging modified western techniques. A. S. Walford, the European agriculturalist, aimed at improving the cultivation and productivity of the one-man plot in the Reserves, and for the purpose of his experiments an unlettered African small-holder worked a demonstration plot in the school grounds. It was his intention that the teachers would on their return to the Reserves continue to play a part-time role as demonstrators of some of their progressive methods. Much careful work was therefore done on improving the efficiency of

[1] Dougall to Jones, 2 Jan. 1927, File N-1, P.S.F.A. See M. Macpherson, *They Built for the Future: A Chronicle of Makerere University College* (Cambridge, 1964), p. 12.

[2] J. W. C. Dougall, interview, Oct. 1966. See Plate VII.

[3] J. W. C. Dougall, interview, Oct. 1966.

PLATE VII

Government-built houses for Africans at the Jeanes School. (From *Jeanes School Kabete, and the Work of the Village Guide*.)

traditional agricultural aids, such as the grain bin and the plough, always restricting the scale of the improvement to the small-holder's budget.[1] It is interesting to note the similarity of these ideas to those associated with Washington in the Southern States. Neither Washington nor the Jeanes School considered it their business to attempt any basic changes in land tenure or in the political status of those whom they wished to inspire; it was their common principle that they should cast down their buckets where they were, and make what small improvements were possible.

The connection with the Southern States was far from a nominal one. Despite the absence of American Negroes, it was Dougall's and Benson's aim to capture for their own students the spirit of sacrificial service which was so evident in the work of the American Jeanes teachers.[2] Consequently a great deal of both the theoretical background to community work and the leisure activity in the Jeanes School drew its inspiration from the Washington tradition. Some of the variety of this influence is described by Benson:

> Much of the pioneering of our methods was Dougall's work and he in turn had traced it from the States. Booker Washington, Armstrong and others were most certainly our heroes in the school. We were modelled on those sorts of experiments like his and the Moga community schools where there was this strong practicality. We talked a great deal about Negroes. We sang Negro spirituals in Swahili. We had those community meetings, and had a lot of singing. In our open air theatre we had much value from plays to illustrate agricultural points. While in our courses on History of Education, we would treat interesting and outstanding examples of these great Negro pioneers.[3]

Although only Dougall among the Jeanes staff had had direct experience of the American South, the school was kept in close touch with all the relevant literature on Negro development and education

[1] A. S. Walford, interviews, Oct. 1966 and May 1969.

[2] Jones, *The Jeanes Teacher in the United States*, *passim*.

[3] T. G. Benson, interview, Sept. 1966. In addition to this, he personally used B. T. Washington's books for his courses on the history of education. As far as direct connection between the Jeanes teachers themselves and their American Negro counterparts went, the African Jeanes men did send a list of questions about methodology to their Jeanes counterparts in the States, the majority of whom were women; see Jeanes teachers of Kenya to Jeanes teachers of America, 27 July 1926, Benson Papers. There was considerable interest at the staff level in the experiments in Indian village education being carried out at Moga by W. J. McKee, described in his *New Schools for Young India: A Survey of Educational, Economic and Social Conditions with special reference to more effective education* (Chapel Hill, 1930).

by Jones, who understandably believed the reputation of his own educational theories to be bound up with the success of the school.[1]

Probably, however, it was another member of the Phelps-Stokes team, Aggrey, who became best known among the students. Members of the staff gave much publicity to Aggrey's philosophy, suggesting in the process that he would have given his approval to Jeanes methods. That this could be done without distorting Aggrey's thought in any way is significant; the very ambiguities of his public expressions had made it possible to use them in support of a Jeanes School as much as an Achimota. Consequently Aggrey's life was serialized in the government-sponsored magazine of the Jeanes School, *Habari*,[2] and lessons were drawn from it to support some of the less popular aspects of the curriculum:

> They [American students] do many kinds of work but none can be more worthy and honest than the work that Aggrey did as printer and journalist in order to pay for his education. He was proud of the work he had done in this way and often said to his students that it had taught him as much as lessons in college. Aggrey always remained sympathetic and understanding towards those who worked with their hands and he never felt because his hands were clean and he wore a white collar that therefore he was better than a farm labourer or a mechanic. The explanation lay largely in the fact that his education had been a thorough one not only through books but through manual work of different kinds.[3]

Even years after Aggrey's death in 1927, his parables, and especially the famous one of the chicken and the eagle, which counselled Africans to patience and self-determination at one and the same time, were frequently retold to the Jeanes teachers.[4]

In all this emphasis on Negro models and heroes, the staff were interpreting in their own way the strong recommendations of the Phelps-Stokes reports to direct history teaching and social studies in Africa away from their traditional pre-occupations with the great men of Europe and America to a new pride in their own Negro

[1] Jones to Benson, 10 Aug. 1932, Southern Education Foundation (hereafter S.E.F.) Papers. The S.E.F. was the result of the 1937 merger between the Peabody, Slater, and Jeanes Foundations.

[2] *Habari* (A Newspaper for the Natives of Kenya Colony, edited by the Department of Education, editor J. W. C. Dougall), vii, Feb. to Sept. 1928, seven articles on Aggrey.

[3] 'Dr. Aggrey Part II', *Habari*, vii, Mar. 1928, 12–13. For further illustration of Aggrey's ambiguity, see pp. 243–4.

[4] R. A. C. Oliver, interview, Oct. 1966.

people.[1] This reorientation was therefore in some sense parallel to the Negro History Week campaigns that DuBois and Woodson promoted in the United States, with the important difference that the Jeanes School paid most attention to Negroes with interests in community and rural development. An important additional factor, however, in Jones's advocacy of this new approach to school history was his fear that much traditional history teaching was responsible for political unrest in Africa and Asia. It was therefore entirely consistent with this belief to wish young Africans to be protected from the inference that the greatness of the western nations was 'the result of strife, rebellion, and revolution and various other forms of demands for rights'.[2] The suggested curricular reform was a further example of how a progressive educational principle could coexist with a reactionary political motive.

It had been hoped, in the original discussion of objectives, that the Jeanes School might pioneer insights into African mentality and psychology, the results of which could in turn be embodied in the teaching materials of the new education. This aim, too, might well have come to very little without outside pressure, this time in the form of a visit to the Jeanes School of the president and secretary of the Carnegie Corporation in 1927. The Corporation had decided to expend a considerable sum on native education in South or East Africa, on the development of teaching materials that were adapted to the African mentality and environment, and through Oldham's persuasion were led to believe that the most auspicious place to begin the experiment was the Jeanes School.[3] What was felt necessary in such a project was not only the regionalization of western textbooks according to the best principles of primary school teaching, but a more radical investigation into the facts of African mentality, without which the mere regionalization of the curriculum would not be sufficient. Dougall explained the need after the discussions with the Carnegie visitors:

> An even more serious lack of adaptation, though one which is more difficult to distinguish is that the method by which a lesson is taught and conclusions reached, is based not on African psychology and the intimate knowledge of native custom and idea but on the pedagogical axioms of England and America. It is taken for granted that the African native thinks as we do, whereas the experience of teachers in touch with native mentality

[1] Jones, *Education in East Africa*, pp. 18, 19. [2] Ibid., p. 18.
[3] Oldham to Ormsby-Gore, 11 Jan. 1929, File Q-E, E.H.

points to the fact that either his premises or his modes of reasoning are different from ours.[1]

With the decision to attach to the Jeanes School, through Carnegie money, a man trained in the practical applications of psychology and anthropology to the life of Bantu peoples, very large prospects opened up. It meant that the materials on native customs and folklore that the African Jeanes teachers were already collecting could be analysed, and then provide the basis for truly Africanized textbooks. There might then have been the possibility of the school's fulfilling the research role for which the staff had been recruited but had so far been too occupied to implement. In the event, most of these hopes were disappointed.[2] The man appointed by the Carnegie Corporation was a psychologist, R. A. C. Oliver, who found for the first three years of his service in Kenya almost no interest in or encouragement for his work by the Education Department. Nor did he become an integral part of the Jeanes team in collating teaching materials, but spent most of his time constructing a non-verbal group test for Africans, which was never put to systematic use by the Education Department.[3] Paradoxically, the appointment originally intended to reveal and emphasize the differences between European and African mental processes eventually had exactly the opposite result. Just before Oliver left the country in 1933, the famous medical controversy about the size of the Kenyan African's brain blew up, and was seized upon by settler opinion to suggest that science proved native education to be a positive danger to African sanity. Oliver was summoned to the Education Department for the first time to give his views, and was able to reassure Scott, the director, that the connection between mental and physical attributes was extremely tenuous, and that the tests which he had been quietly carrying out with European and African children demonstrated the substantial capacity of the African to perform at the same level as the European child.[4]

[1] Dougall to Oldham, 29 Oct. 1927, File Q-G, E.H. See also J. W. C. Dougall, 'Characteristics of African Thought', *Africa*, v. No. 3 (1932), 249–65.

[2] The most solid contribution to this end was *The Village Teachers Guide: A Book of Guidance for African Teachers* (London, 1931), compiled by the members of the Jeanes School Staff, Kabete, Kenya.

[3] R. A. C. Oliver, interview, Oct. 1966.

[4] Ibid. The controversy arose from the use by a Kenya doctor, Gordon, of his own and a Dr. Vint's work on mental patients to demonstrate that they were

Even if the school did fall short of its aim to be the centre for the production of progressive teaching aids for African village schools, it did pioneer a pride in the African past in an era when it was generally dismissed as either unsuitable or irrelevant, and prepared its students to reintroduce the old games, folk tales, and African music as a central part of early schooling. This had after all been the fourth 'Simple' of recreation in Jones's programme for African schools, and he had anticipated at that early date the opposition that would inevitably result from attempting to discriminate the good from the bad elements in African play.[1] It took courage for Dougall and Benson actually to implement these ideas, and they were soon charged by missionaries and Christian native pastors with countenancing 'evil practices',[2] or 'trifling with native custom'.[3] Every medium was used, however, in the attempt to give much-needed recognition to African culture; at Speech Days, songs or hymns were set to African tunes;[4] and drama was similarly used in the every day life of the school: 'The old customs and ways of the African tribes are continually presented. It helps the changing African to see the good things clearly while it is not difficult to see that the bad things are gently ridiculed and their evil effects brought out on the stage.'[5] It must be remembered that such principles were particularly complicated to explain in the late twenties and thirties, when a particular African custom, female circumcision, had tended radically to divide opinion about the African past.

It is, of course, a byword in educational circles that there is little necessary correspondence between the progressive activity that teachers will assent to in training college and its embodiment in the life of the schools. It is worth noting, however, before following the Jeanes teachers back to the Reserves, that something revolutionary had been achieved in a few years by the enthusiasm of a few

---

'in fact confronted in the East African with a brain on a lower biological level'. For correspondence with the Colonial Office Advisory Committee, and cuttings of Gordon's article, 'Amentia in the East African', see Box 200, 'Africa General', E.H.; cf. also E. Huxley, *White Man's Country*, i (1870–1914), p. 221.

[1] Jones, *Education in East Africa*, pp. 31–5.

[2] Julian Huxley, *Africa View* (London, 1931), p. 330; Huxley had been sent out to East Africa to report on certain aspects of biologically influenced curricula.

[3] Dougall to Oldham, 9 Mar. 1930, File on Kenya-Education-Education Adviser-Dougall (hereafter File Q-I), E.H.

[4] For typical Speech Day programme, see Appendix III.

[5] *KEDAR 1930*, p. 72.

Europeans. In a country where the only alternative primary teacher-training was the old pupil-teacher system, the Carnegie money had achieved the beginnings of a new approach in a most neglected sphere. A little of this atmosphere, and some of the skills intended to humanize the village schools, can be seen in the activities of the first Jeanes refresher course:

> A small baby's cot made out of rough wood by the same teacher attracted much attention, and a talk was given on the value of this article to the mother. Other useful articles made at the school were shown, a rough blackboard, of beaver boarding, a rat-proof 'debi' with lid of wood made from a bit of a petrol box, cupboards and flyproof safes, chairs, stools, all made on the spot . . .
>
> A lesson, talks on ships and the sea by a Coast-man, was followed by two tales told by the old teachers. Then all the men took part in African games, the women mostly watching, and finally the women played a quieter game by themselves.[1]

By 1934 there had passed out into the Reserves almost a hundred Jeanes teachers. Few of these could become leaders of native opinion in anything beyond the most limited local area. Nevertheless, there was a handful of men who thoroughly understood what was required of them, and came fully to merit Dr. Loram's description of the 'good African'.

The one who came closest to being the African counterpart to Miss Virginia Randolph, the outstanding American Negro Jeanes teacher,[2] was Justin Itotia. An examination of his interpretation of the Jeanes system reveals the peculiar rewards and difficulties of the life.

There was first his home, deliberately built not on the level of his own technical competence (for he could build more elaborately) but of the villagers' capacities to imitate; it had therefore a roof of grass and walls of wattle and daub, eight feet high. He justified the height chosen to a visitor:

> He agreed that ten feet might be better, 'But', he said, 'I am not merely building this house to live in. I want other people to build such houses also. It has to serve as a demonstration. Today our people live in huts with walls only four feet high. If we put them in a house with walls ten feet high, they might feel lost. But I think we can get eight feet.'[3]

[1] 'Report of the First Jeanes Refresher Course, 2nd-6th April, 1928' (Kenya, File x/15281/28 (No. 1), P.R.O.) Jones to Dougall, 6 Aug. 1928, Jeanes School, Kabete, File, Carnegie Corporation of New York Archives.

[2] For Miss Randolph and missionaries from Africa, see p. 186.

[3] 'An Experiment in African Education in Kenya: A New Idea. Justin, A

The interior, too, showed the Jeanes characteristic of ingenuity in the use of simple materials everywhere available; all furniture had been homemade, and a ceiling had been hung by using flattened kerosene tins. There was nothing ostentatious or unjustifiably expensive, no repetition of what Booker Washington had so scorned—the large gramophone and sewing machine in Negro households that had only one fork among them.[1]

In Justin's office, perfection was again evident; there was a file of *Habari*, and many notebooks filled with Kikuyu proverbs and folktales which he had collected from the neighbourhood, and had succeded in having published in *Africa*.[2] Even his dress signified the same interest in preserving and developing African traditions, for he wore a little cap of antelope fur, thus marking his leadership of an African-style Scouting movement, pioneered by his Jeanes colleague, Jeremiah Segero.

Both men, the one in Kikuyu and the other in Nyanza, had dug into their traditional culture, and had produced African adaptations of Scouting. Segero dropped the standard Scouting uniform, and with the approval of Baden-Powell (then retired in Nyeri) designed a new one using Colobus monkey skin, and instead of drawing on the wolfcub-Mowgli ideas, he devised a code of behaviour derived from the characteristics of the Colobus monkey:

> Why does a Mugosi [Scout] wear the skin of the Colobus monkey? Because when a man goes into the forest he can see the Colobus monkey, for this monkey is a leader . . . Again you never see one such monkey alone. There are always a crowd of them together. In the same way the Vagosi like to go about together in a group.
>
> If you look closely at the Colobus monkey you will see that his hair is long and white and has no tangles in it. It is smooth and glistening . . . A Mugosi is like this in the way he behaves. His actions are straightforward. His conduct is candid and direct so that he helps others to see the way . . .
>
> The Colobus monkey wakens early in the morning when it is nearly

---

Pioneer', *Round Table*, xx, No. 79 (1930), 570. The article is Anonymous, but according to T. G. Benson (interview, May 1969) the writer was A. R. Patterson; see below, p. 170.

[1] See Washington, *Up From Slavery*, pp. 142–5.

[2] J. Itotia and J. W. C. Dougall, 'The Voice of Africa', *Africa*, i, No. 4 (Oct. 1928), 486–90. Itotia's other publications were: *Thimo cia Agikuyu; Kihumo kia Endwo ni Iri na Iriri;* and *Mutiga Iri na Iriri Aromana Kuuraga*. These he sold through the Justin Itotia Bookshop, Wangigi Market; for a copy of *Mutiga Iri*, see U.C.N./H.D.-R.P.A., A/1/5.

daybreak. A Mugosi is like this because by his courtesy and manners, he arouses others to appreciate what the good life is . . .[1]

Similarly, Justin's African Scouts and Guides, the 'Endwo ni Iri', were coached in the heritage of Kikuyu wisdom, and through Justin they gave a new currency to some of the old Kikuyu games, such as spearing the running hoop. These were exactly the sort of features that the training at the Jeanes School had recommended for preservation.

This pattern was continued outside Justin's house. All on an imitable scale there was a lawn, a tree nursery, cypress hedges (still trim today), and a European-style kitchen garden and orchard in which were included some trees and shrubs with medical qualities attested by long tradition. Unlike many Europeanized Africans he did not reject root and branch his father's profession of witch-doctor, but carefully kept all his father's implements and medicaments in a special storehouse. Indeed, Justin continued as a Jeanes teacher to administer one particular specific against colds, brewed from herbs and the fat of a sheep's tail. Also in his compound there was the Jeanes improved grain store, and the goats and hens had been moved out from their traditional place in the family house to a demonstration coop and goat house.[2]

It has been suggested earlier that for the Jeanes teacher to find a medial position between the old and the new would be difficult, and would involve an unusual combination of patience and ingenious simplicity. In the eyes of A. R. Patterson, Deputy Director of Medical Services, however, Justin had met the challenge with conspicuous success, and had begun the process of changing Africa from below:

I have spoken of the magnitude of Justin's achievement, and the words are not wrong. Born and bred in the squalor of Africa, he had built a home which it was a pleasure to visit, squalor had utterly disappeared and he had made no mistakes; there was nothing of Europe but what should be

[1] 'African Scouting', *Habari* (Nairobi), viii (Apr. 1929), 120–1. J. W. C. Dougall in a circular letter of 26 Dec. 1928 (Benson Papers) described something of this indigenization of the Scout movement, 'The "Wagosi" are very proud of themselves and look the part of perfection when on parade. They wear black shirts and khaki shorts with bracelets and anklets made from the skin of a small black monkey . . . On their heads they have a narrow band of the same skin with a small plume.' For a picture of the 'Vagosi' see 'African Scouting' p. 118. T. G. Benson and Rose Kimacia, interviews, 10 May 1969.

[2] 'An Experiment in African Education in Kenya', p. 568.

there, though some things were still wanting. I thought of other homes I knew, the squalid untouched villages, the improved houses of the towns where an equal if different squalor sometimes reigns, and ragged pictures paper the walls, of some houses which had been built for show and are not used, and serve no purpose, but to point to ignorance. I realised the length of the road he had travelled and the magnitude of his achievement, for not only had he remade Africa, but he had spoiled nothing as he worked.[1]

The Jeanes teachers' homes and gardens were admittedly only a small part of the programme; they could, however, help to make credible the suggestions for improvement offered by the teachers as they went about the neighbourhood, attempting to galvanize four or five village communities into action. As the teachers followed no set pattern in the improvements they attempted, it is difficult to generalize about them, beyond saying that they strove to stimulate communal concern in whatever branch of the Jeanes work suited their bent. Individual teachers would campaign for tree-planting, rat-extermination and village clean-up days.[2] Of course all teachers were assigned to a certain school circuit by their supervising mission, and would tour these regularly, aiming at gradual improvement in the techniques used by the village teachers. Following their original brief, they would painstakingly show these teachers how further subjects of social significance might be introduced, and how the three R's could be reinterpreted through the infusion of African material.

It had never been intended that Jeanes men and their wives should simply be concerned with school education as such, but rather, following Jones, they should seek so to reform school education that there was nothing taught in the schools which was not also relevant to the education of the whole community. The trouble with such a community-conscious principle in education was that it overestimated the extent to which the school could influence political and social life in the community outside, and undervalued the role of the village school as the first step in the escape from tribal conservatism. Moreover, it was then possible to view the Jeanes system as a means of preventing detribalization, and as a curtailment of the advantages of western education for the young in favour of slow advance by the whole community; it was just such an interpretation that the inspector of schools in Kenya put upon the Jeanes idea: 'The object of their training [the Jeanes men] is to keep the education

[1] Ibid., pp. 571–2. [2] *KEDAR 1930*, pp. 88–90.

of the rural school closely in touch with rural requirements, and to avoid giving village children an education which will divorce them from interest in village life and cause them to seek employment in the towns.'[1]

Whatever political construction is put on this aim of preventing the alienation of the school population from their more backward elders, it is plain that the Jeanes men and their wives, in working towards it, were playing a number of roles that have since been differentiated. In the years before the Government had provided through its Agriculture and Health Departments for African demonstrators in these and related fields, the Jeanes men carried a general writ for community development and village welfare, with the village school as their base. From this followed their close connections with the local Chiefs and the District Officers, and their continual goading of locally-formed committees to demand and work for dispensaries, schools, latrines, maternity classes, and adult education.

In such diversified activity the nature of their contribution can only be properly appreciated by reading their quarterly reports to the Jeanes School, with their carefully recorded statistics and accounts of village achievements.[2] Thus in the reports of Elisha Shiverenge, a Jeanes man serving with the F.A.M., there is no single thing that could possibly be called spectacular, unless it be his enthusiasm for working in an exceptional number of situations. Within the period of a few months he reported, among much else, the following: demonstrations of granaries and larders; layout of improved house; formation of progress committees, parents' committees, and associations of local teachers; patent rat-catching device, with teams of local boys to operate it; involvement of local Chiefs in stone buildings for schools; revitalized Sunday School work; maternity instruction, and preventative action on tapeworms; pressure on District Commissioner for dispensary; latrine measurements; his own demonstration house.[3]

In such reports Jones's chapter on 'Educational Objectives and Adaptations' in his Phelps-Stokes reports come nearest to fulfilment in Kenya. His own plans, however, had been for a continent-wide adoption of the Jeanes system, and no sooner had the Jeanes School

[1] *KEDAR 1926* (Govt. Printer, Nairobi, 1927), p. 13.

[2] Examples of these early records of community work can be seen in the Benson Papers.

[3] Elisha Shiverenge, Quarterly Reports, in Benson Papers. I am indebted to Mr. Opadia Kadima for his translation of these reports.

in Kenya found firm support than he had mapped out a scheme for 'Jeanesizing' each African country. His master plan for achieving this, 'American Cooperation for Africa', outlined for every colony a particular school or schools that could be Jeanesized.[1] South African schools could be reoriented through Dr. Loram;[2] in Sierra Leone, Keigwin, the Director of Education, had long been a student of the system and had had direct experience of the American South;[3] Zanzibar had already made an official appeal for reorganization;[4] Northern and Southern Rhodesia had two government schools ready to be converted; three schools were likewise capable of adaptation in Nyasaland. Similar possibilities existed in Nigeria, the Congo, Portuguese East Africa, and Angola, and even in Abyssinia, where Jones had first-hand knowledge that the Prince of Abyssinia had shown definite evidence of co-operation with schools of the Jeanes type. For all this the cost, he reckoned, would be some 136,850 dollars, and he felt sure that within two years Jeanes schools could be established in a majority of these areas.[5]

Unlike most continental education schemes for Africa, it came some way towards fulfilment. For Keppel and Bertram of the Carnegie Corporation had been so impressed, on their visit to the Jeanes School in Kenya in 1927, with what they considered 'without question the most important single step in the advancement of the African native',[6] that they were prepared to provide the means for the substantial implementation of Jones's hopes. Within only one year, through an appropriation of almost 100,000 dollars, the governments of Nyasaland, Northern Rhodesia and Southern Rhodesia had established no less than five Jeanes schools; Liberia had an American Negro Jeanes teacher by 1928, and in 1930 Portuguese East Africa introduced the Jeanes training. Lastly a further 35,000 dollars ensured that the Jeanes scheme in Zanzibar was started in 1938.[7]

A little earlier, in 1935, a decade of experimentation in Jeanes work

[1] T. J. Jones, 'American Cooperation for Africa', 19 Feb. 1927, File A-19, P.S.F.A.

[2] See p. 227. [3] See further, pp. 234–5.

[4] The appeal came to nothing until the Director had personally visited the States in 1934; see p. 185.

[5] Jones, 'American Cooperation for Africa'.

[6] R. M. Lester, *The Corporation and the Jeanes Teacher* (printed for the Carnegie Corporation, New York, 15 May 1938), p. 7.

[7] Jeanes schools were thus confined largely to the eastern and east-central areas of Africa; although the Corporation appropriated $ 25,000 for the development of Jeanes schools in S. Africa, nothing resulted.

had passed since the beginnings in Kenya, and it was thought appropriate to draw the strands together and review progress. There was therefore held in Salisbury, Southern Rhodesia, again under Carnegie auspices, the Interterritorial Jeanes Conference.[1] American and especially Phelps-Stokes interests were well represented; Dr. Loram, by now transferred to a professorship of education at Yale, was the Chairman, the Associate Director of the General Education Board, who has been responsible for backing the first American Jeanes teachers, was Vice-Chairman, and Dougall was Adviser. As befitted one who had been involved for longer than most in Jeanes work, T. G. Benson, now principal of the Kenya Jeanes School, took a long, hard look at the need for change in the original aims.[2] The time for the omnicompetent Jeanes man was passing, and what had once seemed pioneering work in preventative medicine and agricultural demonstration was being undertaken by the better trained professionals of the Medical and Agricultural Departments. Within the decade also, teacher training had so improved that there were now some lower-primary-school teachers whom the Jeanes men dared not attempt to supervise. Benson advised their withdrawal from what was now an over-ambitious role, in order to specialize much more intensively in communicating teaching skills and in school supervision. The conference recommended that if the Jeanes teacher was to continue to be effective he must have received a prior certificate in a teacher-training school before he was Jeanesized, and it was suggested by implication that Jeanes schools should awaken an interest in community development in people who were already professionals in some other line, rather than make the Jeanes teachers semi-competent in a multitude of what were now separate professions.

Back in Kenya this change in emphasis was soon apparent after the Carnegie grant ended. There was an increasing use of the school for short community courses by various groups, and a decrease in the number of pure Jeanes teachers. Agricultural demonstrators, health workers, lower-primary teachers, all attended, and there was provided even for the Kikuyu Independent School teachers the opportunity for refresher courses.[3] With the inauguration of the first course for chiefs in 1937 came the realization that, just as the Jeanes

[1] The report of the conference, *Village Education in Africa*, was published in 1936.

[2] T. G. Benson, 'The Community Work of the Male (Jeanes) Teacher after Training', in *Report of the Interterritorial Jeanes Conference*, pp. 55–72.

[3] *KEDAR 1938* (Govt. Printer, Nairobi, 1939), p. 76.

teachers could no longer span the whole range of community development, so now the staff had to be supplemented by visiting experts from the Forestry, Veterinary and Medical Departments.[1] Indeed, this Chiefs' course was just one of the links between the Jeanes School and the present-day Kenya Institute of Administration (K.I.A.), which gradually took over the old Jeanes site. The earlier institution had within the one building made the first faltering steps towards African co-operative organization in Kenya, and had simultaneously trained community-development workers and native administrators;[2] and still in 1969, co-operative training, community development, and administration were being held together within the vastly expanded K.I.A.

The Jeanes School had most nearly embodied Phelps-Stokes principles as adapted to African education, both in its original aims and in its practical application of them in Kenya. Over fifteen years the process tested some of Jones's educational premises, especially the idea that change could be initiated from the bottom, and that the lowest and least considered level of the educational system could influence not only the subsequent stages, but also the total life of rural Africa. Another premise was that the rural African was not yet irrevocably married to the traditional western curriculum, and might be persuaded to accept education reinterpreted in terms of community development. But, in practice, the most influential social and educational factors worked in quite the opposite direction; Makerere College and Alliance School, even at several removes, had more influence on the village school syllabus; and it is not without significance that the decade that began with the Jeanes teachers working without power and prestige to change life in the Reserves from the bottom should have ended with the first Chiefs' course.

The more general hidden premise of Jones was that, just as in the Southern States, so in Kenya the patterns of white supremacy were unalterable in the foreseeable future, and therefore any recommendations must be made within this framework. It followed from this that, eschewing radical political remedies for rural backwardness, Africans must work along Booker Washington lines for self-improvement and the amelioration of the general standard of living, before political

[1] *KEDAR 1937* (Govt. Printer, Nairobi, 1938), p. 80.

[2] It was no accident that A. S. Walford, who had worked to initiate consumers, savings, and loan co-operatives at the Jeanes School in the era before African Co-operative law had been laid down, should be made registrar of Co-operative Societies in Kenya in 1952.

action could be justified. In this light, for all Jones's encouragement of community action, progress was ultimately to be determined by the enthusiasm of individuals; Africa was to be changed by the idealism of voluntary service.

Yet, however limited the opportunity for radical reform in such conditions, something positive was certainly achieved. Inspired by the zeal of the European idealists on the staff, the Jeanes men and women did stand courageously for the beauty and value of African arts and leisure activities, and for a brief period were the only workers in the untouched field of community development.

CHAPTER VII

Some Negro Models for African Educators

THERE WAS a dimension to the Phelps-Stokes Fund's interest in African education that was both more ambitious and more comprehensive than the particular stimulus it gave to the foundation and curriculum of the Jeanes schools. This was the larger hope that both government and mission school systems in Africa might increasingly come to be modelled on the educational ideals and the political philosophy of Hampton, Tuskegee, and their kindred institutions.

The frame of reference in both the Phelps-Stokes reports had been obviously taken from the American South,[1] and there was sufficiently frequent recourse to particular educational innovations at Hampton and Tuskegee, or to the importance of Samuel Armstrong and Booker Washington, to catch the casual reader's attention. Moreover, the circulation of the reports was not left to chance; Jones, in consultation with the Phelps-Stokes European and South African representatives, J. H. Oldham and C. T. Loram, drew up a considerable list of influential missionary leaders and colonial officials to be supplied with copies.

In addition to this, certain types of American Negro experience had repeatedly been given publicity by three members of the commissions on tour. For, as was pointed out in Chapter Four,[2] the Phelps-Stokes Commissions were not only commissions of inquiry but equally commissions to popularize a particular educational system. In East Africa, Jones, Aggrey, and Dillard had the same gospel to communicate, and no opportunity was lost to proclaim it. Indeed, Aggrey spoke in public thirty-three times in Kenya alone within three weeks, and, in many of the formal and informal conferences with missionaries, Dillard and Jones had drawn attention to their specialist interests in American Negro education.[3]

The effects both of the reports and of the impression made by

[1] See p. 131. [2] See p. 103.

[3] See private journal of J. W. C. Dougall, secretary of the East African Phelps-Stokes Commission, entries for 29 and 30 Feb. 1924, File 'Education-Central Africa' (hereafter File Q-H), E.H. Also Hooper to Oldham, 2 Mar. 1924, File Q-K, E.H.

the members of the Commissions would have inevitably faded with time, however, had there not immediately been mounted a campaign extending over twenty years to ensure that this did not happen. The Phelps-Stokes Fund decided, on Jones's suggestion, that the only policy which could conceivably transmit the lessons of Hampton and Tuskegee on a continent-wide scale was to let missionaries and officials from Africa see the American South for themselves.

Oldham and Loram readily supported this recommendation, since the visits they had made to Hampton on their own initiative a decade earlier had so profoundly influenced their own thinking.[1] Although, therefore, a number of informal visits to the States had been arranged successfully after the first commission,[2] all three principal proponents of the visitor scheme thought it expedient that it should have the official sanction of the Colonial Office. This meant that the Colonial Office Advisory Committee on Native Education should give its backing. It is some measure both of Oldham's influence and of the Colonial Office's readiness to institutionalize links with American Negro educational methods that almost the first official act to be recommended to its secretary, Hanns Vischer, was an educational tour of the Southern States.[3] The Advisory Committee thought it worthwhile to send their secretary to observe American Negro schools, even though the maximum time he could spend was twelve days. This very condensed visit was no doubt partly compensated for by what Oldham described as his personal 'coaching' on America,[4] and by the fact that Jones was able to accompany him on most of his travels in the South. It is worth noticing, in view of the restricted time available to Vischer, which schools Jones thought most truly illustrative of education relevant to Africa. Predictably, these were Tuskegee, Hampton, and Penn, along with a few more rural schools in Alabama. This itinerary, it will be seen, remained the basis of several hundred longer tours that followed Vischer's.

This early official Colonial Office approval for acquainting educators from Africa with certain models of American Negro schooling owed much to W. A. Ormsby-Gore, the Under-Secretary of State

[1] Cf. pp. 51–2.

[2] For instance, A. W. Wilkie (Gold Coast); H. Hollenbeck (Congo); W. E. Owen (Kenya); A. D. Helser (N. Nigeria); D. J. Oman (Director of Education, Gold Coast).

[3] Vischer to Under-Secretary of State for the Colonies, 12 Dec. 1923, C.O. 554/60, P.R.O.

[4] Oldham to Jones, 15 Nov. 1923, File Q-E, E.H.

for the Colonies, who wished to ensure the 'closest co-operation' between the Phelps-Stokes Fund and the Advisory Committee.[1] The feeling was firmly reciprocated by Anson Phelps Stokes, president of the Fund:

> I am glad to say that the British Colonial Office realise the importance so keenly of having African educators see Hampton, Tuskegee, the work of the Jeanes Fund Teachers, the Lincoln School and various experiments in agriculture and industrial training that they have just sent over at their expense, at Dr. Jones' suggestion, Mr. Saville . . . and I think that hereafter the Government will continue to meet the expenses of men over whom the Colonial Office has control who would especially profit by American experience.[2]

As for educational leaders among the missionaries, the Fund would as far as possible take care of their expenses, guided by Stokes's optimistic belief that 'a very small expenditure now will insure the adoption of wise policies in matters of Negro education in most of the African colonies'.[3]

The Phelps-Stokes Fund could not, however, carry the cost of transporting a large number of missionaries from all over Africa to the Southern States entirely on its own. The scale of the enterprise was therefore enlarged when the Phelps-Stokes appropriation of 2,500 dollars for 1924 was equalled by the International Education Board for the following two years. To act as a clearing-house for the missionary applications, and also as a selection board, a committee of Jones, Oldham, and Vischer was established in 1924 to administer the 500-dollar travel grants.[4] A further welcome addition to the visitors' budget came in May 1926, with an extraordinary appropriation of 35,000 dollars (from the Rockefeller Board) to the Phelps-Stokes Fund for general African purposes, of which 10,000 dollars were earmarked for the visitors' programme.[5] The policy continued steadily year after year, so that by 1931, from Phelps-Stokes

[1] Ormsby-Gore to Oldham, 9 June 1923, File Q-E, E.H.

[2] Phelps Stokes to W. Rose, 21 Oct., 1924, File A-1, P.S.F.A. This Lincoln Normal and Industrial School is not be confused with Lincoln University, or Lincoln Academy, N. Carolina. Saville was principal-elect of Makerere College, Uganda.

[3] Ibid.

[4] Minutes of the Annual General Meeting of Phelps-Stokes trustees, 19 Nov. 1924, File A-1, P.S.F.A.

[5] Minutes of semi-annual meeting of Phelps-Stokes trustees, 28 May 1926, File A-5, P.S.F.A.

sources alone, there had been expended nearly 38,000 dollars.[1] Such a sum had enabled more than two hundred and fifty white educators to visit Hampton and Tuskegee,[2] and in many colonies had effectively ensured that the majority of influential opinion now had experience of the American background.

Several general characteristics of these comparative education tours are important, not least the restricted type of Negro education considered worth the visitors' attention by the Phelps-Stokes Fund. Here Jones does seem to have been somewhat over-anxious lest his visitors should take a different view of Negro education, and indeed of the whole Negro situation in the States, from his own. Such was this fear of misunderstanding that he arranged with Loram's and Oldham's co-operation some measures which he hoped would help to counteract any other impression of the Negro in the States which his guests might acquire from reading the more radical white or Negro statements. To this end there appeared an item of 250 dollars in the Phelps-Stokes annual budget from 1926 onwards, to be allocated to 'books on race problems for African visitors'.[3]

These turn out to be a very select number of works on the Negro and his education which were to be presented in advance by Oldham and Loram to all sponsored African missionary and government visitors to the U.S.A.[4] An orientation guide to their American visit was thus provided in the shape of Monroe Work's *The Negro Yearbook*, B. T. Washington's *Up From Slavery*, T. J. Woofter's *The Basis of Racial Adjustment*, and T. J. Jones's *The Four Essentials of Education*. If Work's yearbook was uncontroversial and objective, the other three constituted an introduction to a somewhat one-sided interpretation of Negro education and politics.[5] The same was true of the bibliographies which Jones had prepared for distribution by J. H. Oldham and C. T. Loram in the event of anyone's asking for a

[1] $37,726 according to the twenty-year report of expenditure of the Phelps-Stokes Fund, File A-5, 1933, P.S.F.A.

[2] J. Merle Davis, *Modern Industry and the African: An Inquiry into the effect of the Copper Mines of Central Africa upon Native Society and the work of Christian Missions made under the auspices of the Department of Social and Industrial Research of the International Missionary Council* (London, 1933), p. 342; see also C. P. Groves, *The Planting of Christianity in Africa, iv, 1914–1954* (London, 1958), p. 113.

[3] Annual estimates of the Phelps-Stokes Fund.

[4] Minutes of Annual Meeting of Phelps-Stokes trustees, 17 Nov. 1926, P.S.F.A.

[5] T. J. Woofter, a graduate of the University of Georgia, had been one of the two main collaborators with Jones on the survey *Negro Education*.

more comprehensive list. The expanded library included Peabody's history of Hampton Institute, *Education for Life*, and Oldham's *Christianity and the Race Problem*. The only book that did deal at all with the intellectual Negro was a series of essays by Negroes, edited by Dr. Alain Locke of Howard University, under the title *The New Negro*, and about this Stokes warned Oldham: 'Locke's book on the Negro is very valuable to show what the intellectual Negro is thinking about. It might, however, be misunderstood by certain people in Africa.'[1] These measures to form in advance attitudes to Tuskegee and Hampton were accompanied by favourable commentaries on the Penn School, for Loram had arranged, on the instruction of the Fund, for the distribution of a hundred copies of *Homes of the Freed* by Penn School's headmistress, Miss Cooley.[2] These were dispatched to Africa, along with some articles by Loram on 'The Penn School Community work as applicable to African Conditions'.[3] On top of this, it was only with some difficulty that Jones was prevented from installing similar formative selections on each of the most popular transatlantic liners.[4]

It might seem of little consequence that a selection of books purporting to introduce the reader to American Negro life and education should pay no attention at all to the role of W. E. B. DuBois as a writer on and interpreter of Negro conditions in the States, for it might reasonably be assumed that the omission could be repaired adequately by the visitors while in the country. In practice, however, schedules on the Southern tours were so tight that, as in Vischer's case, visitors came away without becoming acquainted with the work of the Negro liberal arts colleges or with their leading protagonist.[5] Of course it was not the purpose of the tour to give a comprehensive picture—simply to illustrate those forms of Negro education most relevant, in Jones's view, to Africa. But it was not perhaps to the advantage of the main body of these missionaries to be

[1] Phelps Stokes to Oldham, 6 Dec. 1926, Box 315, E.H., now I.M.C.A., Geneva.

[2] Minutes of Annual meeting of Phelps-Stokes trustees, 17 Nov. 1926, P.S.F.A.

[3] Ibid.

[4] Phelps Stokes to Oldham, 25 May 1925, Box 315, E.H. now I.M.C.A., Geneva.

[5] J. W. C. Dougall, interview, May 1966. Miss B. D. Gibson, interview, May 1966. Archdeacon G. W. Morrison to Oldham, 30 Aug. 1921, Box 315, E.H. now I.M.C.A., Geneva. For a typical itinerary in the Southern States, see p. 183, n. 3.

so scrupulously protected from other interpretations of Negro educational progress.

In this respect, Jones's attitude to Negro colleges and his interest in propaganda for the Tuskegee system do seem more appropriate to the era of *The Souls of Black Folk*, at the turn of the century, with its violent educational and political disputes about priorities for Negro advancement, than to a time when these early differences were being considerably reduced. Nor was Jones without support for this outmoded view of Tuskegee as a tool to be used against DuBois and his ideas. A small group of leading English missionaries was similarly convinced that it was the task of the Phelps-Stokes Fund and Tuskegee jointly to present a constructive alternative to DuBois. In the month after DuBois's Second Pan-African Congress they felt this even more strongly, as an officer of the Phelps-Stokes Fund explained to Dr. Moton:

> It is imperative that far more publicity be given to other sides of the questions involved. The English friends, who have been with us lately, criticise us very severely because DuBois and his activities and his publications are so well known on the other side, and so little is known of the constructive literature. This whole question needs a conference. It is essential that we get out a magazine of the nature of the *Crisis* with a large circulation which shall be the voice of the other party.[1]

Quite apart from this question of rival political propaganda, it is doubtful if Jones was wise to insist that educationally a rigid line could be drawn between the efficacy and relevance of the Tuskegee-Hampton group and the other aspiring, if wretchedly endowed, Negro colleges. Nor indeed would it necessarily have altered missionary admiration for Tuskegee, if the situation had been presented in less extreme terms.[2] Without such concessions, DuBois was perhaps justified in calling attention to some of the factors that had altered since Washington's day. In a critique of the Fund's policy, 'If I had a Million Dollars: a Review of the Phelps Stokes Fund',[3] he charged the Fund with perpetuating a myth:

> We particularly dissent from the thesis which the Phelps Stokes Fund and others have repeatedly put forth: Namely, that education based on the

[1] Miss Tourtellot to Moton, 17 Oct. 1921, R.R.M./G.C. (1921), T.U.A.

[2] Cf. Oldham's comment on the Negro colleges; Oldham to L. Curtis, 11 Feb. 1921, Box 315, E.H., now I.M.C.A., Geneva.

[3] W. E. B. DuBois, 'If I had a Million Dollars: A Review of the Phelps-Stokes Fund', *Crisis*, xxxlx, No. 11 (Nov. 1932), 347.

Hampton-Tuskegee idea has been the real cause of the success of Negro education in the United States. We firmly believe that the contrary is true and that with all that Hampton and Tuskegee have done, and they have done much, nevertheless their peculiar program of industrial education has not been successful and has been given up, while the essential soundness of the Atlanta, Fisk and Howard program of general and higher education and teacher training has with all its omissions proved the salvation of the Negro race.[1]

Thus it was not an entirely uncontroversial itinerary that the missionaries followed, and for this reason it is all the more necessary to examine some of the more important institutions on its path, for these were in the space of a few years to become common reference points for anyone professing a knowledge of African education.

The first, both in importance and in length of visit, were Tuskegee and Hampton, and missionaries normally stayed from four to seven days in each;[2] this was justified on Jones's premises, for the two institutions were centres for a great variety of those community service activities to which the Phelps-Stokes Reports had drawn attention. Most important also, from the point of view of showing to African missionaries institutions that were not cut off from the local community, both Hampton and Tuskegee were the local headquarters for the Federal Department of Agriculture's Extension Service Bureau, administered through two experienced Negro agents, and it was usually possible to demonstrate in some way the skills acquired by the pupils being taken back to be used in the service of their homes. Most visitors were very impressed in this connection by the Booker T. Washington movable school on wheels, which would trundle out of Tuskegee, laden with equipment, to demonstrate a number of simple improvements by using the common materials of the countryside in a more ingenious way.[3] Use made of the central institution by the local farmers could also be readily shown. The trade buildings and farms were equally impressive, especially to missionaries who found it hard to instil a love of either industry or

[1] Ibid. Despite this polemical paragraph, DuBois was no blind admirer of Negro college education; see particularly his Howard University Commemoration Address, 'Education and Work', printed in the *Journal of Negro Education*, i (1932), 60–74.

[2] Hampton Institute Visitors' Books, 1919–37, H.A.I.

[3] Cf. *Report of Mr. and Mrs. G. B. Johnson on a Visit to the U.S.A. to Study the Organisation, Aims and Methods of Rural Schools, February-April 1934* (Zanzibar, 1934), p. 9.

agriculture in Africans. A not uncommon reaction came from Mrs. Grace, a C.M.S. missionary from Uganda, who had long struggled against African distaste for agriculture in high school, and was thus the more delighted to find one of their own Uganda boys under Tuskegee influence: 'He interested us profoundly with his enthusiasm for agriculture and his belief that it will be the saving of Uganda . . . to find a young man like Kato in this place imbued with the ideas of Tuskegee on agriculture is absolutely thrilling when one thinks of the effect on the Baganda.'[1]

There was, however, in addition to all the traditional activities, one new and to Jones not particularly welcome feature which the missionaries might observe at Hampton and Tuskegee: a college course. Such a departure in those very institutions where he had believed his principles of adaptation had been most nearly perfected caused him great distress; he commented irritably on a *Southern Workman* article justifying these changes:

> The ingenuous admission that Hampton's former 'adaptation to different needs has now been replaced by the usual courses given in other schools and colleges' is a most pathetic confession of ignorance both of the great modern trends of education and of the ideals for which Hampton has always stood. This ignorance is further confirmed by a succeeding sentence justifying the 'adoption of more courses conforming to the standards of the modern college and so making Hampton less different from other schools'.[2]

Tuskegee, as usual, followed Hampton's lead in this matter, and when DuBois visited it in 1928 for the first time in a quarter of a century, his visit symbolically coinciding with the recent inauguration of the four-year B.Sc. degree course, his simple 'Fancy a college at Tuskegee' showed plainly where he considered some concession had been made from Tuskegee's earlier rigidity.[3]

Next to Hampton and Tuskegee on the visitors' itinerary were Calhoun Coloured School and Penn School, two of the very few schools which Jones's *Negro Education* report had in 1917 described as 'excellent' for their community-mindedness and adaptation to what he believed the real needs of the Negroes.[4] Ten years later

[1] Diary of Mrs. E. M. D. Grace's visit to Negro schools in the U.S.A., P.S.F.A., p. 11. See further p. 74.

[2] Jones to Miss R. Cooley, 13 Mar. 1929, R.R.M./G.C. (1928), T.U.A.

[3] W. E. B. DuBois, article on Tuskegee, *Crisis*, xxxvi (Feb. 1929), 67–9.

[4] Jones, *Bulletin No. 39*, pp. 58, 483.

Calhoun was much less able, because of its finances, than Hampton, its mother school, to resist the pressures against the traditional curriculum; and at the very time that it was required to appear as the model of an adapted school for the African visitors, Jones was receiving confidential reports that 'the old clear-cut aims are no longer the aims'; community work, agriculture, and industries had all lapsed; but, worst of all, he learnt that 'with the Academic department, we come to a happy exception. It seems to be understood that the school aims to attain as rapidly as possible to the required standards for an accredited state high school.'[1]

Things were beginning to move in the same direction even in the relative isolation of Miss Cooley's Penn School on St. Helena Island, which had seemed to Loram so eminently suitable for simple imitation in Africa. Conformity to the white school system was the demand there too; and Jones could only comment in some dismay:

> . . . the forces controlling Negro education, notably Negro public opinion and State standardisation, are forcing the literary objectives to the neglect of the social realities required by the Negro. Even Miss Cooley and Miss House are dreading the increasing trend in this direction. I am genuinely perplexed as to the ability of a school like Calhoun to withstand this seemingly overwhelming movement. Even Alabama State aid seems to depend upon the development of high school standards at Calhoun.[2]

In this situation it had been an added blow to hear through J. W. C. Dougall the previous month that the Jeanes School, Kabete, which was to be the vanguard of the new adapted education in Africa, had been confronted by the same demands: '. . . the fact remains that the African in many cases does not want what we think is best for him. This is emphatically true of the education based on the Four Simples with which the name and work of Dr. Jesse Jones is indissolubly associated.'[3]

Very little of the tensions caused by these reappraisals was apparent to the visitors, however, and the Director of Education for Zanzibar and his wife were no exception, even as late as their visit of 1934. They paid no attention to the addition of college-grade work at Tuskegee and Hampton in their full report, noting rather that,

[1] Miss M. McCulloch to Jones, 26 Dec. 1928, File G-6, P.S.F.A.
[2] Jones to Miss McCulloch, 3 Jan. 1929, File G-6, P.S.F.A.
[3] J. W. C. Dougall, 'Training Visiting Teachers for African Village Schools', *Southern Workman*, lvii (Oct. 1928), 403–14.

unlike Africa, manual work was not regarded as undignified by the pupils.[1] In Calhoun they could scarcely modulate their praises for the way the school environment corresponded to the simplicity of the children's needs, and was adapted to local requirements: 'What impressed us most was the way in which the school's activities are made to serve the purpose of preparing these boys and girls for their future life on the plantations of Alabama.'[2]

No tour of the South was complete without a study of the Jeanes system of visiting teachers, especially for missionaries from the east and central African countries which had established Jeanes schools. This usually involved accompaning one of the devoted Jeanes women in her brave attempts to instil into depressed Negro teachers in one-room schools an interest in creative manual and industrial subjects beyond the three R's.[3] Occasionally the missionaries and other Phelps-Stokes visitors were fortunate enough to meet either Dr. Dillard or the first and most famous of the Jeanes teachers, Miss Virginia Randolph, who had, with tremendous personal sacrifice of time and energy, creatively interpreted Washington's motto of working without complaint for the 'inch of progress'.[4] Her unremitting simple service to her people never failed to appeal, and not least to Sir Gordon Guggisberg, ex-Governor of the Gold Coast. Guggisberg's biographer, R. E. Wraith, has commented interestingly that 'even Achimota never fully satisfied him, and it was not until he visited the Negro Colleges of the Southern States of America that he felt himself among kindred spirits'.[5] It is not perhaps surprising, therefore, that the founder of the Jeanes school movement in America should so appeal to him: 'I saw Virginia Randolph today and was greatly struck by her. A fine type and much nearer my own primitive people than anyone else I met.'[6]

After seeing these five institutions, there might be time briefly to visit the great co-operative college president and Christian statesman,

[1] *Report of Mr. and Mrs. G. B. Johnson*, p. 9. [2] Ibid., p. 10.

[3] For a sympathetic survey of the efforts of these Jeanes industrial teachers, see Jones, *The Jeanes Teacher in the United States*, and Brawley, *Dr. Dillard of the Jeanes Fund;* for the Jeanes teacher in retrospect, Myrdal, *An American Dilemma*, pp. 887, 1417.

[4] Quoted in Meier, *Negro Thought in America*, p. 107.

[5] R. E. Wraith, *Guggisberg* (London, 1967), p. 132. Wraith uses the term 'Negro Colleges' rather loosely to refer principally to Hampton and Tuskegee. See further F. G. Guggisberg and A. G. Fraser, *The Future of the Negro* (London, 1929).

[6] Guggisberg to Mrs. Gregg, 12 Oct. 1927, H.A.I.

John Hope, at Atlanta University,[1] or to spend a day in Washington at the Bureau of Agriculture, where the agricultural expert from the East Africa Phelps-Stokes Commission, Dr. Shantz, could point to a wealth of experiments in the Negro South that might well be tried in Africa. Frequently also in New York interviews were arranged with Miss Mabel Carney, of Teachers College, Columbia, whose courses on rural education came to be regarded increasingly by the Fund as a very valuable additional feature for missionaries who could afford to stay longer.[2]

Such was the framework of the tours, with occasional alterations made by Jones to suit individual interests. Some generalizations can be made in describing their constituent parts, but not in assessing their effect upon the African visitors. These results, if such a positive term may be used in this connection, must seem inconclusive and disjointed, for it was a question of largely uncoordinated groups of missionaries and officials reacting in different ways, at both a theoretical and a practical level, to a common stimulus. In an attempt, however, to gauge some of these reactions a little more precisely, a few of the missionaries and government educationists from East Africa, especially from Kenya, will be examined more closely.

The first British missionary society in Kenya to receive an invitation from the Fund to send one of its members to visit America was the C.M.S., and the particular missionary suggested by Oldham to the Phelps-Stokes Fund as being especially influential in the development of native education was Archdeacon Wilfred Owen.[3] The decision was an interesting one. Owen was very far from being a non-political missionary. He had been a continual goad in the Kenya Government's side through his championing of African rights, and in the two years prior to his visit in January 1922 had been, in the company of Leys, McGregor Ross, and Oldham, an important element in the nucleus of protest against African wage cuts, forced labour, and the settler mentality. In the face of what looked like an imminent clash between settler, missionary, and African interests, Oldham had, however, been extremely impressed on his most recent visit to the States by the success of certain steps taken by both Negroes

[1] Cf. R. Torrence, *The Story of John Hope* (New York, 1948).

[2] Miss Carney's course on rural method, especially for Africa, was recommended by the Fund for missionaries and African students in the States. Some of these included J. W. C. Dougall, A. D. Helser, P. Koinange, M. Yergan, K. Simango, E. Ita (see further p. 236 ff).

[3] Oldham to Owen, 24 Oct. 1921, Acc. 83, C.M.S.A., London.

and whites to lessen the tensions of America's own post-war period. There was the creation by Jones of the Interracial Commission,[1] which worked from Atlanta at interpreting the races to each other and at attempting the prevention of racial violence through negotiation. Moreover, in the spring Oldham had spent over a week at Tuskegee, where, in his first close contact with Negro leaders, he had realized the extent to which such a system as Washington's could bring out the latent best qualities in the Negro people:

> What strikes one most in contrast with national and racial situations elsewhere is the extraordinary sanity of outlook of the Negro leaders and the absence of any kind of sourness of disposition notwithstanding the discrimination and disabilities of which they are daily reminded. They exhibit restraint and balance of judgement, a power of recognising and reckoning with facts, patience in working towards a far distant goal, constructive efforts and a cheerful optimism to which I know no parallel. This is no doubt partly due to the magnificent tradition established by Booker Washington.[2]

There seemed perhaps the need to have someone in Kenya who could identify with and guide African politics along lines of constructive interracialism. Owen was the most credible choice for such a task.

Like Vischer two years later, Owen divided most of his time between Tuskegee and Hampton, with both of which he was extremely impressed,[3] and made no contact at all with the other Negro colleges. Much was going on in his own Nyanza district of Kenya, however, while he was studying techniques of interracial co-operation and Tuskegee's self-help schemes for Negro farmers. The Young Kavirondo Association had come forcefully to public attention for the first time just two days before Christmas 1921,[4] possibly partly in response to Harry Thuku's suggestion (it certainly maintained a close relationship with his E.A.A.)[5] Then a mass protest meeting of 4,000 was sponsored by the Association on 7 February, and in July the Governor, Sir Edward Northey, judged a personal meeting

[1] See pp. 54–5.

[2] Oldham to Curtis, 11 Feb. 1921, Box 315, E.H., now I.M.C.A., Geneva.

[3] Owen to Moton, 4 Feb. 1922, R.R.M./G.C. (1921), T.U.A. Owen greatly admired the 'wonders of Tuskegee', which he hoped they would be able in time to emulate in Africa.

[4] Lonsdale, 'Archdeacon Owen and the Kavirondo Taxpayers Welfare Association', p. 1; cf. also Thuku to Njeroge, 23 Dec. 1921, enclosed in Bowring to Churchill, 25 Jan. 1922, C.O. 533/275, P.R.O.

[5] See p. 66.

necessary.[1] After Thuku's arrest in March 1922, something of the growing confidence of the Young Kavirondo Association had been lost, but it still said a great deal for Owen's sensitivity to popular grievance, and perhaps also for his recent interracial experiences in the U.S.A., that he was able on his return in November 1922 to transform this body from a machine for protest to a vehicle for constructive efforts for native welfare. This achievement was noted by the Director of Education in an annual report:

> The Kavirondo Welfare Association is a remarkable organisation . . . It came into being at the time of the Native political unrest in 1921–22. Archdeacon Owen upon his return from leave in 1922 took control of it, and diverted political agitation toward social development, with the result that the very Africans who in earlier years sought to drive him from Kavirondo now make him their refuge in trouble and the repository of their aspirations. Politics are now but little heard.[2]

The Kavirondo Taxpayers Welfare Association (K.T.W.A.), to give it its full name, was certainly a remarkable example of that type of co-operation to establish which the Phelps-Stokes Commission devoted much of its time in Kenya. Owen was president, District Commissioners and Chiefs held honorary positions, and serious attempts were made to prevent clashes between the traditional religions and Christianity. Its ideology, enshrined in the code of honour sworn to by every member, was exactly Booker Washington's ideal of self-help, adapted to African conditions. For this reason this code of moral and economic self-improvement deserves to be quoted in full:

> I promise to keep the laws of the Association; to plant 200 trees and to replace those that die; to build proper latrines and to prevent flies from breeding in them; to kill off rats as far as possible and to report any rats found dead; not to foul the water in rivers, springs or wells; not to aid or abet the marriage of girls under 16 years of age; not to mix cow's urine with milk; to supply beds for my household, and to supply bedclothes; to clothe myself properly and to keep my clothes clean; I promise not to get drunk.[3]

That this parallel with his experience in the American South was

[1] Lonsdale, 'Archdeacon Owen', pp. 1–2; cf. for the whole episode, Oginga Odinga, *Not yet Uhuru* (London, 1967), pp. 24–9.

[2] Jones, *Education in East Africa*, p. 124.

[3] Ibid., p. 125. See further Bennett, 'The Development of Political Organisations in Kenya', p. 120.

not mere coincidence was made clear in a series of articles by Owen in the *E.A.S.*, the most important of which judged the missionary, government, and settler record on native education policy by Washington's criteria. All these three immigrant communities, Owen agreed, had interpreted native education to fit in with their own needs, whether for literate evangelists, clerks, or intelligent, semi-skilled labourers. Such policies were radical misinterpretations of Washington's famous dictum, 'We shall prosper in proportion as we learn to dignify and glorify labour and put brains and skill into the common occupations of life'.[1] What the immigrants too seldom realized was that the first place where labour must be dignified and skills applied was in the development of the Reserves; and it was to precisely that task that the K.T.W.A. addressed itself. In reaching the conclusion that for African fulfilment the ordinary conditions of life and work must be improved in the Reserves, Owen showed little sympathy for Washington's opponents, 'who thought that the way to prosperity lay through higher education and a free use of the vote', and who 'embarked on a political campaign marked with much bitterness'.[2] From this it becomes clear that in Owen's mind a parallel had developed between the DuBois school of Negroes in America and the detribalized Africans in Kenya. This connection was strikingly made when he described the characteristics of the detribalized Africans: 'They become Ethiopians and Pan-Africans and cast their vision to the utmost bounds of racial questions, instead of trying to make their own tribe worthy of the respect which must be earned before it can be accorded it.'[3] There was, therefore, a sense in which the K.T.W.A. functioned as a means of preventing detribalization, and in this respect approximated in its intentions to one of the aims of the Jeanes School.

The point, however, that must be clearly made about the K.T.W.A. is not that Owen did not continue to champion African rights through it, but that it was an interracial, white-led organization, while the Young Kavirondo Association had been an independent political

[1] W. E. Owen, 'Native Policy. Education. Its Objects and Methods. Where Missions and Settlers have Erred. An American Model'. *E.A.S.* (wkly edn), 8 July 1922; see further W. E. Owen, 'Native Policy. Essays towards a clear and Moral Code. The Noahite Policy and the New World', *E.A.S.* (wkly edn.), 6 May 1922.

[2] Owen, 'Native Policy. Education.'

[3] W. E. Owen, 'Native Policy. The Problem of the Detribalised Native. How not to make matters worse', *E.A.S.* (wkly edn.) 27 May 1922.

movement. His American experience had thus convinced Owen that advance on 'Welfare lines'[1] must be the priority for African development, and that politics were the consequence rather than the cause of such advance. He invoked Tuskegee for emphasis:

> Booker T. Washington insisted most strongly that the uplift of the American Negro depended first and foremost on the Negro developing all his powers of hand and skilful work to the uttermost. I myself stand for the spiritual, social and political advance of the Native tribes. I put political last with intent, for the history of our own Empire teaches us that the masses have advanced to political power on the record of and by the merits of intellectual and social advance.[2]

A further direct result of Owen's experience in the States was his quest for a Kenyan African of Washington's qualities. This was soon to become a common theme among missionaries—an interesting conception of a figure who would be non-revolutionary, and incorporate in his person such talents for interpreting white and black to each other that radical changes in the political structure need not occur. It is not for this reason coincidental that this near-mythical figure should be projected shortly after the massive civil disorder over Thuku in 1922:

> We need an African Booker T. Washington, one who will bring all available forces into cooperation towards the great end. Until such a man arises (and even more so afterwards) you will be well advised to gather to yourselves all who are friendly disposed towards your high ideals, and we also (I speak as a European) will be well advised to take advantage of every opportunity you give us of working together with you for the true advancement of this land. May I suggest the formation of an organisation such as Washington and his successor Dr. Moton . . . found most helpful. It is called Racial Cooperation . . .[3]

After the Phelps-Stokes visit to Kenya of the next year, and the impact of Aggrey, this notion of an African Booker Washington became even more current, and not only among missionaries.[4] That the Governor of Kenya himself saw Aggrey as fulfilling the requirements was evident from his admitting to Jones that 'he would prefer

[1] W. E. Owen, letter in the *E.A.S.*, 23 June 1923, on the occasion of the Kikuyu Association protest to the K.T.W.A. over the appointment of Dr. Arthur to represent African interests.

[2] Ibid. [3] Ibid.

[4] See Bishop R. S. Heywood of Mombasa to the Phelps-Stokes Fund, 16 June 1924, File A-5, P.S.F.A.

to have Dr. Aggrey connected with the Kenya Government than a regiment of British soldiers, because his constructive statesmanship in explaining Europeans to natives and natives to Europeans, would be more potent than any military force'.[1]

Aggrey was prepared to play such a role of mediator between the races, and did so in a small way in regard to the K.T.W.A. even in the short time he was in Kenya. He recognized in Owen's work for the association those principles which he himself lived by, and praised him in terms that whites frequently applied to Aggrey himself: 'I have talked about you as being an ideal Britisher in affording safety valve to the engine of native discontentment. If every district could have an Owen there would be the absence of subterranean meetings and a deep rumbling that may prophesy a coming earthquake.'[2] More than this, in reporting back to the Colonial Secretary, E. B. Denham, after addressing the K.T.W.A., Aggrey was prepared to provide, with Owen's help, the names of reliable, constructive Africans who could be consulted by the Government when necessary. They must be scrupulously chosen, for, wrote Aggrey with some importance, 'we cannot afford to make mistakes . . . This is our chance. We must not fail'.[3]

It is not surprising that Jones, too, saw the great co-operative possibilities in Owen's organization, but he was prepared to do more than recommend its example when writing the East Africa report; he believed that some direct financial encouragement should be given to Owen for his 'constructive efforts to improve race relations in Kenya', and at his request the Fund voted him 150 dollars in 1925 and a further 100 in the following year.[4] Although these were of course token amounts, they did mean that the Phelps-Stokes Fund maintained contact with Owen in a direct way until the end of 1927.

The first of the missions to follow the C.M.S. lead was the C.S.M., and although the result of its contacts with the Southern States is not so easily demonstrable as in the case of Owen and the K.T.W.A., certain significant points do emerge from the tours of at least three of its most influential leaders, Dr. J. W. Arthur, Dr. H. R. A. Philp,

[1] T. J. Jones, 'Solving the Race Problem in Africa', broadcast talk, 19 July 1931, copy in File A-19, P.S.F.A. Aggrey was commonly given the courtesy title of 'Dr.', even though he never completed his studies.

[2] Aggrey to Owen, 15 Apr. 1924, Acc. 83, Owen Papers, C.M.S.A., London.

[3] Ibid.

[4] Minutes of Annual Meeting of Phelps-Stokes trustees, 18 Nov. 1925, File A-5, P.S.F.A.

and G. A. Grieve. The C.S.M. stations had received excellent testimonials from the Phelps-Stokes visitors in 1924,[1] and much that these men would now learn in America provided confirmation or slight variation of educational policies for which they had for some time stood.

The first of the Scots to tour the South were Mr. and Mrs. G. A. Grieve in April 1925, and during their time there, particularly at Tuskegee, they believed they had learnt much that would be most useful on their return.[2] What was not known at that time was that within the year Grieve would be the principal of Kenya's first junior secondary school, the Alliance High School, and in a position greatly to influence the character and curriculum of this level of education. While no direct causal relationship is suggested, the American point of view was one of the formative influences that placed agriculture and Bantu studies on the syllabus as two of the four required subjects.[3] Although of course by this time some of the ideas of progressive African-adapted curricula had achieved a currency that they did not have when the Phelps-Stokes Commission first toured West Africa, it is interesting to note how consonant with these were the stated aims of the school. It was hoped that the influence of Bantu studies would offset the effects of using English as a teaching medium, and encourage unity with the local community:

> There is no desire to divorce the interests of the students from their own native life and customs. No European education would be considered complete without knowledge of the development of the civilisation and culture on which it is based. So it ought to be with the African. Bantu Studies therefore occupy a due place in the school and as staff increases it is hoped to make some definite advance along the lines of African culture.[4]

To both Dougall's and Jones's disappointment, however, this initial correspondence with the ideals of the Jeanes School was shortlived; for all the attempt to maintain an important place for vocational training and community centredness, Alliance High School's position at the apex of the junior secondary pyramid in

[1] Jones, *Education in East Africa*, pp. 125–8. For Grieve's use of Jones's report in re-organizing the literary work at Kikuyu 'along practical lines', see Arthur to Jones, 31 July 1924, File on Alliance High School, P.C.E.A.

[2] Grieve to Moton, 2 May 1925, R.R.M./G.C. (1925), T.U.A.

[3] *The Alliance High School Kikuyu* (Nairobi, 1928), p. 15; copy in Grieve papers, Edinburgh University Library. See also *KEDAR 1928*, p. 33.

[4] *The Alliance High School Kikuyu*, p. 7.

Kenya encouraged a competitive academic atmosphere. By Dougall's criteria at least, this made the school 'increasingly artificial. The pupils are divorced from home interests and home conditions. The knowledge is imparted through a foreign medium. Theory predominates even in agriculture. The course on Bantu Studies is just another class-lesson.'[1] By 1934, agriculture, or working in garden plots, remained a compulsory subject, but was, as in some American colleges, more useful in providing a source of fees for the poorer students than in preventing the school's becoming in the pupils' eyes a two year 'stepping-stone between their primary school and Makerere College'.[2]

Dr. Horace Philp of the Scots Mission at Tumutumu was the next to take up Jones's invitation. Since it was by 1925 common knowledge in Kenya mission circles that Owen had been much helped by his visit, a certain amount of intermission rivalry now operated. Philp was then able to put the case to his Mission Board in these terms:

> As the American institutions at Tuskeegee [sic] and Hampton are supposed to be the last word on how Negro education should be run it would be of considerable advantage to me personally to see these institutions with the view of seeing how we can improve our methods here . . . I consider our work here as important as his [Owen's] in Kavirondo.[3]

November, therefore, found Mr. and Mrs. Philp at Hampton, where, in addition to enlarging their own experience, they were instrumental in forging a direct link between American Negro methods and their own mission: they successfully suggested that E. A. Cromack,[4] a white agriculturalist of two years' experience in Hampton Institute, might take up similar work in the Scottish Kikuyu Mission, as this was a subject now being given much prominence.[5]

Here it is again worth noting how widespread the notion had become, as a result of the Phelps-Stokes reports, that an American trained in the Hampton tradition would best introduce the new

[1] Dougall to Oldham, 24 May 1931, File Q-I, E.H.; see also Oginga Odinga, op. cit., p. 36.

[2] *KEDAR 1937*, p. 72.

[3] Philp to McLachlan, 26 July 1924, MS. 7608, Church of Scotland Foreign Mission Papers, National Library of Scotland.

[4] *Kikuyu News*, xcv, p. 16; and Gregg to McLachlan, 20 Jan. 1926, Gregg Papers, H.A.I.

[5] 'Organisation of Agricultural Education for Africans': Report of Committee, 22 Nov. 1928 (stencilled copy in E.H.); 'Memorandum of the Director of Education: Agricultural Education', E.H.

farming methods to African pupils. Only a month before the Philps were at Hampton, a Ugandan contingent of C.M.S. missionaries had been there, and their joint memorandum to the Phelps-Stokes Fund showed how Cromack might just as easily have been recruited for Uganda:

> It is impossible to overestimate the gain that would come to Uganda from the visit for two years or more of one of the experienced men of the Hampton staff. We find ourselves constantly saying: 'If only we could get some of these people over to Uganda to help us with the problems that we are up against.' Not only would such a man bring the experience gained in years of education of negroes on the soundest lines, but he would also bring that intangible and priceless thing—the Hampton spirit.[1]

Although these Uganda missionaries were anxious to have a Hampton Negro graduate as well as white instructors, the difficulties that stood in the way of recruiting Negro missionaries have been fully shown elsewhere.

Dr. Arthur's visit of 1927 by chance raised this same issue of a role for the American Negro college graduate in the Kenya mission field; for it so happened that Arthur was at Hampton at the same time as Max Yergan, with whom it is almost certain that he had worked in co-operation exactly a decade before in the Carrier Corps.[2] Together one Sunday evening, presumably both aware of the almost unsuperable barriers, they pleaded with the students in chapel to go to East Africa. 'Go out to that country,' Arthur repeated the message at Tuskegee the next week, 'Be like Max Yergan; God wants you to take up that cross and follow him.'[3] E. A. Cromack certainly went, and stayed for a tour in Kikuyu until 1930; but how much his Negro counterparts were seriously sought out by missionaries who believed, as did Arthur, so strongly in the civilizing and educating mission of European agriculturalists and commercial men in Kenya must remain in some considerable doubt.[4]

[1] Memorandum of H. Mathers, H. M. Grace, H. F. Wright, 23 Oct. 1925, File B-3, P.S.F.A.

[2] For contact between Kenya missionaries and the Y.M.C.A. volunteers, see Hooper, *Africa in the Making*, p. 18. Arthur had been subscribing to *Southern Workman* since late 1923.

[3] J. W. Arthur, chapel address, 17 Apr. 1927, stencilled copy in T.U.A.

[4] J. W. Arthur, 'The Kenya Colony and Protectorate', *The East and the West*, xxi (July 1923), 240. In 1924 Arthur had vetoed a concrete proposal for a native Indian missionary (from the Presbyterian Church in India) to come and work among Asians or Africans in Kenya; Arthur to W. Paton, 22 Aug. 1924, Box A/37, P.C.E.A.

Visiting the Negro schools was not a policy that Jones proposed only to missionaries from Europe, for, as a glance at the American-led A.I.M. and the F.A.M. shows, the leading missionaries of both denominations gave considerable attention to what could be adopted from Hampton and Tuskegee.

As early as 1922, and possibly connected with the publication of the West Africa Phelps-Stokes Report, Dr. Virginia Blakeslee of the A.I.M. was in correspondence from Kenya with Moton, asking advice from him on the best methods of teaching various industries in a projected African girls school.[1] The scheme lapsed, however, until the Phelps-Stokes Commission toured Kenya. Encouraged by this new stimulus, Dr. Blakeslee personally visited Hampton and Tuskegee and their daughter schools in 1925. Not content with the short-term tour of so many missionaries, she spent the next two years 'studying the various schools of America's Southland to help in forming a sound policy for our school.'[2]

The outcome in 1927 was a new type of girls' training programme among the Kikuyu and Masai at Kijabe, designed to minimize the usual rift between school and community, by holding only the morning instruction on the three R's in the station school, while all the classes adapted to the home, health, and the industries of the local neighbourhood took place in the villages themselves.[3] Some of these experiments were far from popular; and although there is no opportunity here to sort out the numerous factors, apart from the circumcision issue, that led to the hostility between the staff and students of the A.I.M. schools which developed over the next few years, perhaps one factor in the mission's conspicuous lack of sympathy towards student demands for a higher level of education was its conviction that the best model for Kenya's development lay in the utter simplicity of Miss Cooley's little Penn School on St. Helena Island.[4]

The last mission to be examined for its post-Phelps-Stokes contacts with Hampton and Tuskegee is the F.A.M., which, more than any other, thoroughly accepted Jones's belief that experience of Negro schools in America was a pre-condition for success in Africa. This was no sudden conversion, for there had been a long history in the

[1] Miss Blakeslee to Moton, 6 Apr. 1922, R.R.M./G.C. (1922), T.U.A.

[2] H. V. Blakeslee, *Beyond the Kikuyu Curtain*, (Moody Press, Chicago, 1956), p. 165. See also Minutes of Meeting of Kenya Field Council, Kijabe (A.I.M.), 30–1 Aug. 1926, and 16–17 Dec. 1926, (Field Headquarters, Nairobi.)

[3] Blakeslee, op. cit., p. 167.

[4] *Inland Africa* (Brooklyn), ix (May 1925), 10.

F.A.M. of affinity with Tuskegee's industrial methods. One of their pioneer missionaries, Willis Hotchkiss, had in 1910 approached Washington for permission to visit and study Tuskegee,[1] and four years earlier had written for Hampton's *Southern Workman* on Kenya.[2] When another of the older school of American Quaker missionaries, Jefferson Ford, visited Hampton in 1921 on his own initiative, he had immediate reassurance from his Board that this was in accordance with their policy: 'We have long felt that it would be well if some of our missionaries to the African field could spend several months at Hampton carefully studying their method and plan of work. Our program on the African field must be carried out along similar lines to those which are being pursued by negro educators in the South.'[3]

In Ford's case, as so often happened at Hampton and Tuskegee in the twenties and thirties, visitors from East, South and West Africa coincided, and there was thus provided in these centres an opportunity for cross-fertilization of educational ideas from all over the continent. Within ten days in October 1921, for instance, this informal process of contact involved the Wilkies from the first Phelps-Stokes Commission, the Director of Education from the Gold Coast, Miss Gollock of Edinburgh House, J. E. K. Aggrey, Hunter from Lovedale, and Jefferson Ford.[4] It was not surprising, therefore, after his meeting some of these Hampton enthusiasts, that Ford came away the more convinced that Hampton could provide the model for the successful combination of academic, trade, and agricultural branches in one school.[5] Later the next year he too took advantage of the pages of the *Southern Workman* to draw a distinction between the Hampton-based policy of the Friends' Mission and some of the other more academic missions in Kenya.[6]

After the Phelps-Stokes Commission had visited the Quaker Mission in Kenya, Jones had been so impressed by their equipment

[1] Washington to W. Hotchkiss, 7 Feb. 1910, Box 406, B.T.W./L.C.

[2] W. R. Hotchkiss, 'A Glimpse into Central Africa', *Southern Workman*, xxxiv (Sept. 1905), 493, and 'Some Suggestions on Native Education in B.E.A.', in *Evidence of the Education Commission of the East Africa Protectorate* (Nairobi, 1919), pp. 120–1.

[3] W. Beede to J. W. Ford, 26 Oct. 1921, Ford File, Friends' Africa Mission Archives (hereafter F.A.M.A.), Richmond, Ind.

[4] Hampton Institute Visitors' Books, 1919–37, H.A.I.

[5] Ford to Beede, 12 Oct. 1921, F.A.M.A.

[6] J. W. Ford, 'Industrial Work in African Missions', *Southern Workman*, li (Mar. 1922), 121–5.

and by the opportunity which these rural-minded Mid-Westerners had of creating a 'second Tuskegee' in Africa[1] that he sent to the general secretary of the Friends' Board in Richmond, Indiana, a much more detailed set of recommendations for improvements than there had been room for in the East Africa report.[2] Specialists in education and agriculture must be the priority, and both must have the Hampton-Tuskegee outlook to be of optimum value. With these suggestions, Jones began a period as an informal educational advisor to the Friends; he was asked to the General Meeting in Indiana in 1925, suggested particular Negro colleges for missionary visits, and sent to East Africa a copy of the East Africa Report for each of the Mission families.[3]

Negro orientation tours for five more Friends were organized during the next four years, and on a visit to Tuskegee one of them drew attention to a feature that was usually too obvious to receive comment: the fact that Tuskegee was operated entirely by the Negro himself. Mrs. Alta Hoyt's recording of this simple fact is a reminder of just how novel such an experience of an all-Negro institution was for many of the Kenya missionaries:

> In comparing Hampton and Tuskegee, one is just about as good as the other so far as good solid work is concerned, but it has been very interesting to me to see both schools because Tuskegee is operated entirely by the Negro himself while Hampton is run with the management mostly in the hands of the whites . . . It is most interesting to see how capable the Negro is in the management here.[4]

The inferences about African capacity for organization that might follow from this observation she did not elaborate, but the incident is important for demonstrating how, apart from curricular improvements, it was possible for Tuskegee to act as a liberalizing agent.

The educational specialist whom Jones had recommended as indispensable to the Friends' Mission was Everett Kellum. His training reflected the new ideas about missionary preparation, as the Mission Board fell in with Jones's preferences:

> As to the plans for Mr. Kellum, I would suggest that he endeavor to

[1] F. N. Hoyt to Moton, undated but shortly after 21 July 1925, R.R.M./G.C. (1925), T.U.A.

[2] Jones to Beede, 6 May 1925 and 3 June 1925, File D-32, P.S.F.A.

[3] Beede to Jones, 22 July 1925, File D-32, P.S.F.A., and further correspondence in this file.

[4] Mrs. Hoyt to Beede, 29 Jan. 1926, Hoyt File, F.A.M.A.

spend some time at the Tuskegee and Hampton summer schools . . . I believe that Dr. Moton and Dr. Gregg of Hampton would be willing for an extended visit which would enable him to catch the spirit of the two schools. I doubt whether a visit to Columbia would be of much value unless he could arrange to take the full summer course with Miss Carney. However I think that the Tuskegee-Hampton experience would be more valuable than the summer school at Columbia.[1]

Eventually Kellum was able to spend a full week at Hampton and two and a half weeks at Tuskegee, following this with a tour of observation with the Southern Jeanes teachers and some excursions with the movable school.

No less rigorous was the preparation of the Friends' women missionaries; Miss Parker took a similar tour the year after Kellum. But it was Elizabeth Haviland whose training period came nearest to what might be considered a paradigm of apprenticeship for the African field; two years were spent teaching at Calhoun Coloured School, a rural preparation course was taken at Cornell University, and she sailed for Kenya via the Le Zoute conference on Christian mission in Africa.[2]

By 1929 all these missionaries who had had the opportunity to visit the South had returned to Kenya. The F.A.M. proceeded, however, to enter a period of some considerable difficulty which lasted from 1929 until 1934, and not a little of the discontent among the Africans centred on the degree to which the Mission was industrial.

Yet it was the industrial side that had originally won Phelps-Stokes approval. When Jones had visited the Mission's Kenya headquarters in 1924, one feature which earned his strong commendation was the manner in which the Friends had, through the skilful exploitation of the natural resources of timber and water on the mission estates, won a measure of settler esteem. One of the missionaries was mentioned in the Phelps-Stokes Report for having 'won the position of consultant for neighboring European settlers, thus affording an admirable example of cooperation between Missionaries and the settler community'.[3] It is particularly significant, in the light of the later reaction, that the Mission received further praise for the way it taught 'the Native how to take advantage of the waterfalls for milling purposes';[4] the presence in Kaimosi mission of 'water-power machinery for

[1] Jones to Beede, 27 Feb. 1928, File D-32, P.S.F.A.
[2] E. Haviland File, F.A.M.A.; Smith, *Christian Mission in Africa*, p. 180.
[3] Jones, *Education in East Africa*, p. 130. [4] Ibid.

sawing and grinding, and extensive acreage of land'[1] were seen as additional reasons why that station could be converted into a thriving central station. These activities were the product of the Quaker ethos, which stressed the autonomous, self-supporting mission, and, particularly in that period before the Quakers could see fit to receive grants-in-aid, the industrial enterprises were as much to supplement mission income as to train African artisans. It was this pioneering spirit, reminiscent of the way in which Booker Washington had first made good with the Southern white community by making competitively-priced bricks and wagons,[2] which convinced Jones that the Quakers now had the chance to fashion a second Tuskegee.[3]

The architect of this industrial programme, and its leading exponent in the F.A.M., was Fred Hoyt. After a battle for recognition of his industrial methods, he had with Phelps-Stokes encouragement been able to demonstrate to the Education Department in 1924, that the 'Government method of training apprentices in manual labour to do little fiddling things like make picture frames, cigarette trays etc.' was 'impractical for this pioneer country'.[4] He had taken advantage of his leave in 1926 to make study tours of Tuskegee and Hampton, and, like Ford, found confirmation that his work was on the right lines. It is the more interesting, in view of this, to note that in the 1929 explosion of discontent in the Normal Training School, when thirty-two students were suspended for refusing to take the loyalty oath, their first grievance was not against technical education *per se*, but rather against their participation in the mission's commercial enterprises; what they demanded were skills like typing and telegraphy, which would be directly useful for their own futures.[5]

Much deeper implications of the Friends' industrial philosophy were exposed in 1934, when an African Friend, Andreya Jumba, secretary of the North Kavirondo Central Association, bypassed the local mission council and lodged a formal protest with the Friends' Board in Indiana. Exactly how Mr. Hoyt had become the centre of this storm and the chief object of the Africans' discontent was explained to the Board later by Dr. A. A. Bond, of the mission's medical staff:

[1] Ibid., p. 131. [2] Washington, *Up From Slavery*, pp. 189–91.

[3] Hoyt to Moton, undated, R.R.M./G.C. (1925), T.U.A.

[4] Hoyt to Beede, 25 June 1924, Hoyt File, F.A.M.A.; cf. also Levinus K. Painter, *The Hill of Vision: The Story of the Quaker Movement in East Africa. 1902–1965* (Nairobi, 1966), pp. 91–3.

[5] Kellum to Friends' Board, 10 Oct. 1929, Kellum File, F.A.M.A.

There is a feeling that the land which the Mission holds here is not being used altogether for the direct benefit of the native Africans . . . I believe that no other single act for which our mission has been responsible ever lost us so much prestige as this one did . . . That brings to mind a criticism that has been made against the Mission for indulging in commercial enterprises in the country . . . [it] constitutes unfair competition inasmuch as missions are subsidised to some extent by outside funds. Mr. Hoyt has sawn a great deal of lumber which is piled at the Mill, and he grinds much meal for mining companies. The natives feel that it is a money-making enterprise from which they profit little. Personally I believe that the operations in connection with our Mill have for years done far more harm to the missionary cause than good.[1]

The clash that arose out of this issue, even if it did accentuate the division between the conservative and liberal elements in the mission, had the overall effect, as Dr. Bond saw, of making the Africans 'group all white people together in their thinking'.[2] Certainly the mission's conspicuous links with the mining companies and other settlers gave some renewed justification for the attitude to missions which Thuku had popularized twelve years before.[3] It showed in addition some considerable obstacles in the way of this particular interpretation of Tuskegee's industrial principles, and the need for the greatest caution in developing a co-operation with the settler community that did not compromise the mission's educational and spiritual goals.

The C.S.M., the C.M.S., the A.I.M., and the Friends were all thus in a variety of different ways affected by the relevance of much that was being done in the Negro schools of the Southern States;[4] but Jones was anxious that government officials, too, should acquire this perspective. The Director of Education, J. R. Orr, was offered the travel grant early in 1922 on Owen's recommendation, but was unable to take it up.[5] Three years later, Edward Denham, the Colonial Secretary, was made a similar offer, but he too had to

[1] Bond to H. Cope, 23 Sept. 1934, Bond File, F.A.M.A.

[2] Bond to E. T. Elliott, 30 June 1934, Bond File, F.A.M.A.

[3] Report of Thuku's speech in Maxwell (Chief Native Commissioner) to Sir Edward Northey, 9 Mar. 1922, in C.O. 533/276, P.R.O.

[4] In general the Catholic missions in Kenya seem to have been little interested in the educational perspective of the Southern States, partly because of a language barrier, and partly because they believed that many of the recommendations of the Phelps-Stokes Commissioners had been anticipated in their own stations. (Personal communication from Dr. Kieran.)

[5] Miss Tourtellot to M. J. Hunter, 16 Feb. 1922, File 314, E.H., now I.M.C.A., Geneva.

refuse for the moment.[1] He did, however, meet many of those whom he would have met in America by attending the Le Zoute Conference in 1926, and finally found occasion to visit Hampton and Tuskegee in 1932, by which time he had been transferred from Kenya to British Guiana. The Chief Inspector of Education, E. E. Biss, was voted 400 dollars at a Board meeting of the Phelps-Stokes Fund,[2] but there is no evidence that he was able to make the journey. Finally the Governor, Sir Edward Grigg, was also unsuccessfully invited to visit America.[3]

Most of the visits mentioned so far had taken place during the twenties. For the decade that followed, the Phelps-Stokes Fund was to have strong support for its African visitor programme from an important agency, on whose initial establishment, ideology, and financing the Fund had considerable influence. This was the Agricultural Missions Foundation (A.M.F.). It came into being to meet a demand that the Phelps-Stokes Fund had been largely instrumental in creating. For, during the procession of Fund-sponsored visitors to the South, there had been a slowly growing awareness among missionary leaders of the dearth of truly rural-minded candidates for Africa. Their absence was keenly felt, too, by many missionaries in the field, who knew that there had been a contradiction in the policy that they had been practising to date. It had been their intention to develop a healthy native life in the Reserves, yet they had been party, through the government incentives, to training large numbers of semiskilled artisans who were no sooner trained than they left for the urban centres. These joined the many other Africans who had left the Reserves without going through mission hands. The result was the growth of the urban African population, which, in Kenya at least, gave concern to missionaries who had seen in the Thuku incident of March 1922 the new possibility of African mass demonstrations.

Not only from concern or nostalgia for the rural life,[4] therefore, did missionaries long to develop a more challenging alternative in the Reserves, but also in order to provide an antidote to detribalized politics. Owen has been mentioned earlier as conceiving his Welfare

[1] Jones to Ormsby-Gore, 7 May 1925, File Q-J, E.H.

[2] Minutes of semi-annual meeting of Phelps-Stokes trustees, 16 Apr. 1930. File A, P.S.F.A.

[3] Visitors' List 1927, File A, P.S.F.A.

[4] For early criticism of missionary romanticism of rural life, see Murray, *The School in the Bush*, pp. 305, 324, 361.

Association partly as a control on detribalization, and another politically sensitive missionary, Handley Hooper, felt the same need for agricultural development. He had recently discussed with Jones the dangers of the 'vagrant and detribalized proletariat . . . which has no cares of land or property to temper the menace of its smouldering discontent':[1]

> Everyone is waking up to that menace but not the means of counteracting it; we need the encouragement of far more agricultural activity in the Reserves, apart from the training offered at one centre. If only we might have a Christian here who was also a trained agriculturalist who knew enough to experiment and to discover the staple crops which could become a paying proposition for the native small holder . . . such work would speak for itself, apart from the pupils whom he might be training and would be open to the observation of thousands of natives.[2]

The trained Christian agriculturalist was notoriously hard to come by. As was noted in the previous chapter, it had taken the most painstaking efforts of Loram, Jones, Oldham, and the Colonial Office appointments board to find just one modern agriculturalist for the Jeanes School.[3] It had been impossibly ambitious of Orr in Kenya to expect to find thirteen European agriculturalists to implement his proposals to make agriculture the basic subject in African schools.[4] There were almost no suitable personnel available, at the very time when Hampton and Tuskegee were demonstrating the possibilities of highly-developed work in agricultural education. It was therefore natural for the 1928 I.M.C. Conference at Jerusalem to devote a whole session to missions and rural problems,[5] and not

[1] Hooper to Jones, 10 Aug. 1922, File Q-J, E.H.

[2] Ibid. There was a very obvious crop that did not need to be suggested to the Africans by trained Christian agriculturalists: Arabica coffee. Its culture was a white monopoly, except for limited African culture in parts of Embu and Meru country; see *History of East Africa* vol. ii (Oxford, 1965), 343. For further evidence of African demand for this crop, see *Correspondence between the Kikuyu Central Association and the Colonial Office 1929–1930* (Nairobi, n.d.), especially letter of 14 Feb. 1929; copy of this pamphlet in the Arthur Papers, Edinburgh University Library.

[3] See p. 160.

[4] 'Observation of the Director of Education on Agricultural Education for Africans'. (This was the comment of the new Director of Education for Kenya, H. S. Scott, on his predecessor's plans.) Copy in E.H.

[5] *The Christian Mission in relation to Rural Problems: Report of the Jerusalem Meeting of the International Missionary Council, March 24th–April 8th, 1928*, Vol. vi (London, 1928).

surprising that Jones delivered one of the four central addresses.[1] Planning started that same year which resulted in 1931 in the formal organization of the A.M.F.[2]

The founder members were a small group of agricultural college presidents, missionary leaders, and philanthropists, and they received much guidance from Jones.[3] All were Americans with passionate convictions about the agricultural lacuna in missionary training; but from England J. H. Oldham had been working on precisely the same problem, and by coincidence arrived in America to submit his particular point of view to the Carnegie Corporation shortly after Jones had submitted a similar proposal on behalf of the A.M.F.[4] The scope of the A.M.F. was world-wide, but in Jones's mind it had a peculiar relevance to the American and British missionaries serving in Africa. If it could obtain the necessary funds, it was conceivable that it might be the salvation of those values of African rural life so threatened at the time by detribalization and the academic curriculum. How it might be an ally in his own protracted battle to adapt African education to the simplicity of African village life can be seen in the proposal to the Carnegie Corporation: Jones wrote that only a small proportion of American and British missionaries

> have had specific rural training for the missionary task in Africa which is predominantly rural. African civilisation and culture being essentially agricultural, call for a dominantly rural Christian enterprise and a missionary personnel that has had an adequate training in the elements of rural life including agriculture, with due reference to the present primitive basis of culture and to the immediate development of a civilisation and culture that shall be primarily based on agriculture and rural life, and secondarily on modern industry and urban life.[5]

This coincided with Oldham's own presentation of the needs of the predominantly rural communities of Africa. He too desired missionaries to utilize the American experience in agricultural and rural life

[1] T. J. Jones, 'Factors of a Programme for Rural Missions', *The Christian Mission in relation to Rural Problems*, pp. 88–99.

[2] *Quarterly Notes* (Bulletin of the I.M.C.), No. 35 (July 1932), 5. For fuller details of the A.M.F. and its establishment, see John Reisner Papers, A.M.F., Interchurch Centre, New York.

[3] Warnhuis to Reisner, 28 Apr. 1953, Warnhuis Papers, M.R.L.

[4] J. H. Oldham, 'Memorandum to the Carnegie Corporation on Rural Betterment in Africa', Nov. 1932, File L-1, P.S.F.A.

[5] Jones to the Carnegie Corporation, 23 Nov. 1932, Box 313, E.H., now I.M.C.A., Geneva; also Jones to Keppel, 12 Aug. 1932, A.M.F. File, Carnegie Corporation Archives, New York.

programmes, which were 'essentially the thing that Africa needs'.[1] It was largely the result of his pressure that the scope of the Carnegie Corporation's appropriation in favour of the A.M.F. was widened to include British missionaries. In answer to these dual applications, the Carnegie Corporation was prepared between 1932 and 1935 to appropriate close to 50,000 dollars to the A.M.F.[2]

Where the A.M.F. principally differed from the Phelps-Stokes Fund in its visitor policy was in the length of the study period, which now became usually six months. A period of residence was specified at a Northern university with agricultural traditions (often Cornell), but a central feature of the Fellowship remained the Southern tour which ran on identical lines to the typical Phelps-Stokes itinerary.[3] The similarity was marked by Moton's being on the Boards of both organizations.

By 1945 the A.M.F.'s achievements were numerically impressive: ninety-three travel and study Fellowships had been granted for missionaries from Africa, and over two hundred itineraries had been arranged for the observation and study of creative rural schools and community projects in the South.[4] No less than ten missionaries from Kenya and Uganda were afforded this longer stay. One of these, Robert MacPherson, re-emphasized an important point that had arisen in connection with Mrs. Hoyt ten years earlier:[5] that the tours to the Southern States, even if they paid no attention to the Negro liberal arts colleges, could give an important insight into the possibilities of African development. Whatever lessons on agriculture were or were not learnt in Tuskegee by the visitors, there was, simply in the all-Negro operation of an educational machine vastly more complicated than anything attempted in East Africa, an incalculable incentive to faith in the African. Macpherson explained its effect on himself and a fellow missionary:

> We are missionaries working amongst primitive people in Africa. It is sometimes difficult to avoid the assumption (so prevalent among white races in that continent) that the African is of a child type, with child psychology and outlook and that he will remain so through succeeding generations . . .

[1] See Oldham, Memorandum to the Carnegie Corporation.

[2] $10,000 voted on 13 Jan. 1933; $5,000 annually for two years beginning 1933/34; $31,000 final grant of the Carnegie Corporation to A.M.F., 19 Nov. 1935.

[3] See p. 206, n. 1, for a typical Southern tour.

[4] Pamphlet on A.M.F. achievements (*c.* 1945), File C-24, P.S.F.A.

[5] Mrs. Hoyt to Beede, 29 Jan. 1926.

We feel that to be *shown* (as has been so unmistakably demonstrated to us at Tuskegee and other places) that this assumption is baseless, has been an experience of great value to us. As missionaries in Africa, one of our beliefs is that it should be possible for the African to rise above the level of superstition and ignorance in which we find him. And as a direct result of this tour we return to Africa fully convinced that learning and the arts, culture and progress are not impossible to the African just because of his colour.[1]

It is not unfair to the ideologues of the A.M.F. to stress that their central concern in bringing missionaries to the Southern States was by no means to have them convinced of the possibilities of African advance in the fields of 'learning and the arts, culture and progress': quite the reverse. With the emphasis on the rural village community went an implicit rejection of the urban African's aspirations in these four areas; or rather, although missionary leaders and the current educational theorists on Africa stressed that the education of the rural masses and the evolution of an African leadership were parallel movements, there can be little doubt that their preoccupation was with the rural people. Such was the power of what may be called the the agricultural syllogism (Africa *is* predominantly rural, therefore it will remain so) that there was little criticism (except African)[2] of the rigid and sometimes 'moral' dichotomy between town and country.[3] Educational prescriptions were made for the country, and a few were recommended for the town, but both were offered with a strong sense that the country life must be preserved from urban infection and instability. Oldham made the point very clearly to the Carnegie president in 1932:

... whatever industrial development there may be in certain parts of Africa, the fundamental basis of its life is agricultural. If this is the case, the primary object of both the administrative and the educational policies

[1] Robert MacPherson, of the Scots Mission (Kenya), and W. H. Turnbull, (N. Rhodesia), 'Notes on a Visit to the Southern States, 1 Jan.-2 Feb. 1935', Box 313, E.H., now I.M.C.A., Geneva. The Rev. R. MacPherson, interview, Oct. 1968.

[2] A. Victor Murray was one of these exceptions. A lecturer in the Selly Oak Colleges, Birmingham, he had held a travelling research scholarship to study native education in Africa from Apr. 1927 to Jan. 1928. The result of this tour, *The School in the Bush* (London, 1929) was quite the most thoughtful study of African education during the 1920s and 1930s. It aimed a good deal of criticism at Washington's, Jones's, and Reisner's philosophical assumptions about country life; Murray, op. cit., pp. 324–5. See also p. 242.

[3] Murray to Oldham, 2 June 1933, File on Education-Rural Communities, E.H.

of governments should be the creation of a healthy, progressive peasantry and the development of a stable rural life.[1]

Even, therefore, if there is considerable evidence that both J. H. Oldham and his very able secretary, Miss B. D. Gibson, wished to make room for the emergence of highly skilled African élites,[2] it is equally important to assess what he was interpreted by mission boards to be recommending as a priority. From this angle the F.A.M. Board in Indiana was not untypical in construing Oldham's message as directly relevant to the containment of African unrest, and as an encouragement to simplify further the school curriculum; its chairman answered Dr. Bond's reports of African discontent in Kenya accordingly:

I am interested in hearing what you have to say about the degree of unrest among the natives. Dr. J. H. Oldham, Secretary of the International Missionary Council, was recently in Indianapolis, and a few of us got to meet with him. I believe his feeling was that we need to shift our plans from the more American standard of missionary work to a plane a little nearer to the natives, and do just a few simple things which will transform their village life more, rather than calling out of numbers which are more or less isolated from the village groups.[3]

This interpretation of Oldham's thinking does not begin to do justice to the very serious attention he had been paying to the challenge of modern industry on the Copperbelt,[4] but it is significant that it was his interest in the status of the African in the village, and not in the city, that he in effect made the subject of the only Advisory Committee policy paper on African education in the 1930s. This *Memorandum on the Education of African Communities*,[5] for whose drafting he was almost entirely responsible, he acknowledged as being the direct result of two closely related influences—Jones's '*Four*

[1] Oldham to Keppel, 10 Oct. 1933, Oldham Papers in Dr. Kathleen Bliss's possession.

[2] Miss B. D. Gibson notes significantly, in an undated paper from the 1930s. 'There is a danger in Dr. Jones' principle of education of shutting down the lid on the whole community—because it is a farming community no one shall have a chance to be anything but a farmer.' File Africa; General Education; Education of Rural Communities', E.H.

[3] Elliott to Bond, 2 Dec. 1932, Bond File, F.A.M.A.

[4] Oldham played a considerable role in the financing and organization of the Copperbelt study by J. Merle Davis, *Modern Industry and the African*.

[5] *Memorandum on the Education of African Communities*, Colonial No. 103, 1935.

Essentials and the whole circle of ideas connected with them',[1] and the philosophy of the A.M.F.[2]

This memorandum was not the only, even if it was one of the most notable, products of A.M.F. philosophy. Apart from the more 'devotional' literature, with its sometimes romanticized and metaphysical assumptions about country life,[3] there were two seminal books produced under the influence of the A.M.F. ideals or by their direct aid. Each was illustrative in its way of missionaries in Africa who had properly absorbed the 'rural mind': A. D. Helser's *Education of Primitive People*,[4] and J. G. Steytler's *Educational Adaptations: with Special Reference to African Village Schools, with Special Reference to Central Nyasaland.*[5] These two men, and the schools in northern Nigeria and Nyasaland where their ideas came to life, were the sort of products which both the Phelps-Stokes Fund and the A.M.F. policy hoped to create.

Both books were a considerable testimony to their authors' care and ingenuity in adapting to the primary school the simple materials of a village and its people's lore. Their political philosophy too was nearly identical: gradually to find a place for the African between the extremes of the traditional and the western. Steytler thus turned his pedagogical attention to the old problem that dogged the era of indirect rule—how to improve without radically changing—and he illustrated his methods by posing again thirteen years later a question that Dougall had raised in the early days of the Jeanes School: 'how to build an house which is superior to that in vogue though inferior to that inhabited by Europeans'.[6] In this way his programme involved the 'least dislocation' of the African mind and spirit, as it progressed to that 'half-way house' between African and European, an environment 'blended to suit the African's aptitudes, capacities and culture'.[7]

Helser's ends and means were a little more difficult to reconcile;

[1] Oldham to Jones, 1 Jan. 1935, File L-1, P.S.F.A. The reference is to Jones, *The Four Essentials of Education.*

[2] Oldham to Reisner, 22 Oct. 1935, File on rural communities, E.H.

[3] In the estimation of the A.M.F., the most outstanding books in this genre, distributed by the Fund, were: L. H. Bailey's *The Holy Earth* (New York, 1943), and E. K. Ziegler's *A Book of Worship for Village Churches*, (New York, 1939).

[4] New York, 1934. [5] London, 1939.

[6] Ibid., p. 217.

[7] Ibid., p. xxiv. For an excellent discussion of 'half-way house' theories of African culture in the indirect rule era, see Foster, *Education and Social Change in Ghana*, pp. 163–5.

the larger aim of his work in Africa he had explained to Jones as the creation of an educated African élite: 'My whole aim and purpose is to fit myself in the best possible way to serve my beloved Africa. The hope of my life is to see a group of coloured men of the Aggrey type trained and set in responsible positions throughout Africa.'[1] Aggrey had had, however, no 'half-way house' education, as his twenty years in American universities demonstrated. Nor would Helser's methods, for all their imagination and novelty, ever create a 'Black European', as Aggrey was very widely called in East Africa.[2] An extended excerpt from *Primitive Education* will show something of his creativity within a framework of conservatism, which was characteristic of the age:

> Since the activities of each of the 'hoeing bees' is about the same, I shall just describe the activities of one group. Arriving at the farm, each member of the group puts down all clothing except a loin cloth. The leader divides the group into hoeing parties. He divides the farm into two equal parts. The leader in each of these two parties divides his part of the farm into two parts, cutting off about three-fifths for the morning and leaving two-fifths for the afternoon hoeing. The teacher is along with his group to help hoe and to follow the group to make sure that a good job of hoeing is being done. At first the girls help to hoe side by side with the boys . . . Someone leads the singing as he hoes, and all hoe in rhythm. When ever-body begins to get tired the girls put their hoes on a little heap and parade around the boys to the rhythm of music and the clapping of hands. The boys hoe with new vigour and the sweat soon begins to make lines down the faces. The songs praise the strongest and best hoers. If a hoe handle happens to break, its owner is acclaimed the 'best provider of all'. If the group is fortunate they secure a drum to help keep things lively. Some of the smaller girls take their calabashes and bring fresh drinking water . . . The hoeing is completed about 4.00 . . . About 5.00 they all parade triumphantly into the village. They have done what their fathers and mothers have done, but they have done it with a new vim and with a new joy . . .
>
> Few big changes are suggested. The teacher and his wife, and the dispenser and his wife are a part of the community all day, and every day. A little happier here and a little healthier there makes a big permanent change in the life of the individuals and in the life of the community in time. A large part of the practices of the primitive villagers are highly desirable and a new glory is given to them.[3]

It was surely a small symbol of Helser's indebtedness to the South

[1] Helser to Jones, 22 May 1930, File D-19, P.S.F.A.
[2] Hooper to Oldham, 2 Mar. 1924, File Q-K, E.H.
[3] Helser, *Education of Primitive People* (New York, 1934), pp. 301–3.

that fig trees, the present of Miss Cooley's Penn School, should flank his tiny, isolated mission in Garkida, Bornu, northern Nigeria.[1]

One last major occasion in the period before the Second World War when colonial officials were given an opportunity to acquire an American Negro perspective for their African work was a Seminar Conference in 1937. This conference on 'The Education of Negroes and the Native African' was arranged by Dr. Loram under the auspices of the General Education Board and the Carnegie Corporation.[2] Principles and problems common to African and American Negro education were thrashed out between directors of education and inspectors from Africa, and state agents for Negro education in the South. Theory was discussed largely at the University of North Carolina and at Yale, while the practical observations were made over an extended period at Hampton. East Africans were again well represented: R. H. Wisdom, the Chief Inspector of Schools and Acting Director of Education from Kenya; Harold Jowitt, Director of Education, Uganda, and Travers Lacey, Director of Education in Nyasaland, who was to bring this experience to Kenya as its new Director in 1939.[3]

It was by this time twenty-five years, almost to the week, since J. H. Oldham had thanked Dr. Frissell for 'one of the richest experiences' of his life,[4] but the appeal of Hampton was as fresh and relevant to Jowitt:

> Hampton provided us with a delightful experience and for one I am glad that it came at the end of our tour, for it came as a fitting benediction and maybe helped us to gain perspective. I felt there was a glow over the whole place and derived warmth and inspiration from it . . .
>
> I count it a great privilege to have lived for a short while in this atmosphere and from it carry away no little inspiration. Maybe it will help me to go my forty days, and to have a better stab at my job.[5]

The twenty years between the wars had thus left unchanged the conviction that had united Loram, Oldham, and Jones in the early

[1] For this and further evidence of the close indebtedness of Helser to the Phelps-Stokes Fund, and Jones in particular, File D-19, P.S.F.A., and Appendix IV.

[2] Loram to A. Howe (President of Hampton Institute), 5 Jan. 1937, and subsequent correspondence, H.A.I. For a most valuable account in two volumes of the personalities and events of the conference, see W. E. Holt, 'Memoirs of a Conference on Negro Education and Tour in U.S.A., 1937', MSS. Afr. S. 914, Rhodes House, Oxford.

[3] Ibid. See also *KEDAR 1938*, p. 13.

[4] Oldham to Frissell, 15 Oct. 1912, Oldham File, H.A.I.

[5] Jowitt to Howe, 29 Oct. 1937, Howe Papers, H.A.I.

1920s. Loram's Seminar had been an institutionalized version for Colonial Officers of what had been going on under the Phelps-Stokes Fund. The A.M.F. was a development and reinforcement of a concept which no one had done more than Jones to stress. When in 1935 the Foreign Mission Convention of North America issued its policy statement on missionary preparation, its debt to Jones's inspiration was too well known to need any acknowledgement:

> Probably the most important of all experiences and observations for missionaries who are not acquainted with America's educational achievements for Negroes in the Southern States, is a tour of the schools in these states. The most notable of these are: Hampton and Tuskegee, Calhoun and Penn, the Jeanes Visiting Teachers, and the Rosenwald Schools, the Farm Demonstration and the Home Demonstration of the U.S. Government.[1]

[1] Foreign Missions Conference of North America: *Preparation of Missionaries for Africa* (New York, 1935), p. 25.

CHAPTER VIII

African Students in the States: A Phelps-Stokes Fund Concern

A FURTHER feature of the Phelps-Stokes follow-up was its role as adviser and benefactor to African students in America. This function was eventually to supplant the white visitor policy in importance, and to become one of the chief characteristics of the Fund's activity today. In the early twenties, however, it was a policy initiated and shaped by Jones as a corollary of the suggestions to European and American missionaries in the Phelps-Stokes Reports.

There occurred, nevertheless, a change in Jones's thinking about African students abroad even in the short interval between the publication of the 1922 West Africa report and the East and Central Africa one of 1925. While the former, without giving the subject much thought, merely assumed that arrangements could be made for aspiring students to reach universities in Europe and America,[1] the East Africa report sounded a note of high caution on the 'serious handicap' it must be for an African to undertake this 'entrance into the perplexing and conflicting tides of European or American life'.[2] This new concern for the 'danger to mind and morals'[3] of Africans that overtook Jones was not only attributable to the wave of educational and political protectionism for the African way of life, but was also a direct result of some of the difficulties he had already experienced in protecting Africans in the States from radical Negro and white thought and from the development of a pan-African consciousness.

In Chapter Three some East African parallels to Jones's attitude were noted in the ban first placed by Governor Coryndon on African student exits to American Negro colleges[4]—a ruling which had later hardened into semi-official Colonial Office policy for East African dependencies under Churchill.[5] The same arguments reappeared in the deliberations over the proposed Alliance High School in Kenya, and were an important factor in the Director of Education's decision

[1] Jones, *Education in Africa*, p. 66.
[2] Jones, *Education in East Africa*, p. 44. [3] Ibid.
[4] See Ch. III, pp. 71–2. [5] See Ch. III, p. 71.

to proceed with the project: 'There are now Natives demanding such a literary education though not knowing what it meant, nor its effects: there are those who are speaking of going abroad for education. We have to satisfy that demand locally.'[1]

For Jones the dilemma was to weigh the undoubted danger, as he saw it, of study abroad against the gains that would accrue to the student from absorbing the Hampton or Tuskegee spirit. Jones wished in his conversations with those who feared American colleges for African youth to make the same point that the first president of Hampton Institute, Samuel Armstrong, had made to E. W. Blyden fifty years before; Blyden was then as fearful of taking up Hampton's offer of scholarships for African students as many colonial officials would be later. He had commented:

> As a rule without a single exception, those [Africans] who go abroad for education return on stilts—altogether out of sympathy with their own people. They may be giants when they return, but they walk on their heads. The infants on foot who have stayed at home, are stronger than they for the purposes of the country.[2]

Armstrong, in reply, admitted the general point of the unwisdom of sending Africans to the United States, but wished to make an exception for Hampton on the grounds that its atmosphere gave the students only 'moderate cravings'[3] and satisfied these in such a way that the student did not find himself out of sympathy with his people on his return. With Tuskegee founded just a year after this exchange, Jones was able by the twenties to plead for both Hampton and Tuskegee as exceptions to the Blyden rule; and he naturally received considerable support for his position from an influential nucleus of people in Edinburgh House circles and the Colonial Office Advisory Committee on Education, many of whom the Phelps-Stokes Fund had helped come to America to study Hampton and Tuskegee's African relevance. Among the most important of these were J. H. Oldham, Miss B. D. Gibson, Miss G. A. Gollock, Professor Diedrich Westermann, Alek Fraser, Sir Michael Sadler, and H. Vischer.[4]

[1] Notes on meeting between Director of Education (Kenya) and the executive committee of the Kenya Missionary Council, 21 May 1925, in file on Christian Council Correspondence, E.H.

[2] *Southern Workman*, ix (Feb. 1880), Editorial. [3] Ibid.

[4] Both Oldham and Fraser had visited Hampton in 1912, but revisited both Hampton and Tuskegee with Phelps-Stokes encouragement in 1919 and 1921 respectively.

Jones's interest in influencing African students went, however, beyond the provision at Hampton and Tuskegee of subjects which were the basis of his educational philosophy; international political considerations played an important part in his advocacy of this allegedly safe environment for the orientation of future leaders of African opinion. It had been noted at the beginning of the Phelps-Stokes East Africa report that epidemics such as Bolshevism could only be controlled by 'enlightened public opinion', for which reason 'both altruism and self interest combine in making it seem desirable that everything possible should be done to remove possible causes of serious friction or danger even in a continent so "remote" from the great capitals of the world as Africa'.[1]

It was not only from the possible danger of international Communism that Jones suggested the protection of Hampton and Tuskegee, but also as an antidote to the efforts of both Garvey and DuBois to win Africans to their interpretations of pan-Africanism. Since the death of Booker Washington, Jones had felt all the more urgently the absence of a leading non-radical Negro voice, which could modify for young Africans the strident tones of the *Negro World* and the *Crisis*, and counteract the effects of other pan-African literature circulating in the continent.[2] If Aggrey's presence on the Phelps-Stokes Commissions, with the unparalleled access it afforded to a succession of mass African audiences, was a partial counterweight to the Pan-African Congresses of DuBois and the growing power of the U.N.I.A., it could not compete over a long period with the 'gossip, rumors and propaganda,'[3] which Jones believed reached Africa partly from American sources.

It was his reaction to this situation that led Jones to devote considerable time, energy, and funds over the next twenty years to the formation of Africans with the Tuskegee-Hampton spirit. The 'good African'[4] was not, however, to prove easy to produce, nor was the spirit of Tuskegee and Hampton to mean the same to African students as it did to the many visiting missionary educationists.

[1] Jones, *Education in East Africa*, p. xiii.

[2] A cutting from the *Daily Telegraph*, 22 Nov. 1921, in Race Folder, E.H.; cf. also E. Allégret, 'The Missionary Question in the French Colonies', I.R.M., xii (1923), 171.

[3] Jones, *Education in East Africa*, p. 44.

[4] For a definition, see p. 232 below.

PLATE VIII

Professor Simbini M. Nkomo, lecturer in history, Tuskegee Institute, 1920–1924, severally described as from Portuguese East Africa, Southern Rhodesia, and South Africa. (*The Foundation*, Atlanta, Georgia.)

The African Student Union

By a curious coincidence, at the very period when Jones was most concerned to display Tuskegee especially as a stronghold against the forces of pan-Africanism, there was a very remarkable young African, Simbini Mamba Nkomo, teaching African history at Tuskegee, with the pan-African convictions appropriate to the founder and executive secretary of the African Student Union (A.S.U.) of America. J. H. Oldham, during his Tuskegee visit of February 1921, was profoundly impressed in talking to him, and noted with some surprise the coexistence in him of two qualities that European missionaries regarded as antagonistic to each other: the Tuskegee spirit and incipient nationalism: 'He is thoroughly loyal and has the Tuskegee spirit. But as I talked to him I touched exactly the same thing that one knows so well in one's Indian friends. It may be long in coming but sooner or later we shall have the same situation in Africa that we are facing in India.'[1] It was precisely the lack of contradiction between these two concepts that was to be an important aspect of many Africans' attitudes to Tuskegee. This was so with Nkomo. His African history lectures were deliberate attempts to communicate this nationalism, and were known to be such by Moton: 'I am sure that I have tried to do all I could for the students who were in my history classes. In all my class work I have laid great deal of stress of *the National spirit* or the Spirit of racial *selfvaluation* which is the foundation of true progress along all lines.'[2] Much had obviously been achieved by Nkomo's lectures and organization when Oldham could remark of the Africans that he met in Tuskegee that 'the striking thing to me is now all these men have an African consciousness; their loyalty is not Liberian or Rhodesian or Gold Coast, but African'.[3] How this consciousness had grown under the direct influence of this man whom Oldham judged better educated than the average missionary is a not unimportant factor in assessing the American Negro milieu in which the African student could range, whether he was domiciled in Atlanta or Tuskegee.

Nkomo had long been fighting for a common organization among African students in the States, and, as early as 1912, when still an

[1] Oldham to Curtis, 11 Feb. 1921, Box 315, E.H., now I.M.C.A., Geneva.

[2] Nkomo to Moton, 30 April 1921, R.R.M./L.C. (1921), T.U.A.

[3] Oldham to Curtis, 11 Feb. 1921. There were actually at Tuskegee at the time of Oldham's visit two Ugandans, one South West African, two Liberians, and Nkomo.

undergraduate at Greenville College, Illinois, he had circulated the leading Negro colleges, asking them to build up local African student's chapters. His next step was to attend the North American Students' Conference in June 1915, and, as its first African delegate, he promoted his plans for an African Students' Christian Association. Diligently he circularized the results of his efforts in an address: 'To the African Students of Every Tribe', calling for an association 'to promote unity and love among all the students from different tribes of great Africa'.[1] It was not, however, until after the war that Nkomo was able to hold his first African Student Conference in Chicago in 1919 which attracted an attendance of as many as fifty Africans and eight hundred visitors. But his aims were much wider than the organization of an occasional expatriate Africans' conference; rather, any such step towards unity must have its counterpart in Africa itself. Accordingly petitions were sent continually to John R. Mott, president of the World Student Christian Federation, asking that an African be sent from America to Africa to visit all the missionary society schools, and organize African student societies in each, with a programme of study. Thus a continent-wide network would be built up, which would without doubt 'hasten the development of African people'.[2]

Although none of this might seem the sort of radical activity that might afford Oldham any anxiety, there is a sense in which no such pan-African programme could avoid being political. Indeed, Nkomo's picture of African students' concerns at this early period is significant: 'I am just telling you what the educated Africans in America discuss about when they meet. Their interests are awake and they are constantly watching with keen minds whether *white men* or Europeans would finally destroy the African races before the end of twentieth century.'[3]

It is important to note also that this early African pressure group did not isolate itself from its American Negro brethren, but, im-

[1] S. M. Nkomo, 'To the African Students of Every Tribe', address, in Box 68, Y.M.C.A. Historical Library, New York and 'The African Student Union', *The Student World* (New York), xvi, No. 2 (Apr. 1923), 54–8. For Nkomo's African background, see S. M. Nkomo, *How I found Christ in the Jungles of Africa* (Greenville, n.d.).

[2] Nkomo to Moorland, 24 May 1920, Moorland Collection, Howard University.

[3] Ibid. For some discussion on the African student organizations at this time in Britain, see J. S. Coleman, *Nigeria: Background to Nationalism* (University of California Press, 1958), pp. 202–4.

mediately after its first conference in Chicago, strong links were established through Nkomo with Negro leaders. Dr. Jesse E. Moorland, the senior secretary of the Coloured Men's Y.M.C.A., became chairman of the African Students' Fund, and through him Nkomo was soon introduced to Max Yergan, who at that point still believed his departure as international Y.M.C.A. secretary for East Africa was imminent. It may safely be assumed that Nkomo shared in the bitter disappointment that followed Yergan's rejection on grounds of race, as they had both fervently believed with Moorland that this would be 'the beginning of a real connection between the Christian trained colored Americans and the great body of African young men and women on African soil'.[1] At any rate, the issue of the American Negro as missionary to Africa was central to African Student Conference agenda from this point.

The beginning of the 1920 academic year saw Nkomo with a history post in Tuskegee, but still continuing, through Chicago University summer school, his post-graduate work on the very partisanly-entitled thesis, 'The Customs of the Bandowo Folk considered with a view of adding certain new arguments to the generally accepted view of the Unity of the Bantu race'.[2] In a manner reminiscent of the omnivorous Aggrey, he took additional courses on Imperial England, the history of constitutional law, and American history, and justified these to Dr. Moton, who had been suggesting work in the Normal Department, on the grounds that 'the great need of our race is not that they do not know how to teach but they need to understand what they teach'.[3] Unlike Aggrey, however, he could not turn the other cheek to racism, and here it is worth illustrating a little of the pride in Africa which Nkomo radiated and which had a demonstrable effect on many African members of Tuskegee and of the A.S.U.

On an occasion in November 1921, when Dr. L. B. Moore, the Negro dean at Howard University, had been drawing in a public speech at Tuskegee a stereotyped picture of African indolence,[4]

[1] Moorland to the A.S.U., 18 June 1920, Moorland Collection, Howard University.

[2] Univ. of Chicago M.A. thesis 1922. Also Nkomo to Moton, 14 Oct. 1921, R.R.M./L.C. (1921), T.U.A.

[3] Nkomo to Moton, 14 Oct. 1921.

[4] Such addresses were not infrequent at Tuskegee and Hampton, e.g. Hugh Saville, 'African Characteristics', *Southern Workman*, liv (Sept. 1925), 421–6, where Saville, president-elect of Makerere at the time, addressed the Hampton students on African untruthfulness, laziness, immorality, and distrust. Another frequent type was the invocation of the spirit of the founder (Washington or

Nkomo's rebuke to Moton certainly contained very little of that Tuskegee spirit which Jones was looking for:

> In behalf of two hundred million Africans who were so humiliated by Dr. Moore's speech by calling them lazy creatures who go wild, naked and wait on bananas to fall on them and then they get up and eat them, I was forced to write him a letter refuting his statements as fallacious ones. The historical facts are lacking in all what he said. I love the African race and have faith in them and I do not like to hear anybody white or black person speak slightly of the great African race. Any one who does it is a disgrace to the African race. My learned Dr. has lost faith in his own race.
>
> We have lost our relatives in fighting for our native land, Africa, that we love. The reason why white man came over and took our land is not because we were lazy and did not use our land.[1]

Undoubtedly Nkomo believed that there were few more suitable places than Tuskegee to broadcast his notion of African self-esteem, and there was no attempt to conceal the location of the A.S.U. executive secretary's office when, the week after Oldham left, he issued his call to African students of the world to organize themselves on the pattern of African students in the States. Nor was Nkomo's plan limited to West African, or Subsaharan students, but included in its American membership students from Egypt to Transvaal and from Ethiopia to Zanzibar. The redemption of Africa, so ran the manifesto, could only come from the co-operation of Africa's educated minority, realizing the extent of their obligation to the 200,000,000 without education. For the moment the appeal was for every institution of any significance in Africa to form its own A.S.U., 'looking forward to the day when representatives from various parts of Africa can meet in a general convention to discuss the problems of common interest which bear on African people'.[2] Enclosed with the manifesto went a copy of the constitution and by-laws of the A.S.U. of America, specifying among much else that the president must be a native African.[3]

It must be supposed that both manifesto and constitution had a

Armstrong); for a brilliant recreation, see R. Ellison, *Invisible Man* (New York, 1947; 'New American Library' edn., n.d.), pp. 105–21.

[1] Nkomo to Moton, 1 Nov. 1920, R.R.M./L.C. (1920), T.U.A.

[2] Nkomo to a wide range of African schools, 16 Feb. 1921, R.R.M./L.C. (1921), T.U.A.

[3] See *Constitution and Bye-Laws of the African Student Union, June 1919* (Tuskegee, n.d.), article iv.5.

wide circulation, as there were in Tuskegee alone Africans from West, East and South, and Central Africa. What would not, however, be expected was that the material would be regarded as dangerous, and, as happened in Lovedale, South Africa, that the students would be prevented from reading Nkomo's message.[1] Principal James Henderson warned Dr. Moton immediately why he had taken such action:

> I do not believe that the course of history is to be reversed and that the uplifting of Africa is to be effected by a purely black man's combination . . . Further our constant efforts have been directed to securing the fullest possible cooperation between the white and black races and naturally we do not welcome movements tending in the opposite direction.[2]

Dr. Henderson's misreading of Nkomo's scheme, the aim of which was to awaken the Africans into being more than quiescent partners in a white plan of redemption, was shared by Jesse Jones. He intervened immediately after their third annual conference to correct the misapprehensions in their attitudes to Africa and to white people. Most particularly he was at pains to reprove them for their very unfortunate 'misunderstanding as to the coming of the white man to Africa'. 'I called to their attention', he continued, 'the conviction that the elimination of the white man from Africa would be a denial of the testimony of all history, which proves clearly that no people can rise without the aid of other people.'[3] As has been seen elsewhere, Jones was extremely sensitive to even the mildest expression of criticism of permanent white settlement in East Africa, and Nkomo's claims certainly ran counter to Jones's 'inexorable' social forces which would take more and more Europeans to the highlands of Eastern Africa 'to work out salvation for Africa'.[4]

An earlier brush between the A.S.U. and Jones had involved two of the first students to be sent to Tuskegee through the direct encouragement of the Phelps-Stokes Commission to West Africa.[5] These two students from the Gold Coast, C. H. Clerk and Michael Ansah, were

[1] It should be noted in extenuation of this action that there had been a riot in Lovedale a year before Nkomo's literature arrived, but if things were back to normal, as was claimed by the Phelps-Stokes Commission, it is difficult to understand Dr. Henderson's ban; cf. Jones, *Education in Africa*, p. 204.

[2] Henderson to Moton, 4 Apr. 1921, R.R.M./L.C. (1921), T.U.A.

[3] Jones to Moton, 20 Dec. 1921, R.R.M./G.C. (1921), T.U.A.

[4] Jones to Oldham, 31 Aug. 1925, File Q-J, E.H.

[5] A. W. Wilkie, a member of the first Phelps-Stokes Commission, had visited Hampton and Tuskegee in 1921. He directed the Scottish (formerly Basel) Mission in the Gold Coast, and had backed the project.

therefore very much test cases for the far-reaching claims that Jones had made for Tuskegee, and it was his firm intention that they should be allowed to absorb the Tuskegee spirit in peace. Thus when he learnt that they were being urged by Nkomo to attend the A.S.U. Conference in Talladega College, he brought pressure to bear on Moton to prevent their going; the only grounds he gave Moton for such an action were his feelings that 'it is better for both of these young men to remain at Tuskegee pretty constantly this year so that they may obtain the full benefit of their work there'.[1]

There was little that Jones could do for his protégés the following year, however, when Nkomo launched the most outspoken Fourth Annual Conference in Tuskegee itself. The Conference agenda sufficiently revealed the tone:

> Misrepresentations concerning Africa; Abolishing Restrictions on the Coming to America, for study, of African Students; Native Missionaries; Cooperation between Europeans and Africans; the Returning Students and the Mission Boards; How American Negro Students may cooperate with African Students; Liberia and Its Problems.[2]

Added point was given to the conference's deliberations on African students' returning as missionaries on an equal footing with whites, and to the unifying of Africa, by the presence of Kamba Simango, of Portuguese East Africa, and his wife Kathleen Easmon, of Sierra Leone.[3] For a battle was being joined at this very time over the salary that the Simangos should receive when working with the American Board in Portuguese East Africa; accusations and disclaimers of racial discrimination in the operation of pay scales were flying between Dr. Gregg of Simango's old college, Hampton, who was championing Simango, and the American Board, while Jones was entering the fray to ensure that this model Hampton graduate should not be embittered by rough treatment at the mission's hands.[4] With the presence at the Tuskegee conference of Dr. D. D. Martin of the

[1] Jones to Moton, 17 Nov. 1922, R.R.M./G.C. (1923), T.U.A.

[2] W. J. King, 'The African Students' Conference', *The Student World*, xvi, No. 2 (Apr. 1923), 49–50. See Plate IX.

[3] The African background and the beginnings of Simango's fascinating missionary career are well presented in Fred R. Bunker's 'Hampton in Africa—Shall it Be?', *Southern Workman*, lvi (May 1927), 213–23. See also N. Curtis, 'From Kraal to College: The Story of Kamba Simango', *Outlook*, cxxix (14 Sept. 1921), 61–3. Kathleen Easmon was accompanied on her tour of the United States by her aunt, Mrs. Adelaide Casely Hayford; see pp. 132–3.

[4] C. H. Patton to Gregg, 25 Apr. and 18 May 1923, Simango File, H.A.I.

The front row from left to right: Prof. Monroe Work, Dept. of Records and Research, Tuskegee; Unidentified; Dr. Willis J. King of Gammon Theological Seminary; Dr. D. D. Martin of the Stewart Missionary Foundation for Africa; Francis R. Gow, music professor on Tuskegee Staff, from Capetown; Kamba Simango of Portuguese East Africa; Mrs. Kathleen Easmon Simango, from Sierra Leone; Simbini M. Nkomo, Prof. of History, Tuskegee Institute; Rev. Bethel.
The back row contains ten of the African students who attended the Conference from Selma, Talladega, Hampton, Columbia University and elsewhere. (*The Foundation*, Atlanta, Georgia.)

Stewart Missionary Foundation, and Dr. W. J. King of Gammon Theological College, both of whom had given their lives to fighting for a just place in the African mission field for American Negroes, the real issues were exposed at a very practical level.[1]

The conference records of the A.S.U. are valuable, moreover, in affording for East Africa at any rate the only contemporary African reaction to many of these most serious issues, and their study and assessment of the Phelps-Stokes Report for West Africa was a case in point. To students who had had to leave their respective countries for further education, Jones seemed to have placed the emphasis in his Report too exclusively on one area: 'We have read with interest Mr. Jones' report and are glad for his emphasis of the need and and importance of technical and secondary schools. We feel that in addition to this that there must be an increased emphasis on higher education if Africa is ever to relieve other countries of the responsibility of carrying its leadership.'[2]

Here, as in so many other situations, the A.S.U. presented its members with the concrete need to prepare themselves for leading their own people, and inspired them with the determination to take independent action if need be. This spirit penetrated as far as Kenya, and there is a tantalizing fragment of evidence that a similarly independent body in that colony was inspired by Nkomo's vibrant pan-African sympathies to appeal to his organization to start a school in Kenya. It must remain speculative, but it is not impossible that this plea, coming in the year after what Nkomo called the 1922 Nairobi 'race riot',[3] could have been from one of those who started founding independent schools at that time, and if so it would be an indication that some sector of that movement had a more than local outlook.

Suddenly and tragically Nkomo died in 1925, bringing to an end for a time this particular coalition of African and American Negro youth in a common cause. His presence at Tuskegee had been a great attraction for the Africans, Nyabongo, Clerk, and Ansah, who all, not insignificantly, left as soon as he did. If for Jones and the Phelps-Stokes Fund the safety of Tuskegee consisted of an atmosphere in which white domination in Africa and America went unchallenged,

[1] See *The Foundation* (Atlanta), issues from 1900 to 1930, for a commentary on this particular struggle.

[2] 'Fifth Annual Conference of the African Student Union', *Tuskegee Student*, xxxiv (March 1924), 5.

[3] Nkomo to Moorland, 25 Apr. 1923, Moorland Collection, Howard University.

then they were rightly suspicious of a man who could proclaim openly to his Negro brethren in America: 'South African Native will rule South Africa. The world will hear from the "Bantus", and it will not be a joke. I may be dead, Yergan and others may be dead, but the world will hear from the "Bantus".'[1]

Tuskegee—The 'Safe' Negro Institution

One reason why this digression on the A.S.U. has been justified is that it has helped to illustrate a little of the complexity involved in protecting Africans in America from their more radical brethren. The explanation for what would otherwise now seem paradoxes is that the divisions between the conservative and radical Negro leaders were never so hard and fast as Jones had led missionaries and colonial officials to believe. The temptation to oversimplify the enmity between the Tuskegee and Atlanta schools of thought, or between Garveyism and Tuskegeeism, obscured the fact that DuBois was a close personal friend of Moton,[2] and Garvey one of the staunchest admirers of Tuskegee spirit.[3] Although, therefore, Jones habitually viewed Moton as one of the bulwarks against DuBois's pan-African movement, he would certainly have been surprised to learn that Moton was 'in hearty accord with the Pan African movement',[4] and had told DuBois in 1921 that he would be glad to be put down as a member.[5] Nor had Moton any objection to having DuBois as a visiting lecturer, and in November 1928 the Tuskegee students were allowed to hear at some considerable length DuBois's commendations of the fighting spirit of the young Africans in the States and at home, and were encouraged to fight for their own rights.[6] The two levels at which Moton had continually to operate were no better shown than in his inviting DuBois and his daughter to visit Tuskegee shortly after Jones had himself asked Moton to participate in winning the Sultan of Zanzibar over to an anti-DuBois position.[7]

[1] Nkomo to Moorland, 10 Sept. 1923, Moorland Collection, Howard University.

[2] W. E. B. DuBois, Memo to the Board of Directors of the N.A.A.C.P. on his trip to France in December 1918, File on Panafrica, 1919, N.A.A.C.P. Papers, L.C.

[3] Garvey to Moton, 2 Nov. 1921, R.R.M./G.C. (1921), T.U.A.

[4] Moton to DuBois, 9 Mar. 1921, R.R.M./G.C. (1921), T.U.A.

[5] Ibid.

[6] W. E. B. DuBois, 'The Present Condition of Africa', stencilled copy of speech delivered at Tuskegee, 25 Nov. 1928, T.U.A.; see Plate X.

[7] DuBois to Moton, 21 June 1924; Jones to Moton, 14 Apr. 1924, R.R.M./G.C. (1925), T.U.A.

Dr. W. E. B. DuBois with Dr. Robert Russa Moton on the occasion of DuBois's visit to Tuskegee in November 1928. The Washington statue is in the background. (Tuskegee Archives.)

For Garvey a similar case could be made out: in their two African tours, Jones and more especially Aggrey had had frequent occasion, while giving publicity to the co-operative statesmanship of first Washington and then Moton, to squash the various myths about Garvey's power. 'If you love your race, tell it around that Marcus Garvey is their greatest enemy,' Aggrey had to tell groups of curious Africans in Southern Africa,[1] and Dr. Dillard had found the same intense interest in Garvey among the students he talked to informally at Lovedale.[2] Yet only three months before the Phelps-Stokes commissioners were putting the record straight on Garvey, and presenting more worthy models of American Negroes, Mr. and Mrs. Garvey had been spending the weekend at Tuskegee as Moton's guests; Garvey had given what he hoped would become an annual donation of fifty dollars to the institution, and had lectured to the students from the chapel on black pride.[3] In a masterly yet tactful reinterpretation of the spirit of Tuskegee, he demonstrated how accommodationism and the passive acceptance of low-status jobs in unskilled trades were no part of the Tuskegee spirit, but rather stubborn independence and limitless ambition:

> I trust that the Tuskegee spirit that you have will make you realise that your place in the world will be cut out by yourself, will be made by yourself, and not by others. Repeating myself, no one can keep you down but yourself. The new doctrine that some of us are preaching is of that kind and we are endeavoring to inspire this present generation to look forward to the highest in society, in industry, in politics . . . When you go out into the larger world to grapple with men and human affairs you must do it with the feeling and conviction of men believing that your place is there; that God has placed no limit on you and you are just going to rise to the place that you have got in mind.[4]

It was no individualistic programme of self-betterment alone that the students heard from Garvey, but also the political necessity for a 'great black government', and for a 'greater Tuskegee', supported as much by Negro business enterprise as by the white philanthropists.[5]

[1] Smith, *Aggrey of Africa*, p. 122.

[2] J. H. Dillard, 'Impressions from East Africa', *Southern Workman*, liii (Aug. 1924), 360.

[3] *Tuskegee Student*, xxxiii, No. 17 (Dec. 1923), 5; Garvey to Moton, 2 Nov. 1923, R.R.M./G.C. (1923), T.U.A. Moton was very ready to contribute to the *Negro World* an article for the Christmas number 1921.

[4] M. Garvey, 'Address to the Faculty, Students and Friends of Tuskegee', 1 Nov. 1923, pp. 5–6, stencilled copy in T.U.A.

[5] Ibid., pp. 10–11.

If Jones would have disapproved of Garvey's analysis of a Tuskegee spirit that did not depend upon the patronizing concessions of the white community, he would have felt even more strongly about another Negro radical among that same week's guest lecturers: Dr. Carter G. Woodson. The latter's critique of the role of the white philanthropist in Negro welfare organizations had been becoming yearly more bitter, and, in the citadel of white patronage, his convictions about the ease with which Negroes could be manipulated by white money would almost certainly have led him to reiterate his belief that 'the Negro is not worth saving unless he can learn to help himself'.[1] Apart from this general point, much of his lecture concerned Africa, a continent whose advance he believed was threatened by white educational decision-making backed by hand-picked African and Negro leaders,[2] and whose true contribution to the progress of mankind could only be properly realized by American Negroes' sending their own expeditions to investigate its condition. The remainder of his speech was a fervent appeal for race pride and race solidarity, identical in spirit with both Garvey and Nkomo's plans for self-sufficiency:

> When we look to others to employ and sustain us, when we are dependent upon white grocers, white mechanics, white undertakers, then we must be looked upon as an inferior group. We ought to some extent to be sufficient unto ourselves. We must develop in us the various powers to do this and that. Then we can look with a great deal of respect upon ourselves and we can claim more from the other man. We must have economic independence, that will make possible our fostering the beautiful side of life in our own group, that independence that will enable us to encourage ambition and inspiration within our own race, to dictate the character and policies of our institutions of learning and show that we can make progress in business, in literature and convince the world that we are equal to any people on the globe.[3]

To the extent that Tuskegee was thus not as conspicuously sheltered from radical Negro policies as Jones and Oldham had described it, Governor Coryndon had at least been more realistic in attempting to levy a comprehensive ban on the entry of his Ugandans to Negro

[1] See A. Phelps Stokes, 'Confidential Memo for the Trustees of the Phelps-Stokes Fund', Box 314, E.H., now I.M.C.A., Geneva, *passim*. This deals seriatim with Woodson's criticisms of Jones in the *Freeman*, 12 Apr. 1924.

[2] A. Phelps Stokes, 'Confidential Memo', p. 21.

[3] Woodson's address is reported in *Tuskegee Student*, xxxiii, No. 17 (Dec. 1923), 5.

colleges than he would have been in following Jones's distinction between the safe and the unsafe. It would, moreover, have been added weight to the case he presented to the Colonial Office, had he been able to show that both Ugandans, Nyabongo, and Kato, were thus given direct access through Tuskegee to Garvey's and Woodson's ideas.

It is important, however, not to over-emphasize this spasmodic incursion of more radical ideas into Tuskegee, but to see it rather as an additional reason for some of Tuskegee's African students to seek an educational atmosphere where such experience was a more integral part of student life. With this introductory background to the difficulties of sheltering Africans at Tuskegee in mind, it is now appropriate to look in more detail at specific instances of student acceptance and rejection of Tuskegee, as far as these affected the general policies of the Phelps-Stokes Fund.

Comparatively early in the process whereby missions, in co-operation with the Phelps-Stokes Fund, were experimenting with further education for African students at Tuskegee, difficulties began to arise out of the reluctance of some Africans to remain there more than a few terms. With this growing evidence of their dissatisfaction with Tuskegee, there was re-emphasized in Phelps-Stokes thinking a tendency to divide Africans into two distinct categories, and to make English missionaries aware of the difference. Anson Phelps Stokes acquainted Oldham with this:

> The cases of Aggrey, Wolo and Simango are striking examples of the right type of men to send over. Some others who are here now frankly do not seem to some of us to have the force of ideals which makes them best qualified to get much out of their educational opportunities. If, as will probably frequently happen, missionaries wish boys to come to America, to study in schools like Hampton and Tuskegee, this fact should be very specifically mentioned, as we have found from experience that frequently when they get here they prefer to take the more cultural University courses.[1]

Jones, however, in making the same point to Stephen Duggan, of the International Education Board, was more inclined to describe the activities of the American Negro intellectuals as the real source of danger to African students:

[1] Phelps Stokes to Oldham, 15 Sept. 1924, Box 315, E.H. now I.M.C.A., Geneva. Plenyono Gbe Wolo, born on Kru coast, Liberia, gained an A.B. from Harvard, an A.M. from Columbia University and graduated from Union Theological Seminary.

You may be interested to know that in the case of a few African students whom we have aided, we have found it difficult to keep them in such schools as Hampton or Tuskegee. As soon as they come in touch with the Negro intelligentzia of America, they desire to attend some of the outstanding northern institutions like Columbia or Cornell, or some of the more leading institutions of collegiate grade for Negroes in the South.[1]

What is interesting in this categorization of African students into those contented with Tuskegee, and the other sort, allegedly liable to be led by Negro intellectuals into preferring DuBois-type education, was that neither Aggrey nor Wolo had any of their education in institutions of a simple Tuskegee character; and although Simango had four years at Hampton, he insisted on pursuing his studies at Columbia. These exemplary Africans could number among their Alma Maters Livingstone College, Teachers College Columbia, Harvard University, Union Seminary, New York, and Columbia University. As far as their contacts with radical Negro intellectuals went, too little has been written so far on the near-filial relationship that existed between J. E. Bruce, the Negro nationalist and Garvey supporter, and Aggrey for over eight years.[2] With Carter Woodson, too, there is evidence that Aggrey sought a much closer working relationship than Jones would have thought desirable, and only three weeks before his death in 1927 he was preparing to join and become an active member of the Association for the Study of Negro Life and History, which would be, he thought, of the greatest help to him in his work in Achimota.[3] Kamba Simango's attendance at the third Pan-African Congress in Lisbon in December 1923 was also not entirely expected, when it is known how safe an exponent of the Tuskegee-Hampton system he was considered by his white sponsors.[4]

Of the Tuskegee Africans in the twenties, almost the first to be affected by restlessness were Clerk and Ansah from the Gold Coast, who, becoming disenchanted with Tuskegee after two years, rejected Moton's and the Phelps-Stokes Funds' recommendations of Hampton as an alternative, so determined were they to attend Teachers

[1] Jones to Duggan, 28 Dec. 1926, P.S.F.A.

[2] Aggrey to Bruce, 28 June 1922, MS. 63, Bruce Papers, Schomburg Collection, Harlem. Cf. G. Shepperson, 'The African Abroad or the African Diaspora', International African History Conference, Tanzania, 1965, p. 9 (stencilled copy in Edinburgh University Centre of African Studies).

[3] Aggrey to Woodson, 13 July 1927, Box 6, acc. 3579, Woodson Papers, L.C.

[4] *Crisis*, Jan. 1924, p. 120. I owe this reference to Dr. Jabez Langley.

College, Columbia University. Their intention was to acquire a degree in education which would allow them to decide what training was 'the right type for their people'.[1] With such conformist aspirations the Phelps-Stokes Fund had little time or patience, but what was so singularly forgotten, when Clerk and Ansah were characterized as having 'the minds of children'[2] in their desires, was the example of a much more famous Gold Coast African writing two years earlier: 'Mrs. Aggrey and children write me to leave no stone unturned to secure my Ph.D. degree. For it I have turned hermit . . . I do not want to leave this country without the degree. I will need it and need it badly . . . Dr. Jones, I just can't go to Africa without my degree.'[3] Some Africans were, however, brought over for training in Tuskegee traditions on more of a contract basis, to be given a preparation for participation in a specific experiment on their return to Africa. Two of these were Miss Makanya and Miss Njongwana of South Africa, who came through the co-operation of Dr. Loram to become native experts in the Jeanes methods, which, as has been seen, the Carnegie Corporation was financing for East and South Africa.[4]

Although it had long been their intention to come to the States for community service training, the Penn School, specially chosen for them by Loram, did not provide what they considered the relevant experience.[5] For Loram this was a considerable personal reverse for his theory of the suitability of the Penn School for African imitation, which he had set forth in his policy paper, 'The Penn School Community Work as applicable to African Conditions'.[6] This example was symptomatic of the growing divorce between colonial policy and African aspirations, and it was no coincidence that brought both Sir Gordon Guggisberg, ex-Governor of the Gold Coast, and these two South African women to the same tiny island off the Carolina coast in the same month; their reactions were, however, predictably poles apart.[7]

Transferred to Tuskegee, the women reported after a month that they 'had acquired about all the essential experiences which Tuskegee could give them'.[8] As they prepared consequently to break their Jeanes contracts and go severally to Spelman College, Atlanta, and

[1] Roy to Jones, 11 Aug. 1924, File A-22, P.S.F.A. [2] Ibid.
[3] Smith, *Aggrey of Africa*, p. 110. [4] See p. 173.
[5] Miss V. S. Makanya to Loram, 30 Sept. 1928, R.R.M./G.C. (1928–9), T.U.A.
[6] See p. 181.
[7] Wraith, *Guggisberg*, p. 287.
[8] Jones to Phelps Stokes, 24 July 1928, R.R.M./G.C. (1928), T.U.A.

to Cleveland,[1] Jones was understandably no less disappointed than Loram at the failure to create African Jeanes teachers in the American South. But again, Jones's conviction that 'considerable effort is being made to influence such Africans away from the Tuskegee conception of education and life'[2] involved an unnecessary suspicion of conspiracy. The general theoretical background of social service training, such as any white entrant to the field would demand, was not considered necessary at either Penn or Tuskegee.

It was, however, two of the East African Tuskegee students who shed most light on the rapidity with which missionary and philanthropic patronage could be won and lost; Hosea K. Nyabongo, nephew of the Omukama of Toro, entered Tuskegee in mid-1922, and Ernest Kalibala came on from England in 1925, with enough money from his father for half a year in Tuskegee. After spending six months in trade training in the auto-repair workshops, Nyabongo transferred to Clark College and Gammon Theological College in Atlanta, where through a combination of courses, he might better prepare for university.[3] Also within the year, Kalibala was attempting to leave Tuskegee for Lincoln Academy in North Carolina.

As the Phelps-Stokes Fund had become involved with both students, Kalibala immediately found himself having to justify his move.[4] He did not expand on why the tiny Lincoln Academy should appear 'the long desired school' for him,[5] but carefully explained instead that he was no missionary society's protégé under contract. He could then point out the need, especially in the colonial situation in Uganda, for securing a thorough general education before pro-

[1] When Jones heard of their projected moves to Schauffler Missionary Training College, Cleveland, and Spelman Seminary, Atlanta, he gave it as his conviction that 'they should either remain at Tuskegee or return to Africa'; see letter to Phelps Stokes, 24 July 1928.

[2] Ibid.

[3] D. D. Martin, 'A new African student,' *Foundation*, xii (Nov.–Dec. 1922), 9. For Kalibala's early background see pp. 70–2.

[4] Roy to Phelps Stokes, 18 June 1926, File A-1, P.S.F.A. H. M. Grace, the C.M.S. missionary from Uganda, had successfully sought an appropriation for Kalibala, conditional on his staying at Tuskegee.

[5] Kalibala to Phelps Stokes, 12 Dec. 1926, File B-4, P.S.F.A. One reason for Kalibala's preferring this tiny school to Tuskegee was the presence on the faculty of Prof. Orishatukeh Faduma, a founding member of the National Congress of British West Africa. His active part in the A.S.U. was further reason. See Faduma's 'Africa's Claims and Needs', *Southern Workman*, liv (May 1925), 211–25. Dr. Jabez Langley is collecting material for a biography. Cf. also G. A. Shepperson, 'External Factors in the Development of African Nationalism, with particular reference to British Central Africa', *Phylon*, xxii, No. 3 (1961), 209.

ceeding to specialized vocational studies. This introduced an issue that DuBois had been raising since the turn of the century: the political implications for a dependent people of narrowly vocational studies.[1] Kalibala expanded the point: 'From what I know of the English people, I find that an industrial qualification that is not founded on a good mental equipment will be a great barrier to my usefulness when I return home. I can only be used then as a tool and a footmat.'[2] It was not, however, because Kalibala despised agriculture that he had left Tuskegee for Lincoln, but because he believed it should be vocational in the highly professional sense that medicine and the Christian ministry were: 'I see that agriculture is a very important study and requires more preparation than I see in Tuskegee. I shall be more satisfied to go to Tuskegee and take up High agricultural work after preparation in other subjects.'[3]

What was more important than the circumstances of this transfer from Tuskegee to Lincoln was that it gave occasion for an African to reflect upon the priorities of colonial education policies in East Africa, which at this point in both Uganda and Kenya were increasingly influenced by the need to meet demands for skilled native labour. The development of Makerere as primarily a government technical college, and the new N.I.T.D. in Nairobi, did not constitute a trend of which Kalibala could approve,[4] and it was precisely because Tuskegee fitted so naturally into 'the mere industrial training that the Missions and Government are planning which is but little better compared with the natural condition of the people',[5] that Kalibala could not approve. Better, well-equipped native teachers he diagnosed as Uganda's most pressing need. In a situation where only the missions had teachers with any qualifications, Kalibala sounded a faint note of warning for European missionaries who held proprietary rights over Uganda's educational development, and thus anticipated by some ten years the clash that was to come between the missions and the returning qualified native educator: 'It is not that the mission alone going to level up our country, we, we the native, equip and hold the plough'.[6]

[1] See DuBois, *Souls of Black Folk*, 'Of the training of Black Men', pp. 74–8, and 'Of Mr. Booker T. Washington and Others', pp. 42–54. The *Crisis* frequently recurs to this theme; see especially W. E. B. DuBois, 'Education', *Crisis*, xv, No. 4 (Feb. 1918), 173–8, and 'Education in Africa', *Crisis*, xxxii, No. 2 (June 1926), 86–9.

[2] Kalibala to Jones, July 1926, File B-4, P.S.F.A. [3] Ibid.

[4] See pp. 122–3. [5] Kalibala to Phelps Stokes, July 1926. [6] Ibid.

Within three years of this incident, Kalibala was so to regain the Fund's favour as to be regarded as the most capable African in America;[1] Nyabongo's break with the Fund, however, was nothing if not final. The combination of factors that led him in 1934 to a complete rejection of its patronage, and an accompanying most outspoken critique of interference with African students in America, may well have had its roots as far back as the active role he played in the A.S.U. under Nkomo.[2] His term as president of the A.S.U. in 1929 would have further sharpened his vision, especially as Azikiwe was one of the Africans who would have been associated with him at Howard throughout this term of office. The same year he was approached by Jones, and it was suggested that he had made a mistake in going to Howard and ought rather to have gone to an agricultural school.[3] Although he did not take the issue up with Jones at that time, four years later he returned to the matter in another connection, and, with the evidence of other African students to support him, launched a generalized attack on what he thought Phelps-Stokes misconceptions about African education:

> I should like to tell you now, however, that your idea that all African students should take agriculture (or study in a trade school) is absurd. Of course, some of them should study in agricultural, industrial and trade schools; I myself have learned the handiwork of woodcarving. But we are sending out our students from Africa not to perpetuate our homeland as a country of agriculturalists, but to develop it. You assume a condescending air; you think that the African people must devote themselves entirely to agriculture. We are here to acquire all of Western culture that can be useful to us; the elements of Western culture that are suitable for us will be linked to ours, to form the new African culture that is to arise.[4]

The strength of Nyabongo's conviction was significant, not only because of his opposition to African education seen primarily in vocational terms, but also because he pointed out so clearly the stumbling block in the Jeanes and other schemes for adapted education associated with the conservation of 'all sound and healthy elements in the fabric of their social life':[5] namely, that it must be an

[1] Jones to Oldham, 22 Dec. 1930, File B-4, P.S.F.A.

[2] Nyabongo had delivered a paper on 'America helping Africa', at the Fifth Annual A.S.U. Conference; see p. 220.

[3] Nyabongo to Jones, 22 Jan. 1934, File on Nyabongo, P.S.F.A.

[4] Ibid.

[5] *Education Policy in British Tropical Africa: Memorandum submitted to the Secretary of State for the Colonies by the Advisory Committee on Native Education in the British Tropical African Dependencies*, Mar. 1925, Cmd. 2374, p. 4.

African rather than a European prerogative to decide on what might be profitably adopted from the West and what retained from their own traditions.

The immediate cause of his severance of relations with the Fund had, however, been Jones's informing Nyabongo that he had 'remained in the United States for 10 years against the advice of people in Uganda and America'.[1] This would appear at first reading to be an insignificant dispute between Jones and Nyabongo on what length of time the late Omukama of Toro had really intended his nephew to remain in the States; what was really involved in this wrangle was, however, the right of mature African students, having seen the extent of the educational opportunities in America, to prolong their stay beyond even their own original estimate. When, therefore, Jones intervened and gave his opinion, Nyabongo's reaction, as he determined to repay the Phelps-Stokes money he had received, was one of the earliest articulate criticisms of aid 'with strings attached':[2]

> The aim of the Phelps-Stokes Fund is to help us get an education in the United States. This financial aid, however, does not mean that you are authorised to give gratuitous advice to African students. The Fund is supposed to be an aid to us—not a bribe. You may not know it, and I feel it is about time you did: namely—that your attitude is resented by most of the African students in this country.[3]

Before now turning to examine the Phelps-Stokes Fund's difficulties in nurturing even what may be called 'good Africans', it is worth noticing that Nyabongo believed his views to be shared by the large majority of students with whom the Fund had contact. In language strongly reminiscent of Carter G. Woodson, who believed himself to have been similarly interfered with, he defined the African students' dilemma in terms which were by their very nature unverifiable: 'They, however, cannot tell you these things, because they are bound down by the money which the Fund pays them. They must be silent, or they will lose whatever chance they have of getting an education.

[1] Nyabongo to Jones, 22 Jan. 1934. [2] Ibid.

[3] Nyabongo's outspokenness on this occasion does not accord very well with his cautious conservatism shown in Oxford and London the next year, or with the tone of his mild book, *Africa Answers Back* (London, 1936). Ras Makonnen has suggested that it was very likely the result of Ben Azikiwe's and George Padmore's combined pressure (interview, 1969).

They accept the lesser of two evils, feeling also that sincere protest might be interpreted as ingratitude.'[1]

The 'good African' in the United States and in Africa

As it is convenient shorthand, the term 'good African' will be used to describe a student with certain characteristics: a co-operative attitude in race relations, both in Africa and America; readiness to take advice on his education abroad, and abjure politics; pride in remaining African,[2] with a high determination to return to serve his people as soon as possible; a capacity to serve on his return within the existing colonial framework. The overall conviction of Jones in this, his most ambitious task, was that exposure to America need not necessarily make Africans 'walk on their heads'; and if this belief, which he had taken from General Armstrong, needed any confirmation, there was the conspicuous success of its operation in James Aggrey.

There was, however, a very significant contradiction, apart from those already mentioned, involved in using Aggrey as the prototype of the 'good African'; he had stayed in the States for over twenty years, and had insisted on adding qualification after qualification to his name.[3] Perhaps some of the Africans' tenacity in staying beyond the terms suggested by their missionary counsellors and financial supporters must be traced to the very publicity that Jones was responsible for giving to Aggrey's career through the Phelps-Stokes Commissions, and the much read biography and the school readers based on it after Aggrey's death.[4] Jones sometimes seemed oblivious of this facet of Aggrey's appeal to Africans as he debated with missionary boards the problem of protracted study periods in the States: 'I have had this anxiety with regard to a number of African students who have come to America. I am more than ever convinced that African students should come to this country only for a brief period and that after they have been carefully instructed in Africa.'[5]

In the case of several of the 'good Africans' who will now be

[1] Nyabongo to Jones, 22 Jan. 1934.

[2] Or, in Aggrey's words, 'Let Africans remain good Africans, and not become a poor imitation of Europeans.' Smith, *Aggrey of Africa*, p. 139.

[3] Ibid., pp. 61, 109, 111, 251.

[4] Kingsley Williams, *Aggrey the African* (London, 1933); this is a simplified version of Smith's *Aggrey of Africa*; cf. also *An Annotated Bibliography of James Emman Kwegyir Aggrey, 1875–1927* (Salisbury, 1964), compiled at Livingstone College by Louise Rountree.

[5] Jones to Dr. A. T. Schofield, 2 May 1935, File B-4, P.S.F.A.

examined, it was direct contact with Aggrey or Jones that gave them the idea of studying in America, and in particular the idea that Hampton and Tuskegee might be the most suitable colleges. Of these, few more vivid examples of the influence of Aggrey's educated presence in Africa may be found than Peter Mbiyu Koinange's personal testimony, as he considered the effect that attendance at Aggrey's open-air meeting in Nairobi had had on him when the Phelps-Stokes Commission had been in Kenya: 'When I heard that man speak, I quit my job in Nairobi and walked twenty five miles to my home in one day and told my father, I must go to America where that wonderful African was educated.'[1] As to the choice of college in America, the decision in favour of Hampton, which Koinange entered three years later, was very largely determined by his headmaster at Alliance High School, G. A. Grieve, who had himself just returned from a Phelps-Stokes visit to Hampton and Tuskegee.[2]

An example from West Africa showed a similar pattern, as Paul Cardoso traced his initial interest in Hampton to Jones's Lagos visit of December 1920. By the time that he had reached America in 1922, however, his Alma Mater, Kings College Lagos, and his father had decided on the University of California for him. But the strangeness of America, combined with his welcome from the Phelps-Stokes Fund, made him, as he put it, 'not dare to risk going far away at that time from Dr. Jones, the only friend I had on the Atlantic seacoast'. In consultation with Jones, he chose Hampton as his place of study.[3]

The two other Africans whose careers in America were very much bound up with the Phelps-Stokes Fund, and are of central importance to the study of the 'good African', were also from the West Coast: Eyo Ita, whose dream of reaching the States was fulfilled in 1931, ten years after he had met Aggrey in Calabar,[4] and Ross Lohr, of Sierra Leone, who only came to the notice of the Fund in the year of his graduation from Otterbein College, Ohio.

[1] I owe this anecdote to Dr. H. M. Bond. Mbiyu Koinange (he later dropped the 'Peter') was the son of Chief Koinange, who through the Kikuyu Association had led the loyalist African opposition to Harry Thuku (see Thuku's onslaught on him in *Tangazo*, 17 Feb. 1922). Mbiyu Koinange did undergraduate work at Hampton and Ohio Wesleyan University, and postgraduate work at Columbia and Cambridge Universities. Since Kenyan independence he has held several ministerial portfolios.

[2] See p. 193.

[3] P. W. O. Cardoso, 'America and Nigeria', *Southern Workman*, liv (Oct. 1925), 472; see also file on Cardoso, Hampton Institute Registry.

[4] Ita to Roy, 26 July 1931, File B-4, P.S.F.A.

These four men, taken in conjunction with Kalibala in his later years in the States, provided the nearest counterpart to the missionary visitors from Africa. For all of them Jones held the highest hopes, and there seemed little reason not to be optimistic about their reintegration into African life. But that difficulties of adjustment could afflict even Africans apparently most determined to co-operate with the colonial governments in introducing the lessons of Tuskegee and Hampton was a further set-back to some Phelps-Stokes assumptions.

After Aggrey's death on 30 July 1927, Jones felt himself under increased pressure to find an African successor to him, and in this connection these five men had potential. Lohr was the first mature candidate for Aggrey's office, and by August the same year Jones was writing to Moton: 'May I trouble you again as to Lohr, the African student. The passing of Aggrey gives new importance to Lohr, for I am now inclined to think that he has real possibilities for the future. He seems to me the best of all African students with the exception of Simango.'[1] For the next eight years from his adoption by Jones in 1927, Lohr's career was a model course of preparation to be the chief lieutenant of Mr. Keigwin, Director of Education in Sierra Leone. Keigwin had himself first won Jones's admiration when as Director of Native Development in Southern Rhodesia he had been, in the words of the East Africa report, engaged in 'doing a work of unique and outstanding educational importance which will have a marked and beneficial influence on the Natives living within the Colony'.[2] The lines on which he had been working in Southern Rhodesia were further confirmed by his 1925 visit to Southern schools in the U.S.A. at the Fund's expense, and on his transfer to West Africa his ambition 'to pattern the schools of Sierra Leone after the ideals of Hampton and Tuskegee',[3] led him to visit the States again in 1929. There he was brought through Jones to recognize the suitability of Lohr's own training for such a purpose.

Lohr had attended summer schools at Hampton, followed this with a year's teaching at Tuskegee, and like Kalibala received his Master's degree in education from Columbia University. After a further year heading a Southern college's education department, and a year at Hampton, he was ready to co-operate with Keigwin in the

[1] Jones to Moton, 17 Aug. 1927, R.R.M./G.C. (1927), T.U.A.

[2] Jones, *Education in East Africa*, p. 239.

[3] Lohr to G. Phenix, president of Hampton Institute, 24 July 1930, Lohr File, H.A.I.; see also H. S. Keigwin, 'The Influence of Armstrong', *Southern Workman*, lv (Feb. 1926), 54–8.

radical revision of the Sierra Leone system[1] when Keigwin's illness put in his place a director not 'favourable to Africans trained in America.'[2] To this rebuff there was added the complication of the Depression's setting in, and no pressure that Jones and Oldham could bring to bear was effective. Three more years were to pass in suspense before Lohr could bring himself to admit with some sadness the defeat of his hopes, and with them the loss of his training to Africa:

> I came to America on my initiative—neither Church nor government nor any body is responsible for my coming . . . My passport was visaed that I can stay indefinitely in America. Despite this, I was resolved to return. I even took the precaution that my wife's health would stand the climate of Africa before I married her. But as things are now . . . with no prospect back home for a favourable job as far as I can see, not even in other parts of West Africa, I will be glad to pitch my tent at Hampton.[3]

So passed also this opportunity for Lohr to fill for Jones the gap left by the death of Aggrey.

There were vexations of a different sort in store for Cardoso; he too had been made by Hampton very conscious of new motivations for service, such as Armstrong had promised Blyden could be achieved by Hampton at its best: 'Psychologically it has broadened my views. It has filled me with the desire to go home and use the Nigerian farm not for my family's benefit alone but as a demonstration to help other farmers in their problems and to get more out of their land.'[4] Once home, however, Cardoso's demonstration farming was an uphill task, and, despite the encouragement of Fred Irvine, the Hampton-trained agriculturalist at Achimota,[5] Cardoso found little understanding of his methods among the local farmers. Then when the mortgages on his farms had to be given up in the early years of the Depression, many found in this confirmation that he had 'made a sorry mess by taking agriculture'.[6] More than this, prejudice against

[1] Lohr met Keigwin to discuss plans in 1929; see further Lohr to Jones, 29 Oct. 1927, File B-4, P.S.F.A.

[2] Jones to Oldham, 22 Dec. 1930, File B-4, P.S.F.A.

[3] Lohr to Howe, president of Hampton, 3 Oct. 1933, file on Lohr, H.A.I. For Azikiwe's similar difficulties in obtaining employment in Africa after his American education, see R. L. Sklar, *Nigerian Political Parties* (New Jersey, 1963), p. 51.

[4] Cardoso, 'American and Nigeria', p. 473.

[5] Irvine to D. Fenn, Christmas 1930, Cardoso File in Hampton Institute Registry. Cardoso also went for agricultural training to Cornell University before returning home.

[6] Cardoso to Hampton Institute, July 1931, Cardoso File, Hampton Institute Registry.

the standing of the Hampton agricultural degree prevented his joining the staff of Yaba College, a pre-condition for which was a British degree, or an American degree from one of the large Northern universities. Indeed, it is an interesting reflection on the political aspect of university standards that through Jones's advice Cardoso should abandon the University of California for Hampton Institute, and that this inferior qualification should bar him from Yaba; and yet it was the allegedly inferior status of Yaba itself that sparked off the beginnings of the Lagos Youth Movement in 1934—an organization whose successor, the Nigerian Youth Movement, employed Cardoso to edit its quarterly magazine, the *Service*.[1]

Such obstructions as Jones had to face in the cases of Cardoso and Lohr were very largely beyond his immediate control. But Eyo Ita, by reason of the sharp contrast between his American ideals and the grim realities of pioneer farming in Nigeria in the early thirties, gave rise to much greater anxiety: Ita's despair at the frustrations of introducing Tuskegeeism might, Jones feared, result in his embracing political remedies. The process of correcting Ita's waverings on the brink of politics and protest produced from Jones his fullest statement on the returning students and their adaptation to colonial Africa. Ita's possible defection, with its consequences for the good name of the Fund, was the more surprising since his eulogy of Hampton, and more particularly Tuskegee, was unsurpassed by any other Phelps-Stokes visitor. His letters to Jones must have seemed ample justification for the policy of the Fund, combining as they did the recognition of Hampton and Tuskegee as the secret of the Negro's amazing progress in the States, with the grateful acknowledgement of white philanthropy. They had given him a vision and a single hope: 'I only pray for one step more before I sing my "nunc dimittis" and it is this, that I should have the success of transplanting to the soil of Africa the best that I have learnt in these places.'[2] What Jones did not realize, however, was that Ita did not see two similar institutions when he visited Tuskegee and Hampton; he rather saw, as he admitted to Moton, the one as an incentive to racial pride and independence,

[1] Sklar, *Nigerian Political Parties*, pp. 49, 52. In October 1932 Cardoso accepted the principalship of Mabang Agricultural Institute, Freetown (something of a white elephant); despite the set-backs he encountered, he eventually received recognition of his pioneer services through the naming of the Cardoso Agricultural Institute, University of Nigeria, Nsukka. On the whole question of parity of academic standards in African universities, see Ashby, *Universities*, Chs. 7–11.

[2] E. Ita to Roy, 26 July 1931, File B-4, P.S.F.A.

and the other as the direct opposite. His careful distinction between the two is significant, as it illustrates a not infrequent reaction by Africans to these colleges:

> I observed five weeks at Hampton, but I have now come to see that it makes a whole world of difference whether a school is a Hampton or a Tuskegee. Hampton Institute firmly illustrates this principle that no people can ever attain the highest realisation of their potentialities under the control and direction of another, however well-meaning and wide-minded the latter may be. Here is a case in which the 'white' man gives his money, time and life, for the training of the Negro youth, but because the institution is manned by the white heads there runs an undercurrent of a feeling of repulsion, repression and the resultant vile complexes infused in the youth. Here I have found a free self-realisation that opens up the fullest and finest intellectual and physical forces of our youth. Both this institute and Govt. Hospital are great illustration to the Negroes and the world, of what we are and can be.[1]

This description raises again the myth that Tuskegee stood for the principle of black freedom and independence, similar to that noted in Thuku's attitude to it, and this was none the less important even if in reality Tuskegee's freedom was as compromised as Hampton's. Indeed, this view of Tuskegee demonstrates how elusive was the delicately balanced inspiration that Jones wished Africans to absorb from Tuskegee: modest racial pride, such as Aggrey exhibited, but without independence. To encourage the one emotion and not expect its frequent accompaniment was at best short-sighted.

This was not a side of Ita's thinking that Jones at any rate knew of until Ita had returned to Nigeria, via the London School of Economics, and was involved in fighting for the recognition of his ideals, on a salary equivalent to that of a standard-six school-teacher, in a structure 'dead against foreign trained students'.[2] He had accepted wholeheartedly the new ideas of education adapted to agricultural Africa. Following Aggrey, he proposed that 'henceforth education will not Europeanise the African, but on the contrary will Africanise him', and at his school at Ogbomosho, in the Yoruba country, he had all the students cultivating their own plots and organized into one of four industrial clubs: woodwork, pottery, soap, and

[1] Ita to Moton, 14 Aug. 1931, R.R.M./G.C. (1932), T.U.A. For his own reminiscences of this early political interest, and his New York links with Azikiwe, see Eyo Ita, *Sterile Truths and Fertile Lies* (Calabar, 1949), pp. 7–10.

[2] Ita to Jones, 22 March 1934, File B-4, P.S.F.A.

paper.[1] Increasingly, however, he began to feel that his textbook application of Jones's universal 'Simples' of education was failing. The pupils quite refused to drop their interest in Cambridge Examinations and Civil Service appointments; and Jones's principles themselves seemed to be insufficiently adapted to the conditions of an agricultural slump, or to the galvanizing of a local community into radical self-improvement within the colonial system. What could then happen to the message of Tuskegeeism, filtered through a mind groping for a means to communicate social and industrial initiatives to a backward community, must be shown at some length in this passage, in order to understand its effect on Jones:

The gospel of better industry and more production seems equally futile for already the people have more than enough to eat and the surplus finds no market whatever. This would have been all right with our fathers in their happy nudity, and ignorance in the cave life. But having gone out of the 'cave' and eaten from the fruit of the Tree of Knowledge, like Plato's man from the cave, we cannot go back, nor will we allow the gods to shut the gates of life upon us. We will have life. We must have life, fuller and more abundant life. Such is the situation with us, Dr. Jones. You have spoken of General Armstrong as coming to learn of human nature by firing bullets into it. But what will bullets of mere ideas avail in a country like mine, doubly proned to inertia. I wish I could have the means to open a small school where I could teach and give some small industries that might supplement our agriculture. We need the material knowledge to weave our own clothes, build our own houses with bricks and stones from our own fields, make our own glass and china, our pens and papers, since we cannot have them in exchange for our own farm produce.[2]

Ita moved from stressing the agricultural ingredient in education to the conviction that Nigerian nationalism and education must be united. Although he was no narrow nationalist, he felt that truly self-reliant education might only be achieved by the awakening of a nationalist consciousness. This was to be the rationale of his National Education Movement, his establishment of the West African Peoples' Institute, and finally of his move into politics as Vice-President of the National Council of Nigeria and the Cameroons in 1948.[3] But his original questioning of the pre-eminence of agriculture, with its dark

[1] J. F. A. Ajayi, 'The Development of Secondary Grammar School Education in Nigeria', *Journal of the Historical Society of Nigeria*, ii, No. 4 (Dec. 1963), 532–3.

[2] Ita to Jones, 22 March 1934.

[3] Ajayi, 'Grammar School Education in Nigeria', p. 532; Coleman, *Nigeria*, pp. 218–20; Sklar, *Nigerian Political Parties*, pp. 121–3.

undertones of independent action, can only be fully appreciated by placing it in the context of 1935. The educational consensus of American and English experts on tropical areas was that the curriculum of African schools should be further ruralized. This was the year of the Interterritorial Jeanes Conference in Salisbury, Southern Rhodesia, and of the Colonial Office Advisory Committee's *Memorandum on the Education of African Communities*;[1] it coincided, too, with the 41,000 dollar grant from the Carnegie Corporation and other sources to the A.M.F., in support of rural training for American and English missionaries to British Africa. To Jones, then, Ita's writings showed an alarming tendency to reject the counsel of the 'wise and prudent'[2] whom he had once trusted, and to desire something more for his people than merely the next stages in improved agricultural techniques: 'the simple realities known only to those whom Christ called "Babes" '.[3] As for the suggestion that Ita might launch out on his educational-cum-industrial project, Jones, in dissuasion, gave evidence of an attitude to independent African enterprise which could only have been barely inferred from the reading of the African reports.[4] He cautioned Ita:

> My study of schools in Africa and other parts of the world is that independent schools begun by individuals are not successful. There are in America a very few exceptions, notably Tuskegee. In Africa, the successful exceptions are practically negligible. By all means attach yourself to the Government school system or to one of the well-organised missions.[5]

Ita's tentative steps in the direction of a more diversified local economy were similarly dismissed as the result of 'certain abstract conceptions of economic and social theories'[6] picked up in London and New York, and his attention was refocused on agriculture, in language befitting a member of the Board of the A.M.F.: 'The acute need at present not only in Africa but also in America, Europe and Asia is an intelligent consciousness of Mother Earth. Certainly

[1] *Memorandum on the Education of African Communities* (Colonial No. 103), (London, 1935).

[2] T. J. Jones, 'To an Able and Devoted African whose Studies and Experiences in England and America Filled him with Perplexity and Disappointment when he Returned Home', *Southern Workman*, lxiv (Sept. 1935), 279–82.

[3] Ibid.

[4] Jones was, for instance, scrupulously non-committal about the Rev. John L. Dube's independent school in Natal, 'one of the very few institutions in Africa organized and directed by a Native African'; Jones, *Education in Africa*, p. 212.

[5] Jones, 'To an Able and Devoted African', p. 281.

[6] Ibid.

Africa is overwhelmingly rural. God's gift of the soil is only beginning to be adequately recognized by Humanity.'[1]

Whether Jones had a proper understanding of the effect of the slump on West African agriculture is doubtful; if he had, he would not have taken so personally the difficulties of his students and the failure of some of them to make good. This led him even to publish his letter of rebuke to Ita and distribute it internationally, in order to safeguard his reputation and provide a model for others who might have similar difficulties with African students.[2]

A further assumption which Jones had recourse to when a student who had been 'good' in America challenged the colonial government or mission authority on his return was that of left-wing interference with the student *en route*. The underlying notion here did little justice to the African's critical faculties; it suggested that he would not unaided have found anything necessarily repugnant in his status on return. Only three months after the Ita affair, Jones was again on the defensive, this time answering Ugandan missionaries incensed at Ernest Kalibala's failure to be smoothly integrated into the mission.

The initial contretemps over Kalibala's leaving Tuskegee for Lincoln Academy had been quickly forgotten, and throughout his training in anthropology in New York University and his course leading to a Master's degree in education at Teachers College, Columbia, he had gained the complete confidence of the Fund. In addition he received considerable aid from it over this period, and support for study tours to Hampton twice and Tuskegee once. But there were auguries of what might happen on his return, had anyone chosen to consult his Master's thesis, 'Education for the Villages in Uganda, East Africa',[3] submitted in 1934. Its eighty-five pages were a valuable and, for East Africa, very early African criticism of educational theories which were then the stock-in-trade of European experts on indirect-rule education.

Of these one of the most fundamental presuppositions was that there was such a thing as 'Native Education' peculiarly suited to the Africans. This notion and its development in terms of health, sanitation, ability to raise native crops, and moral training, was for Kalibala an 'empty theory':[4]

[1] Ibid. [2] The letter is reproduced in full in Appendix IV.

[3] E. B. Kalibala, 'Education for the Villages in Uganda, East Africa', M.A. thesis, 1934. Teachers College, Columbia.

[4] Ibid., p. 32.

It has no interest in the African child as such. It makes no provision for the development of the potential possibilities of the child. All in all there is nothing in this kind of education but pretense. 'Native Education' is a term frequently used to mean a selected body of ideas suitable to the African mentality, and arranged without regard to the development of the African as a whole person . . . They are the negation of the existing ideals of life and the opponent of the prospective African progressive life.[1]

The political implications of the term that Jones had popularized, 'adaptation', were spelled out no less clearly, and included in the sweep of his criticisms must be all those European experiments which aimed at establishing for Africans some medial position between unchanged traditional life and complete adoption of European ways:

This aim of education shall be thorough. It shall seek three conditions. First, adjustment; second, adaptability and third, transformation. I am very much opposed to the theory of helping the African keep their tribal life. I should be willing to do all I could to keep the African form of tribal life if the present social, economic and spiritual changes were within the keeping of the tribal life. But they are not. Most of the people who advance this theory see the benefit of exploiting the 'uninformed blacks'.[2]

These were, of course, exaggerated terms in which to describe the well-intentioned efforts of those working on experiments of the Jeanes and Malangali[3] type, whose aim was to minimize the break between the old culture and the new; yet they do reiterate Nyabongo's point, so often overlooked in that period, that it must be the Africans themselves who decide what to preserve and adjust, and what to transform.

Kalibala was one of the first East Africans, again, to pick up the political significance for Africa of the use of the word 'simple' in educational writings. It had figured in the memorandum, *Educational Policy in Africa*,[4] which had led to the foundation of the Advisory Committee on Education in Africa; the word was a continual theme of the two Phelps-Stokes Reports, and had reappeared in the

[1] Ibid., pp. 32–3. [2] Ibid., p. 42.

[3] For the Malangali school's attempts at adaptation in Tanganyika, see W. Bryant Mumford, 'Education and the Social Adjustment of the Primitive Peoples of Africa to European Culture', *Africa*, ii, No. 2 (Apr. 1929), 138–61.

[4] *Educational Policy in Africa: A Memorandum submitted on behalf of the Education Committee of the Conference of Missionary Societies in Great Britain and Ireland* (London, 1923), p. 2.

educational recommendations of the East Africa Commission and subsequent reports.[1] It was particularly applied to the type of agriculture thought suitable for African enterprise—the improved one-peasant plot. Kalibala addressed himself to this restriction on large-scale African initiative:

> Farming or agricultural pursuit has been advocated by all the people interested in Africa. By this is meant subsistence farming. The arguments employed here are that Africa is a rural country, that the population there will always remain rural, and that, therefore, the people must be directed to be able to get something to eat. Educational courses on 'How to Live', 'How to Farm', 'The Use of Simple Tools', and many others of similar nature have been developed to meet these needs. I question this policy critically. Subsistence agriculture is a fine move, but not all the people in Africa are starving. If agriculture is conducted on a non-paying basis how will these people pay off their indebtedness?[2]

Kalibala had, however, a contribution to make to the theory of African education which was more valuable than some of these negative criticisms of missionary effort; he realized that in a situation of rapid social change, such as the Ugandan village was undergoing, there should be no such thing as 'a curriculum for village schools in Africa'. Village populations were becoming too transitory for such conspicuously unadapted curricula. If Jones's criteria were strictly to be adhered to, education, Kalibala thought, had to be adapted to the new African life, where the city and the village could no longer have entirely separate programmes:

> It is therefore proper to articulate village education with that of the city. There is no need to exclude or preventialise the children simply because they happen to be born in villages. Where there is no need to introduce all city methods in the village curriculum, there is a need to emphasise the fundamental principles of education wherever they are taught. When the village children follow the dictates of circumstance, education should step in to equip them with the necessary mental ability for self-adjustment and adaptation.[3]

An acquaintance with this and much other level-headed criticism in his dissertation could have given warning of some difficulty in Kalibala's working with the C.M.S. in Uganda on his return, and

[1] *Report of the East Africa Commission*, Apr. 1925, cmd. 2387, p. 29.
[2] Kalibala, 'Education for the Villages in Uganda', pp. 44–5.
[3] Ibid., p. 78. 'Preventialise' is probably a mistake for 'provincialise'.

these ideas were certainly in his head long before the alleged distortion of his thinking by English radicals.[1] At all events, by May 1935, Kalibala, with his American Negro wife, after a short spell as assistant educational secretary for the C.M.S., had broken his connection with the mission to launch an independent school.

There was a paradox in his resignation, however: for the Uganda mission believed Jones answerable for Kalibala's theories. There had been, they alleged, a close correspondence between Jones's educational maxims and the words which Kalibala had used to justify his severance from the mission. How this was so in the case of 'adaptation' has been noticed already, and it is not difficult to imagine how Jones's axioms like 'working with Africans, rather than for them' and 'education for life' could have been similarly interpreted to mean something different from what Jones intended. Indeed, a study in the history of these and other educational ambiguities from Booker Washington through Moton, to Aggrey and Jones, would reveal how many of these leaders' slogans and stories were *doubles entendres*, some deliberately so, some unintentionally, with the interpretation depending on the colour or politics of the audience. The most famous of them all was Booker Washington's, which greeted each visitor to Tuskegee who passed his statue; it appealed to conservative South African missionaries as much as to West African intellectuals:

WE SHALL PROSPER IN PROPORTION AS WE LEARN TO DIGNIFY AND GLORIFY LABOUR AND PUT BRAINS AND SKILL INTO THE COMMON OCCUPATIONS OF LIFE. THERE IS NO DEFENCE OR SECURITY EXCEPT IN THE HIGHEST INTELLIGENCE AND DEVELOPMENT OF ALL.[2]

The particular paradox of Kalibala's resignation was that he named his independent school 'the Aggrey Memorial School', thus identifying himself with that side of Aggrey that appeared in the famous 'eagle' parable, with its apparently unambiguous incitement to independence.[3] This mythical aspect of the independent Aggrey,

[1] Schofield to Jones, 2 May 1935, File B-4, P.S.F.A.

[2] These two sentences, inscribed on the base of Washington's statue, are originally from the famous Atlanta Exposition speech, reproduced in *Up From Slavery*, p. 267.

[3] The story concerns an eagle finally learning to fly after long conditioning to behave like a chicken. The audience could fasten either on the length of the training necessary for the eagle to realize its maturity, or on the victorious flight. For the full parable, see Smith, *Aggrey of Africa*, pp. 136–7. For a further aspect

of course, took little account of what white audiences noted with such satisfaction: Aggrey's uncompromising opposition to Ethiopianism, and the fact that he would never have founded a school independent of mission or government.

The school founded in his honour was, however, a valuable illustration of what Kalibala had adopted and what he had rejected from his own experience in mission schools and in American Negro colleges. The school's prospectus was emphatic on the strictly non-sectarian nature of the institution—as much a comment on the anomalies of mission zoning and spheres of influence in East Africa as on the positive non-denominational life in Tuskegee and other colleges. On the controversial feature of trades, he wanted to avoid the worst abuses of his days in mission school, when he remembered the students being 'herded into cutting lawns, wood, and digging some ditches',[1] and he had written in his thesis that he did not favour the Tuskegee system, in which each student was necessarily bound to one trade. Instead, trades would be used to give the school some measure of self-sufficiency, and provide, in the Tuskegee tradition, opportunity for poorer students to work their way. It is not impossible, however, that something of Kalibala's interest in vocational, agricultural, and industrial education was determined by the fact that he was in the market for American funds, aiming to raise 40,000 dollars in 1938 for a new trades building.[2] The Director of Education in Uganda had, however, felt obliged to protect possible American donors by exposing the hollow claims of Kalibala's appeal to the Phelps-Stokes Fund.[3] Since most of the agencies which would naturally be approached for donations would confirm the good standing of the school with the Phelps-Stokes Fund, the appeal was not successful.

Kalibala turned elsewhere, and within a year had become the first representative in Uganda of the Foreign Mission Board of the

---

of Aggrey's mythical stature, see G. A. Shepperson, 'Myth and Reality in Malawi', Fourth Melville J. Herskovits Memorial Lecture, 13 Apr. 1966, (North Western University Press, 1966), pp. 10–11. See also A. A. Nwafor Orizu, *Without Bitterness—Western Nations in Post-War Africa* (New York, 1944), pp. 289–92.

[1] Kalibala, 'Education for Villages in Uganda', p. 51.

[2] Copy of appeal to 'American Friends of the Aggrey Memorial School', in Kalibala File, B-4, P.S.F.A.

[3] Jowitt to Phelps Stokes, 4 Jan. 1939, File B-4, P.S.F.A.

National Baptist Convention of the U.S.A. (Negro).[1] It is an interesting footnote to this sketch of a 'good African' from Uganda that he should avail himself of the pages of the *Mission Herald* to counter white missionary claims to be the 'dominant benefactors of the Negro masses in Africa', indicting so much missionary teaching for being 'at the expense of the African independent development'.[2] Thus the Aggrey Memorial School was eventually supported by the same Negro body as John Chilembwe's Providence Industrial Mission in Nyasaland.[3]

It has been impossible in this chapter to concentrate exclusively upon East African students in assessing the formative influence of America; it would have been even more difficult to restrict the terms to Kenya, as this would have made it in effect, the study of two students, Mbiyu Koinange and Molonket Olokorinya ole Sempele. Although the latter was in the United States at a time when the Phelps-Stokes Fund was just being founded, the effects of his brief exposure to the American South show another side of the difficulty of forming the 'good African'.

Molonket, the first of the Keekonyokie Masai to embrace Christianity, determined in 1908 to sell his cattle and accompany his close A.I.M. missionary friends, the Stauffachers, on their furlough to America. In his time there he attended a trade school for Negroes in North Carolina, and was also the first East African to join Boydton Academic and Bible Institute, Boydton, Virginia. Reports on his progress were favourable, and for his missionary magazine he gave a report at the end of his studies that augured well: 'I want much the prayers of the people of this land where there is so much of the grace of God, that He may do much for the wicked tribe of the Masai to whom I go.'[4]

However, Virginia then, as in the 1920s, had been quite unable to prevent him from hearing about the 230-odd lynchings that occurred in the United States during his three years' residence, or from seeing 'little white children playing with black dolls, sitting them up and

[1] F. Olmstead to Jones, Dec. 1939, File B-4, P.S.F.A., cf. also the *Mission Herald* (Philadelphia), xliii, No. 6 (Jan./Feb. 1940), 12–15, in which Kalibala's station is stated to be 200 acres in size, and to offer 'unlimited possibilities for educational and religious development'.

[2] E. B. Kalibala, 'Africa—The Unknown Quantity', *Mission Herald*, xliv, No. 3 (July/Aug. 1940), 12.

[3] Cf. Shepperson and Price, *Independent African*.

[4] *Hearing and Doing* (Brooklyn), xvii, No. 2 (Apr./June 1912), 14–15. Cf. G. T. Stauffacher, 'Faster Beats the Drum' (unpublished MS.), p. 99.

throwing stones at them'.[1] Once back in Kenya, he continued for some twenty years to warn his African friends against letting the whites do to them in East Africa what he had observed in the American South; and when the moment was ripe (during the 1929 female circumcision crisis), it was Molonket who led out the majority of African Christians at Narok from the A.I.M., and started an independent church in an abandoned shop.[2]

Perhaps in the case of Koinange, too, his experience in the United States sheds a valuable light on his embracing the Independent School movements when he returned to Kenya in 1938, and on his becoming founder of Kenya Teachers College, an institution independent of government and mission. It was noted earlier that he had come to America under the spell of Aggrey's oratory, but the choice of Hampton was almost certainly that of Mr. A. G. Grieve, his principal, with some additional encouragement from Earl Cromack, the Hampton agriculturalist then teaching at the Scots Mission, Kikuyu. On his arrival in the United States he made his first contacts with the Phelps-Stokes Fund, and proceeded to a Hampton that was as far removed from Jones's stereotype as could be imagined. As an introduction to interracial tensions, his first few days in the autumn of 1927 showed him the Hampton students taking general strike action against the petty restrictions imposed by the white staff on campus life; what may have affected Koinange incalculably more was to sit with the whole college in Sunday evening chapel, as part of this strike, and refuse to perform their famous Negro spirituals in front of the visiting Sir Gordon Guggisberg.[3] The strike atmosphere died down with the suspension of the student committee, and during most of his time in the next four years Koinange felt the inspiration of the Hampton spirit of self-improvement and service. Letters to his old Alliance High School tried to pass this message on:

> Agriculture, Chemistry, Folk Customs, Singing, self-control, entertainments, patriotism or self sacrificing for their country and people are things that make this school so wonderful . . .
>
> Pull yourselves together with the help of your teachers and you will be surprised at all that the Lord will do with your strength to raise dear old

[1] Stauffacher, op. cit., pp. 100–1.

[2] Ibid. pp. 171–3; also the Rev. John Mpaayei, interview, 1968.

[3] This incident was kindly retold to the writer by Dr. St. Clair Drake, a freshman contemporary of Koinange at Hampton. Cf. also W. E. B. DuBois, 'The Hampton Strike', *Crisis*, xxxiv, No. 10 (Dec. 1927), 345–6.

Kenya. Forget you are coloured students and try to observe and invent new things like boys and girls of other countries . . .

But whatsoever you do, good, better, best, never let it rest till the good is better and the better best.[1]

It was in this spirit of co-operatively interpreting Africans to Europeans that in 1931 Koinange addressed a six-page statement to the Secretary of State for the Colonies. This concerned itself with two issues that his father, Chief Koinange, might through lack of English be unable adequately to convey to the Joint Committee on Closer Union in London: 'the education of my people, and their future relations with the white race'.[2] In tone and tact Koinange came closest to Robert Moton's second book, *What the Negro Thinks*.[3] It was in that quietly critical tradition that he found occasion to voice typical native Kenyan grievances. Not the least of these was for parity of educational provision for whites and blacks in Kenya, before the assessment of comparative racial abilities. This was a particularly apposite subject for a year that preceded the publication of Dr. Vint's and Dr. Gordon's widely acclaimed researches on the Kenyan African's brain,[4] with their implications of African mental inferiority. Koinange anticipated:

> If you go to many parts of Africa you will find little neglected waifs of humanity screaming with the spiritual hunger and instinctively cramming their mouths with any rubbish . . . What is appropriate to still the cry of hunger? Would it be justifiable to shut out a-mile-runner from food, drink and shelter for months and then expect him to break the record set by a trained old Pheidippides? The African should be given proper and equal education before his ability is estimated.[5]

Just as in Ita's and Kalibala's cases there were pointers to the conflicts that would arise on their return, so also with Koinange Jones might have foreseen that he had larger educational aspirations for his people than the Government could accept. In 1934 Koinange had presented to Jones a scheme whereby he would on his return

[1] Koinange to 'Schoolmates', 5 Feb. 1928, Alliance High School Files, P.C.E.A., and personal testimony of Dr. H. M. Bond.

[2] Copy of letter (n.d.) in Koinange File, Hampton Institute Registry.

[3] R. R. Moton, *What the Negro Thinks* (London, 1929) has at the end of the twenties a much more outspoken tone than his earlier, more Washingtonite, *Finding a Way Out*.

[4] Cuttings of Gordon's lectures from the *British Medical Journal*, 18 Nov. 1933, and correspondence, in File Q-E, E.H., see also pp. 166–7.

[5] Koinange to Colonial Secretary, 1931.

carry out with the help of the Director of Education an educational programme that would not be confined to the Kikuyu people but would extend to all tribes. Even though he disavowed any 'aim to revolutionise or foster a political party',[1] the extent of his concern to give his life to assuage 'the educational hunger of three millions natives of Kenya'[2] would not be easily met within the framework of the Jeanes School, as he and the Director of Education had once hoped in 1935.[3]

On his return he was offered a headmastership at a fraction of the previous European incumbent's salary, and also a post at Alliance High School, but turned down both to accept the headship of Githunguri Independent School. Shortly, under Koinange's direction, the school was elevated into the trans-tribal Kenya African Teachers College. What is less well known is that he embodied in the College many of the principles which the Jeanes School at Kabete had been advocating for the last decade. Thus there were classes in spinning and weaving, and lectures on Kikuyu traditions and history given by Kenyatta. Although technical training never got off the ground, the school had excellent agricultural plots, and, according to government officials, the best manure system in Kenya.[4] True to the most progressive thinking on indirect-rule education, traditional structures—in Koinange's case the age-grade system—were incorporated in the organization of the school. No better evidence exists for Kenya to refute the notion that Africans were opposed to 'adapted education' of the Phelps-Stokes sort *per se*. What was objected to was adaptation without consultation. This short passage is worth quoting to show its closeness to the European-initiated experiments in the Malangali and Jeanes Schools:

> The age-group system was transformed to serve the community educationally. Every person or age-group in competition with others identified himself with the College. They came to see the School and we had the children sing songs, some songs creating envy and others appealing for help, e.g. hospitality or boarding places for the students. Each age-group made itself responsible for one definite task. The Kismiri group decided

[1] Koinange to Jones, 11 Aug. 1934, File B-4, P.S.F.A.
[2] Ibid.
[3] Koinange to Jones, 16 Jan. 1935, File B-4, P.S.F.A.
[4] M. Koinange, *The People of Kenya Speak for Themselves* (Detroit, 1955), pp. 26–9, and information received from Mr. Kover. Cf. Nottingham and Rosberg, *The Myth of Mau Mau*, p. 179.

to buy land and so did the Kihiumwiri. Shilling decided to give water-pump facilities, other groups to build a school dispensary and others to build the classroom building.[1]

There has, of course, been an element of arbitrariness in selecting such a small number of students for analysis, and any attempt to generalize about African student behaviour in the United States from this sample demands great caution. Ideally the analysis should be extended further; and a great deal of work remains to be done on some subjects which have not been included: the reverberations in the Phelps-Stokes Fund, Edinburgh House, and South African missionary circles when the model African missionary team of Kamba Simango and his wife broke with the American Board in Portuguese East Africa;[2] the Francis Nkrumah who submitted his articles on education for Jones's comment, and whose ambition it was, with Jones's aid, 'to carry on where his teacher and inspirer, Dr. Kweggyir Aggrey, left off';[3] the clash between the South African, Cele, and his Alma Mater, Hampton, when he began to ally himself with the 'Ethiopian' movement;[4] the three Ethiopians who came to the States in 1922, one of whom, Melaku Bayen, founded the Ethiopian World Federation, with Kalibala and Nyabongo on the advisory board;[5] or the Phelps-Stokes relations with S. W. Kulubya's son and Balamu Mukasa from Uganda.[6] These would, however, have only added fresh emphasis to certain general characteristics that have emerged from the present sampling.

Any such extended study also would have to compare the African student movement of America with its British counterpart, and in this wider context T. Ras Makonnen is right to contrast the sporadic protest of the Africans in America with the more thorough ideological commitment of many Africans in London and other British cities. With a few exceptions, such as Azikiwe and Ita, America did not in this pre-war period, produce political Africans of the stature of Kenyatta, Wallace-Johnson, the leaders of the West African Student Union, and others who came under the influence of the circle of

[1] Koinange, *The People of Kenya*, p. 30.
[2] Simango File, B-3, Misc. Students, P.S.F.A.
[3] Nkrumah to Jones, 29 Jan. 1941, File B-4, P.S.F.A.
[4] Gregg to Miss Clark, 17 Feb. 1919, Cele File, H.A.I.
[5] File on Ethiopians, Muskingum College, Muskingum, Ohio.
[6] Files on Mukasa and Kulubya, John Hope Papers, Moorland Collection, Howard University.

radical pan-Africanists.[1] The concern of this chapter, however, has been to measure the political development of African students more precisely against the standards expected of them by the Phelps-Stokes Fund and in particular by Thomas Jesse Jones.

Few would question the vital importance of an agency prepared to devote much of its time and some considerable portion of its funds (18,426 dollars in ten years)[2] to promoting African student welfare in the States during the inter-war period, before scholarships for African students became a part of government foreign policy. There was a desperate need for just this, as Simbini Nkomo had seen in 1920, when, appalled by the deaths of three Africans through overwork and poverty, he attempted to establish an African students' fund.[3] Undoubtedly also, as a result of the Phelps-Stokes Fund's activities in this field, some of the hazards of immigration formalities, visa renewal, and financial crises were removed, and Jones's personal correspondence with immigration authorities, allied philanthropic bodies, and college entrance officials is sufficient testimony to his unstinting efforts in this field.

What is in question is the framework of political and educational assumptions within which the aid was administered, and more particularly the extent to which Jones's conceptions of the education appropriate for Africans led to a certain inflexibility in his advice to Africans in the United States. He attempted to guide Africans for a span of some thirty years, from his grooming of Aggrey in the early years of this century to his horror at Yergan's founding the Communist-linked International Council on African Affairs, which Jones felt might unbalance some hitherto co-operative Africans.[4] But his near-obsessive fears of African contamination by black radicalism had led him to attribute to Tuskegee and Hampton capacities for immunizing African students against it which they have been shown not to possess. Nor were the many Africans whom Jones exposed to the Hampton-Tuskegee system necessarily im-

[1] Ras Makonnen, interview, July 1969. During much of the 1930s African students in Britain had access to such pan-African thinkers as Padmore, C. L. R. James, and Makonnen. Cf. J. R. Hooker, *Black Revolutionary* (London, 1967), Ch. 3, also Coleman, *Nigeria*, pp. 242–3.

[2] File A-5, 1933, P.S.F.A.; also DuBois, 'If I had a Million Dollars', p. 347.

[3] Nkomo to Moorland, 10 Sept. 1923, Nkomo File, Moorland Collection, Howard University.

[4] Jones to Tobias, 8 Sept. 1937, Box 67, Y.M.C.A. Historical Library, New York. Jones particularly feared for Yergan's influence over Dr. Xuma and Prof. Jabavu.

pressed by those aspects which he intended. Tuskegee could often be for Africans a stimulus to attitudes directly contrary to patient non-political co-operation; it could demonstrably become a symbol of separatist black politics, an incentive to aggressive business enterprise, and an inspiration for independent, non-sectarian African schools.

Jones's predilections for agriculture and rural education further illustrated the danger of elevating into a way of life for Africans in training this admittedly important subject. There is little evidence that he was prepared to modify its importance even when slump conditions made agriculture a very unsafe vocation. Indeed, by the thirties, the route from Hampton or Tuskegee to Mabel Carney's rural education courses in Teachers College, Columbia, had hardened into a standard recommendation of the Fund to Africans.

The most serious aim, however, and the one whose failure caused him greatest disappointment, was to restore Africans to their countries untouched by African nationalism and uninterested in challenging the colonial framework. This arose not only, as Alek Fraser of Achimota saw, from a tendency on Jones's part to attribute to Africans the same 'most meagre of political futures'[1] that Hampton and Tuskegee graduates could expect, but also from a more deeply held conviction of African innocence and patience. This basically racialist belief, which of course extended logically to American Negroes, was widely held at the time; it was shared by J. H. Oldham who wrote from Tuskegee that the impression of sanity, patience, absence of ill-will, and the cheerful optimism of Negroes was 'so general and widespread, though of course by no means universal, that one cannot help recognising in it the expression of very admirable and valuable racial qualities'.[2] It was this ultimate conviction about the preservability of such Negro virtues that explained Jones's tendency to inveigh against white radicals and subversive propaganda whenever one of his protégés turned political; and it went some way towards explaining his belief that J. E. K. Aggrey could be the norm rather than the very rare exception.

[1] A. G. Fraser, Circular Letter No. 61 (London), 31 July 1931, File 14, Winifred Holtby Papers, Hull Public Library.

[2] Oldham to Curtis, 11 Feb. 1921, Box 315, E.H., now I.M.C.A., Geneva.

Conclusions

THE HALF century from Tuskegee's foundation in 1881 to C. G. Woodson's 'Miseducation of the Negro'[1] in 1931 saw the constant reworking of a very few great themes in the field of African and American Negro education. Of these none was more representative of the age than the demand by the dominant white groups in the Southern States and the African colonies that Negro education should go off the white standard. If white rationalization for such adaptation could be complicated by the variety of forces advocating special education for Negroes, it was no less possible to characterize Africans and American Negroes according to divisions of opinion on the subject. The period was not one that saw the imposition of a new educational formula on an unwilling people, so much as one in which leading African and American Negro spokesmen agonized over the extent to which they might allow differentiation for their people. The issue was further obscured by a sector of influential white opinion that gravely questioned the wisdom or safety of Negroes' accepting a quite different set of educational standards from the whites.

Something of the peculiar difficulty of adaptation may be understood from the diversity of calls for curricular reorientation in African and American Negro schools. A wide spectrum of opinion thought it entirely appropriate that in certain subjects—especially history, geography, literature and music—Negro children should concentrate on the achievements of their own race. Much of the argument among educationists, however, turned on whether such a 'progressive' culturally-adapted curriculum might not have serious social and political consequences. Curricular change of this sort could so easily be combined with a philosophy of training 'along their own lines', or, less emotively, disparity of academic standards, that some educators were extremely wary of any move in that direction.[2]

[1] C. G. Woodson, 'The Miseducation of the Negro', *Crisis*, xxxviii (Aug. 1931), 266–7. Cf. also C. G. Woodson, *The Miseducation of the American Negro* (Washington, 1933).

[2] Murray, *The School in the Bush*, p. 306; N. M. Leys, *A Last Chance in Kenya* (London, 1931), p. 107. Cf. also Ashby, *Universities*, pp. 240–2.

Indeed, the range of the controversy might best be seen by constructing a scale from completely undifferentiated western education at one end to an education thoroughly 'along their own lines' at the other, and by placing the various white and Negro authorities on this question at their appropriate points along the scale.

At one extreme would come Norman Leys and A. Victor Murray, both extremely sensitive to the political nature of Negro education, and both subscribing to Murray's axiom that 'differentiation without equality means the permanent inferiority of the black man'.[1] At no very great distance from these two would come a large number of African students who had gone abroad for an education identical to that of whites, and who resented the very idea that there was any 'such thing as an African educational problem'.[2] Several of these did have a keen interest in African culture, but made the extremely important point that it was nobody's business but their own to re-interpret African traditions in the modern world. In their various ways, therefore, Kalibala, Koinange, and Nyabongo all shared Victor Murray's conviction that 'we foreigners cannot give him *African* culture, because it is not ours to give. We can only give him European culture, because that is what we have'.[3]

Marginally further along the scale would be placed W. E. B. DuBois. Admittedly no absolutely fixed place could be allotted to a man whose thought had so developed and changed over this half century; but certainly by the thirties this early champion of white standards for the Negro colleges had come some way towards accepting a 'special education' for Negroes.[4] Fully conscious of the dangers sometimes involved in educational theories 'suited' to the Negro, he yet felt there were legitimate reasons for a special education; for the Negro had been so 'hammered' into a separate entity 'by his history, group experiences and memories', that any education concerned to build up Negro pride and solidarity must deal with this history, civics, and literature which were neglected in white institutions.[5] Although, therefore, DuBois did not anticipate the large

[1] Murray, op. cit., pp. 309, 330ff; Leys, op. cit., p. 113.

[2] B. N. Azikiwe, 'How Shall we Educate the African?', *Journal of the African Society*, xxxiii, No. cxxxi (Apr. 1934), 144. Cf. also pp. 240–1.

[3] Murray op. cit., p. 329; cf. also Carmichael and Hamilton, *Black Power*, p. 37.

[4] W. E. B. DuBois, 'Does the Negro Need Separate Schools?', *Journal of Negro Education* (Washington), iv (1935), 328–35.

[5] Ibid. See also DuBois, 'The Negro College', *Crisis*, xl (Aug. 1933), 177.

curricular concessions to Black Studies which have been wrung from many of the great Northern universities during the later 1960s, such a conclusion could be seen as a just development of his lifelong devotion to investigating and raising the status of Negro-African subjects.

Carter G. Woodson, as a result of his lengthy crusade to give scholarly standing to Negro history, was prepared to go a good deal further than DuBois at one time in pressing for a Negro orientation for the history, philosophy, and arts taught in Negro schools. Paradoxically, and if only at the curricular level, the process brought him close to the programme of his old opponent, Jones, as he urged the abandonment of the traditional 'supposedly cultural' courses, and condemned the higher education of the Negro as 'largely meaningless imitation'.[1]

Less outspoken than Woodson, but equally convinced that Africanization of the curriculum was not incompatible with the best that had been achieved in the West or with the development of the African towards full nationhood was A. G. Fraser of Achimota College. After Fraser would come Blyden and Aggrey, both less aware of the political aspect of African education than Fraser, but nevertheless determined to combine African culture with the healthiest elements in western civilization.

Somewhat further still along the road of adaptation should be placed J. H. Oldham and the Colonial Office Advisory Committee on Education whose policy he so greatly influenced. It is becoming increasingly important to make the point that education departments and missions in British colonial Africa did not unthinkingly impose western-style academic education in the various territories; the impression might otherwise be gained from such critiques as Nyerere's *Education for Self Reliance*, that British educators had no qualms about the élitist, academic nature of these institutions. The truth is rather that there is no alarm raised or remedy suggested by Nyerere that had not been mentioned countless times in the colonial period. Whatever the failures in implementation (and this was due less to official apathy than African resistance to educational differentiation), there was seldom a time in the period from 1843 to 1953 which lacked spokesmen for adaptation; like Nyerere, they set up model farm schools and school-farms, planned to make the primary school an integral part of the total village community, and spoke up for an

[1] Woodson, 'The Miseducation of the Negro', p. 267.

egalitarianism that would prevent a privileged élite from leaving the masses behind.[1]

Finally, at some distance again from either Oldham or the Colonial Office Committee, must be placed Booker Washington and Jesse Jones. Both of these saw little political danger involved in the very large measure of adaptation they recommended; equally, they gave small consideration to combining their own educational priorities with adequate safeguards for higher education.

Another constant theme throughout the period was the question of the extent to which Negro schooling should be an 'education for life'. This highly ambiguous slogan (closely related to adaptation) was entirely representative of the era, for it could be used by the two main schools of opposing thought about the Negro or African school. According to the first of these, the school could educate people for a life beyond tribal conservatism or the political oppression of the Southern States; and it could do this despite racial discrimination, creating an élite that could compete in intelligence with the dominant white society. And, second, the slogan could equally well comprehend the view that a Negro or African school must be conditioned by the backwardness and low living standard of the mass of American Negro and African people. Such a view could challenge the school to discard every inessential course, and to equip its pupils for the realities of life in a prejudiced and underprivileged society.[2]

Although it has been broadly possible to associate Armstrong, Washington, and Jones with one interpretation of this slogan, and DuBois, Leys, Woodson, and many African students with the other, there were times, nevertheless, towards the end of the period under review when even DuBois and Woodson wavered. In 1930 DuBois reopened the old dispute between the industrial and academic schools of Negro education, and re-examined in the onset of the Depression just how successfully each of the two methods had prepared its pupils for life. He found that the industrial school, by starting at the bottom, had, with its long outdated manual training, quite failed to build up the solid economic base for Negroes that Washington had sought, and which black leaders and intellectuals

[1] J. Nyerere, *Education for Self Reliance* (Dar es Salaam, 1967), *passim*. P. J. Foster, 'Education for Self-Reliance: A Critical Evaluation', in R. Jolly (Ed.), *Education in Africa: Research and Action* (Nairobi, 1969), pp. 92–3.

[2] For some valuable contemporary examples of this theme, see I. N. Resnick (Ed.) *Tanzania: Revolution by Education* (Arusha, 1968).

have recently acknowledged as an important contribution to modern theories of black economic self-sufficiency.[1] Indeed, DuBois could not refrain from showing that in this respect at least history had been on his side: 'The most revolutionary development in Negro education for a quarter-century is illustrated by the fact that Hampton today is one of the largest Negro colleges and that her trade training seems bound to disappear within a few years. Tuskegee is a high school and college, with an unsolved program of the future of its trade schools.'[2] On the other hand, the college had failed to grapple with the new economic situation and the technology of the 1920s; rather (and here DuBois re-echoed Jones) it had continued 'its old habit of wasting time on Latin, Greek, Hebrew and eschatology', and had forgotten that its main task must be 'to place in American life a trained black man who can do what the world today wants done'.[3] It had failed to do this through lack of relevance—in fact, it had not considered that 'the university education of black men in the United States must be grounded in the condition and work of those black men'.[4] Lest this sound like a final capitulation to the philosophy of Jones and Washington, it must be stressed that he was not merely accepting Washington's emphasis on economic realities, but positively embracing black separatism as the only way to give the economic programme life. Education for life it must certainly be, but for black life, and its quality would no longer be conditioned by co-operation with whites. It could only come from 'the organisation of intelligent and earnest people of Negro descent for their preservation and advancement in America, in the West Indies and in Africa'.[5]

Yet, for all his temporary disillusionment with and denigration of both industrial school and college (which he shared with Woodson),[6] DuBois never accepted the view of Jesse Jones, that by rewriting its curriculum the school could by itself direct Negro and African aspirations towards certain careers, or radically improve rural life in the Southern States or the African village. The school, he was certain, could not change society:

[1] H. Cruse, *The Crisis of the Negro Intellectual* (New York, 1967; London, 1969), pp. 19–20. Cf. also Louis Harlan's forthcoming study of Washington, and G. Breitman (Ed.), *Malcolm X Speaks* (New York, 1966), p. 39.

[2] DuBois, 'Education and Work', p. 13.

[3] Ibid., p. 10.

[4] DuBois, 'The Negro College', p. 176.

[5] W. E. B. DuBois, 'On Being Ashamed of Oneself', *Crisis*, xl (Sept. 1933), 200.

[6] Woodson, 'The Miseducation of the Negro', p. 267.

> These are the three disciplines which are the basis of intelligence, and which no school can fail to teach thoroughly and definitely, and call itself a school. Whenever a teachers' convention gets together and tries to find out how it can cure the ills of society there is simply one answer; the school has but one way to cure the ills of society and that is by making men intelligent. To make men intelligent, the school has again but one way, and that is, first and last, to teach them to read, write and count. And if the school fails to do that, and tries beyond that to do something for which a school is not adapted, it not only fails in its own function, but it fails in all other attempted functions. Because no school as such can organise industry, or settle the matter of wage and income, can found homes or furnish parents, can establish justice or make a civilised world.[1]

This same quite fundamental disagreement over the possible functions of a school was transferred to Africa. Educators like Jones and Loram, and with them large numbers of missionary and colonial authorities, believed the school to have been responsible for creating in Africans the distaste for manual work and the overwhelming desire for clerical occupations. It was consequently argued that the school could be the primary agent in undoing the alleged damage, by the simple expedient of curricular change towards a more vocational bias. Thus in East Africa, through the Jeanes system, and by determined campaigns for industrial schools in parts of West Africa,[2] an attempt was made to reverse the pattern of African aspirations. The very limited success of all such experiments in new types of education was caused less by insufficient finance than by the failure to realize that it was the rewards of the colonial occupational structure that determined African aspirations, and not the fact that the schools were too literary.[3] In pointing this out for Africa, it was perhaps A. G. Fraser who came closest to what DuBois had long stressed in the States: that education must be for full national life:

> Now no national education should be directly vocational. It should train men and women to be intelligent, adaptable, useful and trustworthy in any vocation they may follow, but a national education must have a far wider outflow than any vocation or group of vocations can supply. There is a great outcry in India and a lesser one in Africa against the results of our literary education in these lands, on the ground that it has trained

[1] W. E. B. DuBois, 'Curriculum Revision', address to Georgia State Teachers Convention, 12 Apr. 1935, DuBois Papers, Park Johnson Archives, Fisk University.

[2] Foster, *Education and Social Change in Ghana*, Ch. V, *passim*.

[3] Ibid., p. 164.

too many clerks and glutted the market. Then, in wondrous inconsequence, the complainants ask for vocational training in its place. But the very reason why so-called literary education has failed is that it has been vocational. Heaven knows, it has often been anything but literary. It has failed because it was vocational and has only been too successful in training students for one vocation.[1]

The last of the really major themes in this half century was the assumption that Africa should learn from the example of the American South. Although this became the conviction of the Phelps-Stokes Fund in 1920, and remained a powerful element in its policy-making for the next twenty years and more, a rich diversity of educational links between Africa and the Southern States had been built up long before the first Phelps-Stokes Commission reached Freetown, Sierra Leone, on 4 September 1920.

The tendency of the Phelps-Stokes Fund, and in particular of Dr. Jesse Jones, was to proscribe as dangerous many of these relationships between American Negroes and Africans, and concentrate upon a single path;[2] through Tuskegee methods alone both in Africa and America could Negroes be educated to be constructively content. For all its popularity with white educators, however, Jones's Tuskegee formula for contentment had little effect upon African or American Negro aspirations in politics and education. Some of the forces working against Jones's programme have been described, but the greatest obstacle lay in this, his favourite conviction, that the Negro could by education be immunized against politics. Ultimately not even Tuskegee believed it could do this for its students, as one of Tuskegee's Negro faculty admitted to W. E. Owen of Kenya:

I asked one of the heads, a negro, whether the young men and young women were happier after passing thro' the Institute than they were before entering it. My question made him pause and after thinking a while he said, 'I think that it probably makes them less happy', and when I asked him

[1] Fraser, Circular Letter No. 61.

[2] Jones had no understanding of Fraser's point, that whites must prepare Africans for full national sovereignty, nor ever contemplated the possibility that Africans might attain that political maturity before their American Negro brethren; see Jones to Fraser, 14 Sept. 1931: 'The American Negro has now, and will increasingly have in the future a larger control of his destinies than any African that I know in any of the African Colonies.

"O Alec dear, of earth the cream
In Africa the shining light
Would you could grasp Tuskegee's dream
And guide the Natives on aright." '

Papers in possession of Dr. Kathleen Bliss.

why he said so, he replied that it was because they became more sensitive to injustices and slights and felt their lower position in the estimation of whites more keenly than before. Well then, I said, why not alter the course of training so as to avoid making them more unhappy, and indeed are you doing them a kindness in making them more sensitive. He replied to this that the stage of unhappiness was inevitable, and that it lay full in the path of progress and could not be avoided.[1]

[1] *E.A.S.* (wkly edn.), 17 June 1922.

Appendix I

From Dr. Jones's address to the National Education Association in Salt Lake City, 1913, 'The High School and Democracy'.

On teaching Latin:

'. . . If Miss Smith, teacher of Latin, wishes really to help the great wave of democracy, she must follow Mary to her mother's home and see the mother battling to educate her family of five children and feed and clothe the entire family on ten or fifteen dollars a week. She must learn what is Mary's attitude toward her hardworking father and mother. She must ascertain Mary's pleasures and evening companions. She must study the relation of housing and food to the death of Mary's baby brother. She must determine in her own mind and, if possible, help Mary to determine what useful sphere in life Mary is going to fill. These various excursions into Mary's life will probably lead Miss Smith to the study of her community and she will learn why the health officer does or does not know that William had diptheria, why a city of 17,000 has no sewerage system, why their typhoid fever death list is twice what it ought to be, why there are so many beautiful homes, why the schools are so well constructed and many other conditions good and bad of which she had not dreamt. Finally at the end of the school year when her mind is full of this living information, Miss Smith, the Latin teacher, will decide to teach Latin in such a living style that it can no longer be called a dead language, or she will throw Latin overboard and teach another subject which Mary needs more in her daily contact with a mother that slaves all day, with children who need to be fed and clothed and washed, in a city that does not give anything away, in a democracy that only asks a man or woman to produce something useful whether it is of matter, mind or spirit . . .'

(Copy in Hampton Institute Archives)

See p. 37.

Appendix II

Letter of Thuku to Tuskegee; see p. 75. (Tuskegee Institute Archives)

The East African Association
P.O. Box 598.
NAIROBI, 8th September, 1921.

The Secretary,
Tuskegee Institute,
Albama, U.S.A.

Dear Sir,

From the books and newspapers I read dealing with the condition of Negro races in America I find that your Institute from the time of its establishment has been engaged in up-lifting the Negro races there and that you are the likely person, being its Secretary, who may be looked to, for advice by those engaged in a similar work. I therefore take the liberty of addressing you the following and any information or advice you may be able to give me will be gratefully appreciated.

I am a native and the Secretary of the East African Association lately established with the object of promoting the welfare of the African native races in British East Africa now called Kenya Colony. In this capacity I might state that the number of natives, so far as this Colony is concerned, is 2,800,000 and almost all of them are practically in the primitive stage of civilization although, this country has been under the rule of the British people for the last two decades. Their declared policy of the Administration is to govern for the benefit of the natives and some petty efforts are made by them ostensebly to impart technical and elementary education to the natives but at an expense totally disproportionate to the revenue extracted from them. From this and from the nature of ligislation as applicable to us and from similar other evidence (details of which are hardly necessary to be enumerated here at this stage) it can be safely concluded that the children of the soil have been ceaselessly exploited under pretext of civilising them and the country is governed primarily not for the aboriginal races but, to all interests and purposes, for the governing race. The advent of the British people in this country was supposed to be for the up-lifting of our races but from the experience, such as we have been having during the last twenty years, the fact protudes beyond the possibility of doubt that such is not their intention and the whole is a hollow boast and to this horrid myth, the steady deterioration which has been gradually taking place in every condition of native life amply testifies. The process we have been brought under by foreign influences, if allowed to go on unchecked and unrestrained, is bound to annihilate and wipe out our native races from the land of their fore-fathers at no distant date.

Under the circumstances a serious duty devolves upon this Association and upon educated natives of whom there are few, to try to avert such a catastrophe and to find out ways and means for their unification, and preservation. The first essential, of course, is education, but this can not be secured without the aid of able and devoted men and what is most deplorable is, such men among us are none. We suffer beyond imagination from the want of such men and leaders of our own race to guide us in every walk of life and the result is that our progress in the sphere of Trade Industry, Agriculture and the last but not the least important politics is seriously hampered. We must frankly confess that we are not without warm friends and sincere sympathisers among European Missionaries and benevolent Indians (East Indians) to whom we owe so much of our improved life of few of us. These friends have been helping us as much as they can, and in their own way; but with all this, we are convinced that this is totally inadequate and insufficient to dispel our present illiteracy and ignorance we have steeped in and to safeguard our position as human beings or to avert the impending danger which seems so imminent to our view.

The necessity therefore of having our own man—a skinsman brother, and a leader, who has devoted his life and renounced everything for the elevation and up-lifting of a primitive race like ours, which is even now scarcely free from the shackles of the slavery days will be too obvious for further elaboration. It gives me the greatest pleasure to learn that despite the stubborn adverse evil influences the Negro race in America has been successful in producing many large hearted men like Booker T. Washington and establishing Institutes like the Tuskegee. We regard such men as our saviours and the Tuskegee as our asylum where the hunted down-trodden and oppressed Negro may hasten to seek for help or advice in all times of danger. Such being the feeling I am therefore anxious to be informed if a Booker T. Washington or a Du Bois can be spared for founding a 'Tuskegee' in the African wilds and for the holy Mission of up-lifting and emancipating the hopeless, hapless, struggling 3,000,000 nude Native souls from deep ignorance, object porvity, and grinding oppression of the white settlers of this Colony of Kenya.

One thing I must make clear before I close this appeal for help and it is that we have no money for any purpose whatever but we have gratitude for our benefactors present or future.

I enclose under separate cover newspaper cuttings and other literature though scanty on our native affairs in this country for your information.

Trusting that this appeal will receive the earnest attention of your Institute and the Negro public of the United States of America and thanking you in anticipation on behalf of the Native races of this country for the advice and help we may receive at your hands.

I am dear Sir,Yours faithfully,
Harry Thuku
Hony. Secretary.

Appendix III

Speech Day Programme. See p. 167.

(T. G. Benson Papers)

JEANES SCHOOL SPEECH DAY

Tuesday Aug. 6th 1929, 4.45 p.m. in the School Hall.

1. *African Tribal Songs.*
   (*a*) *Kikuyu Rattle Song.*
   The song centres round the rattle (Gicandi) and its ornaments. The singers ask riddles in turn. A full explanation would fill a book.

   (*b*) *Luo Wedding Song.*
   The bridegroom's age-equals gather together and sing in praise of him, his work, his skill, his shield etc. The musical instrument of 8 strings (Thom) is of ancient origin. The man mentioned at the end, Gor, was a famous old Chief of South Kavirondo.

   (*c*) *Abananda* (Bantu Kavirondo)
   i. *K'arimiwa.* According to a tradition of the tribe a weakly hunchback saved people from the cannibals by his cunning. They now sing in praise of him.
   ii. *Mishere ulule.*
   The singer recites the names of people and tribes and says what they each do, making puns on their names.
   iii. *Lubenzu.*
   The song of the bird and the beautiful maiden. She begs the feathers and is enticed far away from her own home. The bird represents the young man who will one day come and woo her.
   iv. *The War Horn* sounds and all rush to the call.

2. Presentation of Permanent and Provisional Jeanes Certificates by the Hon'ble the Director of Education.

3. Jeanes School Hymns (Swahili).
   1. God our Father. African Tune.
   2. Praise the Lord. African Tune.
   3. Nobody knows the trouble I've seen. Negro Spiritual.

   Speech: Chief Koinange.
4. Recreational Games and Drill.
5. Show of Handwork.
   1. Men's carpentry.
   2. Women's sewing.

Appendix IV

Letter of T. J. Jones, 'To an Able and Devoted African whose Studies Filled him with Perplexity and Disappointment when he Returned Home', *Southern Workman*, lxiv, No. 9 (Sept. 1935), pp. 279–82:

Dear Friend,

A very happy New Year to you. I have thought of you often since you returned to your Native Nigeria, and your letters have given me some idea of your thoughts and emotions as you have again entered the currents of life among those you have known from childhood. I am not at all surprised that you are subjected to the variety of feelings mentioned in your letters. As I watched your development at Columbia University, I had increasing fears that your continued study of abstract interpretations of human affairs would add to your perplexity when you were again compelled to deal with simple realities among your home people. Do you remember Christ's prayer: 'I thank Thee, Father, Lord of Heaven and Earth, that Thou hast hid these things from the wise and prudent and hast revealed them unto babes'? When you left Calabar and your Native Nigeria and arrived in America, you gave every evidence that you had an accurate knowledge of the every day life of the simple people in West Africa. You came sincerely seeking to learn the next steps necessary to their development. You listened eagerly to those who were regarded as 'wise and prudent'. You were remarkably successful in passing all University examinations with honor. I am proud of your scholarly attainments both at Columbia University and at the London School of Economics. Undoubtedly you acquired much useful knowledge, but the disappointments and discouragements expressed in your letter confirm my fears that some of your present interpretations are out of focus. You are probably depending too exclusively on those whom Christ called the 'wise and prudent' and you are possibly neglecting the simple realities known only to those whom Christ called 'Babes'.

Your excellent letter clearly reveals the conflict between your commonsense understanding of the actualities of life, on the one hand, and your acquired belief in certain abstract conceptions of economic and social theories on the other hand. Your commonsense impels you to recognise the importance of health and sanitation, of the soil and agriculture, of sound family life, and of mental and spiritual development for all the people. Your acquired beliefs in social and economic abstractions impel you to seek solutions for problems that are vaguely understood by you. Two such problems to which you refer are the marketing of products and your relationships to educational organisations in Nigeria. In both instances you seem to disregard numerous and vital factors involved in the problem.

Marketing, in the sense implied by you, involves intricate conditions and forces far beyond, not only your experience and studies but also the experiences and understanding of the American and English lecturers whom you heard. Similarly your relationships to existing educational policies and organisations in Nigeria can be successfully developed only on the basis of long and intimate experience and through understanding. My urgent advice to you is that you remember Christ's prayer of thanksgiving and follow the impulses of your own commonsense rather than the vague implications of the so-called 'wise and prudent' whom you heard in London and New York.

Turning now to what I believe is your conviction, namely what you call the 'gospel of health and industry and agriculture and modern equipment of machinery and culture for living' I submit the following suggestions:

1. That you make every effort to understand those large and vital fields and service; I regret exceedingly that you did not have time to learn more about them when you were in England and America.

2. Among the sources of information which I hope are available, are the following:

(*a*) Mr. Helser's mission school at Garkida in Northern Nigeria and also his books. If possible you should visit that station.

(*b*) Careful reading and study of 'Overseas Education' published by the British Advisory Committee for Education in the Colonies. If possible you should study all the issues of this remarkable magazine.

(*c*) Of course you should become acquainted with everything published by the Nigeria Dept. of Education; Mr. Hussey, the Director of Education, is a remarkable man.

(*d*) There are several excellent schools in Nigeria whose work you should carefully study. You can learn their names through Mr. Hussey.

(*e*) You should learn as much as possible about the Nigeria Departments of Agriculture and Health and Public Works.

3. My study of schools in Africa and other parts of the world is that independent schools begun by individuals are not successful. There are in America a very few exceptions, notably Tuskegee. In Africa, the successful exceptions are practically negligible. By all means, attach yourself to the Government school system or to one of the well-organised missions.

4. Your desire to organise industries in glass and paper is in the wrong direction because they cannot be introduced into Africa for a long time to come. Nor are they relatively important to Africa at present.

5. The acute need at present not only in Africa but also in America, Europe and Asia is an intelligent consciousness of Mother Earth. Certainly Africa is overwhelmingly rural. God's gift of the soil is only beginning to be adequately recognised by Humanity.

6. You should know about the Jeanes visiting teachers and Jeanes Schools in East Africa. They are especially designed for villages and the open country in every part of the world.

Time does not permit me to write more at the present time. I am enclosing copies of my address, 'What is Education' and my Tuskegee Founder's Day Address—'Booker Washington, Apostle of Self-Determination and Cooperation.' What I have written briefly in this letter, you will find more fully developed in the Phelps-Stokes Education Commission Reports and especially in the earlier chapters of "Education in East Africa". I urge you by all means to read the first four chapters of that volume.

I have every confidence in your ability and character and devotion. I am most eager that you shall succeed in your efforts to serve the fine people of your Native Nigeria. Remember that remarkable Beatitude:

"Blessed are the gentle, for they shall inherit the gratitude of Humanity." (See pp. 239–40.).

Bibliography

I. PRIMARY SOURCES

A. INTERVIEWS

Miss Rosebud Aggrey, second daughter of James E. K. Aggrey.

Mrs. J. W. Arthur, widow of Dr. J. W. Arthur, Scots Mission, Kikuyu.

T. Godfrey Benson, principal of the Jeanes School, Kenya, in succession to J. W. C. Dougall, from 1932.

Dr. Horace Mann Bond, one-time president of Lincoln University, Pa., now dean of the School of Education, Atlanta University, Ga.

Major Walter Brown, commandant and dean of men, Hampton Institute, during 1920s and 1930s.

The Rev. Andrew Doig, one-time holder of an Agricultural Missions Foundation Fellowship to America.

Dr. James W. C. Dougall, secretary of the East Africa Phelps-Stokes Commission, first principal of the Jeanes School, Kabete, Kenya, and educational adviser to the Protestant Missionary Societies of Kenya and Uganda.

Dr. St. Clair Drake, undergraduate at Hampton Institute, contemporary with Peter Koinange.

Mrs. A. G. Fraser, widow of Alek Fraser of Achimota.

Mr. A. G. Fraser, son of the late Alek Fraser, and colleague of J. E. K. Aggrey at Achimota.

Miss B. D. Gibson, secretary to J. H. Oldham.

Dr. Lewis Jones, for reminiscences of W. E. B. DuBois and J. E. K. Aggrey.

E. B. Kalibala, student of Tuskegee, Lincoln Academy, Columbia and New York Universities in the 1920s and 1930s.

The Rev. Robert MacPherson, missionary of the Church of Scotland in its various Kenya missions from 1925.

Ras Makonnen, founder member of the Pan-African Federation, colleague of Padmore and Nkrumah.

The Rev. John Mpaayei, secretary of the Bible Society of Kenya.

Professor R. A. C. Oliver, one time Carnegie Fellow appointed to the Jeanes School, Kenya.

Dr. Frederick Patterson, son-in-law of Robert Russa Moton, and third president of Tuskegee Institute, now president of the Phelps-Stokes Fund.

Dr. Emory Ross, one-time secretary of the Congo Protestant Council, and president of the Phelps-Stokes Fund.

Harry Thuku, secretary and chairman of the East African Association, 1921–2.

Mrs. Edith Washington Shehee, daughter-in-law of Booker T. Washington.

A. S. Walford, agriculturalist at the Jeanes School.

W. E. F. Ward, colleague of J. E. K. Aggrey and A. G. Fraser.

Dr. Max Yergan, Y.M.C.A. secretary in the East Africa campaign, 1916–17.

(Interviews with the above people were all conducted during the period 1965–9.)

B. ARCHIVE MATERIAL: in manuscript or unpublished

(*a*) *Philanthropic Funds*

Carnegie Corporation of New York:

Papers on the Jeanes Schools in Kenya, Nyasaland, the Rhodesias, and Zanzibar.

Phelps–Stokes Fund (New York):

Papers of the educational director of the Fund, Thomas Jesse Jones, including correspondence with missionaries, Negro schools and colleges, organizations for Negro welfare, African students in the States, miscellaneous individuals (1919–40); papers of Dr. J. H. Dillard, president of the Jeanes and Slater Funds.

Southern Education Foundation (Atlanta, Ga.):

Papers of the Jeanes and Slater Funds.

(*b*) *Predominantly Negro Colleges and Universities*

Fisk University, (Nashville, Tenn.):

(i) W. E. B. DuBois's printed papers, drafts of articles, and correspondence.

(ii) Rosenwald Fund Archives.

(iii) American Missionary Association Archives.

Hampton Institute (Hampton, Va.):

Papers of Hampton presidents; S. C. Armstrong; H. B. Frissell; J. E. Gregg; Arthur Howe; especially correspondence with T. J. Jones and B. T. Washington; files on Hampton students.

Howard University (Washington D.C.):

(Moorland Collection): papers of John Hope, president of Morehouse College; correspondence of J. E. Moorland with Y.M.C.A. officials, especially J. E. K. Aggrey (1900), M. Yergan, and S. Nkomo. See S. Nkomo, *How I found Christ in the Jungles of Africa: The Story of my Conversion* (Greenville, *c.* 1917).

Morehouse College (Atlanta):

John Hope Papers.

Tuskegee Institute (Ala.):

Papers of president R. R. Moton from 1917 to 1934, general and local correspondence. Boxes of cuttings on the Negro in Africa and America, broken down annually by subject, and arranged under the direction of Monroe Work, first director of the Tuskegee department of records and research.

(*c*) *Other Universities and Colleges*

Makerere University College:
Archives of the Church Missionary Society for Uganda and Nyanza province, Kenya.

Muskingum College (Muskingum, Ohio):
Files on Ethiopian students and correspondence with T. J. Jones, 1922–3.

University College Nairobi:
History Department: Research Project Archives, for numerous papers derived from oral tradition and documentary sources in Kenya. Microfilm of the Friends' Africa Industrial Mission minute-books.

Yale University, department of manuscripts of the University Library.
Papers of Anson Phelps Stokes, chairman of the Phelps-Stokes Fund. Papers of C. T. Loram, one time Sterling Professor of Education, and chairman and director of graduate studies, Dept. of Race Relations.

Edinburgh University:
J. W. Arthur Papers, and photograph albums. G. A. Grieve Papers, especially material on Alliance High School, Kenya. A. R. Barlow Papers.

(*d*) *Missionary and Church-related Archives*

Africa Inland Mission (Field Headquarters, Nairobi):
Minutes of Field Council Meetings, 1912–30.

American Friends Board of Missions (Richmond, Ind.):
Correspondence of missionaries of the Friends' Africa Mission, Kaimosi, Kenya, 1910–39.

Church of Scotland:
Foreign Mission papers, held in the National Library of Scotland (Edinburgh), especially the letterbooks of W. M. McLachlan, also papers and letterbooks not released to National Library, in Church of Scotland Offices, Edinburgh, especially letterbooks of J. W. C. Dougall.

Church Missionary Society (London):
Letterbooks of Africa secretary, H. D. Hooper. Private and confidential report of Dr. Garfield Williams on education in Kenya, 1924. W. E. Owen papers, with diaries and cuttings.

Edinburgh House (Headquarters of British Conference of Missionary Societies of Great Britain and N. Ireland (London)):
Classification of material in these archives has been made more difficult by the transfer to the World Council of Churches, Geneva, of papers related to the International Missionary Council. Boxes of America-related material were transferred, especially important being boxes 313–15, and two boxes of materials on Race. A temporary code has been employed in this work to facilitate reference to the remaining relevant boxes, most of which contain J. H. Oldham's correspondence.

Q-A = box on East Africa: Kenya: Education: General Material.
Q-B = box of correspondence with N. M. Leys, W. E. Owen, W. McGregor Ross; see especially 'Copy of 48 page letter sent by Dr. Norman Leys, Medical Officer, Nyasaland to the Secretary of State for the Colonies, 7.2.18'.
Q-C = Africa: box on Conference of Missionary Societies at High Leigh, 1924. See especially T. J. Jones, 'An Educational Policy for African Colonies'.
Q-D = Africa General: Education: Mission Policy.
Q-E = Africa: General Education. Approach to the Colonial Office. Advisory Committee for Education in Africa.
Q-F = Education: Kenya. Nyasaland; Zanzibar Reports, 1920, etc.
Q-G = Kenya: Education: Jeanes School.
Q-H = Education: Central Africa; including extracts from J. W. C. Dougall's Journal.
Q-I = Kenya: Education Adviser; mainly Dougall.
Q-J = Phelps-Stokes Fund; Thomas Jesse Jones.
Q-K = East Africa: Kenya: Hooper File and Arthur File.
Q-M = Advisory Committee Files.
Q-N = African Education Group.
Q-O = African General Education; African Education Group.
Q-P = Africa General.
Q-R = East Africa: Tanganyika: Education.
Q-S = East Africa: Uganda: Education.

Missionary Research Library of Union Theological College (New York):
(i) A. L. Warnhuis Papers.
(ii) C. H. Fahs Papers, especially for material on Aggrey.
(iii) Papers of the Edinburgh World Missionary Conference, 1910.

National Council of Churches of America (New York)
(i) Archives of the Committee of Reference and Counsel.
(ii) Archives of the Committee on Race Relations.
(iii) Archives of the Agricultural Missions Foundation (especially John Reisner's papers).

Presbyterian Church of East Africa (Nairobi):
Archives of the Church of Scotland Missions at Kikuyu and Tumutumu. Arthur Papers. Education files.

Y.M.C.A. Historical Library (New York):
Reports of Foreign Secretaries during First World War, in British East Africa; correspondence *re* Max Yergan; John Mott Papers.

(*e*) *Official and Semi-official*

East African Indian National Congress (Nairobi):
Files of material relating to African political associations in Kenya and Uganda.

Entebbe Secretariat Archives (Uganda):
Secretariat Minute Papers, for material relating to Young Baganda Association, and education policy.
Hull Public Library (England):
Winifred Holtby Collection, especially for Leys's correspondence.
Kenya National Archives:
(i) Education Department Archives.
(ii) Church Missionary Society (Kenya) Archives.
Library of Congress (Washington D.C.):
(i) B. T. Washington Papers, especially material on International Conference on the Negro 1912, and correspondence with A. Phelps Stokes and T. J. Jones.
(ii) G. F. Peabody Papers.
(iii) National Association for the Advancement of Coloured People Archives.
(iv) Carter G. Woodson Papers.
Public Record Office (London):
Especially Kenya papers: C.O. 533/276 (1922) to 533/363/xf7877 (1926).
Rhodes House (Oxford):
(i) W. E. Holt, 'Memoir of a Conference on Negro Education and Tour in U.S.A., 1937', 2 vols. diary: MSS. Afr. S.914.
(ii) R. T. Coryndon Papers: MSS. Afr. S.6.33
(iii) A. G. Fraser Papers.
(iv) E. B. Denham, 30 vols. diaries.
Schomburg Collection of New York Public Library (New York):
J. E. Bruce Papers.
Tennessee State Archives (Nashville, Tenn.):
Fayette Avery McKenzie Papers; correspondence with T. J. Jones.

(*f*) *Papers in Private Possession*

T. G. Benson Papers, kindly lent to the writer but now at Rhodes House; especially for materials on the Jeanes School, Kabete, Kenya.
Kathleen Bliss Papers: at present a quantity of J. H. Oldham Papers previously in the possession of Miss B. D. Gibson are with Dr. Bliss.
H. M. Bond Papers, especially for his data on African students in the United States.
J. W. C. Dougall Papers, for material and pamphlets on the Jeanes School.
Miss B. D. Gibson Papers: many now transferred to Dr. Bliss.
John Grigg Papers: a professionally catalogued selection of Sir Edward Grigg's correspondence.
Gladys T. Stauffacher, 'Faster Beats the Drum' (unpublished MS.).

C. PAMPHLETS AND REPORTS

Jones, T. J., 'The educational needs of the people of Equatorial Africa', address at 29th annual session foreign mission conference of North America, 1922 (New York, 1922).

Jones, T. J., 'An educational policy for African colonies', in *Christian education in Africa. Conference at High Leigh, Hoddesdon, September 8–13, 1924* (Edinburgh House).

Jones, T. J., *Booker T. Washington: Apostle of self-determination and cooperation* (Founders Day address, Tuskegee Institute, 8 Apr. 1934; copies in the Phelps-Stokes Fund Archives and at Edinburgh House).

Kenya Colony and Protectorate: Education department annual reports (Nairobi, 1921–39).

Phelps-Stokes Fund Special Reports:

Jones, T. J., *Educational adaptations. Report of ten years' work of the Phelps-Stokes Fund, 1910–1920* (New York, c. 1920).

Phelps Stokes, A., 'Confidential memorandum for the trustees of the Phelps-Stokes Fund regarding Dr. Carter G. Woodson's criticism of Dr. Thomas Jesse Jones' (Phelps-Stokes Fund, New York, 1924).

Twenty year report of the Phelps-Stokes Fund, 1911–1931, with contributions from C. T. Loram, J. H. Oldham, T. J. Jones, M. N. Work, and A. Phelps Stokes (New York, 1931).

Phelps Stokes, A., *Report on education, native welfare, and race relations in East and South Africa* (Carnegie Corporation of New York, 1934).

Education for life: the Phelps-Stokes Fund and Thomas Jesse Jones. A twenty-fifth anniversary (New York, 1937).

Negro status and race relations in the United States, 1911–1946: The thirty five year report of the Phelps-Stokes Fund (New York, 1946).

D. PERIODICAL;

The Crisis: A record of the darker races (monthly publication of the National Association for the Advancement of Colored People, New York), 1911–35. See especially:

W. E. B. DuBois, 'Negro education', xv, Feb. 1918;

W. E. B. DuBois, 'Thomas Jesse Jones', xxii, Oct. 1921;

W. E. B. DuBois, ' "Kenya"—A study of East African conditions as revealed by Norman Leys', xxxi, Feb. 1926.

W. E. B. DuBois, ' "Education in Africa"—a review of the recommendations of the African education committee', xxxii, June 1926.

W. E. B. DuBois, 'Missionaries', xxxvi, May 1929.

C. Tobias, 'Max Yergan', xl, July 1933.

W. E. B. DuBois, 'The Negro college', xl, Aug. 1933.

International Review of Missions (London):

A. G. Fraser, 'Impressions of Hampton Institute', i, 1912; B. T. Washington, 'David Livingstone and the Negro', ii, 1913; H. B. Frissell, 'The value of industrial education', iv, 1915; J. H. Oldham, 'Christian missions and the education of the Negro', vii, 1918; J. H. Oldham, 'The Christian opportunity in Africa: some reflections on the report of the Phelps-Stokes commission', xiv, 1925; R. R. Moton, 'The education of

Africans', xii, 1923; xv, July 1926, *passim*; A. V. Murray, 'Christianity and rural civilisation', xix, 1930.

Southern Workman (monthly publication of Hampton Institute):
T. J. Jones, 'Social studies in the Hampton curriculum', xxxiv, 1905; R. E. Park, 'The international conference on the Negro', xli, 1912; M. Yergan, 'A YMCA secretary in Africa', xlvii, Aug. 1918; K. Saunders, 'A forward move in Africa' (Max Yergan in B.E.A.), xlix, Feb. 1920; W. E. Owen, 'Unrest in Kenya colony', liii, June 1924; J. H. Dillard, 'Impressions from East Africa', liii, 1924; J. E. K. Aggrey, 'The Prince of Wales college', lv, Jan. 1926; H. S. Keigwin, 'The influence of Armstrong', lv, Feb. 1926; Fred R. Bunker, 'Hampton in Africa—shall it be?', lvi, May 1927; J. W. C. Dougall, 'Training visiting teachers for African village schools', lvii, Oct. 1928; T. J. Jones, 'Letters by Thomas Jesse Jones: (i) "To an American on a journey to Africa"; (ii) "To an able and devoted African whose studies and experiences in England and America filled him with perplexity and disappointment when he returned home" ', lxiv, Sept. 1935.

Tuskegee Student (the publication of Tuskegee Institute, Ala., from 1924 called *Tuskegee Messenger*):
R. R. Moton, 'Problems and development of the Negro race', xxxii, 1922; 'African student union', xxxiii, Mar. 1923; 'Fifth annual conference of the African student union', xxxiv, Mar. 1924.

E. PRINTED BOOKS

DuBois, W. E. B., *The Souls of black folk. Essays and sketches*, (Chicago, 1903).

Jones, T. J., *Negro education: a study of the private and higher schools for colored people in the United States* (Department of the Interior, Bureau of Education, Bulletins, 1916, Nos. 38, 39, Washington, Government Printing Office, 1917).

Jones, T. J., *Education in Africa: A study of West, South, and Equatorial Africa by the African education commission, under the auspices of the Phelps-Stokes Fund and the Foreign Mission Societies of North America and Europe* (New York, 1922).

Jones, T. J., *Education in East Africa. A study of East, Central and South Africa by the second African education commission under the auspices of the Phelps-Stokes Fund, in cooperation with the international education board* (New York, 1925).

Smith, Edwin W., *Aggrey of Africa. A study in black and white* (London, 1929).

Smith, Edwin W., *The Christian mission in Africa: A study based on the work of the international conference at Le Zoute, Belgium, September 14th to 21st, 1926* (London, 1926).

Washington, B. T., *Up from slavery, an autobiography* (New York, 1901).

II. SECONDARY SOURCES

A. PAMPHLETS AND REPORTS

'Africa conference' held under the auspices of the committee of reference and counsel of the foreign mission conference of North America at Hartford, Conn., October 30–November 1st, 1925.

African training institute: Annual report of the British and African incorporated association (Colwyn Bay, Wales) 1907–10, copies in Union Theological College, New York.

Bigham, R. J., *Shall we commercialize the Negro?* (Nineteenth Formal Opening Day Address, Gammon Theological Seminary 1901, South Atlanta, Ga.)

Bowen, J. W. E. (Ed.), *Africa and the American Negro. Addresses and proceedings of the congress on Africa held under the auspices of the Stewart missionary foundation for Africa, December 13–15, 1895* (Atlanta, Ga., 1896).

Carnegie, A., *The Negro in America: An address delivered before the Philosophical institution of Edinburgh, 16th October 1907* (Committee of Twelve for the Advancement of the interests of the Negro Race, Phila., n.d.).

Christian action in Africa. Report of the church conference on African affairs held at Otterbein College, Westerville, Ohio, June 19–25, 1942 (New York, 1942).

Christian occupation of Africa, 1917. Conference of Mission Boards concerned with Africa, held in New York City, Nov. 1917.

Educational policy in Africa. A Memorandum submitted on behalf of the education committee of the conference of missionary societies in Great Britain and Ireland (London, 1923).

Turner, F. P., and Sanders, F. K., *The foreign missions convention at Washington 1925* (New York, 1925); see address by T. J. Jones, 'Why the missionary forces must in many fields deal with agriculture and simple industries'.

General Education Board: An account of its activities, 1902–1914 (New York, 1915).

Hampton Institute: Annual reports of the principal, 1900–1915.

Haygood, A. G., *Address of the Rev. Atticus G. Haygood, D.D., LL.D., of the Methodist episcopal church, South, at the fourth annual opening of the Gammon school of theology, Atlanta, Georgia, Oct. 27, 1886.*

Kenya colony and protectorate. Annual reports. Native affairs department, 1921–1930.

Jeanes School Kabete, and the work of the village guide (Nairobi, 1931).

Kenya Legislative Council Debates, 1923–7.

J. R. Orr, 'Lessons derived from twelve years' administration of African education' (Dec., 1923).

Report of the education commission of the East Africa Protectorate, 1919 (Nairobi, 1919).

Kikuyu Central Association. *Correspondence between the Kikuyu central association and the colonial office, 1929–1930* (Nairobi, n.d.).

Lester, R. M., *The corporation and the Jeanes teacher* (printed for the information of the Trustees, Carnegie Corporation of New York, May 15, 1938).

McGrath, E. J., *The predominantly Negro colleges and universities in transition* (New York, 1965).

Lonsdale, J. M., 'Archdeacon Owen and the Kavirondo taxpayers welfare association', in 'Proceedings of the East African institute of social research conference held at Kivukoni college, Dar es Salaam, Jan. 1963'.

Lugard, F. D., *Political memoranda 1913–1918*, Memo No. 4, Education (London, 1919).

Parliamentary Papers:

Advisory committee for native education in British Tropical Africa: Education policy in British Tropical Africa (xxi, Cmd. 2374, 1925).

Advisory committee on education in the colonies: Memorandum on the education of African communities (Colonial No. 103, 1935).

Board of education. Special reports on educational subjects. Educational systems of the chief crown colonies and possessions of the British Empire, including reports on the training of native races (xxvi, Cmd. 2378, 1905).

Imperial education conference papers. Education systems of the chief colonies not possessing responsible government (London, 1915).

Report of the commission on closer union of the dependencies in Eastern and Central Africa (Cmd. 3234, 1929).

Joint select committee on closer union in East Africa (Commons 156, 1931, vol. ii, minutes of evidence).

Papers relating to native disturbances in Kenya . . . 1922 (Cmd. 1691, 1922).

Preparation of missionaries for Africa. A statement prepared under the direction of the missionary personnel and Africa committees as revised in 1935 (New York, 1935).

Report of the inter-territorial 'Jeanes' conference held in Salisbury, Southern Rhodesia, on 27th May to 6th June 1935 (Lovedale Press, 1936).

Report of the Jerusalem meeting of the international missionary council, March 24th–April 8th, 1928, vi, (London, 1928).

Scott, H. S., 'Some aspects of native education in Kenya', *London University Institute of Education, studies and reports No. 9* (Oxford, 1936).

Sheffield, J. R. (Ed.) *Education, employment and rural development: Report of the Kericho (Kenya) conference 25th September to 1st October 1966* (Nairobi, 1967).

Shepperson, G., *Myth and reality in Malawi. The fourth Melville J. Herskovits memorial lecture delivered under the auspices of the program of African studies, North-Western University, 13th April, 1966* (Evanston, 1966).

Spiller, G. (Ed.), *Inter-racial problems. Papers communicated to the first universal races congress, 1911* (London, 1911).

Stauffer, M. (Ed.), *Christian students and world problems; report of the ninth international convention of the student volunteer movement for foreign missions, Indianapolis, Indiana, December 28th 1923 to January 1st 1924* (New York, 1924).

Vischer, H., 'Report for the chairman of the advisory committee on native education in tropical Africa' (15 December 1925), copy in Edinburgh House.

Washington, B. T., *Some European observations and experiences* (Tuskegee, *c.* 1900).

World Missionary Conference 1910. Report of commission iii (Edinburgh, 1910).

Zanzibar Protectorate. *Report of Mr. and Mrs. G. B. Johnson on a visit to the U.S.A., to study the organisation, aims and methods of rural schools, February–April 1934* (Zanzibar, 1934).

B. PERIODICALS AND NEWSPAPERS

The Advent Review and Sabbath Herald (Washington), 1923–33.

Africa. Journal of the international African institute (London). W. B. Mumford, 'Education and the social adjustment of the primitive peoples of Africa to European culture', iii, 1929; J. W. C. Dougall, 'School education and native life', iii, 1930; W. B. Mumford, 'Malangali school', iii, 1930; J. W. C. Dougall, 'Characteristics of African thought', v, 1932. G. Bennett, 'From paramountcy to partnership: J. H. Oldham and Africa', xxx, Oct. 1960.

African Times and Orient Review (London)
'The negro in conference at Tuskegee institute', i, 1912; B. T. Washington, 'Tuskegee Institute', i, 1912.

American Historical Review (New York)
L. R. Harlan, 'Booker T. Washington and the white man's burden', lxxi, 1966.

American Mercury (New York)
J. Robbins, 'The Americans in Ethiopia', xxix, 1933.

Annals of the American Academy of Political and Social Science
B. T. Washington, 'Industrial education and the public schools', Sept. 1913.

Atlantic Monthly (Boston)
B. T. Washington, 'The fruits of industrial training', Nov. 1903.

Canadian Journal of African Studies (Montreal)
King, K. J., 'James E. K. Aggrey: collaborator, nationalist, Pan-African', iii, 1970.

Church Missionary Review (London)
G. T. Manley, 'Industrial education in Africa', lxxi, 1920; W. E. Owen, 'The missionary in politics', lxxii, 1921; J. R. Orr, 'Education in Kenya colony', lxxiii, 1922; H. Vischer, 'Some aspects of African education', lxxvi, 1925; E. M. D. Grace, 'Negro education in America', lxxvii, 1926.

Colonial Review (London)
Sir Christopher Cox, 'The impact of British education on the indigenous peoples of overseas territories', ix, 1956.
East African Standard (Nairobi), 1922–6.
East Africa (London)
'The last word on native education: the Phelps-Stokes report—A mine of information', i, No. 32, 1925.
The East and the West (London)
J. W. Arthur, 'The Kenya colony and protectorate', xxi, 1923; C. F. Andrews, 'The Kenya problem', ibid.
Edinburgh Review (Edinburgh)
Sir F. D. Lugard, 'Education in tropical Africa', ccxlii, 1925.
Educational yearbook of the international institute of teachers college, Columbia University (New York) 1930–3.
Foreign affairs (Washington)
W. E. B. DuBois, 'Worlds of color', iii, 1925.
Foundation, The, (Atlanta), 1911–24.
Habari (Swahili, Government-sponsored monthly, Nairobi), 1922–8.
Hampton Script (Hampton, Va.), 1927–31.
Independent (New York)
B. T. Washington, 'Industrial education in Africa', lx, 1906.
Inland Africa (Brooklyn), 1909–30.
International Review of Missions (London), 1912–39
N. Leys, 'A problem in East African Missions', viii, 1919; B. D. Gibson, 'Negro agricultural extension work in the United States', x, 1921; C. T. Loram, 'The Phelps-Stokes education commission in South Africa', x, 1921; C. H. Dickinson, 'Samuel Armstrong's contribution to Christian missions', ibid; A. G. Fraser 'Aims of African education', xiv, 1925.
Journal of African and Asian Studies (New Delhi)
K. J. King, 'The young Baganda association: some notes on the internationalisation of early African politics in Buganda' (Autumn, 1969).
Journal of African History (London)
G. A. Shepperson, 'Notes on Negro American influences on the emergence of African nationalism', i, 1960; B. A. Ogot, 'British administration in the Central Nyanza district of Kenya, 1900–1960', iv, 1963; J. M. Lonsdale, 'Some origins of nationalism in East Africa', ix, 1968.
Journal of the African Society (London)
E. W. Blyden, 'West Africa before Europe', ii, 1902/3; M. S. Evans, 'The international conference on the Negro', xi, 1911/12. B. T. Washington, review of 'The Negro in the new world', x, 1910–11; B. N. Azikiwe, 'How shall we educate the African?', xxxiii, 1934; T. G. Benson, 'The Jeanes school and the education of the East African native', x, 1936.
Journal of British Studies (Hartford, Conn.)
Ann Beck, 'Colonial policy and education in British East Africa, 1900–1950', v, 1966.

Journal of Negro Education (Washington)
W. E. B. DuBois, 'Education and work', i, 1932; W. E. B. DuBois, 'Does the Negro need separate schools?', iv, 1935. (See also Dorothy Porter, *Index to Vols. 1–31* (*1932–1962*).)
Journal of Negro History (Washington)
C. G. Woodson, 'Thomas Jesse Jones', xxxv, 1950.
Kikuyu News (Edinburgh), 1912–29.
Leader of British East Africa (Nairobi), 1910–22.
Mission Herald (Phila.)
E. B. Kalibala, 'Africa—the unknown quantity', xliv, 1940.
Negro World (New York)
'The sort of education Africans need', xxi, 1926.
Overseas Education (London)
J. Segero, 'Work of a Jeanes school teacher', i, 1929.
Phylon: The Atlanta University Review of Race and Culture (Atlanta)
H. R. Isaacs, 'The American Negro and Africa: some notes', xx, 1959; G. A. Shepperson, 'External factors in the development of African nationalism, with particular reference to British Central Africa', xxii, 1961; G. A. Shepperson, 'Pan-Africanism and "Pan-Africanism": Some historical notes', xxiii, 1962.
Past and Present (Oxford)
T. Ranger, 'African attempts to control education in East and Central Africa', No. 32, 1965.
Political Studies (Oxford)
G. Bennett, 'The development of political organisations in Kenya', v 1957.
Round Table (London)
'An experiment in African education in Kenya' (anon.), xx, 1929/1930.
Student Movement (London)
H. D. Hooper, 'African and Negro progress', xxiv, 1921.
Student World (New York)
W. J. King, 'The African students' conference', xvi, 1923; S. M. Nkomo, 'The African student union', ibid; J. E. K. Aggrey, 'The native students of Africa', ibid. M. Yergan, 'The native students of South Africa', ibid.
Transition (Kampala)
K. Kyle, 'Gandhi, Harry Thuku and early Kenya nationalism', vi, 1966.

C. PRINTED BOOKS

Ajayi, J. F. A., *Christian missions in Nigeria, 1841–1891* (London, 1965).
Anderson, J. E., *The struggle for the school* (Longmans, London, 1970).
Armstrong, S. C., *Education for life* (Hampton Institute Press, 1913).
Ayandele, E. A., *The missionary impact on modern Nigeria, 1842–1914* (London, 1966).
Bennett, G., *Kenya. A political history. The Colonial Period* (London, 1963).
Blyden, Edward W., *Christianity, Islam and the Negro race* (London, 1887).

Bond, H. M., *The education of the Negro in the American social order* (New York, 1934).
Brawley, B., *Doctor Dillard of the Jeanes fund* (New York, 1930).
Broderick, F. L., *W. E. B. DuBois: Negro leader in a time of crisis* (Stanford, 1959).
Brotz, H. (Ed.), *Negro social and political thought, 1850–1920. Representative texts* (New York, 1966).
Bullock, H. A., *A history of Negro education in the South from 1619 to the present* (Harvard, 1967).
Buxton, T. F., *The African slave trade* (London, 1839); *The Remedy* (London, 1840).
Cambell, T., Davis, J., and Wrong, M. (Eds.), *Africa advancing* (New York, 1945).
Churchill, W. S., *My African journey* (London, 1908).
Clendenen, C., and Duignan, P., *Americans in black Africa up to 1865* (Hoover Institution Series, No. 5, Stanford, 1964).
Clendenen, C., Collins, R., and Duignan, P., *Americans in Africa, 1865–1900* (Hoover Institution Studies: 17, Stanford, 1966).
Coles, Samuel B., *Preacher with a plow* (Cambridge, 1957).
Coleman, J. S., *Nigeria: Background to nationalism* (California, 1958).
Cooley, R. B., *School acres. An adventure in rural education* (New Haven, 1930).
Cronon, E. D., *Black Moses. The story of Marcus Garvey and the universal Negro improvement association* (Madison, 1955).
Cruse, H. *The crisis of the Negro intellectual* (London, 1969).
Cunard, Nancy, *Negro. An anthology made by Nancy Cunard, 1931–1933* (London, 1934).
Curtin, P. D., *The image of Africa* (London, 1965).
Davis, John A. (Ed.), *Africa seen by American Negroes* (Présence Africaine, Dijon, 1958).
Davis, J. Merle (Ed.), *Modern industry and the African* (London, 1933).
Dike, K. O., *Trade and politics in the Niger Delta* (Oxford, 1956).
Dougall, J. W. C. (Ed.), *The village teacher's guide* (London, 1931).
Dougall, J. W. C. (Ed.), *Missionary education in Kenya and Uganda. A study of cooperation* (London, 1936).
Dougall, J. W. C. *Christians in the African revolution* (Edinburgh, 1963).
DuBois, W. E. B., and Washington, B. T., *The Negro in the South* (Phila., 1907).
DuBois, W. E. B., and Dill, A. G. (Eds.), *The Negro American artisan* (Atlanta University Publication No. 17, 1912).
East African Red Book 1925–26 (East African Standard, 1925).
Edwards, Adolph, *Marcus Garvey 1887–1940* (London, 1967).
Elkins, S. M., *Slavery. A problem in American institutional and intellectual life* (Chicago, 1959).
Ellison, R., *The invisible man* (New York, 1947).

Evans, Maurice S., *Black and white in South East Africa. A study in sociology* (London, 1911).

Evans, Maurice S., *Black and white in the Southern States: A study of the race problem in the United States from a South African point of view* (London, 1915).

Foster, P. J., *Education and social change in Ghana* (London, 1965).

Frazier, E. F., *The Negro people in the United States* (New York, 1949).

Frazier, E. F., *Black Bourgeoisie: The rise of a new middle class in the United States* (New York, 1957).

Furse, Sir Ralph, *Aucuparius: Recollections of a recruiting officer* (London, 1962).

Fyfe, C., *A history of Sierra Leone* (Oxford, 1962).

Fyfe, C., *Sierra Leone inheritance* (London, 1964).

Gatheru, R. M., *Child of two worlds* (London, 1964).

Graham, Sonia, *Government and mission education in Northern Nigeria, 1900–1919, with special reference to the work of Hanns Vischer* (Ibadan, 1966).

Groves, C. P. *The planting of Christianity in Africa, iv, 1914–1954* (London, 1958).

Guggisberg, Sir Gordon, and Fraser, A. G. *The future of the Negro* (London, 1929).

Harlow, V., Chilver, E. M., and Smith, A., *History of East Africa*, ii, (Oxford, 1965).

Hayford, C., *Ethiopia unbound* (London, 1911).

Helser, A. D., *Education of primitive people* (New York, 1934).

Herskovits, M. J., *The myth of the Negro past* (New York, 1941).

Hobley, C. W. *Kenya from chartered company to crown colony* (London, 1929).

Holden, Edith, *Blyden of Liberia: An account of the life and labors of Edward Wilmot Blyden, LL.D., as recorded in letters and in print* (New York, 1946).

Holmes, B. (Ed.), *Educational policy and the mission schools. Case studies from the British Empire* (London, 1967).

Hooker, J. R., *Black Revolutionary* (London, 1967).

Hooper, H. D., *Leading strings. Native development and missionary education in Kenya colony* (London, 1921).

Hooper, H. D., *Africa in the making* (London, 1922).

Hopkins, A. J., *Trail blazers and road makers. A brief history of the East Africa mission of the United Methodist Church* (London, n.d.).

Hunter, G., *Education for a developing region: A study in East Africa* (London, 1963).

Huxley, Elspeth, *White man's country. Lord Delamere and the making of Kenya* (London, 1935).

Huxley, J., *Africa view* (London, 1931).

Isaacs, H., *The new world of Negro Americans* (New York, 1963).

James, C. L. R., *The black Jacobins* (revised edn., New York, 1963).
Johnston, Sir Harry H. *The Negro in the new world* (London, 1911).
Jolly, R. (Ed.), *Education in Africa: research and action* (Nairobi, 1969); especially Foster, P. J., 'Education for self-reliance: a critical evaluation' and Anderson, J. E., 'Education for self-reliance—the impact of self-help'.
Jones, Lance G. E., *Negro schools in the Southern States* (Oxford, 1928).
Jones, Lance G. E., *The Jeanes teacher in the United States: 1908–1933* (Chapel Hill, 1937).
Jones, T. J., *The four essentials of education* (New York, 1926).
Jones, T. J., *The essentials of civilization* (New York, 1929).
Jones-Quartey, K. A. B. *A life of Azikiwe* (London, 1965).
Kenyatta, J., *Facing Mount Kenya* (London, 1938).
Kidd, D., *Kafir socialism and the dawn of individualism* (London, 1908).
Kimble, D., *A political history of Ghana, 1850–1928* (Oxford, 1963).
Kingsley, M., *Travels in West Africa* (London, 1897).
Koinange, M., *The people of Kenya speak for themselves* (Detroit, 1955).
Latourette, K. S., *A history of the world service* (New York, 1947).
Lewis, L. J. *Education policy and practice in British tropical areas* (London, 1954).
Leys, N., *Kenya* (London, 1924).
Leys, N., *A last chance in Kenya* (London, 1931).
Locke, A., (Ed.), *The new Negro* (New York, 1925).
Loram, C. T., *The education of the South African native* (London, 1917).
Lucas, E., *English traditions in East African education* (London, 1958).
Lugard, Lord, *The dual mandate in British tropical Africa* (London, 1923).
Lynch, H. R., *Edward Wilmot Blyden, Pan-Negro patriot 1832–1912* (London, 1967).
MacPherson, Margaret, *They built for the future* (Cambridge, 1964).
Mair, Lucy P., *Native policies in Africa* (London, 1936).
Mangat, J., *A history of Asians in East Africa* (Oxford, 1969).
Mathews, B., *Booker T. Washington: Educator and interracial interpreter* (London, 1949).
Mayhew, A., *Education in the colonial Empire* (London, 1938).
McIntosh, B. G. (Ed.), *Ngano: Nairobi historical studies No. 1* (Nairobi, 1969).
Meier, A., *Negro thought in America, 1880–1915. Racial ideologies in the age of Booker T. Washington* (Ann Arbor, 1963).
Meier, A., and Broderick, Francis L., *Negro protest thought in the twentieth century* (Bobbs Merrill Co. Inc. 1965).
Mockerie, P. G., *An African speaks for his people* (London, 1934).
Moton, R. R., *Finding a way out. An autobiography* (London edition, 1920).
Moton, R. R., *What the Negro thinks* (London n.d., circa 1928).

Murray, A. V., *The school in the bush. A critical study of the theory and practice of native education in Africa* (London, 1929).

Myrdal, G., *An American dilemma. The Negro problem and modern democracy* (New York, 1944).

Nyabongo, Prince Aliki K., *Africa answers back* (London, 1936).

Nyerere, J. K., *Education for self-reliance* (Dar es Salaam, 1967).

Patterson, F. D., and Hughes, W. H., (Eds.), *Robert Russa Moton of Hampton and Tuskegee* (Chapel Hill, 1956).

Odinga, O., *Not yet Uhuru: An autobiography* (London, 1967).

Oldham, J. H., *Christianity and the race problem* (London, 1924).

Oldham, J. H., *White and black in Africa. A critical examination of the Rhodes lectures of General Smuts* (London, 1930).

Oldham, J. H., and Gibson, B. D., *The remaking of man in Africa* (London, 1931).

Oliver, R., *The missionary factor in East Africa* (London, 1952).

Painter, L. K., *The hill of vision. The story of the Quaker movement in East Africa, 1902–1965* (Nairobi, 1966).

Peabody, F. G., *Education for life. The story of Hampton institute told in connection with the fiftieth anniversary of the foundation of the school* (New York, 1919).

Philp, H. R. A., *A new day in Kenya* (London, 1936).

Resnick, I. N. (Ed.), *Tanzania: Revolution by education* (Arusha, 1968).

Roosevelt, T., *African game trails* (New York, 1910).

Rosberg, C., and Nottingham, J., *The myth of 'Mau Mau': nationalism in Kenya* (Stanford, 1966).

Ross, W. McG., *Kenya from within: A short political history* (London, 1927).

Ross, E., *Out of Africa* (New York, 1936).

Rudwick, E. M., *W. E. B. DuBois: A study in minority group leadership* (Phila., 1960).

Schweizer, A., *On the edge of the primeval forest* (London, 1922).

Scott, E. J., and Stowe, L. B., *Booker T. Washington: builder of a civilisation* (New York, 1916).

Shepperson, G. A., and Price, T., *Independent African. John Chilembwe and the origins, setting and significance of the Nyasaland native rising of 1915* (Edinburgh, 1958).

Sklar, R. L., *Nigerian political parties* (New Jersey, 1963).

Smith, Edwin W., *The golden stool. Some aspects of the conflict of cultures in modern Africa* (London, 1926).

Sorrenson, M. P. K., *Origins of European settlement in Kenya* (O.U.P., 1968).

Spencer, S. R., *Booker T. Washington and the Negro's place in American life* (Boston, 1955).

Stauffer, M. (Ed.), *Thinking with Africa: Chapters by a group of nationals interpreting the Christian revolution* (London, 1928).

Steytler, J. G., *Educational adaptations. With reference to African village schools, with special reference to central Nyasaland* (London, 1939).
Torrence, R., *The story of John Hope* (New York, 1948).
Ward, W. E. F., *Fraser of Trinity and Achimota* (Ghana University Press, 1965).
Washington, B. T., *The future of the American Negro* (Boston, 1899).
Washington, B. T., *Working with the hands* (New York, 1904).
Welbourn, F. B., *East African rebels: A study of some independent churches* (London, 1961).
Welbourn, F. B., and Ogot, B. A., *A place to feel at home* (London, 1966).
Westervelt, Josephine H., *On safari for God: An account of the life and labors of John Stauffacher a pioneer missionary of the Africa inland mission* (New York, n.d.).
Wilson, John, *Education and changing West African culture* (New York, 1963).
Woodson, C. G., *The education of the Negro prior to 1861* (New York, 1915).
Woodson, C. G., *The history of the Negro church* (Washington, 1921).
Woodson, C. G., *The Negro in our history* (Washington, 1922).
Woodson, C. G., *The miseducation of the American Negro* (Washington, 1933).
Work, M. N., *Negro year book, 1918–1919* (Tuskegee Institute, 1919).
Work, M. N., *Negro year book, 1925–1926* (Tuskegee Institute, 1925).
Work, M. N., *A bibliography of the Negro in Africa and America* (New York, 1928).
Work, M. N., *Negro year book, 1937–38* (Tuskegee, 1937).
Wraith, R. E., *Guggisberg* (London, 1967).
Wright, A. D., *Negro rural school fund incorporated, 1907–1933* (New York, 1933).

D. THESES

Abbott, Sally, 'The education policy of the Kenya government, 1904–1935' (Univ. of London, Ph.D. thesis, 1969).
Carson, Suzanne, 'Samuel Chapman Armstrong; Missionary to the South' (Johns Hopkins University, Maryland, Ph.D. thesis 1952).
Carter, Felice, 'Education in Uganda, 1894–1945' (Univ. of London, Ph.D. thesis 1967).
Harr, W. C., 'The Negro as an American Protestant missionary in Africa' (Univ. of Chicago Ph.D. thesis 1945).
Kalibala, E. B., 'Education for the villages in Uganda, East Africa' (Teachers College Columbia University, New York, M.A. thesis 1934).
Kalibala, E. B., 'The social structure of the Baganda tribe' (Ph.D. Harvard, 1946).
Kieran, J., 'The Holy Ghost Fathers in East Africa, 1863–1914' (Univ. of London Ph.D. thesis 1966).

Lonsdale, J. M. 'A political history of Nyanza, 1883–1945' (Univ. of Cambridge Ph.D. 1964).

McIntosh, B. G., 'The Scottish mission in Kenya, 1891–1923' (Univ. of Edinburgh Ph.D. thesis 1969).

Nkomo, S. M., 'The customs of the Bandowo folk considered with a view of adding certain new arguments to the generally accepted view of the unity of the Bantu race' (Univ. of Chicago M.A. thesis 1922).

Russel, B. T., 'What are the policies, practices and attitudes of the foreign mission boards in North America with reference to the sending of American Negroes as foreign missionaries' (Presbyterian College of Christian Education M.A. thesis 1945; copy in Missionary Research Library, New York).

Shah, S. R., 'A history of Asian education in Kenya, 1886–1963' (University College Nairobi M.A. thesis 1968).

Wright, Marcia, 'German evangelical missions in Tanganyika, 1891–1939, with special reference to the Southern Highlands' (Univ. of London Ph.D. thesis, 1966).

Index